Balance of Payments and Economic Growth

Balance of Payments and Economic Growth

JOHN M. LETICHE
UNIVERSITY OF CALIFORNIA, BERKELEY

AUGUSTUS M. KELLEY • PUBLISHERS
CLIFTON 1975

First Edition 1958

(New York: Harper & Brothers, 1958)

Reprinted 1967 and 1975 by

Augustus M. Kelley Publishers

Clifton New Jersey 07012

By Arrangement with John M. Letiche

Library of Congress Cataloged.
The original printing of this title as follows:

Letiche, John M., 1918–
    Balance of payments and economic growth ₍by₎ John M.
Letiche. New York, A. M. Kelley, 1967.

   xiii, 378 p. illus. 22 cm.   (Reprints of economic classics)

   Reprint of the 1958 ed.
   Bibliography: p. 321–364.

   1. Balance of payments. 2. Economic development.   I. Title.

HG3881.L45 1967   332.1′5   66–21681
ISBN 0–678–00267–3

PRINTED IN THE UNITED STATES OF AMERICA
by SENTRY PRESS, NEW YORK, N. Y. 10013
Bound by A. HOROWITZ & SON, CLIFTON, N. J.

To my father

and

in memory of my mother

Contents

Preface

In this book I have endeavored to present a series of critical studies on the theory of the balancing of international payments. It is in two parts. The first deals briefly with the historical origins of modern doctrine and gives, in Chapters 3-6, an analytical account of classical and modern theories. It is shown that a generalization of classical theory can provide a more adequate explanation of the balancing process than has been given by some of the more recent and more complicated analytical devices. The second part consists of case studies applying this more generalized theory and analyzing relationships between economic growth and international equilibrium, as well as disequilibrium. The central theme of the book is that the international mechanism of adjustment comprises the entire process of domestic and external forces which affect the balance of payments: how and why internal and external forces are, or are not, harmonized. It is shown that the classical and more modern theories have been too narrowly conceived. An attempt is made to expand the analysis of the interrelationships between internal and external balance and imbalance.

My main objective in writing this book is that it serve as a useful supplement to the textbooks on international economics. I hope that the extensive discussions of economic development and of the role of cyclical, monetary, and fiscal factors in the equilibration of international accounts will make it of interest also to teachers, students, and government officials in these fields.

Acknowledgments are due to the editors and publishers of the *Journal of Political Economy*, the *Quarterly Journal of Economics*, and the *Encyclopædia Britannica* for their kind permission to include in this book material which appeared in my articles, "Isaac Gervaise on the International Mechanism of Adjustment," *Journal of Political Economy*, February, 1952, pp. 34-44; "Differential Rates of Productivity Growth and International Imbalance," *Quarterly Journal of Economics*, August, 1955, pp. 371-401; and "Balance of Payments," *Encyclopædia Britannica*, copyright 1958. These articles, however, have been substantially elaborated in the process of incorporation in this book.

The first part of the book is an outgrowth of ideas first presented in a doctoral dissertation submitted to the University of Chicago. It has been further developed, extensively revised, and refined. With the exception of a few pages, the actual exposition is entirely new. I am grateful to the John Simon Guggenheim Foundation for a fellowship which provided the opportunity to concentrate on the studies which form the second part of this work.

My heaviest intellectual indebtedness is to Professor Jacob Viner, who has been a constant source of inspiration, encouragement, and advice. I am grateful to other friends and colleagues: the late Professor Norman S. Buchanan, and Professors Philip W. Bell, John B. Condliffe, Howard S. Ellis, Gottfried Haberler, Bert F. Hoselitz, D. Gale Johnson, Arthur H. Leigh, Erik Lindahl, Lloyd W. Mints, and Tibor Scitovsky, who read portions of the manuscript and gave me the benefit of highly valued criticism and comment. Acknowledgments are also due to a long line of able students who either raised stimulating questions or assisted in statistical computations, in checking references, and in meeting the physical burden of using libraries. In particular, I cannot forbear to mention the following: Walter F. Abbott, John F. Benton, Joe Conard, Meredith Clement, William H. Fink, and Russell Moran. My thanks, in addition, are due to the

Institute of Social Sciences and the Bureau of Business and Economic Research of the University of California, which provided the funds that enabled me to recruit the aid of these students and furnished the typing facilities.

To my wife, Emily Kuyper Letiche, I am deeply indebted for literary criticism; to my son, Hugh, for general assistance. They have both sacrificed much for this book, and I hope that the reader will have occasion to share their satisfaction in its completion.

J.M.L.

Berkeley
January, 1959

Part I

The Balancing of International Payments

1

Background of Classical
Mechanism Theory

THIS chapter deals with the general background from which emerged the traditional theory of the balancing of international payments, a theory which was developed almost wholly by the English classical school of economists and its later followers.

The technical assumptions of traditional mechanism theory, as found in the major writings of Hume, Ricardo, Senior, J. S. Mill, and Cairnes, are not uniform; but their similarity is more striking than their diversity. This similarity is in part the result of a common outlook on philosophical, political, and economic affairs.

Fundamentally, the philosophy of theoretical discussions in the nineteenth century was based on Newtonian and Lockian concepts. These concepts were defined in terms of their properties rather than of their historical or functional setting. Newton's own definition of time affords an excellent example: "Absolute, True, and Mathematical Time, of itself, and from its own nature flows equably without regard to anything external, and by another name is called Duration."[1] As early as 1691, we find Sir Dudley North applying these concepts to the laws of nature. Society was regarded as a mechanism that worked in accordance with its own laws, requiring no man at the wheel.[2] This application to economics of concepts derived from the experimental sciences had serious limitations, and not the least of these was the failure to abandon them even after scientists had found them erroneous. Professor Bridgman has shown, for example, that Einstein, in proving that the length of a moving object is a function of its velocity, gave up the Newtonian view and argued that the proper definition of a concept is not in terms of its intrinsic properties but in terms of actual operations.[3] These operations are assumed to be carried out in an environment which is uniquely specified. They can be tested, however, only by actual experiment, and for that reason have limited range in the field of economics. Yet one aspect of this view of concepts has an important bearing in the field of economics as well as in physics; viz., that changes in premises may be called for by new facts or by changes in recognized or stated objectives.

Hence, for an understanding of the premises and conclusions of classical mechanism theory, and for a consideration of its relevance to modern conditions, an appreciation of the environment and objectives which the classical writers envisaged is a primary requisite. But to refer even in briefest terms to the great age of liberalism, which was "saturated with the conviction that the unfettered action of the individual is the mainspring of all progress,"[4] a sense of continuity is indispensable.

THE DISINTEGRATION OF MERCANTILISM

The breakdown of mercantilism still awaits its historian, but there

[1] Isaac Newton, Scholium, Book I of the *Principia* (1687), in *Sir Isaac Newton's Mathematical Principles*, trans. Andrew Motte (1729), and rev. Florian Cajori, 1934, p. 6. (For complete references, see Bibliography, pp. 321-364.)

[2] Cf. Sir Dudley North, *Discourses upon Trade* (1691) 1907, pp. 21-27, 36-37; and the Preface, which was not written by North.

[3] P. W. Bridgman, *The Logic of Modern Physics*, 1927, p. 6. "The only justification for our concepts and system of concepts," states Einstein, "is that they serve to represent the complex of our experiences; beyond this they have no legitimacy." Albert Einstein, *The Meaning of Relativity*, 1945, p. 2.

[4] L. T. Hobhouse, *Liberalism*, 1911, p. 78.

are several relevant aspects of that history which for our purpose may be summarized as follows.

In England the disintegration of the feudal system partly coincided with, and was partly followed by, the emergence of representative institutions. Industrialization followed, by a lapse of nearly a century, the democratic development which was symbolized by the Bill of Rights of 1689. This development was extremely complex and irregular.

During the period of the Stuarts the people became jealous of the power of state as exercised by the Crown. This jealousy persisted into the eighteenth century. And with the rise of the merchant class—operators of shops and of shipping, entrepreneurs in manufacturing, brokers, and traders—there emerged an important pressure group, able to make independent political demands on the central authority, as soon as cleavages appeared between the religious, political, and economic activities of the King and his subjects. Generally, these merchants seemed to justify government interference when "needed," particularly when the regulations were in harmony with their own interest.[5] But in time this harmony of interests declined, and the merchants joined in a movement *against mercantilist controls*, giving lip service to laissez faire though occasionally showing why their particular industry should be granted protection.[6] There were few, if any, advocates of government interference as a general and systematic policy, or of interference as good in itself. In general, English thought

[5] There were, of course, many controls to the common interest of the pamphleteers, and they invariably stressed the importance of the merchant. British "artisans were universally allow'd the best upon Earth for Improvements," noted James Puckle, A *New Dialogue between a Burgermaster and an English Gentleman*, 1697, p. 20. Another writer proclaimed that "all Trades receive their Vigour and Life from the Merchant." John Oldmixon, *The British Empire in America*, 1708, Vol. I, pp. xxi-xxii.

[6] The English functional (and somewhat inconsistent) approach to the role of government in business during the latter part of the seventeenth and early part of the eighteenth centuries is well represented by the position of John Cary. In effect, it is a position for careful and studied control. The government, he wrote, should consider all possible means to improve and to make more profitable the flow of commerce. It should determine "what is necessary to be prohibited, both in our Exports and Imports." But, he warned, "when that great and glorious Assembly hath medled with Trade, they have left it worse than they found it; and the Reason is, because the Laws relating to trade, require more time to look into their distant Consequences, than a Session will admit; whereof we have had many instances." John Cary, A *Discourse on Trade*, 1717, pp. 86-88.

was "libertarian" even in the mercantilist period. Thus the historic struggle between King and Parliament, with the gradual emergence of the commercial interest, furnished an important source for the breakdown of mercantilism.

The Reformation naturally bred individualism and thereby furnished a theological source for the breakdown of mercantilism. Introduced from above by Henry VIII with the Act of Supremacy of 1534, it had inadvertently sanctioned religious and, by implication, political nonconformity. The Puritans held that the individual himself had access to God, and that he himself could interpret the Holy Writings. Their stress upon the importance of the individual was uppermost. They emphasized individual rights, administered their churches along democratic lines, and generally were prepared for democratic procedures. But these Dissenters were a repressed group. They so remained long after the restoration of the Monarchy, being permitted neither to attend the regular universities nor to be members of Parliament. At the end of the eighteenth century they opened Dissenting Academies, which, in many respects, were superior to Cambridge and Oxford. "The English universities of the eighteenth century," writes Sir Leslie Stephen, with some exaggeration, "are generally noted only as embodiments of sloth and prejudice."[7] The Dissenters, however, were generally more critical in their thinking. Since in an important sense they represented a movement for individualism, the state was against them; but they contributed to the theological force which played no small role in the disintegration of mercantilism.

There occurred also a rise of some political and psychological ideas that led to individualism. Beginning in the seventeenth and extending through the eighteenth into the nineteenth century, the development of the scientific outlook and method, the expansion of political philosophy, and the spread of individualism strongly influenced one another. The remarkable expansion of physics, astronomy, and mathematics gave rise toward the end of the seventeenth century to a new

---

[7] Sir Leslie Stephen, *The English Utilitarians*, 1900, Vol. I, pp. 43-51. This was true only of the Anglican universities; it was not true of the Scottish. And whatever was true of the teaching was by no means wholly true of the "dons" as scholars. Moreover, it is extremely difficult to find any clear *direct* relation between religious individualism and laissez faire in the economic field.

scientific outlook on the universe. It envisaged the world as a vast mechanism, determined by mechanical forces, working according to natural laws comprehensible to the human reason. The success of the physical sciences stimulated the belief that human nature and social life might be explained in analogous terms. It was thought that if the forces determining man's character and mental process could be discovered, a science of society could be constructed on a firm basis. This view does not imply that one must have faith in a doctrine of natural harmony of interests, in the sense of a harmony preordained or inherent in the nature of man living in a society unregulated by government. In fact, the political philosophers who were important in the seventeenth and eighteenth centuries, such as Hobbes and Locke, did not adhere to such a doctrine. Faith in natural harmony may stem from faith in a beneficent Director of the Universe. Adam Smith, for example, was an antimechanical philosopher who believed men had God-created psychologies which made them operate in a beneficent manner. There was a Director of the Universe who created earth and heaven and then left it to run, having built into it psychological forces which would make it run on an even keel.

A system so defined does not require, but it permits, a theory of individualistic social organization. Government interference may be part of such a system, with justice being necessary only as an arbitrator and the role of the state not being potentially great.

Thus historical, theological, and political forces all contributed to the breakdown of mercantilism. But the greatest force of all was the mechanical, for predominantly mercantilism disintegrated—it was not repealed.

Just as the medieval economy, with its merchant guilds and regulatory powers of the crafts and the courts merchant of the towns, showed itself to be too rigid for the expanding opportunities of the domestic system of industry, so the mercantile economy of the sixteenth, seventeenth, and a good part of the eighteenth centuries—with its panoply of protective tariffs and prohibitions on the export of bullion, wool, and naval stores; bounties and sliding-scale duties upon the export and import of corn; Navigation Laws and Statute of Artificers; colonial system and control over consumption—showed itself to be too rigid for the expanding opportunities of the factory system.[8]

In England, the extensive guild and state regulations, which were vested in the hands of the justices of the peace or the Privy Council, had to give way to the gradual increase of capitalist industry. "In the long run," writes Clapham, "the gilds failed; and outwork became the predominant—though never the sole—form of capitalistic industrial organization in Britain."[9] Obsolete rights and customs were unable to withstand the revolutionary effects of the enclosures and other industrial changes of the age. Pressure of agricultural unemployment, coupled with some rising standards of life and the novel sense of power, weakened the force of guild and state regulations. The improvement of roads and canals, the decay of the apprentice system, the absorption of small farms into large ones, the expansion of capitalistic industry and finance, all contributed to the disintegration of mercantilism. In truth, the regulations had disintegrated so rapidly that "So far as any effective governmental regulation was in question, the English official attitude [practice?] was in fact laissez faire by the year 1700."[10] The Statute of Artificers (1562), which proposed to adjust wages to the rising prices of provisions (but in effect did not do so), continued substantially unchanged well into the eighteenth century, though with the exception of agricultural laborers it was not generally enforced. The usury laws were ingeniously evaded. The control of sumptuous consumption was virtually abandoned. Mun complained that Englishmen were "besotting our selves with pipe and pot, in a beastly manner, sucking smoak, and drinking healths, until death stares many in the face."[11] Lax administration, coupled with neglect and some disregard of laboring interests, intensified evasions and

---

[8] However, while the medieval economy to a great extent was consistent with the static attitudes of the day, the mercantile economy was not. For a provocative discusson on the general background of mercantilism, cf. Joseph A. Schumpeter, *History of Economic Analysis*, 1955, pp. 143-155. An excellent description of the controls in the sixteenth, seventeenth, and eighteenth centuries is to be found in Eli F. Heckscher, *Mercantilism*, trans. Mandel Shapiro, 2nd ed., rev., 1955, Vol. I, Chap. 6.

[9] J. H. Clapham, *An Economic History of Modern Britain*, 1950, Vol. I, p. 178.

[10] Conyers Read, ed., *The Constitution Reconsidered*, 1938, p. 72; cf. also Heckscher, *op. cit.*, pp. 63-77.

[11] Thomas Mun, *England's Treasure by Forraign Trade* (1664), 1903, p. 99.

rendered many state economic controls ineffective. "Thus," write the Hammonds, "England and Scotland, from the time of the Union of 1707, composed the largest free trade area in Europe, and the new economy had nowhere in Europe so wide or so convenient a theatre."[12]

In the sphere of foreign trade, mercantilist controls were retained over a longer period. There the regulations were aimed at foreigners. They catered to stronger prejudices and consequently operated in a psychological setting more conducive to the maintenance of controls. Moreover, it is simpler to regulate foreign than domestic trade. But even here, for the period before 1689, the extreme "bullionist" trade regulations had become obsolete by 1560. The outstanding changes in legislation and in administrative practice occurred long before 1620 or did not occur until long after.[13]

The institution of the Staple, which served as an instrument of regulation of individual transactions, expired in 1558. The Statutes of Employment, which required that foreign merchants pay for the English commodities which they bought, in part at least, in coin or bullion, had become inoperative long before the end of the sixteenth century. The Royal Exchanger, with his control over exchange transactions, went out of existence practically, if not legally, in the reign of Elizabeth. The restrictions on the export of coin and bullion also had been relaxed during her reign.

However, the restrictions on the export of gold were more strictly enforced in the reign of James I, in accordance with a proclamation of 1603. Even stricter regulations were laid down by Charles I in 1628. It was not until 1663 that gold and silver bullion and *foreign* coin could be freely exported. And it was not until 1819 that English coin or bullion derived from it could be legally exported.

Clearly, the disintegration of mercantilist controls over exchange transactions and over the movement of foreign and English coin or

[12] J. L. and Barbara Hammond, *The Rise of Modern Industry*, 3rd ed., 1927, p. 59. For an excellent discussion of the development of internal trade and transport, see T. S. Ashton, *An Economic History of England: The 18th Century*, 1955, Chap. III.
[13] Cf. Jacob Viner, *Studies in the Theory of International Trade*, 1937, pp. 4-5.

bullion was a primary requisite for the evolution of a "self-regulating" international mechanism of adjustment.

Legally, there was no important relaxation over foreign trade between 1689 and the treaty with France of 1786. However, in 1671, William Carter, a customs official, published a pamphlet describing his difficulties in enforcing the prohibitions on the shipment of wool. In 1672 and 1688 he published two more pamphlets, urging improvement of the laws and the machinery of general enforcement.[14] Davenant, another public official, drew attention to the difficulties of enforcing foreign-trade controls during the eighteenth century.[15] To be sure, some officials were chiefly concerned with maintaining their own positions, but the literature teems with elaborate proposals for all sorts of trade and bullion "registry schemes."[16] But it was found impossible to administer less ambitious policies even in the trade with the colonies, not to mention trade with foreign countries. Many provisions of the Navigation Laws had become obsolete. Even the monopolies in manufacturing, which Englishmen were to have, "and which Mercantile exaggeration treated as the essential conditions of political power and of intellectual progress . . . perhaps, did more to lower the moral character of Englishmen than to retard the higher development of the colonies: for the colonists found unexpected ways of using their minds."[17] This mechanical disintegration of mercantilism became almost commonplace, and partly for that reason administration became weak and corrupt.

It seems that although the practical, intellectual, and political factors in the breakdown of mercantilism were closely related, in fact, much of the gradual practical breakdown occurred first. There then followed an intellectual synthesis. When Adam Smith published his

[14] William Carter, *England's Interest by Trade Asserted*, 1671; *A Brief Advertisement to the Merchant and Clothier*, 1672; and *An Abstract of Proceedings to Prevent Exportation of Wool Unmanufactured*, 1688.
[15] Charles Davenant, "Discourses on the Public Revenues, and on Trade," *Works*, 1771, Vol. I, p. 392.
[16] Cf., e.g., William Mildmay, *The Law and Policy of England, Relating to Trade*, 1765, p. 73.
[17] Alfred Marshall, *Industry and Trade*, 1921, Appendix D, p. 733. Cf. *ibid.*, Appendix C, p. 707; and Earl J. Hamilton, "The Role of Monopoly in the Overseas Expansion and Colonial Trade of Europe Before 1800," *American Economic Review*, May, 1948, pp. 48-51.

Wealth of Nations in 1776, the theoretical breakdown was complete; but the practical breakdown was as yet incomplete, and the political breakdown had hardly begun.

LEGISLATIVE QUIESCENCE, 1760-1830

The period ranging from the accession of George III in 1760 to the era commencing a little before the Reform Act of 1832 was one of legislative quiescence. Among the reasons for this quiescence was the fact that, although the initial phase of the Industrial Revolution was to a large extent destructive in nature, the age was marked first by intense satisfaction with things as they were, and then by timid reaction to everything foreign or Jacobinical. These tendencies reinforced one another and resulted in legislative stagnation.

From approximately 1760 (or, indeed, from 1689) to 1790, pride in English institutions, particularly in the British Constitution, united with widespread optimism to check political reform. Then this early period of optimism was reinforced by Toryism. The black reaction against revolutionary violence, which lasted from about 1790 to 1820, in turn obstructed improvement in the law. As the memory of the French Revolution slowly receded into the background of men's consciousness, optimism reappeared; but the legislative quiescence and stagnation remained. Generally, the laws passed during these 70 years (1760-1830) were aimed "at the suppression of sedition, of Jacobinism, of agitation, or of reform."[18] The English lawmakers seemed chloroformed to change. From the "Glorious Revolution" to the Reform Bill, the first duty of the ministry seems to have been not the passing of laws, but the guidance of national policy. As far as change recorded in the statutebook or the law reports was concerned, Dicey suggests that ". . . the Constitution rested in 1827 on the foundation upon which it had been placed by the Revolution of 1689. In the daily working of parliamentary government, it is true, vast alterations had been made during the lapse of more than a century, but these alterations were the result of political conventions, of

[18] A. V. Dicey, *Lectures on the Relation between Law and Public Opinion in England during the Nineteenth Century*, 2nd ed., 1914, p. 63.

understandings, which left untouched the law of the Constitution."[19]

It is not surprising that an incongruity developed between the rapidly changing economic conditions and the practical unchangeableness of the law.

The period of the most rapid economic transition, whereby England led the world in a sweeping phase of evolution, occurred after 1780, and continued well into the nineteenth century. The slow improvement in public order, in medical efficiency, in cleanliness, and in food, fuel, and clothing resulted in lengthening the average span of life. In spite of all the acute miseries of the period, the English death rate, which was already falling quite steeply by 1780, continued to fall sharply until about 1820—from about 30 per thousand in 1780 to about 20 in 1820. The total population rose from approximately 9,000,000 in 1781 to 14,000,000 in 1821, and to 21,000,000 in 1851. On balance, national conditions improved for the population as a whole; but, at least in certain localities, the rise in the number of unskilled laborers seriously aggravated the long-drawn-out period of pauperization.

As the economy changed its structure and location, laws and institutions remained in one place, while men and women had moved to another. If they happened to move into a chartered town, they lived under a closed corporation and its municipal magistrates. If they were outside such precincts, they were under the rule of justices of the peace and the antiquated court leet. In either case, English standards of bureaucracy were bad. What the state did, it did badly. Too often the higher officials of the civil service were neither efficient nor honest, growing rich on bribery and blackmail. In other countries, particularly in Prussia, the higher ranks of the civil service were composed of efficient, hard-working, and faithful officials. In England, they were for the most part amateurs. The justices of the peace, who governed by absolute and patriarchal sway over three-quarters of England, were unpaid local magistrates. They were nominally state officials, legally responsible to quarter sessions, but they were in fact responsible to no one, and their powers and functions governed all

---

[19] *Ibid.*, p. 84. However, the Tory "liberals" were responsible for some reform, even in the tariff, between 1815 and 1830.

sides of country life.[20] As a rule, they had no proper staff in their pay. The total English civil service at the end of the eighteenth century was very small. Even as late as 1825 the Home Office, whose chief function was to deal with labor, had a total staff of 18 persons, and there was virtually no police force.[21] Voluntary persons acted as informers and were paid when convictions were handed down.

In new towns such as Leeds, Sheffield, and Manchester, which developed in the northern part of England, there was no aristocracy to enforce the regulations of the old guilds, and hence the mercantilist practices were abandoned. Here the economic and social relations, "Which went to built up a Parish Oligarchy or a Government by Consent, either had never existed or were in process of rapid disintegration."[22] The public business of the township of Manchester, "containing, by 1790, a population of about 60,000, whether relating to street nuisances or to police, poor relief or the collection of rates, had plainly outgrown the capacity of the annually chosen, unpaid amateur officer."[23] The inhabitants of these new towns were unknown to one another; many, as newcomers, were uninterested in the local affairs and unacquainted with the local customs. Past social ties no longer strengthened bare legal relations. Respectable citizens would often pay a heavy fine rather than serve as constable, surveyor, overseer, or churchwarden. Well-to-do-citizens who desired to obtain a lifelong exemption from these obligations paid from two to three hundred pounds for the certificate of exemption, or the "Tyburn ticket," as it was called.[24] Those who did serve were often "scarcely removed from idiotism," says one writer; "and not fit to govern anything," says another.[25]

[20] Cf. Sidney and Beatrice Webb, *English Local Government from the Revolution to the Municipal Corporations Act: The Parish and the County*, 1906, pp. 418 et seq.
[21] "Until 1829 the capital of England did not possess a regular body of police." Dicey, *op. cit.*, p. 122.
[22] Webb, *op. cit.*, p. 61.
[23] *Ibid.*, p. 71.
[24] *Report of the House of Lords Committee on the Poor Laws*, 1817, p. 153.
[25] Cf. a letter by Rev. Richard Canning of Ipswich in *The Christian's Magazine*, Vol. III, 1763, p. 26; and *Observations on the Abuses and False Interpretations of the Poor Laws* by the Earl of Sheffield, 1818, p. 34, quoted in Webb, *op. cit.*, pp. 63-64.

In those areas where reputable justices of the peace did exist, the pressure of public opinion often compelled them to leave if their views did not conform to the vast majority of the inhabitants. If they decided to remain, proud and haughty as they were, expressing the views of the nobility, the justices would frequently permit evasions rather than truckle to government. More generally, the rapid growth of the factories and the attendant circumstances "hardly disturbed the complacency of the long inactive oligarchs, who were so well accustomed to neglect their old duties that they were not likely to attend to the new ones."[26] It was this nonresistance that permitted multifarious evasions of the remaining mercantilist controls. In one parish after another, conclude the Webbs, "the slight legal framework . . . fell hopelessly asunder and the situation became almost incredibly bad."[27]

The prohibitions against the exportation of machinery and the emigration of skilled artisans could not always be enforced; indeed, many of them were probably not expected to be. When necessary, Europeans and Americans smuggled out machinery and adjusted it to meet their demands, often with the aid of imported artisans. A record exists, showing that as early as March 4, 1775, a committee met in North Carolina to promote subscriptions for the encouragement of manufactures. It was not long before mechanics like Samuel Slater landed in America (1790). In 1811, when Francis C. Lowell of Boston visited Manchester to obtain information on the power-loom industry, it was still a criminal offense to export from England either models, parts, or working drawings of machinery. "However, he seems to have overcome these difficulties and such pricks of conscience as may have disturbed him. He returned to Boston in 1813 and, with the assistance of a Patrick T. Jackson and Nathan Appleton, purchased a water-power site in Waltham, Massachusetts, obtained an act of incorporation, and began the manufacture of cotton goods

---

[26] George Macaulay Trevelyan, *British History in the Nineteenth Century,* 1782-1901, 1928, p. 161.

[27] Webb, *op. cit.,* p. 63. The *Gentleman's Magazine* of January, 1787, p. 5, reports that "in case of law-suits . . . the jury are obliged to depend on the memory of some old men."

by power looms in America."[28] In England, this process of legal quiescence had become widespread, decadent, and almost always reactionary.

Except for the Customs and Navigation Laws, and even here there was much evasion and obsolescence, mercantilism really disintegrated; it was not repealed. The practical decadence and legislative quiescence furnished an ideal environment for radical political and economic change.

UTILITARIANISM: A RADICAL CREED

At the close of the Napoleonic Wars, the task of legal reconstruction was still almost untouched. Goldsmith's cosmopolitan Chinaman described the situation as follows: "This is the most perfect state of civil liberty, of which we can form any idea; here we see a greater number of laws than in any other country, while the people at the same time obey only such as are *immediately* conducive to the interests of society; several are unnoticed, many unknown; some kept to be revived and enforced upon proper occasions, others left to grow obsolete, even without the necessity of abrogation."[29] This legal sloth was probably prolonged by the more general need of Parliamentary reform.

The truth of the matter seems to be that the laws were not only antiquated, but were often so savage as to shock every man of common decency. English aristocracy had great power, which, fortunately, it used more sparingly and laxly than is customarily assumed. Jurymen revolted against the immorality of penalties out of all proportion to moral guilt. The crumbling foundation of the old legal system had

[28] J. B. Glover and W. B. Cornell, *The Development of American Industries,* 1941, p. 211. While emigration of artisans was still illegal, 16,000 British artisans had arrived in France during the years 1822-1823. The principal foremen in the cotton factories of France, Belgium, and Holland were from Lancashire, Glasgow and Manchester. Cf. C. K. Hobson, *The Export of Capital,* 1914, p. 109; and Clapham, *op. cit.,* pp. 487-494. The abundance of evasion and smuggling made these prohibitions ineffective and they were repealed in 1847 (6 and 7 Vict. C. 84).

[29] Oliver Goldsmith, *The Citizen of the World* (1760), 1900, Vol. I, p. 245. See also Vol. II, p. 124.

become a simple anomaly to the new radicalism. The need of the day was thoroughgoing legal reform.

Conditions in England between 1815 and 1830 displayed discord between social change and unchanging laws. There was urgent need for people who had studied English law and who were able to elaborate proposals for its practical amendment. Such qualifications were found in Bentham and his disciples.

Bentham was the son of a London attorney, and he shared the beliefs and ideas of the middle-class tradesmen, merchants, and professional men of his time. When he revolted against what he had been taught at Westminster and Oxford, he naturally took up the philosophy which was in the air. That philosophy was utilitarian in substance. It represented the views of Locke and Newton: reason, free thought, the abandonment of prejudices and special privilege.

Bentham founded a method, not a doctrine. He hoped to become the Newton of the moral world. Utilitarianism, which came to him simply as a general principle, in his hands became a powerful instrument applied with most fruitful results to questions of immediate practical interest. And nothing was of more practical interest than commerce. It is not surprising that Bentham as early as 1787 wrote a book on the *Defence of Usury*.[30] This book contained probably every pertinent argument against laws which checked freedom of trade in moneylending; but these laws were only finally repealed in 1854, 22 years after Bentham's death. Still, there can be no doubt that above all utilitarianism was a movement for the reform of the law.

Maintaining that all government is in itself one vast and corrupt evil, protecting ancient customs modified by haphazard legislation, and restricting the action of individuals in no sense necessary for the safety of the country, Bentham believed that the less government the better. But, as governments are a necessary evil, their functions must be limited to the sole legitimate aim of the "greatest good to the greatest number," and they must be watched constantly by public opinion, or through the diffusion of universal responsibility. This was Bentham's leading rule. He called it "Minimize Government."

In practice the rule meant individualism as regards legislation: the

[30] Jeremy Bentham, *Defence of Usury*, in W. Stark, ed., *Jeremy Bentham's Economic Writings*, 1952, Vol. I, pp. 123-207.

sweeping away of government restraints on individual energy, the abolition of government corruption and monopoly power, the removal of historical anomalies, and the repeal of unnecessary checks on individual freedom. In short, the struggle of the utilitarians for individual freedom was also a struggle against government restriction, discrimination, monopoly, corruption, and abuse.

Bentham's hatred of monopolies and artificial privileges, largely granted and protected by government, seems to have been derived from his careful study of contemporary and past facts at least as much as from his general principles of liberty. This also seems to have been true of his predecessors David Hume and Adam Smith. Hume shows that when individual monopolies were granted most freely in England, very few of them were granted to encourage and reward those who had discovered new and constructive methods in manufacture; most of them were given to favorites, or sold for sums not comparable in value to the injury inflicted on the people.[31]

Adam Smith was also convinced, on both *a priori* and empirical grounds, that apprenticeship and settlement laws; laws of succession hindering free trade in land; bounties, duties, and prohibitions in foreign trade; and legal monopolies were activities of government which operated against national prosperity.[32] As Viner said:

> Smith had encountered few instances in which government was rendering intelligent and efficient service to the public welfare outside of the fields of protection and justice. The English government of his day was in the hands of an aristocratic clique, the place-jobbing, corrupt, cynical, and class-biased flower of the British gentry who clung to the traditional mercantilism not so much because of a strong faith that it met the problems of a growing trade struggling to burst its fetters, but because they did not know anything else to do.[33]

To be effective a creed must be credible at the time, and congenial to the aspirations of the mass of mankind. Bentham's creed was exactly that. It provided reformers with a formula.

---

[31] Cf. David Hume, *History of England* (1754), 1840, Vol. II, Chap. XLIV, and Appendix III, pp. 97-113.

[32] Cf. Adam Smith, *Wealth of Nations*, ed. Edwin Cannan, 1937, pp. 120-123, 361-372, 420-439, 472-490, 595-596, 612, 844.

[33] Jacob Viner, "Adam Smith and Laissez Faire," *Journal of Political Economy*, April, 1927, p. 221.

Bentham and his disciples proposed to reform the law of England, not by revolution, but by securing for all Englishmen the right of property and of individual liberty which all in theory enjoyed, but which, through grave defects in the law, were in fact denied to large numbers. The striking phenomenon of this movement was not its conservatism but its fundamental radicalism, the fact that English thought and institutions were able to achieve radical reforms through parliamentary means rather than through physical force.

Although laissez faire was not an essential part of utilitarianism, practically, it was the most vital part of the doctrine. It gave the movement for the reform of the law both its power and its character. It was a radical assertion against every restriction on political and economic liberty not justified by some definite reason of utility. This denunciation of needless restraints, coupled with the struggle for personal liberty, gave the utilitarian movement its whole spirit and life as a militant creed. In his celebrated essay *On Liberty*, John Stuart Mill proclaimed that "the sole end for which mankind are warranted, individually or collectively, in interfering with the liberty of action of any of their number, is self-protection. That the only purpose for which power can be rightfully exercised over any member of a civilized community, against his will, is to prevent harm to others."[34]

The importance of this principle is derived from the fact that it was generally accepted by the leading writers and statesmen of the mid-Victorian era. Nor is it necessary to distinguish between jurists and economists on this point. To be sure, the leaders of the Manchester school were not philosophical radicals. They were enlightened men of business who desired commercial reforms, and in the field of politics they supported and helped carry out the ideas of Bentham more assiduously than did any other body of English liberals. Even trade unionists and theologians conformed to the doctrine of democratic Benthamism. With such widespread support, it is not surprising that the Reform Act of 1832 ushered in a period of individualism and reform which lasted at least until 1870, a period of compara-

---

[34] John Stuart Mill, *On Liberty*, 1873, p. 23. Cf. also Jeremy Bentham, *Truth Versus Ashurst* (1792), 1823, pp. 8-9; and Dicey, *op. cit.*, p. 125.

tive freedom, peace, and economic progress unmatched in the history of modern civilization.

There was thus a delicate transformation, first from medieval prohibition (linked with moral sin) to political offense (linked with evasion and obsolescence); and then, as the supervisory powers of the state became more extensive and more unwieldy, there was a second transformation, from government sin (linked with monopoly and corruption) to a freer and more competitive form of economic organization.

RELATION BETWEEN FREE TRADE AND PEACE

Social, political, and economic integration was perhaps the predominant characteristic of the early nineteenth century. It provided the foundation on which the industrial structure of England flourished. The benefits of free trade, without the need of government controls over the exchanges, became a commonplace among economists as well as men of commerce. Ricardo remarked as early as 1809 that "The exportation of the specie may at all times be safely left to the discretion of individuals; it will not be exported more than any other commodity; unless its exportation should be advantageous to the country. If it be advantageous to export it, no laws can effectively prevent its exportation. Happily in this case, as well as in most others in commerce where there is free competition, the interests of the individual and that of the community are never at variance."[35] The Bank of England followed these precepts. John Clapham reports that in 1824, when heavy lending abroad was turning the exchanges against England, the bank saw no reason to interfere.[36]

Tory liberalism had reformed the tariff before 1832. Preferences had been largely abolished, and were restored and extended in 1842. The policy of protection and imperial preference failed, and in 1846 Peel successfully put through a measure reducing the protective and

[35] David Ricardo, *The High Price of Bullion, A Proof of the Depreciation of Bank Notes*, in Piero Sraffa and M. H. Dobb, eds., *The Works and Correspondence of David Ricardo*, 1951, Vol. III, pp. 55-56.
[36] Committee of 1832, Q. 4847, cited in Sir John Clapham, *The Bank of England, A History*, 1945, Vol. II (1797-1914), pp. 94-95.

preferential duties. During the period 1846-1870, preferential tariff treatment was virtually abolished and tariff levels drastically reduced. There followed an era of phenomenal expansion. By 1860 the United Kingdom had, in effect, attained a free-trade position. Even the capital-starved countries which sought protection for their "infant industries" did not question the logic of the comparatively free system of multilateral trade and its monetary complement, the gold standard. Indeed, the generally successful operation of the entire system provided little occasion to examine the nature of its foundation.

The system of relatively free multilateral trade was the logical counterpart of the system of free private-enterprise national economies. With some exceptions, these private-enterprise economies were held in flexible balance through the interplay of dynamic economic forces. Adaptations occurred more or less automatically, through the cost-price structures of the trading countries, which were linked together by fixed exchange rates. The faith in the mechanism and perseverance of this "automatic" multilateral trading system contributed greatly to the success of its operation.

The absence of major wars, coupled with a phenomenal expansion of production and population, furnished a satisfactory environment for the development of a well-tuned, interdependent structure of world trade with substantial harmony between debt structures and ability to pay. The lack of excessive rigidities in prices and mobility eased the problem of adjustment between debtor and creditor countries, although it must be borne in mind that fundamental adjustments, in the structure of British production were constantly being made to meet changing conditions of demand.[37] This flexibility occurred in an environment two aspects of which deserve particular attention. Imports were readily accepted for the payment of exports or countries supplying industrial exports did not demand immediate payment for their goods. And the mechanism of adjustment was reinforced not only by the generally accepted rules of the game but also by some legislation.

[37] A. G. B. Fisher, "Some Essential Factors in the Evolution of International Trade," *Transactions of the Manchester Statistical Society*, session 1942-1943, p. 11. The impact of Britain's economic development on its internal and external balance will be discussed in detail in Chaps. 8 and 9.

Interested in obtaining raw materials at the lowest possible price, English merchants developed sources of supply as an adjunct of home trade. They found it convenient and profitable to carry on the production of sugar and other tropical commodities in the West Indies. Not only were imports largely balanced by exports, but a great entrepôt trade was developed. There emerged, a satisfactory balance between domestic production, imports, and exports.

Unfortunately, many nineteenth-century English economists accorded an exaggerated importance to the continuance of free trade in maintaining the peace of the world. Ricardo, with customary reserve, wrote that free trade "binds together, by one common tie of interest and intercourse, a universal system of nations throughout the civilized world."[38] Senior attributed to mercantilism many of the causes of war.[39] But John Stuart Mill went further. In an early chapter of his *Principles* he wrote that:

. . . commerce first taught nations to see with good will the wealth and prosperity of one another. Before, the patriot, unless sufficiently advanced in culture to feel the world his country, wished all countries weak, poor, and ill-governed, but his own: he now sees in their wealth and progress a direct source of wealth and progress to his own country. It is commerce which is rapidly rendering war obsolete, by strengthening and multiplying the personal interests which are in natural opposition to it. And it may be said without exaggeration that the great extent and rapid increase of international trade, in being *the principal guarantee* [italics inserted] of the peace of the world, is the great permanent security for the uninterrupted progress of the ideas, the institutions, and the character of the human race.[40]

[38] David Ricardo, *The Principles of Political Economy and Taxation* (1817), 1913, p. 81.

[39] Nassau Senior, *Three Lectures on the Transmission of Precious Metals* (1828), 1931, pp. 35, 51.

[40] John Stuart Mill, *Principles of Political Economy*, ed. W. J. Ashley, 1929, Book III, Chap. XVII, p. 582. In a later passage, Mill showed greater reserve: "The feelings of rival tradesmen, prevailing among nations, overruled for centuries all sense of the general community of advantage which commercial countries derive from the prosperity of one another: and that commercial spirit, which is now *one* [italics inserted] of the strongest obstacles to wars, was during a certain period of European history their principal cause." *Ibid.*, p. 678. It is questionable whether these passages, literally interpreted, mean that "Mill sees in international trade *the chief factor* [italics inserted] of peace." Such is the interpretation of Edmund Silberner in his interesting descriptive study, *The Problem of War in Nineteenth Century Thought*, 1946, p. 165.

In later years he realized that the existence of a great volume of free foreign trade is not a guarantee of peace. Writing to his friend Gustave D'Eichtal during the Franco-Prussian War, he said: "A long time ago I arrived at the sad conviction that, in spite of the incontestable reality of modern progress, we are not yet safe from the great misfortunes and the great crimes which our century was flattering itself of having succeeded in banishing from the earth."[41] From the close of the Napoleonic period until the outbreak of the Franco-Prussian War, this expectation of peace was an implicit assumption of English economic thought, and was, in fact, a necessary condition for many conclusions which were assumed to follow from more mechanical assumptions. When peace was not assumed, circumstances such as industrial power able to withstand foreign competition, industry sufficiently developed to supply the needs of national defense, and a powerful navy capable of keeping open the lanes of commerce seemed to have removed the possible fear that freedom of commerce would weaken the military, political, or economic position of Britain.

If "free trade" was not a sufficient condition for peace, the large and expanding volume of unrestricted trade at least removed most of the economic causes of war. The free system of multilateral trade—with convertibility of currencies at fixed rates of exchange and with flexible cost-price structures—assisted numerous small countries as well as large to live in freedom without being forced to adopt beggar-my-neighbor measures as a defense against the threat of war. The expectation of peace did more to encourage the freedom of trade than the freedom of trade did to encourage peace. Yet history may record a fundamental truth in the classical position: the existence of a reasonable degree of nondiscriminatory trade between the major countries of the world may be necessary for the maintenance of peace among them.

THE ROLE OF LAW AND MANAGEMENT
IN THE MECHANISM

It is generally assumed that during the nineteenth century England was the "manager" of the international gold standard, and that the

---

[41] J. S. Mill, *Letters*, ed. Hugh Elliot, 1910, Vol. II, p. 270; also cited in Silberner, *op. cit.*, p. 66.

Bank of England was a nuclear agency through which this management was applied. There is no evidence for this position. In the crisis of 1783, the Bank of England for the first time deliberately and successfully met an outflow of gold by a contraction of credit. And as late as 1839, the "Chairs" (the directors of the Bank of England) relied on the easy doctrine of allowing "the public to act upon the Bank."[42] From January to October of 1839, treasure dropped from £9,500,000 to £2,300,000 but no monetary contraction occurred.[43] In fact, income from discounts rose on Threadneedle Street from £31,000 to £69,000, and in the branches from £69,000 to £113,000.[44] Prices rose while treasure declined, clearly indicating that a mechanism of adjustment was wanting. The Bank Act of 1844 was intended, among other things, to enforce legally such a mechanism of adjustment in the domestic market. This was to be accomplished by requiring the Issue Department of the bank to limit the issue of notes uncovered by bullion to £14,000,000, above which amount it could issue or contract notes only in exchange for gold. But as far as the international aspect of the gold standard was concerned, there has appeared no evidence whatever to support the common belief that the bank "managed" the gold standard. The Bank of England neither accumulated excess gold reserves in good times nor released excess gold reserves in time of strain. It did not undertake to exert a stabilizing influence on world prices, or to counteract inflationary and deflationary tendencies as they manifested themselves. On the contrary, the Bank of England operated with extremely inadequate reserves. They were inadequate not only for the global task of stabilization but even for the preservation of convertibility of sterling without frequent recourse to undesirable deflationary pressure by the bank on the English economy.

It would seem that the remarkable longevity of the Bank of England must largely be attributed to the conservatism of its management and to the moderation of English politics. From 1694 to 1797 its prestige is probably to be explained by the fact that well-informed opinion considered that its operations were as successful as might

[42] Clapham, op. cit., Vol. II, p. 166. See also F. A. von Hayek, ed., Introduction to Henry Thornton, An Inquiry into the Nature and Effects of the Paper Credit of Great Britain, 1939, p. 38.

[43] Clapham, op. cit., p. 162.

[44] Ibid., Appendix, p. 433.

be expected from any other private or government agency; and from 1797 to 1914 its preëminence in world banking is probably to be explained by its longevity and by its efficient clearing-house facilities for the exchange business of the world, in an environment of political liberalism and *economic expansion*.

Hence, the large measure of success that the international gold standard experienced appears to have been due, in a negative sense, to the legally enforced, conservative behavior of the monetary mechanism of the Bank of England. But in a positive sense it was due much more to the period of economic expansion with which the entire mechanism had to deal.

SUMMARY: INSTITUTIONAL ENVIRONMENT AND TECHNICAL ASSUMPTIONS

The aim of this chapter has been to present a statement of the general background out of which emerged the classical theory of the self-regulating balancing process. Since the general background covers the whole intellectual content of the eighteenth and nineteenth centuries, the discussion has been restricted to those aspects of the institutional environment which suggest what changes in premises may be called for by new facts or by changes in recognized or stated objectives. For the emergence and development of the traditional balancing process, the following institutional factors appear to have been primary requisites:

1. The disintegration of mercantilism.
2. The evolution of a radical utilitarian creed.
3. The spread of monetary-banking investment institutions and instruments.
4. The growth of free private-enterprise national economies, with reasonably flexible cost-price structures and comparatively stable exchange rates.
5. The legal domestic implementation of some basic "mechanism rules."
6. The expectation of peace.
7. The development of a large volume of long-term and short-term private lending and competitive trade.
8. The existence of economic expansion.

The technical assumptions of classical mechanism theory were meant to apply to this, or a similar, environment. They may be briefly summarized:

1. Free competition prevails in each country entering into foreign trade.
2. Free competition exists in international trade except as governments levy import or export duties or grant export bounties.
3. The bulk of trade is carried on by firms or individuals motivated by a desire to maximize profits.
4. Labor and capital migrate within the same country more easily and freely than among different countries.
5. Costs and prices are appreciably more variable than employment; hence full-employment conditions are taken for granted in long-term analysis.
6. Factors of production of equal quality tend to have the same productivity and earn equal rates of pay in all their employments.
7. Transportation costs are assumed to be zero, internally and internationally.
8. Entrepreneurs expect current prices to continue for that part of the future which is relevant to their decisions.
9. An international gold standard prevails, i.e., multilateral convertibility in the modern sense of the term plus approximately stable exchange rates.
10. Monetary and credit systems work either automatically or under central management in such a way as to bring the monetary and real factors easily and readily toward domestic and internaional equilibrium.
11. The maximization of national real income or of aggregate world real income is considered to be the most important economic objective, with some recognition, but not of practical importance, of the possible conflict between countries as to their relative level of real income or of its distribution.

Although these assumptions have undergone technical revision, with some, on occasion, having been dropped and others added, for the most part they have continued to form the basis of traditional mechanism theory.

2

First General Equilibrium
Treatment of the
International Mechanism

THE greatest contribution to the theory of the international mechanism of adjustment prior to the writings of David Hume and Henry Thornton—if not prior to Ricardo—was made in 1720 by Isaac Gervaise.[1] The discussions by Gervaise entitled "Of the Different Kinds of Value," "Of the Balances of Trade," and "Of Exchange" are truly remarkable. His treatment of income effects and his general equilibrium analysis of the international mechanism of adjustment are in many respects superior to those prevalent today. In effect, Gervaise outlined the first theory of general equilibrium in the

[1] For an account of the life and business career of this remarkable man, see my scarce tract of Isaac Gervaise, *The System or Theory of the Trade of the World*, with a foreword by Jacob Viner, 1954. Gervaise was one of the very few economists before Adam Smith who maintained a consistent free-trade position. His objectives, assumptions, and analysis belong to the classical tradition. For these reasons, and because his presentation provides a useful frame of reference for further development, I have placed this chapter here rather than in an appendix, notwithstanding the fact that Gervaise wrote in the preclassical period.

international field, whereas most current presentations are still partial in their approach. He generalized the analysis of the mechanism of adjustment both for relatively stable and for fluctuating exchange rates. The customary present-day treatment deals first with the analysis of stable exchange rates and then proceeds to an analysis of fluctuating exchange rates, as if the processes of adjustment under relatively stable and under fluctuating exchange rates were independent phenomena. Analysis of stable exchange rates usually assumes gold-standard conditions and too frequently overlooks the fact that exchange rates are often stabilized more rigidly after a country is forced off the gold standard. Analysis of fluctuating exchange rates seldom explicitly considers the specific environment or relevant context. To Gervaise the same underlying factors appear to be operating under both conditions, differences in the quantitative importance of the variables under changing conditions always considered. Stable and fluctuating exchange rates are thus not unrelated phenomena. Both are instruments called into operation as part of a generalized process of adjustment or maladjustment through time.

FIRST GENERAL EQUILIBRIUM THEORY OF THE BALANCING PROCESS

Gervaise's basic propositions may be stated algebraically as follows:

Production + imports − exports = Net consumption,

or

$$\text{Production} + \text{imports} = \text{Net consumption} + \text{exports}, \quad (1)$$

$$\begin{array}{l} \text{Production} \times \text{prices (for a given} = \text{Money income (for that period} \\ \text{period of time)} \qquad \text{of time).} \qquad\qquad (2) \end{array}$$

Gervaise points out that if certain commodities were transportable and there were no tariffs or transportation costs, identical internationally traded commodities would be sold at the same price in all markets. Under normal conditions, trade relations would result in the distribution of the precious metals according to the relative national real incomes of the respective trading countries. Parenthetically, Gervaise notes that nations with rich gold and silver mines would be able to sustain a larger proportion of the precious metals than they otherwise would have been able to sustain—but only as long as their mines last and to the extent of their richness. During a war or some other national catastrophe, a nation may be denuded of its precious metals by employing a greater share of its resources "in the Defense of the State,"[2] and other countries may benefit. Ordinarily, however, if a country acquires a greater proportion of the precious metals as compared with the previous levels of money income—money being distributed according to national real income—and the cause of that attraction ceases, the country in question will not be able to retain the greater proportion of the precious metals. For, as Gervaise observes, if a country started with a certain equilibrium level of production, a level required to satisfy a desired and attainable level of national consumption, the increased quantity of money would, by raising money incomes (eq. 2), break the equality (in eq. 1) between the level of consumption and the level of production. The increase in incomes, with no corresponding increase in production, would lead to an excess of consumption over production, for "the number of Rich [consumers] is too great in Proportion to the Poor [producers]." And, since

$$\text{Net consumption} + \text{exports} = \text{Production} + \text{imports} \qquad (1)$$

an excess of consumption over production must mean an excess of imports over exports. Barring loans or default, the excess of imports would be paid for in gold, reducing the stock of gold and therefore, *mutatis mutandis,* causing a decline in the level of money incomes of the country in question, until its proportion of gold to that of the commercially active world gold stock was equal to its proportion of real income to that of world income, on the one hand, and until its level of consumption was equal to its level of production, on the other hand.[3]

This in itself, for 1720, was an important contribution to the understanding of the relation between domestic and international equilibrium. Yet the insights of Gervaise into a relevant and generalized theory of the mechanism of adjustment were even more ingenious.

[2] *Ibid.,* p. 4.
[3] *Ibid.,* p. 5.

CREDIT, INFLATION, AND THEIR EFFECT ON TRADE

Penetrating with surprising simplicity and terseness to the root cause of private credit creation, namely, the wish of the seller to consummate a sale rather than risk losing it in the future, Gervaise considers the case of a nation having increased its credit relative to that of other countries. This disproportionate increase in credit results in higher money incomes and in higher prices. "Credit," writes Gervaise, ". . . adds unto all things, an Increase of the Denomination of Value, proportion'd to the Increase of the Denominator by Credit."[4] Further, he points out that the increase of credit will operate in a way similar to an equal increase of mined gold, so that the country undergoing the credit expansion will retain only its proportion of the increased credit, prices now being higher all around. Explicitly, Gervaise explains the gold efflux entirely through the effect of the credit expansion on money incomes. But, since he assumes a fixed level of production and clearly states the effect of credit upon prices, he may have subsumed the price effects under the income effects. If, however, an explicit treatment of price effects is wanting, his treatment of income effects is both clearer and superior to that of the modern income approach. For his, in effect, is a rate-of-expenditure approach, recording any impact of obsolescence and/or capital decumulation upon the balance of payments—an approach which we should find extremely useful in examining current problems in the international mechanism of adjustment.

Gervaise makes it quite clear that simple metallic-currency systems (presumably he would have said the same for ideal gold-standard conditions) provide no guaranty against world inflations or deflations. Metallic currencies merely tend to prevent an individual country from stepping out of line.[5]

Gervaise's discussion of the mechanism of adjustment under inflationary conditions is particularly noteworthy. Stressing the relation between inflation and the resource-allocation problem, he observed

[4] *Ibid.*, p. 8.
[5] *Ibid.*

that inflation stimulates excessive production for the home market as compared to exports. The nation, "being unable to furnish unto the rest of the World, the same quantity of Labour [goods] it furnish'd" prior to the credit expansion, "the Rich in that case being either richer than they were, or in greater number, consume more than before; so that . . . less is exported from that nation than was before the Excess of its Denominator."[6] In less antiquated terminology: as a result of credit expansion, money incomes are raised, and consequently the consumption of "native" commodities (i.e., domestic plus exportable commodities) is increased, thereby reducing the amount of goods available for export. This reduced volume of exports relative to imports is responsible for the decline in the inflow, and hence in the stock, of precious metals and continues until a new equilibrium position—if possible—is reached, and conversely for the case of deflation.

The inseparable connection between domestic monetary policy and the balance of payments is made emphatically clear. But relative stress is laid upon the tendency for exports to decline during a period of inflation rather than for imports to rise, an important turn of emphasis which has received insufficient theoretical or empirical attention, particularly since Gervaise postulated a meaningful hypothesis which is capable of being tested under varying inflationary conditions.

THE "BALANCE-OF-TRADE" CONCEPT

Gervaise broadens his analysis to introduce the concept of the balance of trade, which he defines as the difference between exports and imports. When disturbances arise solely from trade, this balance "neither is very great, nor lasts long,"[7] for the trade itself causes continuous equilibrating adjustments about a natural level of exports and imports. But under inflationary conditions a lasting discrepancy may arise between imports and exports. In analyzing how such disequilibriums arise and the process of adjustment or maladjustment which they engender, Gervaise made his greatest contribution toward a

[6] *Ibid.*, pp. 8, 9.
[7] *Ibid.*, p. 9.

general theory of the international mechanism of adjustment.

Starting from an equilibrium position between exports and imports, Gervaise, with the aid of an arithmetical example, illustrates how a country undergoing inflation incurs an excess of imports over exports, and then proceeds to show how this indebtedness may be discharged. At first, the indebtedness is met by the exportation of "Coin or Bullion"; for as long as coin remains the legally defined unit of account, it represents the only international means of payment that does not rise in value in terms of paper. All other debt-discharging instruments, e.g., internationally traded goods, are affected by the inflation—rise in price in terms of the domestic currency—and hence are a costlier means of discharging foreign debt. Consequently, the outflow of gold and the negative balance of trade will run against the country until the domestic inflation is checked, i.e., until the total volume of means of payment—gold plus currency plus credit—is again in "proportional Equilibrium of the rest of the World."[8] But how can such an equilibrium be reached?

Equilibrium in the balance of trade may be reached, continues Gervaise, if the country in question possesses a stock of gold large enough not only to permit a gold outflow of sufficient volume to curb the domestic inflation (and thereby restore equilibrium between domestic production and consumption, and thus between imports and exports) but, in addition, to leave enough gold within the country to permit the maintenance of convertibility. If, however, the amount of gold available is so small that, after the country is entirely denuded of its gold holdings, the total amount of domestic means of final payment is still excessive (i.e., consumption exceeds production and therefore imports exceed exports), then convertibility has to be abandoned, in effect, at the point where the excess of imports has so reduced the quantity of gold holdings that they are merely sufficient to support the existing amount of domestic credit. Beyond this point, the level of imports has to be reduced to a volume that can be paid for by the reduced level of exports. This contraction in the volume of imports would lead, in time, to a reduction of domestic credit until a new equilibrium between consumption and production was estab-

[8] *Ibid.*, p. 12.

lished. The result of inflation, concludes Gervaise, "consists only in the Inhabitants living for a time in proportion to that swelling, so as to make a greater Figure than the rest of the World, but always at the cost of their Coin, or of their Store of real and exportable Labour [goods]."[9]

According to the foregoing analysis, inflation tends to reduce the volume of exports and, in time, of imports, thereby lowering the total volume of foreign trade. This, too, is a meaningful hypothesis which is capable of being tested under ideal conditions.

EXCHANGES AND THEIR EFFECTS

We have observed that for the reëstablishment of equilibrium between exports and imports, credit contraction is a primary requisite. But what of the transition? Although Gervaise spoke, as it were, in terms of comparative statics, his major emphasis was on the nature of the transition. He realized that the underlying inflationary factors causing the reduction of exports as compared with imports may not quickly disappear after convertibility and stable exchange rates are no longer attainable. Indeed, among the great merits of his analysis is its generalized and somewhat dynamic treatment of the process whereby a country moves from stable to fluctuating exchange rates. His insistence upon regarding relatively stable and fluctuating exchange rates as part of a continuous process of adjustment or maladjustment to the same underlying disturbance, e.g., domestic inflation, is a contribution of the first rank. He demonstrated that, except for the limited range of possible fluctuations of the exchanges under an international metallic standard, there is no basis for differentiating the theory of foreign exchanges between two currencies having a common metallic standard from that between two currencies of different standards. Yet he did not impute a significant function in the mechanism to the exchange-rate fluctuations within the limits of the specie points.

Specifically, tracing the mechanism of adjustment of a country undergoing inflation, Gervaise points out that if the excess of imports

[9] *Ibid.*, p. 13.

has caused such an outflow of gold that convertibility can no longer be maintained, then it may be impossible to pay for the imports by exports at the going rate of exchange. Foreign creditors, fearing the risk of transporting gold and being unwilling to wait until the balance of trade returns to equilibrium, will sell their accumulated foreign balances at a discount, the extent of the discount varying with the degree of the country's import surplus.

When the exchange rate of the country undergoing inflation falls markedly (ranging downward from the gold-export point) and gold becomes scarce, foreigners find that they would incur severe losses by selling their holdings of the depreciated currency. This in itself makes them ever more anxious to exchange their foreign holdings into any international means of payment whose value has not depreciated. In order to minimize their losses, they use their foreign-currency holdings to buy goods in the country undergoing inflation and ship them wherever they may yield the greatest revenue. But this increased demand for internationally traded goods raises their price in terms of the depreciated currency. Consequently, when merchants try to sell the goods elsewhere in terms of gold, they are compelled to reduce their prices, for competitors from third countries will offer similar goods at lower, uninflated levels. Hence exporters, finding that their receipts are unavoidably reduced by exporting goods to the inflated country, cease to accumulate foreign balances in it and export to it no more than they are sure of importing from it. Thus that nation which has lost its stock of gold will be obliged to use its stock of exportable internationally traded commodities, a condition which will persist until the volume of credit is reduced.

Meanwhile, however, the reduction of exports by the country undergoing inflation stimulates the exports of third countries whose money incomes and prices have not risen. This, in turn, creates a brisk domestic demand in these third countries, making it possible for them to import "produce or materials" from the country undergoing the inflation; for, although the selling prices of the inflated country are high, the dearness is compensated by the difference in exchange. But this, in turn, forces these domestic goods—"raw materials and pro-duce" which ordinarily do not cross national frontiers—to rise in price in the country undergoing inflation even beyond the differences in the exchanges and consequently relative to the price of previously exportable finished manufactures.

As costs of manufacturing in the export fields rise relative to selling prices, exporters in the inflated country may find neither the same profit nor the same demand as before for their products. They are therefore forced to lay off some of their men. By degrees, the workers are compelled to quit their usual occupations and to move to those that are catering to the domestic inflationary demand.

Luxury and "superfluous" industries flourish at the expense of necessities. Nor are subsidies to manufacturers of necessities likely to be of much assistance. For any subsidy given to specific manufacturers merely results in attracting workmen from other similar occupations: "So that what is transported of the encouraged Manufacture, beyond nature, only ballances the Diminution of the others."[10]

Hence, while Gervaise comes very close to the present-day explanation of the way in which a country with a depreciated credit currency reaches equilibrium with an outside world having a metallic standard, he stops short, and his analysis takes on an extremely realistic form, a form which is, in effect, a particular case of a more general case; and the particular nonequilibrating case which Gervaise discusses is, on *a priori* grounds, as likely to occur as the particular equilibrating case which is generally accepted as current doctrine.

Gervaise closes his discussion of the mechanism of adjustment with a testimonial to free trade. When domestic production is not large enough to supply the demand of the inhabitants, he writes:

. . . the best and safest Way is freely to suffer Their Importation from the rest of the World; Taxes on Imports being no more than a Degree of Prohibition, and Prohibition only forcing those Manufactures to extend themselves beyond their natural Proportions, to the prejudice of those, which are, according to the Disposition of the Country, natural beyond the intire Demand of the Inhabitants; which lessens or hinders their Exportation, in proportion to the prejudice they receive by the Increase of those Manufactures, which are but in part natural, and whereof the Importation is prohibited.[11]

[10] *Ibid.*, p. 22.
[11] *Ibid.*, pp. 22-23.

And so Gervaise concludes: "That Trade is never in a better condition, than when it's natural and free."[12] For, even if certain benefits from protection are seen, "it is difficult to perceive its Countercoup, which ever is at least in full proportion to the intended Benefit."[13]

MONOPOLY, TARIFFS, AND THE DETERMINANTS OF FREE TRADE

Before turning to his concluding section on remedies for internal and external instability wrought by inflation, Gervaise strongly censured the inefficiency of bigness and the imperfections and corruptions of monopoly. Giant organizations, which he considered under the heading of "corporations," were of no advantage to the state, except when private people were unable to attain such communal ends as improving navigation, etc. Large units, he maintained, "deprive Man of his natural Right to make the best of his Industry according to his genius, or Inclination."[14] Another charge against bigness was its tendency toward monopolistic and monopsonistic practices: "It's exceeding hard to find a number of Men as careful and laborious, as is necessary in buying and selling, and at the same time so generous and disinterested, as not to turn things to their own private advantage, when occasion serves."[15]

While Gervaise states in uncompromising terms that monetary instability, tariffs, and monopoly must be held in strict control, he consistently adheres to the principle that free enterprise is the essence of liberalism. His judgment on the ultimate determinants of foreign trade is no less incisive, for he suggests in several places that, government interference aside, they are to be explained predominantly by the relative scarcity and abundance of the factors of production, the quality of the factors always considered:

Whenever I mention the quantity of Inhabitants, I always suppose, that regard which ought to be had, to the Situation, and Disposition, of the different Countries of the World; the same quantity of Inhabitants,

[12] *Ibid.*, p. 23.
[13] *Ibid.*
[14] *Ibid.*, p. 27.
[15] *Ibid.*

not producing the same Effect, in all Countries, according as their Dispositions differ: which I shall shew hereafter.[16] [And later:] Neighbouring Nations have, generally speaking, a certain natural Portion, either great or small, of the same Produce and Manufactures, according to their Number of Inhabitants, and as they are disposed and situated.[17]

DOMESTIC AND INTERNATIONAL EQUILIBRIUM

Gervaise next proceeds to furnish his remedies for the interrelated problems of domestic monetary stability and of balanced international accounts.

If a country finds that its exchange rate is overvalued, the remedies are either deflation—"proportion the People to the Denominator"[18]— or a lowering of the exchange rate. But, since a policy of deflation "is most difficult, and almost impossible"[19] to enforce, a lowering of the exchange rate must be preferred. This may be accomplished either (1) by taxation—using the funds to establish a sinking fund for national debts or setting the proceeds aside for future contingencies, i.e., the establishment of a fund which could be used to supplement the normal supply of the domestic currency at the reduced rate of exchange—or (2) by raising the price of coin.

A rise in the price of coin, maintains Gervaise, would reduce the amount of outstanding credit, since a greater proportion of the volume of monetary transactions could now be conducted with the same amount of coin. Raising the price (i.e., denomination) of coin would accordingly bring about the desired monetary contraction. But Gervaise cautioned against severe contraction, maintaining that the hardship caused would be greater, the longer and the more severe had been the credit expansion. If the credit expansion were "new and sudden," it might rapidly disturb the allocation of incomes but not the allocation of resources, for the mobility of resources between "necessary" and "superfluous" manufactures is not a short-term process. Consequently, as long as the misallocation of resources is not serious, trade may not greatly suffer. However, when the credit expansion is of long standing, the resource structure becomes badly skewed, with

---

[16] *Ibid.*, pp. 3-4.
[17] *Ibid.*, p. 22; cf. also pp. 24, 26.
[18] *Ibid.*, p. 29.
[19] *Ibid.*

an excessive amount of factors being sucked into the production of "luxuries" and an inadequate amount remaining for the production of "necessary manufactures." So that, if after several years of such expansion a nation suddenly followed a policy of stringent contraction, the remedy, in effect, might be disastrous. Granted that the demand for "luxuries" would be greatly reduced and the demand for "necessities" increased, but so rapidly and to such an extent that, in the short run, the manufacturers of necessities would be unable to meet the extraordinary demand facing them. Only in the long run would an adjustment be reached, i.e., a period of time sufficiently long to attract from the "luxury" industries the workers which the manufacturers had lost to them during the period of inflation. But this may entail a long period of misery and privation. For these reasons, Gervaise stands resolutely against a policy of rapid and stringent monetary contraction, advocating, instead, a policy of gradualism, with the maintenance of a sufficient stock of foreign reserves to cushion the effect of a serious external drain.[20]

In concluding his discussion on the mechanism of adjustment,

[20] It is interesting to note that Henry Thornton, some eighty years later, similarly elaborated on this point. The lack of balanced judgment on this entire issue makes it worth while to quote, in extenso, Thornton's brilliant testimony on the effects of a severe restriction of the paper of the Bank of England. When such a restriction is "Sudden and Violent," he testified, "it must tend, by the convulsion to which it will lead, to prevent gold from coming into the country rather than to invite it, and thus to insure the danger of the bank itself" (An Inquiry into the Nature and Effects of the Paper Credit of Great Britain, ed. F. A. von Hayek, 1939, p. 122). Later (1802), with comprehensive brevity, he concluded:

"The Bank, by proceeding to that reduction of its own paper which is necessary to bring gold into the country, may possibly annihilate, before it is aware, a part or even almost the whole of the circulating country bank notes, and much other paper also; and it may, in that case, have to supply gold sufficient to fill the whole void, perhaps more than the whole void, which it has created; for it may be called upon to furnish large additional sums which may forthwith be hoarded in consequence of the alarm thus occasioned. Hence, even though it should increase the supply of gold from abroad; it may augment, in a far greater degree, the demand for it at home. For this reason, it may be the true policy and duty of the bank to permit, for a time, and to a certain extent, the continuance of that unfavourable exchange, which causes gold to leave the country, and to be drawn out of its own coffers: and it must, in that case, necessarily encrease its loans to the same extent to which its gold is diminished. The bank, however, ought generally to be provided with a fund of gold so ample, as to enable it to pursue this line of conduct, with safety to itself, through the period of an unfavourable balance, a period, the duration of which may, to a certain degree, be estimated, though disappointment in a second harvest may cause much error in the calculation" (ibid., pp. 152-153).

Gervaise states that although foreign borrowing constitutes a mark of indebtedness, it nonetheless may be a healthy instrument for the development of a country and is entirely compatible with maintaining equilibrium in its international accounts—as long as the "Confidence" and the "Fear" of foreign investors are kept in balance. If, however, fear outstrips confidence, then foreign borrowing may become a disequilibrating force, with the degree of disequilibrium depending upon the degree of fear and the size of the foreign debt. Monopolistic conditions must also be considered; for if a country procures a larger share of world gold, as compared to its relative share of real world income, then it will be found that other nations "are either subjected or indebted to it."[21]

CRITICISMS AND CONCLUSIONS

While Gervaise is guilty of several technical errors of omission in his analysis of the international mechanism of adjustment, he presents a far more precise and more systematic exposition of the nature of domestic and international equilibrium than does any previous theorist known to me. Consistently maintaining the free-trade position, he states that in each country productive resources will be allocated among different industries in accordance with the productive capacities of the people and their "geographical" situation, clearly suggesting that the relative abundance and scarcity of factors— quality considered—are an important determinant of domestic and international specialization.

The most outstanding features of his discussion are his analysis of the self-regulating mechanism of international adjustment, whereby specie obtains its proper international distribution, and his application of the mechanism, in a generalized form, to both stable and fluctuating exchange rates.

Isaac Gervaise was also responsible for one of the earliest statements of the relation between the specie and nonspecie elements of the currency upon prices. He stated correctly that the total means of payments is *a* determinant of prices. He did not, however, explain the

[21] Gervaise, *op. cit.*, p. 34.

international mechanism of adjustment predominantly in terms of fluctuations in relative prices, although he did suggest the importance of changes in relative price structures. His explanation runs in terms of a "rate-of-expenditure approach." In fact, to my knowledge, Gervaise is a pioneer in the use of this approach to determine the proportion in which the money income of a country must be expended between native commodities and imports to achieve domestic and external equilibrium; that is, net consumption of country X must not exceed its production if it is to have sufficient exports to pay for its imports, and, conversely, production of country X must not exceed its net consumption if all other countries are to be able to maintain a sufficient volume of exports to pay for their imports.[22] Gervaise integrated these two advances—his penetrating analysis of the relation between total means of payment and prices and his effective use of the rate-of-expenditure approach—to provide what was in all probability the first systematic exposition of the mechanism of adjustment in terms of the role of fluctuations in the nonspecie as well as in the specie elements of the currency. In taking this forward step, he analyzed the relation between national and international equilibrium, placing much emphasis upon the level of consumption and exports, production and imports; the role of foreign-exchange rates and costs; and the relative fluctuations of import, export, and domestic prices. These contributions alone are sufficient to assure him a rank of first importance in the history of international equilibrium theory.

Further, Gervaise deserves recognition for his treatment of time lags and unemployment. In stressing the importance of transition, as well as equilibrium analysis, he perceived some of the methodological problems for the solution of which economists are still attempting to develop satisfactory techniques. But even in his hands the tortuous analysis of time lags was not without its limitations. For, although he came close to the present-day explanation of how a country with a depreciated credit currency reaches equilibrium with an outside world having a metallic standard, his formulation stopped short, and, instead of maintaining that equilibrium would be reached, he claimed that unemployment would set in and further disequilibrium take

[22] See above, eqs. 1 and 2.

place. Here Gervaise fell into error, for he did not show under what particular assumptions this disequilibrium would occur, nor did he specify the assumptions underlying his position that a reduction in imports or a rise in the price of gold would necessarily curtail the demand for credit. These aberrations and those stemming from his inadequate treatment of velocity and investment are understandable when one takes into account the monetary and banking practices of his time.

Finally, the importance of Isaac Gervaise as a contributor to the general equilibrium theory of the international mechanism of adjustment rests in no small measure upon his purely scientific formulation of his theories and his clear, mathematically illustrated exposition of them at a time when such precise formulation, free of moralistic preoccupation, was scarcely known to economic literature.

3

Persistence of the
Classical Influence

In THIS and the following chapter a critical appraisal of the currently dominant approach to the theory of the balancing process will be presented. This approach is characterized by an unwarranted segmentation, e.g., analysis under conditions of stable exchange rates, analysis under conditions of freely fluctuating exchange rates, analysis of stability conditions in terms of Marshallian demand and supply elasticities, and analysis that attempts to apply "Keynesian economics" to the theory of the international mechanism.

SEGMENTATION IN THE TREATMENT OF THE INTERNATIONAL MECHANISM

We have observed that perhaps the most outstanding feature of the analysis of Isaac Gervaise is the nature of the self-regulating mechanism of international adjustment, whereby specie obtains its proper international distribution, and the application of this mechanism, in a generalized form, to both stable and fluctuating exchanges. He wisely insisted upon regarding relatively stable and fluctuating exchange rates as parts of a sequence of events through time in which, under conditions of pressure on the exchanges, stable exchange rates commonly give way to fluctuating exchange rates in a continuous process of adjustment (or maladjustment) to the same underlying disturbance (e.g., inflation). Gervaise realized the now commonly overlooked fact that, except for the limited range of possible fluctuations of the exchanges under an international metallic standard, there is no basis for differentiating the theory of foreign exchanges between two currencies having a common metallic standard from two currencies on different standards. The fragmentation of mechanism of adjustment analysis into compartments of stable and fluctuating exchange rates is, of course, not incorrect methodologically, but it has led to serious analytical errors and misplaced emphasis in regard to policy.

The compartmentalization is seldom questioned. All the textbooks on international trade use it. First a chapter deals with currencies rigidly linked together by convertibility into gold. Then a chapter deals with the opposite extreme, with inconvertible paper currencies, the relative values of which are determined by supply and demand in the open market. The value of one currency in terms of the other, it is explained, is subject to variations like the price of ordinary commodities. There are no fixed parities or gold points, and hence it is said that a passive balance of payments will cause, not an outflow of gold, but a depreciation of exchange.[1]

Unfortunately, in dealing with the international mechanism, the partial-equilibrium approach and the errors associated with it have become common currency. This fragmented approach is the more surprising since well-known economists of the eighteenth and nineteenth centuries have dealt with the problem in a remarkably vigorous and much more general manner. The discussions by Richard Cantillon

---

[1] Such presentation is surprising in view of the fact that inductive studies have stressed the importance of gold flows in the presence of depreciated paper and fluctuating exchange rates. See, e.g., John H. Williams, *Argentine International Trade under Inconvertible Paper Money, 1880-1900,* 1920, pp. 21, 111, 146, 154, 164, *passim.*

(circa 1730-1735)[2] and by Henry Thornton (in 1802)[3] are striking illustrations. While the relevant passages are too lengthy to be quoted, it is interesting to note that the presentation, especially that of Thornton,[4] is very similar to that of Gervaise.

Thornton, and later Ricardo, never tired of emphasizing that when the country's prices are relatvely high, gold becomes the cheapest way of effecting remittances, the form (i.e., stable or fluctuating) of exchange rates notwithstanding.[5]

Thornton went further and laid down a general principle which, he maintained, applies to all periods of time, and to every kind of circulating medium which may happen to be in use.[6] In a country in which *only coin* circulates, if through some accident "the quantity of coin should become greater in proportion than the goods which it has to transfer than it is in other countries," the coin would become cheap as compared with goods—or, in other words, goods would become dear as compared with coin—and a profit would arise in exporting coin. This profit, in effect, would soon cease through the actual exportation of the excess coin. In a country in which *coin and paper* circulate at the same time, if the two taken together should in like manner become excessive, a similar effect would follow. A profit would arise in exporting coin, and it would therefore be exported. In a country in which *only paper* circulates, if the quantity would in the same sense become excessive, and assuming the credit of the banks which issued it to be perfect, the paper would depreciate "in proportion to the excess, on an exactly similar principle." Goods would rise in price, and it would be necessary to grant, through a depreciation of the exchange rate, a bounty on exports "equal to that which would have been afforded in the two former suppositions, assuming

---

[2] Richard Cantillon, *Essai sur la Nature du Commerce en General*, ed. and trans. Henry Higgs, 1931, pp. 269-299. The exact date of original writing appears to be unknown. See Introduction and pp. 363-389.

[3] Henry Thornton, *An Inquiry into the Nature and Effects of the Paper Credit of Great Britain* (1802), ed. F. A. von Hayek, 1939, pp. 141-160.

[4] *Ibid.*, p. 159.

[5] David Ricardo, *The High Price of Bullion, A Proof of the Depreciation of Bank Notes* (1810), in Piero Sraffa and M. H. Dobb, eds., *The Works and Correspondence of David Ricardo*, Vol. III, 1951, p. 57.

[6] Thornton, *op. cit.*, pp. 247-248.

the quantity of circulating medium to be excessive in an equal degree in all the three cases."

In a review of Ricardo's *High Price of Bullion*, Malthus also spoke of the international mechanism in general rather than in particular terms. He pointed out that the price of bills of a country whose balance of trade turned passive, owing to a failure of the harvest, may be insufficient to restore equilibrium if the fall of the price of bills was limited to the gold export point. He wrote that if the debt for the corn was considerable, and required prompt payment, the bills on the debtor country would fall below the price of the transport of the precious metals. A part of the debt would therefore be paid in these metals, and a part by the increased exports of commodities.[7] It is possible to cite passages from the writings of Longfield, Torrens, Joplin, J. S. Mill, Cairnes, Senior, Bastable, and others in which the international mechanism is analyzed within the framework of an equilibrium theory far more general than that to be found in most current textbook and periodical presentations.

Obviously this would not be a serious defect of the current literature if the specific classifications of the institutional conditions commonly assumed in the partial-equilibrium approach had useful service to render. But it seems questionable whether the classification into stable exchange rates under gold-standard conditions, and fluctuating exchange rates under nondescript conditions, possesses any inherent superiority over other possible institutional arrangements. The classification used currently is an understandable product of historical circumstance. It may have served a useful purpose for its time. But in dealing with mechanism problems of the mid-twentieth century, it is obsolete.

We seek a theory at a high enough level of abstraction and with sufficient generality to be useful in analyzing as many different institutional situations as possible. If we are to explore this possibility, we must first revert to a more general equilibrium analysis of the international mechanism of adjustment. For it is only by so doing that we can differentiate clearly between fundamental, generalized tendencies and particular cases which happen to be imbedded in a

[7] Cf. *Edinburgh Review*, February, 1811, pp. 344-345.

specific historical environment. Before proceeding to this task, it will be useful to note briefly (1) the misplaced emphasis with respect to policy which has resulted from the classification currently in use, and (2) the quality of the extant analysis within the assumptions of this classification.

MISPLACED EMPHASIS WITH RESPECT TO POLICY

The choice between the gold standard and fluctuating exchange rates includes more than a choice between stable versus fluctuating exchange rates. Stable exchange rates may be possible without a gold standard, and the existence of a metallic standard does not insure exchange-rate stability through the relevant future. Furthermore, a widespread adherence to a gold standard does not guarantee against world inflations or world deflations. Hence the following sets of issues, pro and con, of the gold standard; stable versus fluctuating exchange rates; and stable versus fluctuating price levels are separate though closely related problems.

However, even in the hands of Keynes, the issue between stable versus fluctuating exchanges became an issue of stable exchange rates versus stable prices. In his well-known passage on this matter he wrote:

Since . . . the rate of exchange of a country's currency with the currency of the world (assuming for the sake of simplicity that there is only one external currency) depends on the relation between the internal price level and the external price level, it follows that the exchange cannot be stable unless both internal and external price levels remain stable [or move similarly?]. If, therefore, the external price level lies outside our control, we must submit either to our own price level or to our exchange being pulled about by external influences. If the external price level is unstable we cannot keep *both* our own price level *and* our exchanges stable. And we are compelled to choose.[8]

Into this short passage Keynes imported two unfortunate errors. The assimilation of all foreign countries into one single currency is a misleading simplification and, in effect, begs most of the real issues. And the discussion of average "price levels" is not relevant to the issue.

[8] J. M. Keynes, A *Tract on Monetary Reform*, 1923, p. 154.

Keynes' expression "external influences" is an unhappy one, for it is here used in defiance of the fact that a national economy is linked by more than one tie with other national economies. The transition from the notion of insulating a country from disturbing "external influences" to that of an "independent national economy" is one of degree only. Pushed to its logical conclusion, the absence of "external influences" would mean no external ties whatsoever. Moreover, the entire argument ignores the fact that internal as well as external forces may be responsible for domestic fluctuations. And in the event that external forces are more stable than internal ones, then stable exchanges and closest possible economic relations with foreign countries would dampen the severity of domestic fluctuations.

Strictly speaking, there are no "price levels" in the real world, but price structures; and while international comparisons between changes in national price structures are more difficult than comparisons between average price levels, they are much more instructive and provide a safer basis for policy. Under a system of fluctuating exchanges, a paper-standard currency could, of course, be so managed that the amplitude of short-term fluctuations in some general "price level" would be greatly reduced as compared to what they would ordinarily be under stable exchanges. But the fluctuating exchanges and the stability in the general average price level would tend to increase greatly the amplitude of short-term fluctuations relative to each other of the sectional price structures—e.g., export commodities, import commodities, domestic commodities—as compared to what is conceivable under an international gold standard.

Hence, to the extent that stable versus fluctuating exchange rates became the issue of stable exchange rates versus stable prices, this passage from Keynes had the unfortunate effects of misleading and misguiding. It was misleading since it oversimplified the complexities of the international mechanism and thereby led to error; it was misguiding since the illusory promises of general or average price-level stability under fluctuating exchanges directed the attention of many governments toward nationalistic autarkic policies that usually underestimated the possible contribution which a large volume of foreign trade could make to the average level of real income of a country and overestimated its possible contribution to the instability of that level.

If each country were willing and able to stabilize its internal price level, the international exchange position probably would not cause serious maladjustments. Those arguing in this vein, however, either overlooked or disregarded the difficulty that the international and national economic situation required to enable such objectives to be realized is out of gear with our political environment. Assume, for example, that Argentina, while maintaining a stable average price level, reduces its price for wheat. This would affect the income of Canadian wheat farmers, and the Canadian government might find it necessary to cut its exchange rate, as would Australia and other wheat-producing countries, measures which would obstruct their attempts to maintain internal price-level stability.

Between World War I and World War II, many participants in the debate of stable versus fluctuating exchange rates argued at cross purposes, and only too often presented their case in a way which was unrelated to the economic and political environment of the period. Those arguing for stable exchange rates frequently overlooked the economic advantages afforded by an independent monetary standard, particularly such alleged advantages as the possible dampening of, or even escaping from, a deflation or inflation induced by external factors. In addition, they failed persistently to meet an important issue of those advocating fluctuating exchanges, that stable exchanges may intensify a deflation resulting from internal factors by the prevalence of rigidity downward in the prices of the factors of production.

On the other hand, the advocates of fluctuating (i.e., floating) exchange rates failed to meet satisfactorily the position that in actuality almost no country for which foreign trade has been of great importance has ever been willing for long to tolerate freely fluctuating exchange rates. They did not cope with the fact that fluctuating exchanges are an excellent vehicle for speculation, since (1) customarily there is a small, well-informed group dealing in the exchanges; (2) there is no storage expense; (3) there is no physical deterioration or obsolescence due to changes in tastes or wants; (4) the asset in question is for practical purposes homogeneous, standardized, and without grades; (5) brokerage charges are at a minimum, with the level of commissions by middlemen being lower than in any other field of speculation except national bond markets; (6) the hedge earns income for the speculator; (7) foreign exchange or gold may be the best hedge with respect to expectations of fluctuations in the general price level; (8) there are no physical restraints on the extent of the swing downward in the value of a single country's currency. Further, fluctuating exchange rates usually obliterate any objective as to the exchange value of a country's currency. It is the association of the stature and dignity of a country with the reasonable stability and worth-whileness of its national currency, say, in terms of dollars or gold, that often provides the major restraint on unrestrained inflation. Once the brake of reasonably stable exchange rates is removed, the last significant obstacle to irresponsible monetary and fiscal and commercial behavior, for a long period and for many countries, also is removed. Moreover, experience had proved that fluctuating exchange rates result in risks and uncertainties for foreign trade and investment which are economically costly and for which the development of forward exchange markets and other facilities for hedging provide only a very limited palliative.[9]

When England went off the gold standard in September, 1931, her objective was not fluctuating exchange rates for all, but managed fluctuating exchange rates for England with some important country (or countries) maintaining its currency pegged to gold. First the United States, then France performed this function; for until March, 1933, the British Exchange Equalization Account had operated in the dollar market, and when the United States left gold (officially April

[9] E.g., in New York no more than five or six currencies have ever had active forward markets at one time: the Canadian dollar, British pound sterling, French franc, Swiss franc, belga, and guilder. Cf. Paul Einzig, *The Theory of Forward Exchanges*, 1937, pp. 104-105; Keynes, *A Treatise on Money*, 1930, Vol. II, pp. 333-334. The experience of the United Kingdom and Canada from 1950-1955 confirms Professor Robbins' observation that ". . . when the general financial position is strong, free rates are usually unnecessary and that, when it is weak, they are apt to be a source of appalling danger." Lionel Robbins, "The International Economic Problem," *Lloyds Bank Review*, January, 1953, p. 16; and Samuel I. Katz, "Two Approaches to the Exchange-Rate Problem: The United Kingdom and Canada," *Essays in International Finance*, August, 1956, p. 15. Cf. also the testimony of Jacob Viner in *Hearings Before the Subcommittee on Foreign Economic Policy*, 1955, pp. 616-618.

20, 1933) the British Account transferred its operations to the franc market.[10]

Apparently, some participants in the debate assumed that stable or fluctuating exchange rates are to be imposed by mere fiat. They failed, or refused, to recognize that, in an important sense, stable or fluctuating exchange rates are the external manifestation of more fundamental and deep-seated economic and political conditions.

Perhaps the most unfortunate result of the partial-equilibrium discussion in terms of stable versus fluctuating exchanges was that it impeded the development of a new and better approach to the problem, namely, the shift from emphasis upon nationally maintained stable or fluctuating exchanges to emphasis upon developing international institutions for the multinational determination of exchange rates. In order to be effective, these institutions would have to assist in evolving rules proscribing unauthorized or unwarranted unilateral depreciations or appreciations, and to develop a body of economic principles which would meet the need of flexibility in regard to the relative values of the respective member currencies through time, i.e., a moving anchor within the framework of a relatively stable, multinationally determined exchange-rate pattern. And to achieve such an exchange-rate pattern, rules had to be evolved as to more or less appropriate ways of moving from one exchange rate to another. We shall now turn to the problem of examining whether the quality of present-day theoretical literature provides either definite or satisfactory solutions in dealing with these matters.

SOME RECENT INTERPRETATIONS OF THE CLASSICAL THEORY

Not only has the fragmented approach to the international mechanism proved to be a faulty tool of economic analysis, leading to misplaced emphasis with respect to policy, but much of the analysis

[10] This transfer is reported by N. F. Hall, *The Exchange Equalisation Account*, 1935, pp. 54-61. Cf. also Leonard Waight, *The History and Mechanism of the Exchange Equalisation Account*, 1939, p. 21; and Arthur I. Bloomfield, *Capital Imports and the American Balance of Payments*, 1934-39, 1950, pp. 147-50.

within the framework of its own partial assumptions appears to be unsatisfactory.

A survey of recent contributions to international mechanism theory shows many writers believe that in order to attribute the observed adjustments of the balancing process to changes in relative prices, it would in many instances be necessary to assume that demand elasticities are much higher than those which have actually been measured.[11] Empirical studies for the interwar period purport to show that the price elasticity of demand for imports in the United States was about .5, and in the United Kingdom about .6; consequently, many economists thought that the traditional explanation of the mechanism of adjustment in terms of relative prices either is erroneous or does not apply to modern conditions. The rapid adjustment of a country's balance of payments, they concluded, seemed to occur without the assistance of price changes or changes in central bank policy, and to be largely the result of induced movements of income and employment.[12]

Machlup has stated the position in more general terms:

An analysis based on the assumption of full employment must be more, or almost exclusively, interested in relative price changes and the barter terms of trade. An improvement in the barter terms of trade would be the only way of increasing, with a given state of the arts, the real national income. And it becomes very clear why the "*automatic*" rectification of

[11] Cf. Lloyd A. Metzler, "The Theory of International Trade," in A *Survey of Contemporary Economics*, ed. Howard S. Ellis, 1948, p. 215. We shall not be concerned here with the purely statistical difficulties of technique in measuring foreign demand elasticities. Insofar as the statistical studies are concerned, the high values for the import and export elasticities of demand which have been reported for the period since World War II appear to be as inconclusive as the low values which have been reported for the period between World Wars I and II. For a survey of, and commentary on, these statistics, see my "A Note on the Statistical Results of Studies on Demand Elasticities, Income Elasticities, and Foreign Trade Multipliers," *Nordisk Tidsskrift for Teknisk Okonomi*, Lobe No. 39, 1953, pp. 39-54, and sources there cited. Cf., in particular, Guy H. Orcutt, "Measurement of Price Elasticities in International Trade," *The Review of Economics and Statistics*, May, 1950, pp. 117-132; Fritz Machlup, "Elasticity Pessimism in International Trade," *Economia Internazionale*, February, 1950, pp. 3-26; and G. D. A. MacDougall, "British and American Exports: A Study Suggested by the Theory of Comparative Costs, Part I," *Economic Journal*, December, 1951, pp. 718-724; and Part II, *ibid.*, September, 1952, pp. 490-496, 512-518.

[12] Metzler, *loc. cit.*

the trade balance is claimed to be so speedy in an economy with flexible wage rates and unchanged employment.[13]

But who has claimed all this? Are we to believe that all or the most important nineteenth-century writers, not to mention the contributions which have been made by the economists who have followed in their tradition, assumed that demand elasticities are much higher than those which have actually been measured? That they always, or generally, omitted from their analysis induced movements of income and employment? That they assumed, without important qualification, flexible wage rates and unchanged employment? That when they did assume the latter, and considered the barter terms of trade to be the only way of increasing, with a given state of the arts, the real national income, this necessarily meant to them a speedy and automatic rectification of the trade balance?

Many distinguished economists of the nineteenth century not only did not assume what has recently been imputed to them, but, in addition, refrained from making errors which have been made in the recent literature.

Concerning demand elasticity, Henry Thornton, to whom Viner attributes the first clear formulation of the traditional theory of the international mechanism,[14] wrote in 1802:

> The fair statement of the case seems to be this. At the time of the very unfavourable balance (produced, for example, through a failure of the harvest), a country has occasion for large supplies of corn from abroad: but either it has not the means of supplying at the instant a sufficient quantity of goods in return, or, which is much the more probable case, and the case which I suppose more applicable to England, the goods which the country having the unfavourable balance is able to furnish as means of cancelling its debt, are not in such demand abroad as to afford the prospect of a tempting or even of a tolerable price. . . . The country, therefore, which has the favourable balance, being, to a certain degree, eager for payment, but not in immediate want of all that supply of goods which would be necessary to pay the balance, prefers gold as part, at least, of the payment; for gold can always be turned to a more beneficial use than a very great overplus of any other commodity.[15]

[13] Fritz Machlup, *International Trade and the National Income Multiplier*, 1943, p. 207.

[14] Cf. Jacob Viner, *Canada's Balance of International Indebtedness 1900-1913*, 1924, p. 191.

[15] Thornton, *op. cit.*, p. 151.

Moreover, Thornton realized that the demand abroad for English goods was not the decisive issue, and he therefore pushed the matter further. Stressing the role of expectations of foreigners that the British currency might decline in value, he drew attention to the fundamental problem—the relation between England's total supply of, and total demand for, foreign exchange. If England should attempt to pay in goods, "It would be requisite . . . to render them excessively cheap." And if the Bank of England adopts deflationary policies to bring this about:

> . . . then there will arise those other questions . . . whether the bank, in the attempt to produce this very low price, may not, in a country circumstanced as Great Britain is, so exceedingly distress trade and discourage manufacturers as to impair . . . those sources of our returning wealth to which we must chiefly trust for the restoration of our balance of trade, and for bringing back the tide of gold into Great Britain.[16]

To be sure, Thornton did not speak in precise terms of Marshallian demand elasticities, but, as we shall see, in dealing with the international mechanism his analysis may have been the better for it. He was acutely aware of the difference in the possible short-run effects of price reductions as compared with their long-run effects. The favorable effect which a limitation of bank paper produces on the exchange, he noted, is certainly not instantaneous, and may, probably, only be experienced after some considerable interval of time.[17]

Cairnes was even more definite. Dealing with the possibility of inelastic foreign demand for British exports, he wrote in 1854: "It is not true that the motives to importation and exportation depend upon prices alone; and, should the fall in prices be very sudden and violent, I conceive its effect on the whole would be rather unfavourable than otherwise on the exportation of commodities,"[18] probably implying, in modern terms, a foreign-demand elasticity of less than unity.

---

[16] *Ibid.*, pp. 151-152. Concerning expectations, Thornton adds in a note that if foreigners would expect the British exchange to be "a permanently declining one," then it would "answer to them to draw than to remit, and to draw immediately than to delay drawing," both forces further deteriorating Britain's exchange position. Cf. note, pp. 157-158.

[17] *Ibid.*, p. 152.

[18] J. E. Cairnes, *The Principles of Currency Involved in the Bank Charter Act of 1844*, p. 34; cf. also pp. 33-37.

It was precisely because Thornton believed that a sharp drop in prices might reduce England's total supply of means of international payment that he thought the Bank of England ought generally to be provided with a fund of gold sufficiently large to permit the continuance, for a time and to a certain extent, of a passive balance and an outflow of gold, rather than inflict a deflation upon the country.[19] Indeed, to avoid deflation, he held that the bank should increase (although not invariably) its loans to the same extent to which its gold was diminished.[20]

Judging by the above passages, Thornton and Cairnes certainly did not believe that their presentation of the theory of the international mechanism rested on the assumption of high foreign-demand elasticities. While it might be argued that these are short-run considerations, in effect, both authors (and particularly Thornton) maintained that in regard to the adjustment of balances of indebtedness for more or less permanent disturbing factors, such as "war, scarcity, or any other extensive calamity,"[21] induced movements of expenditure and income were as important as, if not more important than, induced movements of prices.

The role of relative changes in demand as an equilibrating force in the international mechanism has, of course, been pointed out by many economists of the nineteenth century. It would appear that most modern economists consider these early statements to have been spotty utterances or flashes of insight unrelated to the general theories of the authors in question. The purpose of the following illustrations is to dispel this common impression. Not only were changes in demand *not* an omitted factor among many of the nineteenth-century economists, but to Thornton, at least, changes in demand brought about by induced movements of income and expenditure appear to have been an integral part of his theory of the balancing process.[22] In a

---

[19] Thornton, *op. cit.*, p. 152.

[20] *Ibid.*, pp. 152-153.

[21] *Ibid.*, p. 143.

[22] *Ibid.*, pp. 142-143. It need scarcely be mentioned that Thornton dealt adequately with the role of price effects in the mechanism. *Ibid.*, e.g., pp. 144-157, and the "Evidence Given Before the Committee of Secrecy of the House of Commons Appointed to Inquire into the Outstanding Demands of the Bank of England" (1797), pp. 279-310.

chapter devoted expressly to this problem, Thornton maintained that there is in the mass of the people of all countries a propensity to adapt their individual expenditures to their incomes. Imports for domestic consumption are limited by the ability of the individuals of that country to pay for them out of their incomes. Imports with a view to subsequent exportation are similarly limited by the ability to pay of the individuals of the several countries to which the imported goods are afterward exported. "The income of individuals," he writes, "is the general limit in all cases."[23] If through any unfortunate circumstance—war, scarcity, or any other extensive calamity—the value of the annual income of the inhabitants of a country is diminished (as are its exports), external balance will be restored, after a certain time, and in some measure, either through a reduction in imports or an expansion of production of certain industries. Hence the "equality between private expenditures and private incomes tends ultimately to produce equality between the commercial exports and imports."[24]

The heterodox treatment of the mechanism of adjustment by Cairnes no doubt was inferior to that of Thornton. In his most general work[25] he makes no reference to the relative shift in means of payment, or to induced movements of income, as a factor contributing to the adjustment of international balances. Actually, in one place, Cairnes wrote that "A change in the relation of exports and imports in the trade of a country can only be effected through a change in relative prices."[26] But previously, in a more specialized study dealing with "The Course of Depreciation," he observed that English and American prices, and with them money incomes in England and America, under the stimulus of new gold had been advancing more rapidly than prices and incomes in Oriental countries. The result was a change in the relative indebtedness of England and America, leading to a transfer of gold to the Oriental countries.[27] And in a still earlier

[23] *Ibid.*, p. 143.
[24] *Ibid.*
[25] J. E. Cairnes, *Some Leading Principles of Political Economy Newly Expounded*, 1874, particularly pp. 353-374.
[26] *Ibid.*, p. 371.
[27] "The Course of Depreciation. Essay Towards a Solution of the Gold Question," read before the British Association, September, 1858. Reprinted in *Essays in Political Economy*, 1873, p. 71. Cf. also "International Results," *ibid.*, pp. 86-87.

essay Cairnes emphasized the role of relative shifts in means of payment, and of induced movements in income and expenditure.[28]

Referring to any circumstance which might occur to render industry less profitable, or to diminish the general wealth of a country, Cairnes said that the means at the disposal of the community for the purchase of foreign commodities would be curtailed. Without supposing any change in prices, therefore, the demand for such commodities would decline and consequently the volume of imports would be reduced. Conversely, if the wealth of a country were to increase, the inhabitants on the average would have more to spend, and a portion of this increased wealth, without necessarily supposing any fall in prices abroad, would increase the demand for imports. Therefore, says Cairnes, the relation between a country's exports and imports, and, by consequence, the inflow and outflow of gold, depends not only on the state of prices at home and abroad but also on the means of purchase which are at the command of home and foreign consumers.

And referring to crop failures, military remittances abroad, etc., Cairnes points out that the resulting gold transfers alter proportionately the "means of expenditures" of the paying and the receiving country, and consequently the demand for each other's goods. There is thus a provision made for the return of gold, "quite independently of the state of prices."[29]

It is thus untrue that all of the most important economists of the eighteenth and nineteenth centuries omitted induced movements of income and expenditure from their presentation of the balancing process. True, many did and especially at times, but to others it was a key factor in their general system of analysis.

It is equally untrue that they always omitted the possibility of unemployment, though they certainly gave inadequate attention to it. Keynes could have obtained his horizontal supply curve of labor from David Hume, the best-known early expositor of the international mechanism. As early as 1752 Hume had written:

In my opinion, it is only in this interval or intermediate situation, between the acquisition of money and rise of prices, that the encreasing quantity of gold and silver is favourable to industry. When any quantity

---

[28] J. E. Cairnes, *The Principles of Currency Involved in the Bank Charter Act of 1844*, 1854, pp. 34-36.
[29] *Ibid.*, p. 36.

of money is imported into a nation, it is not at first dispersed into many hands; but is confined to the coffers of a few persons, who immediately seek to employ it to advantage. Here are a set of manufacturers or merchants, we shall suppose, who have received returns of gold and silver for goods which they sent to Cadiz. *They are thereby enabled to employ more workmen than formerly, who never dream of demanding higher wages,* but are glad of employment from such good paymasters.[30]

It is interesting to note that Hume assumed the existence of unemployment within the context of a problem dealing with international trade. This in no way obtrudes upon the generally correct interpretation that the economists of the eighteenth and nineteenth centuries usually assumed full employment conditions in their long-term economic analysis. But it does suggest that they were aware of the problem, and deliberately chose that assumption: an awareness of unemployment conditions is not an invention of modern economics.

To have assumed "flexible wage rates and unchanged employment," and to have maintained that under such conditions an improvement in the terms of trade is "the only way of increasing, with a given state of the arts, the real national income," does not and, as we have seen, did not mean to economists of the classical tradition, such as Thornton and Cairnes, "a speedy" and "automatic rectification of the trade balance." If under conditions of unemployment and rigid wage rates the rapid adjustment of a country's balance of payments "was found to be largely the result of induced movements of income and employment," this does not necessarily mean that it becomes "very clear why the automatic rectification of the trade balance is claimed to be so speedy in an economy with flexible wage rates and unchanged employment.[31] In discussing short-term adjustments, they made no such claims. Moreover, full employment does not imply constant real income. And full employment or constant real income does not imply constant money income. Money income effects and real income effects can therefore be significant even if full employment is assumed.

Granted, when unemployment conditions were mentioned in the classical literature, these conditions were not incorporated into a

---

[30] David Hume, *Essays Moral, Political, and Literary*, (1752), 1889, ed. T. H. Green and T. H. Gross, p. 313 (italics supplied). Compare with J. M. Keynes, *The General Theory of Employment, Interest, and Money*, 1936, p. 15.

[31] Machlup, *op. cit.*, p. 207; above, pp. 50-51.

"general" theory of employment. However, once it is also granted that, with reference to long-run equilibrium analysis, the "spending versus hoarding" conflict and the attendant assumption of involuntary unemployment are illegitimate assumptions, unless a specific assumption of long-run perverse monetary policy is added, then much of the recent criticism of the classical analysis appears to be unwarranted. The classical writers, in discussing long-run equilibrium analysis, seemed to have in mind an economy in which wage rates and other factor prices were appreciably more variable than employment and a monetary and credit system which worked to promote smooth and rapid equilibration of the balance of payments. It is of course true that most of them gave primary attention to long-run equilibrium analysis. But they virtually all had occasion to deal with problems of short-term adjustment, and when they did so their analysis and conclusions had fewer errors and more relevance than has usually been imputed to it.

What of the possibility, however, of inelastic demand conditions under the classical assumptions of flexible wage rates and unchanged employment? Is it legitimate to apply the Marshallian demand-elasticity concepts to the theory of the balancing process? And if at all, under what conditions?[32]

STABILITY CONDITIONS IN TERMS OF MARSHALLIAN DEMAND AND SUPPLY ELASTICITIES

The purpose of this section is to survey the analysis of recent writers on the determinants of stability conditions, which in the hands

[32] After having formulated my own discussion of this problem, I found substantial agreement between it and the discussion of Michael L. Hoffman, *The Economics of Fluctuating Exchanges*, unpublished Ph.D. dissertation, Department of Economics, University of Chicago, 1942, pp. 84-93. However, the analysis is here applied to a different problem. Cf. also the comments by R. F. Kahn, "Tariffs and the Terms of Trade," *Review of Economic Studies*, Vol. XV (1), 1947-1948, pp. 14-19; C. Kennedy, "Devaluation and the Terms of Trade," *ibid.*, Vol. XVIII (1), 1949-1950, pp. 28-41; I. Balogh and P. P. Streeten, "The Inappropriateness of Simple 'Elasticity' Concepts in the Analysis of International Trade," *Bulletin* of the Oxford University Institute of Statistics, March, 1951, p. 65; S. S. Alexander, "Effects of a Devaluation on a Trade Balance," *International Monetary Fund Staff Papers*, April, 1952, pp. 263-264; Fritz Machlup, "The Analysis of Devaluation," *American Economic Review*, June, 1955, pp. 255-278; and E. V. Morgan, "The Theory of Flexible Exchange Rates," *ibid.*, pp. 279-295.

of these writers consists primarily of Marshallian coefficients of elasticity.

Under the heading "Where Demands are Inelastic the Automatic Mechanism Works the Wrong Way," Lerner has expressed the position as follows.[33] If unemployment succeeds in reducing wages, costs, and prices, exports would be increased because they are cheaper and imports decreased because with the lower incomes not so many of them could be afforded and cheaper domestic goods would be substituted for them. But this would not necessarily mean a correction or even an improvement in the import balance, for that is concerned not with the amounts of physical goods but only with their values. At the lower price of exports foreigners would buy more of them; but unless the quantity of exports increases in a greater proportion than their prices fall, that is, unless the foreign elasticity of demand is greater than unity, the value of the exports would not increase. If the elasticity of demand is less than unity, the value of exports would decrease and that would make the import balance greater than ever. The situation might still be saved by the decrease in imports. But if the demand for imports is very inelastic, the decrease might not be sufficient to make up for the decrease in the value of exports. If the elasticity of demand for imports is greater than zero by the degree to which the elasticity of demand for exports is below unity, the two influences would just offset each other and the fall in domestic prices would have no effect at all on the import balance; and if the elasticity of demand for imports is less than this, the import balance would actually increase as a result of the fall in price so that gold would flow out even faster than before and the crisis would get worse and worse. At the critical point, where the elasticity of demand for imports is just as much above zero as the elasticity of demand for exports is below unity, the sum of the two elasticities is unity. If this sum is greater than unity, a fall in the price level would tend to correct the import balance and to check the gold flow; if it is just equal to unity, the fall in prices would have no effect on the import balance; and if it is less than unity, the fall in prices would increase the import balance and render the situation even more critical.

[33] Abba P. Lerner, *The Economics of Control*, 1944, pp. 377-380.

Applying this argument to depreciation as a means of reducing the import balance of a country, Lerner goes on to say that if the elasticity of demand for exports is unity, the quantity of exports would increase in the same proportion as the price falls (together with the domestic price level), so that the value of the exports would remain the same. If the elasticity of demand for exports is less than unity, say one-third, the quantity bought would increase only one-third as much as the price falls and then the total value of the exports would fall. Suppose the price of exports falls 3 percent. This would result in an increase in exports of 1 percent, so that the total value of exports would fall about 2 percent. Now suppose the elasticity of demand for imports to be two-thirds (so that the sum of the two elasticities is equal to one). Then the decrease in income and in domestic prices of 3 percent would be equivalent to a 3 percent increase in the price of imports (for that is the relative increase) and would lead to a decrease in the amount bought, and in their value, of 2 percent (two-thirds of the change in their relative prices because the elasticity of demand for imports is two-thirds). The values of imports and exports would move together and the import balance would remain unchanged. If the sum of the two elasticities is less than unity, there would be a "perverse" movement of the import balance.

This state of affairs, concludes Lerner, could not be set right by depreciation. That would avoid all the harmful effects of the preliminary phase with a depression at work to reduce the prices; but if the sum of the elasticities is less than unity, it would not correct the initial import balance any more than the fall in prices would. The import balance would increase in the same way and bring with it a further depreciation in the value of the domestic currency which would only make matters still worse. To correct such a situation, we are told, it would be necessary to *raise* the value of the currency instead of lowering it.[34] The situation would be most difficult to handle if the relevant elasticities were in the neighborhood of one. For in that case, a correction either could not be brought about at all through price changes or could be brought about only at the expense of disturbingly sharp changes in the terms of trade.

[34] *Ibid.*, p. 379.

Lerner's terminology is somewhat curious, for it does not stipulate what kind of elasticity concept is involved: price, income, or some hybrid of the two. We are told that exports will be increased because of unemployment and reduced prices, and imports will be reduced because of lower incomes and lower domestic prices. Consider the following statement: ". . . the decrease in income and in domestic prices of 3 per cent is equivalent to a 3 per cent increase in the price of imports (for that is their *relative* increase) and will lead to a decrease in the amount bought, and in their value, of 2 per cent (two thirds of the change in their relative prices because the elasticity of demand for imports is two thirds)."[35]

To treat reductions in income and in domestic prices as equivalent to a relative rise in the price of imports is, of course, technically erroneous. A decline in income does not necessarily have the same effect as a relative rise in import prices; for in the first case we are dealing solely with income effects, and in the second case with price effects *and* income effects. Again, to switch from price reductions to a reduction in the value of the currency, a switch which the reader presumably is to regard as equivalent, is misleading. The process whereby an adjustment in the trade balance might occur through price reductions is not the same as that of a currency depreciation. The differences involved in the issues that arise in the one case are at least as great as are the similarities. By way of illustration, one may note that an improvement in the cost-price relationships in export industries brought about by falling costs and relatively constant selling prices (the case of deflation) may differ significantly from such an improvement brought about by increased selling prices with relatively constant costs (the case of depreciation). Nor does it necessarily follow that if a depreciation of the currency cannot influence the balance of trade, then "To correct such a situation it is necessary to raise the value of the currency instead of lowering it."[36] Movements in the two directions are most likely not to have symmetrical effects.

Lerner assumes that exports and imports are supplied at constant cost, i.e., that the supply curves of imports and exports are infinitely

---

[35] *Ibid.*, p. 378.
[36] *Ibid.*, p. 379.

elastic. If supply elasticities are different, a somewhat more complicated condition prevails, because in that case a depreciation of 3 percent would not result in a proportional change of import and export prices. Most writers who have recently dealt with the problem of exchange stability have therefore presented an "elasticity of the balance of payments" in the following terms.

Consider two countries, Y_1 and Y_2, and let n_1 and n_2 represent the elasticities of demand for imports in the two countries. Similarly, let e_1 and e_2 represent the elasticities of supply of exports. Examining only the trade balance, and starting from an equilibrium position between exports and imports, it has been shown that a devaluation of either country in the proportion K would bring about a change, favorable or unfavorable, in that country's trade balance, which has the following value, relative to the original value of exports:[37]

$$K \cdot \frac{n_1 n_2 (1 + e_1 + e_2) + e_1 e_2 (n_1 + n_2 - 1)}{(n_1 + e_2)(n_2 + e_1)}$$

It can readily be seen that this expression must be positive if the sum of the two demand elasticities is greater than unity, and that it may be positive, even if the sum of the demand elasticities is less than unity, provided that the supply elasticities are sufficiently small. Distinguished economists have drawn important practical conclusions from these results. If exports are produced under constant supply prices—and they claimed this to be the case for many manufactured products—then both e_1 and e_2 are infinite, and the elasticity of the balance of payments becomes $n_1 + n_2 - 1$. The minimum requirement for stability in this case will therefore be that the sum of the two demand elasticities be greater than unity. If the supply of exports is completely inelastic—and they claimed this to be the case in the short run for certain agricultural products—then the elasticity of the balance of payments is always positive and has a value of unity, regardless of the demand elasticities. "Under such conditions," concludes Metzler, "depreciation always improves a country's balance of payments no matter how inelastic the demands for imports may be."[38]

[37] See, e.g., Joan Robinson, *Essays in the Theory of Employment* (1936), 2nd ed., 1947, pp. 142-143; and Metzler, *op. cit.*, pp. 225-227.
[38] Metzler, *op. cit.*, p. 227.

At first glance, the expositions of the "elasticity of the balance of payments," as illustrated above, give the impression of tidiness, rigor, and cleverness, but it may well be that they provide the kind of intellectual light that blinds rather than guides. These formalistic statements seem to overlook the relationships between the policy followed and the forces which these policies set into motion.

Actually, the substance of the apparently complicated "stability conditions" can be presented very simply in geometric form. However, this has the effect of making the misconceptions even more glaringly clear.

Starting from a position of equilibrium, the stability conditions are satisfied if the elasticity of supply is algebraically greater than the elasticity of demand. But there is no need of speaking in terms of elasticity at all. The presentation in terms of slopes is more simple and more general. The stability conditions are satisfied if the demand functions and the supply functions intersect at some positive rate of exchange and the following relations prevail:

1. The demand curve is negatively sloped and the supply curve positively sloped.
2. The demand curve is negatively sloped and the supply curve is negatively sloped, but the supply curve intersects the demand curve from above.
3. The demand curve is positively sloped and the supply curve is positively sloped, but the demand curve cuts the supply curve from below.

1. In Fig. 1 let DD represent England's demand for United States dollars and SS England's supply of United States dollars. Under the customary two-dimensional demand-supply curve assumptions, the higher the price of United States dollars, the lower will be the quantity demanded. For example, in the case of England's imports from the U.S., at the price of, say £1 = $1, British imports would be relatively low. On the other hand, if £1 = $4, the quantity demanded of U.S. imports would be relatively high. Similarly, in terms of these curves, if £1 = $1, there would be a great volume of dollars supplied to England; for American imports of British goods and services would be high. In addition, Americans would find it profitable to supply a large volume of dollars for various forms of American investments in

Britain at that low rate of the pound. On the other hand, if £1 = $4, then the quantity of dollars supplied would be comparatively low. Assume that the two curves intersect at the rate of exchange £1 = $3. At the exchange rate £1 = $4, the quantity of U.S. dollars demanded is, say, $7 billion, whereas the quantity supplied is $4 billion, resulting in an excess demand of $3 billion. If the pound were depreciated to $3, the quantity of U.S. dollars demanded would be reduced to $5 billion, and the quantity supplied would be increased to $5 billion, resulting in an equilibrium position between demand for and the supply of dollars. Thus, based on the assumptions underlying two-

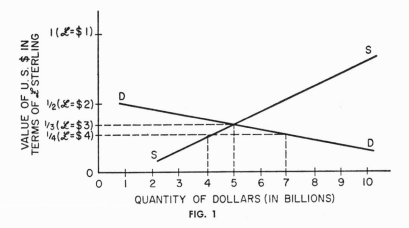

FIG. 1

dimensional demand-supply curves, a sufficient depreciation of the exchange would always bring about an equilibrium in a country's balance of payments.

2. Similarly, as is shown in Fig. 2, if the demand curve is negatively sloped, and the supply curve is also negatively sloped and cuts the demand curve from above, any excess demand for, or excess supply of, dollars could be removed by lowering or raising the value of the British pound respectively. Consider the case of £1 = $4; the quantity of dollars demanded at this rate of exchange would be $8 billion and the quantity supplied would be $6 billion, resulting in an excess demand of $2 billion. If the pound were depreciated to $3, the quantity of dollars demanded would be reduced to $5 billion and this would be

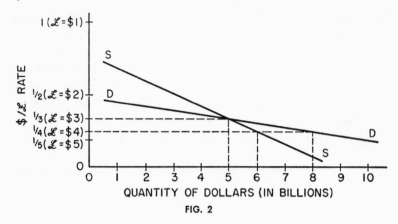

FIG. 2

equal to the quantity of dollars supplied, establishing a position of equilibrium at this rate of exchange.

3. If the demand curve is positively sloped and the supply curve is also positively sloped, with the demand curve cutting the supply curve from below, then again the stability conditions are satisfied. Examine Fig. 3, where such conditions are presented.

Three corresponding disequilibrium cases are represented in Figures 4, 5, and 6. The important point to be made about these cases, as well as about the equilibrium cases presented above, is that the entire form of analysis has little service to render for analyzing important problems of mechanism theory arising from fluctuations in the level

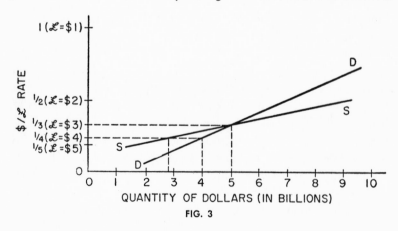

FIG. 3

of income and employment; or, for that matter, from any problems dealing with the mechanism of adjustment arising from monetary disturbances. Yet not only has it, and is it, being used in this form by some of the most eminent international trade theorists, but the analysis is even translated into further elasticity and other mathematical forms.[39]

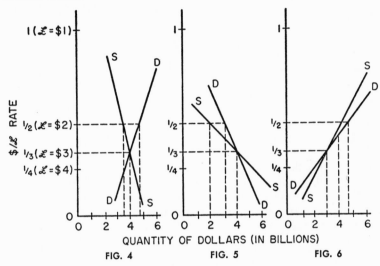

QUANTITY OF DOLLARS (IN BILLIONS)

FIG. 4   FIG. 5   FIG. 6

[39] Expressed in terms of elasticities of demand for currencies, the argument may be summarized as follows. Let England's elasticity of demand for United States dollars be represented by $N_\$$, United States elasticity of demand for British pounds by $N_£$, and England's elasticity of supply of pounds by $E_£$. In terms of Lerner's analysis (corrected for present purposes) the stability conditions would be satisfied if the elasticity of England's demand for dollars plus the elasticity of United States demand for pounds would be greater than unity, i.e.:

$$N_\$ + N_£ > -1 \qquad (1)$$

And since the English demand for dollars implies a supply of pounds, it has been shown that the elasticity of demand of a reciprocal trade curve (i.e., the elasticity of English willingness to buy American goods) is related in the following way to the elasticity of the supply of English pounds (Jacob Viner, *Studies in the Theory of International Trade*, 1937, p. 540):

$$N_\$ + E_£ = -1 \qquad (2)$$

Substituting equation (2) into equation (1), we obtain:

$$N_£ - 1 - E_£ > -1, \text{ or} \qquad (3)$$
$$N_£ - E_£ > 0 \qquad (4)$$
$$\therefore N_£ > E_£ \qquad (5)$$

(Continued)

INAPPROPRIATE PARTIAL ANALYSIS

These recent contributions to the theory of the international mechanism (in terms of Marshallian demand elasticities) would appear to be both inappropriate and unproductive. The entire discussion, be it in algebraic or geometric form, in terms of slopes or elasticities, is applicable only to "real" static equilibrium conditions. It has no applicability whatever to the discussion of international monetary disequilibria, or to the discussion of shifts in domestic two-dimensional trade curves. Mill, and the classical economists who followed his tradition, particularly Marshall and Edgeworth, realized all this; but it is to be regretted that in much, perhaps most, of present-day analysis this is not always the case. As Mill correctly wrote in a letter to Cairnes, June 23, 1869:

I think that the proposition as laid down [i.e., the equation of supply and demand] is something more than an identical proposition. It does not define—nor did it, as I stated it, affect to define—the causes of variations in value. But it declared the *condition* of all such variations and the necessary *modus operandi* of their causes, viz., that they operate by moving the supply to equality with the demand or the demand to equality with the supply.[40]

Starting from a position of equilibrium, the stability conditions of the international mechanism of adjustment are therefore presumably satisfied if the elasticity of supply of a given country's currency is algebraically greater than the elasticity of demand, i.e., since demand elasticity is negative. Disregarding the sign, the elasticity of demand for pounds must be greater than the elasticity of supply of pounds. If the supply curve is negative, too, the demand elasticity must be numerically greater than the supply elasticity—again disregarding the sign. If exports and imports are not equal to begin with, Lerner's stability conditions must be modified as follows (disregarding the sign):

$$N_\$ \cdot \frac{M}{X} + N_\pounds > 1$$

X = exports, M = imports, both in dollars. For the most elegant presentation, see G. Haberler, "The Market for Foreign Exchange and the Stability of the Balance of Payments," *Kyklos*, Vol. III (3), 1949, pp. 193-218; and A. Hirshman, "Devaluation and the Trade Balance," *The Review of Economics and Statistics*, February, 1949, pp. 50-54.

We have already observed that the first substantial contribution to the general equilibrium method of economic analysis was made in the field of international trade by John Stuart Mill and was developed by the English school of economists that followed him. This contribution rested, *inter alia*, upon the perception of the fact that the nature of the magnitudes examined in the international trade mechanism does not permit abstraction from the variations in the value of money inherent to the mechanism of adjustment. How, then, is it possible to speak of Marshallian demand elasticities when dealing with shifts in a country's demand and supply for foreign currencies which by their very nature are assumed to alter price levels and price structures, and are therefore bound to alter the purchasing power of money? Most significant problems involved in the international mechanism are inextricably linked with relative changes in domestic expenditure, gold flows, or exchange-rate movements—all of which almost always cause shifts in "domestic" demand and supply schedules.

To apply the Marshallian concept of elasticity, which assumes the constant purchasing power of money, and which has relevance only to incremental changes *along a demand or supply schedule*, to problems dealing, for the most part, with *shifts* in these schedules is misleading. The misuse of the concept in mechanism theorizing is so widespread—in practically all of its forms—that little service would be rendered by citing individual cases. It will suffice to illustrate the point by referring to the well-known study of the Department of Commerce, *The United States and the World Economy*. Concerning the alleged inelastic demand of the United States for imports, the authors write:

The behavior of United States imports in relation to changes in price is highly distinctive. Over a broad range of commodities, such as a country's total exports or imports, a relative decline in prices generally may be expected to promote sales, while an increase in price works in the opposite direction.

This generalization is not valid, however, with respect to United States imports as a whole because they consist chiefly of primary goods or partially fabricated materials, which are largely noncompetitive, and for which the demand is tied to the course of industrial production. A decrease in foreign prices—whether direct or by means of currency depreciation—thus has *little* or *no stimulative effect* on United States imports, with minor exceptions, and only results in a *fall* in the *total value of our purchases*. This *characteristic of American import trade is particularly unfortunate in times of depression* and *pressure on the balance of payments of foreign countries with the United States. It means that a fall in foreign prices under such conditions does not facilitate but only aggravates the problem of adjustment.*[41]

The fact of the matter is that the demand functions for dollars and the supply functions of dollars in any country for which foreign trade with the United States is important are not independent of one another, and it is therefore illegitimate to discuss the problem in such two-dimensional terms. Aside from the illegitimate application of the inelastic-demand concept in dealing with such problems, the statistical results obtained in regard to it must represent a congeries of promiscuous aggregates. Authors of such statements are apparently thinking of the elasticity of demand for foreign exchange as an "average" of domestic trade-demand-curve elasticities for different commodity imports. To speak, however, "with respect to United States imports as a whole" in elasticity terms is not meaningful. Clearly, it is impossible to postulate a change in the price either of all imports or of all exports and at the same time assume that all other relevant prices remain constant, at least for more than a very short period, which would be necessary in order to make use of any price elasticity of demand. Substantial deflation (or depreciation) cannot but lead to shifts in demand and supply curves as a result of changes in the relative cost and price structures of imports, exports, and domestic goods—independent of the shifts which would occur through changes in income. Moreover, use of the elasticity concept which does not take into account the income effect of price changes is logically invalid for the two-country, two-commodity case and practically even more so for the more general case. Consequently, the statement that the "sum of the demand elasticity" is less than one is a condition of demand in which commodity movements are disequilibrating has no meaning when "elasticity" is used in the sense of simple Marshallian price elasticity.

Further difficulty arises from the failures of many writers to specify

[41] Hal Lary and Associates, 1943, pp. 15 *et seq.* (italics supplied).

their assumptions about monetary and credit policy, fiscal policy, incomes, and employment. The authors of the Department of Commerce study, in asserting that the inelastic character of "American import trade is particularly unfortunate in times of depression," appear to have in mind not merely a downward movement along a demand curve but also a leftward shift of demand curves. It is regrettable that this misconception of the Marshallian concept of elasticity has crept into the most authoritative studies, particularly since Marshall himself gave as his reasons for dealing with international value problems in nonmonetary terms, as distinguished from the monetary approach of his general value theory, (1) the fact that any disturbance in international equilibrium will result in a change in the value of money in the two areas, or in "the standard of prices"; and (2) that if the analysis is in monetary terms, allowance must be made for this change in value. He believed that the attempt to make such allowance results in wholly unmanageable complexities if one proceeds far into the *pure* theory of foreign trade.[42]

The elasticity concept, therefore, when used in the sense of Marshallian two-dimensional domestic trade curves, is inappropriate as a tool for the analysis of the effect of price reductions or of exchange depreciations on the value of exports or imports; for it ignores the effects of changes in relative cost and price structures, in the value of money, and of changes in money incomes, which are too great to be ignored when dealing with important problems in the international mechanism of adjustment.

The elasticity concept expressed in terms of the Marshallian reciprocal demand and supply curves is also inapplicable for dealing with the effects of price reductions or exchange depreciations upon the

[42] Cf. Alfred Marshall, *The Pure Theory of Foreign Trade* (1879), 1930, No. 1, p. 1; *Money, Credit and Commerce*, 1929, p. 157. Professor Samuelson's general comments on the use of the elasticity concept are particularly applicable to the theory and practice of the balancing process. He writes: "Through the influence of Alfred Marshall economists have developed a fondness for certain dimensionless expressions called elasticity coefficients. On the whole, it appears that their importance is not very great except possibly as mental exercises for beginning students. Not only are elasticity expressions more or less useless, but in more complicated systems they become an actual nuisance." Paul A. Samuelson, *Foundations of Economic Analysis*, 1947, pp. 125-126. See also the discussion on pp. 105, 188 n.

current balance, for it is impossible (without serious amendment) to express, in terms of these curves, changes which are not changes in the real demand and real cost situation. Regarding the possibility of aggregation, the arguments raised against the applicability of the Marshallian elasticity-of-demand concept for two-dimensional domestic trade curves, expressed in some quasi-Marshallian form, apply also against Marshall's reciprocal demand and supply curves, since the same problem of aggregation arises if one operates with export and import "bales" of changing content.

Drawn entirely in real terms, each point on a reciprocal demand-supply curve includes a number of "bales" of domestic goods that would be given up on certain terms of trade for a given number of "bales" of foreign goods, each bale representing a fixed quantity of productive services. A movement along a curve indicates alternative trading positions when underlying consumer preferences and real cost conditions are given. A shift of the curve to the left or right indicates a change in the underlying consumer preferences and/or real cost conditions. These curves are useful and valid at the same level of analysis as is static general equilibrium theory. They are useful for the purpose for which they were designed, viz., to give graphical representation to the long-run effect of changes in the underlying determinants of trade.

The reciprocal trade curves are, in short, not applicable to situations where monetary disequilibrium is involved; they cannot be drawn to depict a situation in which tastes, supply functions of resources, and productivity functions remain the same while prices and incomes are unstable in one (or more) of the trading regions. To be sure, they are free of one of the limitations of demand elasticities derived from the domestic curves in that they specifically account for the income effect of changes in relative prices. But they are drawn to depict a final equilibrium position, always expressed in real terms, with money treated as a *numéraire* and expressing the situation after all the internal readjustments have been made.

In either of the usual senses in which the Marshallian elasticity concept is used (in domestic market analysis or in international reciprocal-demand analysis), it is therefore inadequate when monetary instability is assumed or when the problem of primary interest is a disturbance which is essentially monetary in origin.

GENERALITY OF CLASSICAL ANALYSIS AND ITS GAPS

Though Marshall's theory of international value abstracts from absolute money prices, he did not regard it as a theory of barter applied to foreign trade. The theory of barter, strictly speaking, is not applicable to an economy in which money serves as a medium of exchange, as a common measure of relative values, and as a store of value. In drawing his reciprocal demand curves, Marshall took for granted the existence of money and the execution of its respective functions, but he confined his analysis to the nonmonetary manifestations of the balancing process. He strongly adhered to the classical tradition of general, as compared with partial, analysis of the international mechanism. Attempting to present a picture of complete generality which would show the final result of the balancing process, Marshall, in effect, used macroeconomic and microeconomic analysis simultaneously. To avoid complexity—but in order to stress generality —he made it quite clear that while his reciprocal demand-and-supply-curve diagram may be applicable to single countries, whose sole trade is with one another, in the last analysis it should be interpreted as an n-country diagram, with the country of special interest or "your" country set off against all foreign countries combined.[43]

Marshall noted that even in domestic price theory it is logically incorrect to treat the supply of and demand for significant commodities in a common national market as completely independent of

[43] Marshall was concerned lest his diagram be misapplied. Given the multiplicity of potential exports, he argued that, in the long run, most trade of a modern commercial country and the rest of the world involves high elasticities of demand for exports in general—i.e., for the productive power of the area in question. Two-dimensional diagrams, he cautioned, are likely to give false ideas of the possibilities of long-period elasticities, even when they are supposed to represent the supply of and demand for representative bales with changing contents. Cf. Alfred Marshall, "Memorandum on the Fiscal Policy of International Trade" (1903), in *Official Papers of Alfred Marshall*, 1926, pp. 368-388; *Memorials of Alfred Marshall*, ed. A. C. Pigou, 1925, pp. 449-451. See also the discussions by Lionel Robbins, *The Economist in the Twentieth Century*, 1954, pp. 113-114; and Jacob Viner, "International Trade Theory and Its Present Day Relevance," *Economics and Public Policy*, 1955, pp. 111-112, 126.

each other. In the field of foreign trade, he regarded it as logically absurd to treat the supply of and demand for currency in terms of money for each country as independent of each other, and of the amount of national real income, and seriously in conflict with reality if the traded goods under consideration are taken as representative of a large fraction of the total national output or consumption. To Marshall, the most fundamental characteristic of the balancing process was its interdependence: the interdependence of supplies of and demands for foreign currencies, of the entire system of national demand curves for imports and their relation to exports, of national supply curves for exports and their relation to imports. The mutual dependence of exports and imports is specifically provided for in his reciprocal demand and supply curves by an ingenious fusing of the two concepts into one.

In all these respects, most of the recent literature on the international mechanism appears to be at the opposite pole. Its most fundamental characteristic is independence of national demand and supply curves both for imports and exports and for foreign currencies. In the modern literature on exchange theory and stability conditions, all the weight is thrown on price elasticities of independent national demand and supply curves for foreign currencies—even more so than in the pre-Keynesian era, and certainly more so than in some of the best classical literature.

The recent neo-Marshallian contributions to mechanism theory have been productive in focusing attention upon the basic assumptions of classical theory and upon the important gaps which it contained. The classical literature either underemphasized or failed to discuss key aspects of the balancing or imbalancing process which arise from such causes as relative shifts in levels of national real and money income; the differences in relative and absolute quantities of the factors of production and their quality in different regions; dynamic factors of growth and change, or "economic development"; the differences in the structure of industrial and agricultural production; the existence of imperfect factor and commodity markets; the international movement of labor and capital; the existence of fluctuating exchanges under various national monetary standards; the existence of pegged exchanges and the inability or unwillingness of various countries to discharge their international obligations in full convertible means of payment.

The frame of reference of classical mechanism theory was broad and vague enough so that it succeeded in leaving much room for the incorporation of many of these factors into its analysis. It is an open question, however, as to how many of these variables and their mutual interrelations can be incorporated into a general theory of the international mechanism which would be able to provide both true and relevant conclusions. General or not, if the theory of the international mechanism is to have relevance to present-day conditions, the aforementioned factors will have to be considered. For as Marshall observed: "It is not by applying without question the judgments as to proportion which were made by the great men who founded our present system, but by forming our own judgment on the facts of our own generation as they did of theirs, that we can show ourselves worthy to be their followers."[44]

---

[44] Marshall, "Memorandum on the Fiscal Policy of International Trade," p. 368.

4

The Keynesian Contribution

THE Keynesian developments in economic theory which occurred in the 1930's had a profound influence upon almost all fields of economics, and this was no less true of international-trade theory than of other branches of the science.

Keynes' main objective in the *General Theory* was to explain the determinants of the level of income and employment. Primarily his book was a reconsideration of traditional ideas regarding money, interest rates, and prices. It is therefore not surprising to find that the most important changes which the Keynesian literature made in the balancing theory were in the income and monetary aspects of the subject. Let us begin our analysis with Metzler's able survey of this Keynesian influence.[1]

ALLEGED ERRORS IN TRADITIONAL DOCTRINE

The important feature of the classical mechanism, we are told, is the central role which it attributed to the monetary system. The classical theory, the Keynesian writers believe, contained an explicit

[1] Lloyd Metzler, "The Theory of International Trade," in a *Survey of Contemporary Economics*, ed. Howard S. Ellis, 1948, pp. 210-215.

acceptance of the quantity theory of money as well as an implied assumption that output and employment are unaffected by international monetary disturbances. In other words, the classical doctrine assumed that an increase or decrease in the quantity of money leads to an increase or decrease in the aggregate money demand for goods and services, and that a change in money demand affects prices and costs rather than output and employment. It was the Keynesian revolution, the argument proceeds, that cast doubt upon both of these crucial assumptions. Say's Law of Markets—the bulwark of both the quantity theory and the classical theory of the balance of payments— was rejected, and the possibility of general overproduction or general unemployment was finally acknowledged. In the course of this revolution, the monetary system, which had been regarded as a director of economic activity, was relegated to a somewhat secondary position, and economists increasingly emphasized the effect of saving and spending habits upon the circular flow of income.

Thus the Keynesian writers assumed that the foundations of the classical theory had crumbled and that Keynesian economics provided a new explanation of the balancing process in international trade. The new theory, they claimed, was a direct outgrowth of the *General Theory*, though Keynes himself had little to do with it. The essence of this new theory was thought to be that an external event which increases a country's exports will also increase imports even without price changes, since the change in exports affects the level of output and hence the demand for all goods. Movements of output and employment, it was said, play much the same role in the new doctrine that price movements played in the old.

In explaining the position of the Keynesian writers, Professor Metzler states—too sweepingly—that no substantial revisions of the traditional theory were made until Keynes published his *General Theory*.[2] Illustrating the new doctrine, he assumes that country A increases its imports from country B, and that a deficit thus arises in A's balance of payments. At first, the deficit may be financed by a movement of gold or by a transfer of short-term balances. But regardless of the method of financing, a more or less automatic mech-

[2] *Ibid.*, p. 215.

anism will soon offset at least part of the initial disturbance. Income and employment will expand in the export industries of country B, the demand for home goods will therefore rise in that country, and the expansion will spread from the export industries to the entire economy. As output and employment increase, country B will increase its imports from country A, thereby offsetting a part, or perhaps all, of the initial rise of exports to A.

Let us examine the substance of these propositions. In regard to the "explicit acceptance of the quantity theory of money," there is no doubt whatever that the important members of the classical school maintained that the quantity of money was a determinant of the level of prices. Serious criticism of this assumption must therefore be directed not against some crude concept of the quantity theory, which the classical economists did not hold, but against their omission of the Keynesian assumption that, under certain circumstances, the quantity of money has no effect upon prices. And for this perhaps grounds for praise are as strong as grounds for blame. In any event, theoretically, there is no contradiction between a correct statement of the quantity theory and the extreme Keynesian case in which an increase in the quantity of money has no effect upon prices, for under such conditions (a horizontal demand schedule for cash balances) the velocity of the additional quantity of money is in effect equal to zero.[3]

---

[3] By a "correct" statement of the "quantity theory" I mean that M is *a* determinant (and determinate) of P and not that M is *the* determinant of P. It might be argued that, strictly speaking, the quantity theory says that P varies directly and proportionally with M, or that in the Fisher equation, $P = \dfrac{MV}{T}$, the fraction $\dfrac{V}{T}$ is a constant, hence $P = K(\text{constant}) \cdot M$. Accordingly, one might assert that a "correct" statement of the "quantity theory," in which, for example, V drops as M increases, is really not "the" quantity theory. Those writing in the classical quantity-theory tradition, such as Cantillon, Thornton, Ricardo, and Mill, did not adhere to so rigid a position; and it certainly would not apply to short-term problems of the kind referred to in the text. However, there is not full agreement on this in the literature and certain aspects of the aforementioned rigid approach are often referred to as being "traditional." For stimulating discussions of classical, neoclassical, and recent theories of money, interest, and, prices, cf. Don Patinkin, *Money, Interest, and Prices*, 1956, pp. 96-121, 256-269, and notes A, J, and K in the Appendix; J. R. Hicks, "A Rehabilitation of 'Classical' Economics?"

Concerning the implied assumption that output and employment are unaffected by international monetary disturbances, there is evidence showing that a number of early classical writers dealt with this relationship. As Professor Robertson has pointed out, the charge (just or unjust) against the classical theorists was not that they "assumed full employment" but that they took too lightly the fact that such unemployment, even when money wages were more flexible than they are now, was involved in the working of the system.[4] Moreover, they did assume a degree of wage flexibility downward which was not in conformity with the facts of their own day.[5] To repeat, if we are to give the classical economists the best possible interpretation, we should recognize that their analysis appears to rest on the implied assumption that prices (including wage rates) are appreciably more variable than employment. This may have been a mistaken notion, but to the knowledge of the present writer there exists as yet no conclusive evidence to demonstrate that it was erroneous.

The Keynesian revolution could scarcely claim credit for the rejection of Say's Law of Markets. It will be recalled that the discussion concerning the Law of Markets was stimulated by the crises of 1818 and 1825. Primarily it was a debate between Malthus and Sismondi, on the one hand, and Say, Ricardo, and James Mill, on the other. For different reasons, Malthus and Sismondi regarded oversaving as a consequence of the development of capitalism and maintained, accordingly, that a general oversupply of commodities was possible.[6] Say, Ricardo, and James Mill attacked this view, Say serving

---

Economic Journal, June, 1957, pp. 278-289; William Fellner, Monetary Policies and Full Employment, 1946, pp. 136-173; and Franco Modigliani, "Liquidity Preference and the Theory of Interest and Money," Econometrica, Vol. 12, 1944, pp. 45-88, reprinted in Readings in Monetary Theory, 1951, pp. 186-240.

[4] D. H. Robertson, "The Revolutionists' Handbook," Quarterly Journal of Economics, February, 1950, p. 10.

[5] See A. L. Bowley, "The Statistics of Wages in the United Kingdom during the Last Hundred Years," Journal of the Royal Statistical Society, December, 1898, pp. 702-722; March, 1899, pp. 140-151; March, 1901, pp. 102-111; and A. D. Gayer, W. W. Rostow, A. J. Schwartz, and I. Frank, The Growth and Fluctuation of the British Economy, 1953, Vol. II, pp. 939-957.

[6] Cf. T. R. Malthus, Principles of Political Economy, 1821, pp. 6-7: "If consumption exceed production, the capital of the country must be diminished, and its wealth must be gradually destroyed from its want of power to produce; if pro-

as principal expositor and Ricardo giving the concept precise formulation.[7]

The fact that Say's Law has become the target of adverse criticism from Keynes and the Keynesians has given it an importance out of all proportion to its original, and subsequent, meaning. According to some Keynesian writers it is to be regarded as a basic proposition of the Walras-Marshall system.[8] For these reasons, and because of its importance for mechanism theory, we must present a brief statement of this concept with greater care than would otherwise be necessary.

Say perceived that under division of labor, the only means normally available to everyone for acquiring goods and services would be to produce (or take part in production of) some equivalent goods and services. Consequently, production increases not only the supply of goods in markets but normally it also increases the demand for them. It is in this sense that production itself (or supply) creates the "fund" from which flows the demand for its products. Products are thus "ultimately" paid for by products in domestic as well as in foreign trade. Say realized the theoretical implications of this theorem, viz., that a balanced expansion in all lines of production is an absolutely different phenomenon from a one-sided increase in the output of an individual industry or group of industries. Consider an industry that is too small to exert a perceptible influence upon the rest of the economy, and hence upon such social aggregates as national income.

---

duction be in a great excess above consumption, the motive to accumulate and produce must cease from the want of will to consume. The two extremes are obvious: and it follows that there must be some intermediate point [the optimum propensity to consume?], though the resources of political economy may not be able to ascertain it, where taking into consideration both the power to produce and the will to consume, the encouragement to the increase of wealth is the greatest." Malthus states further (p. 8) that the adoption of parsimonious habits in too great degree must "throw the labouring classes out of employment." Sismondi used the very words "consumption . . . is in fact limited by income." M. de Sismondi, *Political Economy and the Philosophy of Government*, 1847, pp. 119-120. Sismondi's views on this matter were first published in 1819. Cf. *ibid.*, p. 113.

[7] See, e.g., J. B. Say, *Traité d'Économie Politique*, 1803, pp. 152 *et seq.*, and A *Treatise on Political Economy*, trans. C. R. Prinsep, 1824, Book 1, Chap. XV, esp. pp. 84-86, 89-93; and David Ricardo, *The Principles of Political Economy and Taxation* (1817), 1937, p. 194.

[8] Cf. the discussion and references in Joseph A. Schumpeter, *History of Economic Analysis*, 1954, pp. 615-625.

The conditions in the rest of the economy may therefore be considered as data for an analysis of this industry. The demand schedule for the product of the industry is derived from the income generated by all the other industries. Since its own contribution to total income is assumed to be negligible, the demand schedule of this industry may be considered as given independently of its own supply, and so may (in general) the prices of the factors which it uses. Hence we have given independent demand and cost schedules that summarize the economic conditions to which the industry has to respond and which determine the output it will produce at each price (supply schedule). The equilibrium output of the industry is defined by this demand and this supply schedule. It would be meaningful to say that, in a particular case, the industry produced "too little" or "too much," and it would not be difficult to describe the mechanism set in motion to eliminate such under- or overproduction. This industry's output, however, is obviously the equilibrium or "right" output only with reference to the outputs of all other industries. In other words, demand schedules, supply schedules, and equilibrium are concepts which may be legitimately used to describe quantitative relations *within* the universe of commodities and services. They do not have meaning with respect to this universe itself. Strictly speaking, it is not meaningful to speak of an economic system's total demand and supply. But when economists do apply the terms demand and supply to social aggregates, one must bear in mind that they mean something entirely different from what they mean in their usual context and acceptance. In particular, this "aggregate demand" and "aggregate supply" are not independent of each other because the component demands for the output of any industry come from the supplies of all the other industries and hence the component demands will in most cases increase (in real terms) if these supplies increase and decrease if these supplies decrease. It is this proposition which renders Say's fundamental meaning.

Interpreted in this way, it is both true and important. Keynes obviously had no objection to this connotation. Regrettably, errors are made to this day from the mistaken application to social aggregates of propositions derived by means of the demand-supply apparatus. As we had occasion to observe, these errors have been serious in mechanism theory. Keynes himself warned his readers not to confuse his Aggregate Demand Function and Aggregate Supply Function with supply and demand functions "in the ordinary sense."[9] However, Keynes adopted a different interpretation of Say's Law, which has been precisely formulated by Oscar Lange.[10] According to this interpretation, the Law consisted of two parts, the impossibility of total excess of supply and the impossibility of general overproduction.

Say believed that universal excess supply was impossible by virtue of the fact that the demand for one commodity is the supply of other commodities. Therefore, there could be no excess of supply over demand for all commodities, for the excess of supply of one commodity implied that there was an insufficient amount of other commodities with which it could be bought. Obviously, the argument is based upon the assumption that no money is hoarded. If each sale of commodities automatically implies demand for other commodities, then each supply creates a potential demand. But Ricardo, long before the "Keynesian revolution," was quite conscious of this assumption. He realized that the argument was based on the proposition that "Money is only a medium by which exchange is effected."[11] However, since money is also a store of value, it can,

[9] J. M. Keynes, *The General Theory of Employment, Interest and Money*, 1936, p. 24, n. 1.

[10] Oscar Lange, "Say's Law: A Restatement and Criticism," in *Studies in Mathematical Economics and Econometrics*, ed. O. Lange, F. McIntyre, and T. O. Yntema, 1942, pp. 49-69. For some recent literature related to Say's Law, but not directly relevant to the problem at hand, see the articles by Patinkin, Hickman, Leontief, Phipps, and Brunner in *Econometrica*, Vols. 16, 17, 18, and 19; Patinkin, "A Reconsideration of the General-Equilibrium Theory of Money," *The Review of Economic Studies*, Vol. XVIII, No. 45, 1949-1950, pp. 42-61; G. S. Becker and W. J. Baumol, "Classical Monetary Theory: The Outcome of the Discussion," *Economica*, November, 1952, pp. 355-376; Patinkin, *Money, Interest and Prices*, note L, pp. 472-476, and sources there cited to the text.

[11] Ricardo, *op. cit.*, p. 194. Nonetheless, Ricardo and Say were often practically wrong in either not realizing or terribly understating the gulf that separated their theorem from the realities of the economic process to which it was meant to apply. I do not wish to be misunderstood. It is of course true that Ricardo upheld Say's Law while Keynes rejected it. In spite of the abundant empirical evidence to the contrary, Ricardo was able to convince the classical economists that Say's Law actually held. But the point I wish to stress in the following passages of the text concerns the history of ideas; to wit, many economists long before Keynes rejected Say's Law.

of course, be hoarded. And under such circumstances acts of supply are not necesarily followed by acts of demand. Similarly, if money is dishoarded, acts of demand are not preceded by acts of supply. Consequently, total supply can be greater than total demand, or total demand can be greater than total supply.

In a word, the first part of Say's Law was based on the assumption that the demand for money is equal to the supply of money, and this assumption was made explicitly by Ricardo. Admittedly, Say's writing was careless; but prior to 1832 Thomas Attwood, in a series of articles published under the signature "The Scotch Banker," stated the matter correctly.[12] These issues have unfortunately caused much confusion. Their importance for present purposes warrants a correct statement of them here.

Consider a closed economy with n commodities (securities can readily be included in the analysis), their prices ranging from $p_1 \ldots p_n$. Let the quantities demanded be signified by $D_1, D_2 \ldots D_n$. Money is not included as one of these commodities and prices are all expressed in dollars. Let the quantity of commodities supplied be indicated by $S_1, S_2 \ldots S_n$. The demand for money will be signified by $D_{(m)}$, the supply of money by $S_{(m)}$.

1. The total demand for money is equal to the quantities of different commodities supplied multiplied by their prices, or:

$$D_{(m)} = p_1 S_1 + p_2 S_2 + \ldots + p_n S_n = \sum_{i=1}^{n} p_i S_i$$

2. The total supply of money is equal to the quantities of different commodities demanded multiplied by their prices, or:

$$S_m = p_1 D_1 + p_2 D_2 + \ldots + p_n D_n = \sum_{i=1}^{n} p_i D_i$$

3. Therefore the total supply of commodities is equal to the total demand for commodities when the aggregate demand for money (as a flow) is equal to the aggregate supply of money, or:

[12] Thomas Attwood, *The Scotch Banker*, 2nd ed., 1832, esp. pp. 37-49; *Observations on Currency, Population and Pauperism*, 1818, pp. 97-117; 150-160, 209-51; *Prosperity Restored*, 1817, particularly p. 40.

$$\sum_{i=1}^{n} p_i S_i = \sum_{i=1}^{n} p_i D_i \text{ when } D_m = S_m$$

Say erroneously maintained that the total supply of commodities was *always* equal to the total demand for commodities, or that the following was an identity:

$$\sum_{i=1}^{n} p_i S_i = \sum_{i=1}^{n} p_i D_i$$

In his diffuse exposition, Say did express himself in several places as if it were an identity. But Ricardo and Attwood, and later Marx and Wicksell, and the later Cambridge and Swedish schools, and most American economists maintained that this was *not* true. The total supply of commodities is equal to the total demand for commodities only when the total demand for money is equal to the total supply of money, or:

$$\sum_{i=1}^{n} p_i S_i = \sum_{i=1}^{n} p_i D_i$$

is an equation, not an identity. Actually, read in its entire context, one gets the impression that Say did not consider it to be an identity. If we are to give him the most favorable interpretation, the first part of Say's Law would assert the impossibility of total excess supply only in a state of perfect equilibrium of the system.

Say, it is true, did not consider that when we demand money, we may be demanding it to increase our stocks of money, not merely to purchase goods. He always treated the demand and supply of money in terms of flows rather than stocks. But the flow of money demand is in fact equal to the flow of money supply only when the amount of money which people want to hold in cash balances is equal to the total amount of money in existence. This presupposes that the banks and other monetary institutions are able and willing to create the amount of money which people wish to hold. All this was well recognized long before the *General Theory*.

So was the fact that the second part of Say's Law was erroneous. The proposition that universal overproduction is impossible implied that all commodities can be sold to cover costs; i.e., it assumes certain relationships between prices of products and prices of factors of production. But if the demand for money is assumed to be identical with the supply of money, then the demand for commodities is equal to the supply of commodities no matter what the prices of commodities may be—no matter what the price structure is. For over a hundred years it has been recognized that whether prices of products are sufficient to cover costs cannot be deduced from the first part of Say's Law. Indeed, Say gave up the entire problem by a terminological sleight of hand, defining products as things which can be sold at a price to cover the cost of production. The "rejection" of Say's Law, therefore, can scarcely be claimed as one of the achievements of the Keynesian revolution.

However, Keynes had something more important in mind. Even the most favorable interpretation of Say's Law does not get to the root of the matter that troubled him. At best, Say's Law would assert only the possibility of equilibrium at all levels of output. But Say and Ricardo—and some deservedly eminent present-day economists —claim that this yields a further proposition which is not equivalent with it. Namely, that an enterprise system operating under conditions of free competition always tends to lead to equilibrium at maximum or "full employment" output. This appears to be the proposition to which Keynes really meant to object.

Marshall and Pigou treated full employment as the "norm" toward which an enterprise system would incessantly tend. If by "norm" we are to understand a property of the logical schema of perfect or complete equilibrium under perfect competition, "with monetary stability" and "flexible prices," then they were right. For it can be proved that within this logical schema, in the long run, there would be no involuntary unemployment and the system would tend toward a full-employment equilibrium position. But if by the term "norm" we are to understand a property of reality, viz., a tendency of the capitalist system, as it actually works, to approach and maintain a full-employment equilibrium position until some force drives it off again, then Keynes was correct. For Say and Ricardo, Marshall and Pigou— and ever so many other economists—were inadequately aware of the qualifications which must be made in asserting the existence of such a tendency. Hence there is no real problem of reconciling classical and Keynesian thought; the two systems were based on different sets of assumptions and, in effect, complement one another.

Keynes exaggerated his theoretical differences with the classical economists. As regards Say's Law, all that had to be done to it was to add the "demand for cash balances," and to make it a second approximation, rather than to "refute it" or "overthrow it." The important contribution which Keynes made was to stress the relevance of certain institutional conditions which differed strikingly from the assumptions of long-run classical analysis and to construct a theoretical system which applied to the abnormal conditions of the 1930's. Some of the most basic concepts which he, and others, introduced have been indispensable in strengthening the classical analysis for any relevant conditions. But some of his propositions and conclusions have taken on a life of their own and have been applied to the international mechanism out of context and without relevance.

A terrible cost of Keynes' genius was the error of theoretical exaggeration; it persists in theory and practice long after it has served its purpose.

It is true that during the 1930's, both prior to and after the publication of *The General Theory*, monetary and banking policy "was relegated to a somewhat secondary position, and economists increasingly emphasized the effects of saving and spending habits upon the circular flow of income."[13] In part this was probably the result of too much having been claimed for the role of banking policy in controlling industrial fluctuations during the 1920's. But then the pendulum swung to the opposite extreme. Too much was claimed for the role of fiscal policy, and too little for the role of banking policy, during the 1930's and 1940's.[14]

[13] Metzler, *op. cit.*, p. 212.

[14] Cf. John H. Williams, "Domestic Fiscal and Monetary Policy," in *Postwar Monetary Plans and Other Essays*, 1944, pp. 63 *et seq.*: "It has been the history of the development of major ideas about economic policy that there has been a warming-up period and a cooling-off period. We have yet to look at fiscal policy in proper historical perspective. I think it will be found to have much the same kind of limitations that characterize the policy (of central banking) out of which it developed. It is a partial and over-simplified analysis, dealing with large aggregates of the income flow." Cf. also Lionel Robbins, *The Economist in the Twentieth Century*, 1954, pp. 61-80.

The influence of Keynesian economics has been to subordinate unduly the role of money and banking in the analysis of both domestic and international economic problems. The effect has been an artificial cleavage between monetary and banking theory and policy, on the one hand, and the theory of the circular flow of income and expenditures, on the other. Indeed, Metzler reports that the most striking single feature of the neo-Keynesian theory of the balancing process is its comparative independence or divorce from banking policy.[15] Since the approach of neo-Keynesian writers to the international mechanism has been based on the circular-flow concept, they have failed to attribute sufficient importance in this connection to monetary and banking theory and policy.

The foundations of Keynesian analysis are short run and static; they were born of a peculiar historical situation. Unfortunately, some neo-Keynesian writers have attributed to this analysis greater generality than is warranted. In the application of their analysis to the international mechanism they have treated as general a system of relationship which is in fact only one (a limiting case) of a host of possible alternative systems which could stem from the same set of fundamentals.

Considering first the short-term aspect of the matter, we shall attempt to show that this so-called divorce of the modern balancing mechanism from bank and price policy is, for the most part, illusory.

KEYNESIAN DIVORCE OF MECHANISM-OF-ADJUSTMENT THEORY FROM BANKING AND PRICE POLICY

Essentially, Keynes' theory of prices differs from the traditional theory in two respects. It used to be assumed that the volume of transactions was determined by the amount of resources and their productivity. Since the latter were assumed to be constant, the volume of transactions was, in turn, assumed to be constant. Traditionally, it was also assumed that velocity was determined by relatively constant habits of the people and therefore could be considered as a constant. Keynes broadened the hypothesis of traditional theory by considering

[15] Metzler, *op. cit.*, p. 216.

the volume of transactions and velocity to be variables rather than constants. He assumed the quantity of money to be a determinant of the level of real income and of the ratio between cash balances held and aggregate income.

Let M be the quantity of money, k the ratio between cash balances held and aggregate income, P the price level, and R the level of real income. Then the Keynesian formulation is:

$$M = k\,P\,R$$

Keynes considered k to be a function of the quantity of money via the rate of interest. An increase in M, given the schedules of liquidity preference and of the propensity to consume, would reduce the rate of interest and it would therefore become profitable to hold a larger proportion of real income in the form of cash balances. k would therefore increase as M increases because of the decline in the rate of interest. Further, at very low rates of interest, Keynes assumed that any increase in the quantity of money would be absorbed in the form of cash balances, i.e., k would increase proportionately to M, and therefore the level of prices and of real income would not be affected. This, obviously, is a limiting case and based on questionable assumptions. The more important relationship is that between the level of real income (R) and the proportion of real income held in cash balances (k). However, here again, Keynes assumed the level of real income to be a function of the quantity of money via the rate of interest. An increase in M, given the liquidity-preference schedule, and the consumption function, would have the effect of lowering the rate of interest, raising the volume of investment per unit of time, and thereby increasing real income. If R should increase in the same proportion as M, banking policy would have virtually no effect on the price level.[16]

But this is also a limiting case. Such conditions might occur during the initial stages of transition from mass unemployment to business revival. But even here, as Keynes well realized, bottlenecks

---

[16] The possible change in k under such circumstances would probably be negligible. See Keynes's well-balanced discussion on "The Theory of Prices"; it runs in terms of effective demand *and* the quantity theory, pp. 298-304 in the *General Theory*.

might occur in certain sectors of the economy and costs and prices would slowly begin to rise. Once the process of expansion got under way, some specific factors of production would become relatively scarce, either in specific industries or in the economy as a whole. These factors would rise in price. Other more abundant factors would be substituted for them. The greater the substitution of factors which have not risen in price relative to those that have, the more rapidly would the law of ultimate diminishing marginal returns begin to operate with respect to the substituted factors. This would be a second reason why costs would rise and prices would follow suit. Once the economy approached full utilization of resources and optimum allocation, a further increase in the quantity of money could scarcely have any effect but to raise the level of prices. After this point, unless k increases proportionately to M (a most unlikely prospect during expansion), an increase in bank credit would necessarily result in a rise in prices. If people expected prices to rise still further, then k would decline and prices rise even in greater proportion to the increase in the quantity of money. Clearly then, even on the basis of the Keynesian model, bank policy in such cases will necessarily have an effect on prices.[17]

If we abandon the unrealistic assumption that the rate of interest changes only through the exchange of money for securities (as it was partially abandoned later by Keynes himself and generalized by Hicks and Robertson), then k and R not only are dependent upon changes in the quantity of money via the rate of interest but also via the direct substitution of money for goods and services.[18] In the short run, k, R, and P are therefore all functions of M, and M is, in turn, dependent upon them.

In summary, then, even within the "Keynesian framework" three sets of possibilities may be distinguished. In the early stages of expansion with extreme unemployment, monetary expansion may in-

---

[17] Keynes was, of course, not so Keynesian as to ignore the price effects of income and employment fluctuations. Cf. *ibid.*, Chap. 21.

[18] Keynes, "Alternative Theories of the Rate of Interest," *Economic Journal*, June, 1937, pp. 241-252; J. R. Hicks, *Value and Capital*, Chaps. 11-13; D. H. Robertson, "Mr. Keynes and the Rate of Interest," in *Essays in Monetary Theory*, 1948, pp. 1-38.

crease real national income without appreciable price increases. As expansion proceeds into later stages, monetary expansion may increase both real national income and the level of prices significantly. Finally, when a condition of "full employment" of resources is reached, further monetary expansion will have a far more marked

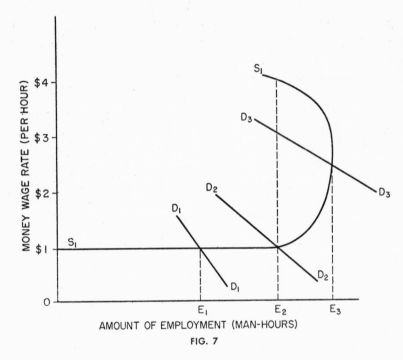

FIG. 7

effect upon prices than upon real national income. In all cases expansion in real income, and price increases, will in turn affect bank credit creation and the availability and cost of nonbank credit. It follows clearly that all these mutually interdependent influences must be of primary importance in any adequate theory of the international mechanism of adjustment.

Some of these influences may be briefly illustrated with the aid of Fig. 7. S_1S_1 is given as the supply curve of labor. Assume D_1D_1 to be the initial demand curve for labor, OE_1 the amount of employment, and E_1E_2 the amount of involuntary unemployment in the initial situation.[19] Suppose now that the banking system successfully expands credit, with the result that the demand for labor increases to D_2D_2 and the amount of employment to OE_2. The resulting rise in real incomes and money incomes which would occur even under the assumption that there is neither an increase in wages nor in prices may be expected to increase imports by an amount depending upon the income elasticity of demand for imports. The point to be stressed here is that effective policy is likely to influence the balance of payments, even though it has had no effect upon the level of prices and wages, provided only that it has increased the total income flow.[20]

It is understood, of course, that within the range of involuntary unemployment (E_1E_2), a similar set of effects would follow an expansion of income and expenditures originating from nonbank sources. When expansion of imports follows an expansion of domestic incomes without significant price and wage increases, the subsequent operation of the mechanism of adjustment is facilitated

[19] Involuntary unemployment is here defined as the amount of unemployment which exists by virtue of the fact that persons desiring to work at the current money wage rate cannot find employment, in this case the number of man-hours represented by the distance E_1E_2. This definition is not identical with the one used by Keynes. According to his definition it would be impossible to distinguish between the existence of involuntary and voluntary unemployment. The latter may be defined as the number of man-hours which would not be offered at the current money wage rate, but which would be offered at higher or lower money wage rates. In the present diagram the amount of voluntary unemployment is indicated by E_2E_3.

[20] As Professor Robertson has well put it: "Due to a strange inconsistency in the scheme of his (Mr. Keynes's) book . . . 'active money' could generally only grow as a result of a previous growth in income, so that the banks could only operate by increasing 'idle money': yet at the same time it was apparently contemplated that, even if 'idle money' were zero, there would still be some (unexplained) way for total money to be increased and the rate of interest to fall, the growth of incomes following as a consequence. Common sense suggests that the natural way for this to occur is by the banks performing the primary function of banking, i.e. lending money to people who want to make productive use of it. But in those days Mr. Keynes was so taken up with the fact that people sometimes acquire money in order to *hold* it that he had apparently all but entirely forgotten the more familiar fact that they often acquire it in order to *use* it." Robertson, *op. cit.*, pp. 11-12 (italics in original). For a discussion on the role of bank policy in expanding or checking expenditures during depressions and inflations, cf. also Jacob Viner, *International Trade and Economic Development*, 1952, pp. 35-37; William Fellner, "Employment Theory and Business Cycles," in A *Survey of Contemporary Economics*, pp. 86-98, and sources cited therein.

by the fact that an expansion of exports will not be inhibited by rising costs.

Assume now that an expansion of credit increases the demand for labor from D_2D_2 to D_3D_3 and employment from OE_2 to OE_3.[21] The resulting increase in incomes and expenditures will raise not only the level of output but also the level of prices and wages. The effect on the balance of payments will operate through both the income effect and price effect, thus combining the aspects emphasized respectively by the classical and the neo-Keynesian approach. Finally, if an expansion of credit were to increase the demand for labor beyond D_3D_3, the predominant effect would be inflation and the price effects and money-income effects would attain greater importance in the international mechanism. The importance of money-income effects in this case would depend upon the *direction* of the additional money expenditures. If this expansion continues to an extreme such that the demand for labor increases beyond the point where the supply curve of labor begins to slope backward, say, on account of money illusion, contraction in real income may occur and inflation with its attendant effects on the mechanism becomes even more pronounced.

Hence, under inflationary conditions, monetary-income analysis is of predominant importance; whereas income analysis in the Keynesian sense, i.e., in terms of real income, may be an exaggeration or even an irrelevance. In most cases, both monetary-income analysis and real-income analysis have important relevance. But the analytical framework of most neo-Keynesian models has represented an intransigent front against banking theory and policy. They have been developed in terms of short-run, simultaneous, realized magnitudes—an approach which has been partially useful in dealing with problems of comparative statics at various levels of output and trade—but they have been much less useful in dealing with dynamic problems of economic change and growth, or with static problems of long-run, complete equilibrium analysis. The approach has been inapplicable to long-run equilibrium analysis because it is illegitimate to assume

---

[21] Keynes termed OE_2 full employment and OE_3 maximum employment. The expansion in employment within this range has thus eliminated the so-called voluntary unemployment. It is probably unnecessary to point out that such terms as "full employment" and "maximum employment" are precise-sounding terms for inherently unprecise phenomena.

the existence of involuntary unemployment in developing a *general equilibrium* theory, be it applied to a closed economy or to the international mechanism of adjustment. Keynes and the neo-Keynesians, of course, had other objectives in mind. They were neither dealing with nor concerned with a *complete general equilibrium* theory. Yet many a disciple of Keynes disregarded the fact that, without an explicit assumption of long-run perverse monetary policy, or an abnormal environment, it is illegitimate to stress as important the decisions between spending and hoarding (involving an immovable horizontal demand curve for cash balances at a rate of interest which is inflexible downward, or an immovable horizontal supply curve of loanable funds at a rate of interest which is inflexible upward). Clearly, such assumptions of long-run perverse monetary policy or abnormal conditions are unacceptable for long-run equilibrium theory. Fortunately, the rejection of such assumptions removes the major obstacle to the reincorporation of banking theory and policy into mechanism theory, although it obviously does not remove their relevance over certain ranges and in certain circumstances.

NEO-KEYNESIAN SUBMERGENCE OF COST-PRICE RELATIONSHIPS

Another important aspect of the neo-Keynesian approach and its implications for the international mechanism is its unwarranted submergence of cost-price relationships, especially of cost-induced inflation. The role of cost-price relationships can be illustrated by the effect of possible changes in the position of the supply curve of labor. The Keynesian assumption that a change in the general level of money wages has no effect upon the level of employment and output is of doubtful validity. There has been as yet no evidence to disprove the *a priori* assumption that disinflation, for example, may reduce the general level of money wages (as compared with all other prices), induce increased investment per unit of consumer demand, and thereby increase the level of output and employment.[22] The outcome

---

[22] Graphically, the change assumed could be represented by a vertically downward movement of the supply curve of labor with the demand curve (sloping downward to the right) intersecting the supply curves in their horizontal range. The graph would indicate an increase in employment provided the demand curve

of such a change in the general level of money wages would depend upon its net influence on total expenditures. And as yet we know little about this matter. The question turns around the kind of environment in which the positive effect of a relative decline in wages upon the inducement to make investment expenditures is greater than the possible negative effect which such a decline may have upon total expenditures out of wages. This net effect on total expenditures depends largely upon business expectations. And the expectations of businessmen certainly depend in part on current and expected cost-price relationships. A similar role is played by the price expectations of consumers.

These cost-price relationships are relevant not only in the aggregative sense but also for specific sectors of the economy. They have an important bearing upon the distribution of expenditures as between traded and nontraded commodities. To illustrate briefly the application of price-cost relationships to the international mechanism under stable exchange rates, which are here in question, we may outline briefly several cases.

1. We may first assume that a country is experiencing an export balance at a time when its domestic economy is in a state of less-than-full employment (i.e., somewhere below E_2 in Fig. 7). If credit is expanded upon the basis of gold imports (or acquisitions of short-term claims abroad), there may, in this case, be small (or no) price-cost effects and the real- and money-income effects would be the predominant equilibrating forces in the balancing process. But even in this case, if the adjustment is brought about by an appreciation of the country's currency, differential price-cost relationships in favor of import industries may play an important role in the adjustment mechanism.

2. Let us now assume that a country has an export balance but its domestic economy is in a state of what Keynes termed "full employment" (i.e., represented in Fig. 7 at some level above E_2). If credit is expanded on the basis of gold imports or upon some other basis

---

had this negative slope (all prices falling by a smaller proportion than money wages), and the aggregate wage income received by the newly employed workers exceeded the fall in the incomes of workers previously employed.

resulting from the existence of the export balance, then some effect on prices and costs may be expected in which export industries would tend to find costs rising relatively to their selling prices, a trend which domestic and import industries may experience, if at all, to a smaller degree. The resulting discouragement to exports would then be clearly related to the cost-price structures.

3. Finally, let us assume that a country is undergoing inflation which turns an export balance into an import balance. Should the inflation be suppressed, and prices and costs maintained by means of direct controls at levels where excess demand persistently appears, then formal or informal rationing would become inevitable. Seller competition in the domestic (and soft currency) markets would become virtually nonexistent. Gradually resources would be pulled away from export industries where competition would have to be met. Excess demand would be directed toward domestic goods and services —and toward imports. The exchange rate, if pegged, would become more and more overvalued, further stimulating imports, discouraging exports, misallocating resources. Inventories and savings (as a percentage of national production) would tend to decline, with damaging effects upon specialization, productivity, and economic growth. This case differs markedly from those mentioned above in that the disturbance originates as a suppressed domestic inflation in which the customary cost-price relationships are prevented from operating by artificial controls. Yet, if allowed to work themselves out, they would be present and operating with either an equilibrating influence (e.g., a depreciated exchange rate) or a disequilibrating influence (e.g., a rise in domestic prices relative to import prices).

These illustrations are, of course, not exhaustive. They simply demonstrate that cost-price relationships are an integral part of any adequate theory of the balancing process, no matter what our assumptions may be concerning the level of employment or the stability of the domestic monetary structures.

Just as there is no ground for differentiating, in any strict sense, between the role of circular income flow and that of banking theory and policy in the international mechanism, so there is no ground for differentiating between the role of cost-price relationships and that of employment theory and policy.

NEO-KEYNESIAN CONTRIBUTIONS TO BALANCING THEORY

There can be no doubt, however, that the investigations of aggregate output and employment analysis have had a strong positive influence upon the quality of mechanism theory. This positive influence lies primarily in the emphasis placed on the roles of propensities to import, income elasticities of demand for imports, and foreign-trade multipliers in the cumulative expansion or contraction of income, which account for a large part of the balancing process. In effect, the equilibration of international balances of payments is often achieved mainly through the adjustment of imports and exports to changes in the levels of production at home and abroad. These contributions to the theory of balancing process stem primarily from Keynes' systematic theory of the determinants of the level of income and employment, and from the work on national income and business cycles which has been done by economists since that time.[23]

Metzler interprets the justification for calling the adjustment through changes in income a "new" or "modern" theory, as compared, say, with the theories of Wheatley, Ricardo, Mill, Bastable, Marshall, Taussig, Ohlin, and others, as follows:

> The difference, in my opinion, is primarily that the earlier expositions lacked a theory of employment or income, and were therefore unable to explain just how far the adjusting process could go . . . when secondary as well as primary changes in income have been taken into account, it is clear that something more than a mere shift in purchasing power has occurred; in addition, there may be a net change in output and employment both at home and abroad. It is the ability to set limits to these changes in pur-

[23] The substantive contributions which Keynes made to the history of ideas (and his *Treatise on Money* may in this respect be as important as his *General Theory*) followed gradually and chronologically the discussion of Say's Law, the banking school–currency school controversy, Wicksell's *Prices and Interest*, the theory of forced savings, Marshall's *Principles*, Pigou's work on income, and the writings of the Swedish economists (e.g., Myrdal, Ohlin, Lindahl, and Lundberg) on expectations and unemployment.

chasing power, or at any rate to determine the conditions on which the changes depend, which distinguishes the new theory from the older shifts of purchasing power doctrine.[24]

It is diL.cult to know precisely what the above statements mean. Had Keynes and his disciples shown "how far the adjusting process could go," this would indeed have been an important contribution. But they have as yet failed to do so, nor have they "set limits to these changes in purchasing power" or determined the conditions on which these changes depend. Without adequate appreciation of the role of monetary and bank policy, and the effect of cost-price relationships upon aggregate output and employment analysis, it is entirely understandable why the neo-Keynesian approach was useful only to a limited extent in developing a satisfactory theory of the balancing process.

Referring to the "limits of the adjusting process," Metzler himself notes the conclusion of most economists that, except under unusual conditions, the adjustment of a country's balance of payments by means of income movements is likely to be incomplete.[25] Indeed, this conclusion is brought out by Metzler's own excellent work on the problem.[26]

When speaking in more general terms, however, here again those theorizing primarily in the neo-Keynesian tradition have made exaggerated claims. Metzler himself states:

The essence of the new theory is that an external event which increases a country's exports will also increase imports even without price changes, since the change in exports affects the level of output and hence the demand for all goods. In other words, movements of output and employment play much the same role in the new doctrine that price movements played in the old.[27]

If this is interpreted to mean that the equilibrating effect of income

[24] Metzler, op. cit., p. 218.
[25] Metzler, op. cit., pp. 219, 220.
[26] Cf. Metzler, "The Transfer Problem Reconsidered," Journal of Political Economy, June, 1942, pp. 397-414; "Underemployment Equilibrium in International Trade," Econometrica, April, 1942, pp. 97-112; and "A Multiple-Country Theory of Income Transfers," Journal of Political Economy, February, 1951, pp. 14-29.
[27] Metzler, "International Trade," p. 213.

changes was neglected in much of earlier theorizing, there could be no objection to it. But this fact hardly establishes the basis for claiming that it constitutes a new general theory. As we had occasion to observe, just as in the modern literature on exchange theory and stability conditions all the weight is thrown on price elasticities—even more so than in the pre-Keynesian era—so in the modern literature on mechanism theory, all the weight is thrown on income elasticities.

Yet the emphasis on the level of output, and on fluctuations in that level, have had the important effect of focusing attention on the problems involved in the adjustment of international balances to a disturbance resulting from depression (or inflation) in a major trading country. While Keynes and the "Keynesians," with their strong inflationary bias, underestimated the forces of adjustment operating on the side of deflation, they nonetheless did point to the serious difficulties facing a country whose balance of payments on current account deteriorates as a result of a sharp drop in income and prices in some other country. Admittedly, Keynesians have overestimated the responsibilities of countries with active balances, and underestimated the responsibilities of countries with passive balances in reaching equilibrium in international accounts. But in obtaining adherence to the view that the problems and responsibilities are those of mutual concern, Keynes and the Keynesians deserve much of the credit.

A most striking Keynesian influence upon the analysis of the international mechanism lies in the field of model building or numerical theory. This is quite understandable since the greatest objective of the economist is to figure out developments that would follow from a given disturbance to the economic system. And, in effect, the simplest Keynesian model held out this promise. The lure proved irresistible. By assuming (1) that certain propensities to save and to import are absolutely stable throughout the periods under consideration, (2) that prices (including foreign-exchange rates and interest rates) are also stable, and (3) that home investment is entirely unaffected by the changes in foreign trade as well as by those in income which may result from foreign trade, Machlup isolated the income effects of autonomous changes in foreign trade from all effects of changes in home investment and in psychological propensities.[28] Ingenious arithmetical model sequences of autonomous-foreign-trade multipliers (Models I-VII) were worked out.[29] Then nonautonomous foreign-induced changes in exports were assumed and the foreign-induced-trade multiplier derived.[30] Lastly, inverse changes in investments in two countries were assumed, the investment multiplier involving two countries derived, the transfer problem considered, and a parallel expansion in two countries with balanced trade examined.[31] A forthright and appropriate conclusion of "Apologies and Confessions: Exact Formulas for Incomplete Theories" followed.[32]

Other writers have been more daring in their application of Keynesian models to the analysis of an international economic system. They have usually assumed that fluctuations in the level of a country's exports "determine" fluctuations in its national income. In part, this relationship is claimed to be instantaneous, an increase in exports constituting an increase in national income and in part working with a certain time lag via the multiplier. It is also assumed that fluctuations in national income determine the level of imports either at the same time or with a certain time lag. Since by definition total imports of all countries equal the total volume of world trade, the interdependence of the model is completed by assuming the volume of exports of each country to be determined by the level of world trade.[33]

Many of the models constructed have been technically strong in rigor, elegance, and internal consistency. They have provided new theoretical tools and some useful insights. But they have not been strong in relevance. The impetus which numerical theory has given

[28] Cf. Machlup, *International Trade and the National Income Multiplier*, 1943, pp. 19, 20.

[29] *Ibid.*, pp. 24-114.

[30] *Ibid.*, pp. 115-129.

[31] *Ibid.*, pp. 155-197.

[32] *Ibid.*, pp. 198-218. In his article, "Underemployment Equilibrium in International Trade," *ibid.*, Metzler assumes that investment, in the short run, may depend upon the level of income, and shows that induced cumulative movements of income may be large enough to offset a balance-of-payments disturbance completely (pp. 99-101). This article illustrates well the elements of strength and weakness of numerical theory when applied to mechanism of adjustment problems. It is assumed that no variations occur in prices (including money wages and other costs), interest rates, or the rate of exchange.

[33] See, e.g., J. J. Polak, *An International Economic System*, 1953, pp. 15-17.

to the measurement of foreign-trade multipliers, foreign demand and income elasticities, etc., is a noteworthy contribution—even though the results of these studies have often been unenlightening.[34] Their analytical framework has usually ignored such fundamental factors as variations of relative costs and prices, of interest and exchange rates. By virtue of the variables considered determining or independent, they have disregarded essential elements of change and economic growth.[35] There are numerous illustrations where the neo-Keynesian models have permitted little more than arithmetical exercises. They frequently raised no hypotheses which could be confirmed or rejected by experience and their solutions often centered in the postulated disturbance and in the *ceteris paribus* assumptions. There have also been a few brilliant exceptions which we shall have occasion to examine.

Some of the neo-Keynesian models have misused the Marshall-Edgeworth type of two-country analysis. Marshall, it will be recalled, had warned that the reciprocal demand-and-supply diagram was not to be interpreted as a two-country diagram which is applicable to a world of many countries. It ought not to be used, for instance, as representing trade relations between Great Britain and the United States, with the locked-up assumption that the United States corresponds to the rest-of-the-world compound. This procedure leads to serious error in working with mechanism-of-adjustment problems. A rise in British production, for example, with a minor recession in the

---

[34] *Ibid.*; see the admittedly unsatisfactory results on the balance of payments of Norway, Sweden, Hungary, Ireland, and China, Chap. VII, "Statistical Results for Individual Countries."

[35] In the United States and England, for example, the character of the problem of economic progress changed between World Wars I and II. It became increasingly that of taking advantage of opportunities to improve the capital replaced and the efficiency with which that capital was used. Any model based on the assumption that fluctuations in the level of a country's exports determined fluctuations in its national income must therefore be misleading. An increase in the obsolescence and replacement rate of capital might, under such conditions, have been of greater importance in determining the changes in real income of a country than the level of exports or the rate at which capital could be accumulated. Cf. John H. Williams, "An Appraisal of Keynesian Economics," *American Economic Review*, May, 1948, pp. 282 *et seq.*, reprinted in *Economic Stability in a Changing World*, 1953, pp. 51 *et seq.*; and William Fellner, *Trends and Cycles in Economic Activity*, 1956, pp. 223-224, 237-270.

United States (exchange rates remaining the same), leads to the conclusion that the British balance of payments will in all probability deteriorate. However, should the production of western Europe be expanding simultaneously, British exports to western Europe would rise. Hence there need be no deterioration but perhaps even a general improvement in Britain's balance of payments. Marshall made it quite clear that while his diagram may be applicable to single countries whose entire trade is with one another, primarily it should be interpreted as an *n*-country diagram, with the country of special interest set off against *all* foreign countries combined. Whenever necessary, each country in turn could be selected for separate examination in a separate diagram in relation to its *relevant* rest-of-the-world compound. Neo-Keynesian models have been extremely restrictive in this regard.

On the other hand, the approach has had a pretension to universality, similar assumptions having been made about, and the same variables applied to, countries at varying stages of economic development. Even more important, their rigid analytical framework has revealed inherent weaknesses for the possible reconciliation of classical and modern theory as regards internal and external adjustment. Though Keynes himself was partially responsible for inspiring this frame of reference, his strong sense of relevance compelled him to abandon it.

The Keynesian contribution to mechanism theory has been extremely important as an elaboration of the classical position. But it is more than that. It should not be looked upon merely as a discussion of the course of affairs during a period of unemployment and readjustment. Output and employment ought *not* to be regarded as playing much the same role in the new doctrine that price movements played in the old—formulations by neo-Keynesians to the contrary notwithstanding. The importance of relative income changes is not restricted to unemployment conditions. An analysis based on the assumption of full employment must *not* be almost exclusively interested in relative price changes. Full employment not only does not imply constant real income, but constant real income or full employment does not imply constant money income. Money-income effects and real-income effects can therefore be significant even if full employment is assumed. In an expanding world economy, changes in productivity and their relation to changes in real and money incomes are of key importance in the balancing process. Keynes, himself, stressed their influence in his posthumous article on the balance of payments.[36]

Barring crises such as war and reconstruction, with full employment, smaller changes in relative prices may, in effect, be required to help produce equilibration of international accounts. As the economic organization of a country improves and moves toward optimum output conditions, changes in relative prices become a stronger equilibrating force in shifting resources between domestic, import, and export commodities. Thus, during such periods of full employment and long-term economic expansion, real- and monetary-income effects may play a more significant quantitative role than price effects in the balancing process. However, there are no *a priori* or empirical grounds for the view that international balance need be consummated with the aid of inflation. On the contrary, as the above analysis has pointed out, inflationary pressures are most likely to generate international imbalance and/or bilateralism.

KEYNESIAN EVOLUTION ON INTERNAL AND EXTERNAL ADJUSTMENTS

The classical economists for the most part assumed away the problem of full employment and dealt with international trade from the standpoint of the best application of given and employed resources. They were able to do so by assuming great adaptability of the internal economy to external forces, stressing internal adjustability of prices, costs, and factors. The neo-Marshallian approach to exchange theory emphasized the virtually exclusive role of price elasticities and, from the early 1930's to the early 1950's, generally accepted the view that their (alleged) statistical values were low. Hence even in this literature the conclusion emerged that it was extremely difficult to achieve external adjustment through the price mechanism. Analysis of the

[36] Keynes, "The Balance of Payments of the United States," *Economic Journal*, June, 1946, esp. pp. 185-186.

logically preceding problems as to whether countries did, in effect, adopt effective domestic financial policies for the maintenance of internal balance, and as to whether they had sufficiently flexible domestic price systems for variations in relative price structures or in foreign-exchange rates *to be able* to exercise a decisive influence on the balance of payments, was disregarded.

The Keynesian literature moved to the opposite extreme. It swept aside the classical assumptions of maintaining the pivots of stabilization (exchange rates) fixed and of relying upon internal adjustments of the domestic economy to bear the full brunt of the balancing process. Laying stress on equilibrating effects through income changes and on the insensitivity of internal adjustments to external forces, it placed primary emphasis on greater exchange-rate variation and on trade controls as a guide to external policy, and on internal stability at full employment and effective demand as a guide to internal policy.

Keynes was among the first to perceive that, for countries subject to severe balance-of-payments strains, such emphasis on internal stability would entail a strong dose of self-sufficiency.[37] He thought it worth the price, however, in order to help insulate the domestic economy from the onslaught of the Great Depression and to help shift part of the cost of external adjustment on countries abroad. His thinking in the early 1930's thus ran in terms of closed, depression economics. Pushed to its logical extreme, this would mean an economy sheltered by a combination of direct external controls and (whenever necessary) currency devaluations in an aim to preserve external stability and yet enable Britain to break off from and tie on to external price levels. Many Keynesians, in fact, advocated such measures. But Keynes disapproved in principle of the use of direct external controls for the long run, either as a means of gaining trade benefits or as a device for granting domestic protection. As world economic conditions improved, and as the conflict between "self-sufficiency" and economic growth became more apparent—as well as more severe —Keynes modified his views.

The practical necessities of the postwar world, as he envisioned

[37] See Keynes, "National Self-Sufficiency," *Yale Review*, June, 1933, esp. pp. 758-762.

them, led him to remind his readers of the important elements of adjustment stressed in the classical literature—particularly the role of costs and prices as they are influenced by wage rates and monetary policy.[38] He thus placed in perspective the role of internal adjustments through changes in relative incomes, costs and prices, and the role of external adjustments through discontinuous changes in exchange rates.

Keynes insisted that for the postwar era exchange-rate changes should be the rare and last resort. He staunchly opposed discriminatory exchange practices, and advocated as rapid a return as possible to *universal* convertibility for trade transactions. Indeed, few have so strongly championed the cause of multilateral clearing with the return to convertibility at the earliest possible time. When the period of transition is over, he said before the House of Lords, and England is again strong enough to live year by year on her resources, their Lordships would be able to look forward to trading in a world of national currencies which would be interconvertible.

For a great commercial nation like ourselves, this is indispensable for full prosperity. Sterling itself, in due course, must obviously become, once again, generally convertible. For, without this, London must necessarily lose its international position, and the arrangements in particular of the sterling area would fall to pieces.[39]

This is a far cry from the Keynes of closed, depression economics, or from the notion that external adjustment depends on the maintenance of internal stability at full employment instead of adjustment through internal change. In his last phase, Keynes was attempting to reconcile the problem of how to achieve internal and external balance at full employment and rising levels of income without the use of direct controls over foreign trade.

He was attempting to work out a theory of international economic policy which in the external field would be realistic to the demands of full employment and domestic growth and at the same time would consolidate the trade relations between the British Commonwealth,

[38] Keynes, "The Balance of Payments of the United States," pp. 178-187.
[39] Speech delivered by Lord Keynes before the House of Lords on "The International Monetary Fund," May 23, 1944, reprinted in Seymour E. Harris, ed., *The New Economics*, 1947, pp. 370-371.

the United States, and other significant trading countries. Keynes, it appears, maintained that when a nation suffers from domestic depression, the expansion of domestic expenditure with the cumulative rise in income is the most practical *internal adjustment* which it can make in working toward external balance at high levels of trade. And there is much truth in this position. To be sure, he underestimated the danger of precipitating inflation in debtor countries long before they might achieve external balance. Nor did he pay particular attention to the importance of freer commercial policy for the effective operation of the balancing process, though the International Monetary Fund was to play a preambular role in the development of a liberal code of postwar commercial policy. Further, he had no occasion to consider the case of external strain stemming from the temporary overexpansion of some internationally traded commodity (e.g., textiles) with the rest of the economy operating at full-employment levels. An expansion of domestic demand under such conditions would merely aggravate the external unbalance.

POST-KEYNESIAN APPLICATIONS

During the depressed conditions of the 1930's, Keynes was right in his capacity as statesman and economist in advising governments to eschew financial contraction. But, in effect, he underestimated the importance of the balancing process through financial contraction at all times. Hence he was apt to neglect a variable which under relatively expansionary conditions may be of the utmost importance. Just as the volume of domestic expenditure may need to be varied upward in the interest of internal and external equilibrium, so it may need to be varied downward in the interest of internal and external equilibrium. The greatest contribution which the post-Keynesian literature can make to the theory and practice of the balancing process is to apply the tools of the national-income approach, with due emphasis upon financial considerations, to the tools of the more traditional price-cost approach. It is the relevance, interdependence, and relative effectiveness of these forces under different conditions which are of paramount importance.

Progress has recently been made in this direction. Consider the case of a country with a deficit on current account brought about by domestic inflation and a fixed exchange rate. The extent of the deficit is kept in check by direct external controls. The problem is to determine the *relative* rate of growth of domestic expenditure and the interdependent relative pattern of price-cost relationships which may be compatible with internal and external balance without the use of direct controls.[40] There is, of course, no direct way of estimating the magnitude of the *extra* demand for imports caused by the inflation. The marginal propensity to import is distorted by the existence of direct controls and by the inflationary price-cost pressures. With full or overfull employment, the marginal propensity to import is in all probability extremely high, and certainly higher than the long-term average propensity to import when the economy is in reasonable internal balance (i.e., when there is no excess demand for goods and factors at a somewhat less than full-employment price level). If this "normal" long-run average propensity to import is fairly stable—as it appears to be for some countries—then by projecting the real rate of growth in national income or gross national product from some stable base year, it is possible to obtain a rough first approximation of what the "normal" volume of imports would have been at the higher level of real income without inflation, as compared with their actual inflationary level. Adjustments may then be made for the even higher volume of inflationary imports which would have occurred had there been no direct external controls.

Adjustments could also be made for some price rise which would have occurred by reason of the "normal" rate of growth in the gross national product. By making similar estimates for exports, the probable extent of the external imbalance may be inferred. Assuming a "normal" rate of growth for the country in question, and a price level relatively stable to that of other countries, one can compare the actual values with the estimated "normal" values of imports, exports, and gross national products. The difference between the actual and

<hr>

[40] The author has had the privilege of examining such investigations and discussing their strength and weakness with government officials and private economists in Denmark and Sweden. The approach has been used by Erik Lundberg and Malcolm Hill in *Some Points of View on the Long-Term Balance of Payments Problems of Australia*, January, 1956 (mimeographed).

"normal" values of the gross national products may provide a rough guide as to the extent of disinflation which may be required to establish internal and external balance without the use of direct controls at the prevailing, fixed rate of exchange. However, these first approximations may reveal, *a priori*, that such disinflation could *not* bring about external balance; i.e., that the "normal" value of imports would tend to exceed the "normal" value of exports. In that event, if the long-term trends are not affected by short-term disturbances or by cyclical movements, it is customary to interpret the emerging pattern of external imbalance as "structural" in character, requiring further price-cost adjustments through devaluation. The problems then remain as to whether or not, under what conditions and at what cost, devaluation will be effective in maintaining external balance.

The advantage of this approach lies more in the nature and scope of the analysis than in the power of precise prediction. It brings to bear all of our available tools upon the problems under consideration. For some decision-making issues it may furnish a reasonable range of estimates regarding the possible consequences of alternative policies. In all these respects the neo-Keynesian and the traditional analyses were less satisfactory.

As a frame of reference for further inquiry, the traditional approach appears to be much more productive than the neo-Keynesian approach. The very fact that the traditional approach was flexible and broad renders it adaptable to absorb all the recent contributions without loss of essential precision. The traditional approach, however, is inapplicable to the analysis of severe economic fluctuations, for it customarily assumed conditions of (hypothetical) monetary equilibrium.

A reconciliation of the two has not been achieved. This is understandable since the traditional approach assumed, for the most part, full employment and a given level of national income. Its main task of analysis, therefore, usually revolved about the determinants of relative prices in attempting to explain the mechanism, terms, and volume of foreign trade. Keynes and neo-Keynesians, on the other hand, were interested in analyzing the determinants of the level of aggregate income. Consequently, in the main stream of their analysis, they paid little attention to the role of relative prices. It is in the changes of the aggregate levels of income that they sought an explanation of the mechanism, terms, and volume of foreign trade. As is characteristic of the history of thought, Keynesian criticisms of classical theory went too far.[41] No one can gainsay, however, that Keynes' analysis had relevance. Though he was trained in a distinct and established school—indeed, his originality and genius were supported on the shoulders of the classical tradition—he possessed that rare capacity to revise premises in accordance with new conditions. In the best spirit of that tradition, he once again modified his premises in his final work on the balance of payments. Regrettably, some of his disciples have shown less flexibility. They have made erroneous criticisms of the classical theory, as they have made exaggerated claims for the neo-Keynesian models. One ought not to impute error to traditional analysis when new conditions or new objectives call for different assumptions and different conclusions.

Although the frame of reference of traditional theory is well suited to incorporate the recent contributions to the balancing process, it is questionable whether a fully general theory can be developed whose solutions would be both true and applicable to all, or most, non-Communist countries under modern conditions. Much partial analysis of a theoretical and empirical nature is first required to meet this test of relevance. In pursuing our analysis toward this objective, we shall attempt in the following chapters to fill in some gaps in traditional mechanism theory.

---

[41] In the Preface to his French edition, Keynes later explained that in writing his book he felt he was abandoning classical orthodoxy and was reacting strongly against it; that he was breaking his chains and gaining his freedom. "This state of mind explains certain defects in the work; it explains in particular why certain passages assume a controversial character." Cf. Préface pour l'édition française, *Theorie Générale de l'Emploie, de l'Intérêt et de la Monnaie*, 1943, pp. 9-13; trans. A. T. Peacock, *International Economic Papers*, No. 4, 1954, pp. 66-67.

5

Harvard Neo-Classicists

THIS chapter, and the following one, are a development of the Harvard neo-classicists. The objective of these chapters is to complement traditional mechanism theory by broadening its premises so that it may be used to explain important cases of international disequilibrium, as well as (hypothetical) international equilibrium. To achieve this aim, it will be necessary first to outline briefly the key postulates of traditional mechanism theory.

POSTULATES OF TRADITIONAL THEORY: STABLE EXCHANGE RATES

Most theorists who have analyzed the mechanism of adjustment have assumed the introduction of some major disturbance into a preëxisting balance-of-payments equilibrium and have traced the sequence whereby other items in the balance, most notably merchandise trade, adjust themselves to the disturbance and restore equilibrium.[1] The analysis has traditionally been carried out in terms

[1] Though the meaning of balance-of-payments equilibrium has not been definitely established, most writers regard the absence of flows of monetary reserves as a primary criterion. For a discussion of the various meanings of the concepts, cf.

of two countries, both of which are on a gold standard. Certain important modifications are usually made when many countries and modern banking procedures are introduced into the analysis. We may illustrate the argument by referring to the mechanism of adjustment to international long-term capital movements under stable exchanges as presented by Ohlin, criticism of which will follow below.[2] Assuming a loan of capital from country B (the United States) to country A (Great Britain), Ohlin states that before the real transfer of goods and services takes place, there occurs an original and prior change in buying power. "This monetary transfer," he writes, "is the direct and indirect cause of the readjustment involved in the real transfer."[3] And the same principle works in domestic interregional transfers.

Specifically, England finds that during the first year of borrowing the total increase in her buying power by far exceeds the expansion of her bank credit, which arises from the increase in foreign bills held by the banks as a result of the fact that part of the loan is not used to pay for imports from the United States during the first year. Ohlin calls the borrowed amount the primary increase in buying power, and considers it equal to the foreign money used to keep the balance of payments in equilibrium (i.e., used immediately to pay for imports from the United States), plus the inflation of credit caused by that part of the foreign loan which is not currently used for the purchase of imports and the acquisition of which by the banks places an equivalent amount of purchasing power in domestic circulation. Ohlin's "secondary" increase is the expansion in purchasing power arising from a more lenient credit policy on the part of the banks which have acquired increased foreign-currency reserves. Since the loan is not entirely used up to purchase imports, the dollar depreciates relative to the pound. This will lead to a further lowering of the discount rate in England and a raising of the discount rate in the United States, with respective expansion and curtailment of credit in the two countries. Rising prices

---

Howard S. Ellis, *Exchange Control in Central Europe*, 1941, pp. 233-242, 309-315, 336-348; Alvin H. Hansen, "A Brief Note on Fundamental Disequilibrium," *Review of Economic Statistics*, November, 1944, pp. 182-184; and Gottfried Haberler, "Some Comments on Professor Hansen's Note," *loc. cit.*, pp. 191-193.

[2] Bertil Ohlin, *Interregional and International Trade*, 1935, Chap. XX.

[3] *Ibid.*, p. 411.

in England, combined with increased velocity and expansion of productive activity, lead to a further expansion of credit. If English gold reserves are insufficient to support such an expansion of credit, then the banks may exchange some of their "foreign bills" for gold from abroad. Ohlin says that "theoretical reasoning and the evidence of experience indicate that this influx of gold is due to" the equilibrating increase in credit, "rather than that the gold flow is the cause of the credit expansion."[4]

Transitionally, the terms of trade between English goods and United States goods change in favor of the English. For when the loan is made by the United States to Great Britain, it means that all commodities in Britain become dearer than before, compared with commodities produced in the United States before the loan was made. Income levels rise in England as compared to the United States. The extent to which a certain shift of the supply curves of the goods sold by the United States will change prices of those goods depends upon the elasticity of demand for those goods in both countries—the greater the elasticity, the less the price drop. Ohlin stresses that a relative change in cost levels, those of the United States falling in comparison with the British, enables the United States to export certain goods which before belonged to the home market, or to the semi-international group, whereas some of Britain's goods disappear from its export trade. The demand for international goods, according to Ohlin, is highly elastic, and consequently the tendency to changed terms of international exchange will be strong only in quite exceptional cases. "For this reason detailed studies of the influence of different degrees of elasticity of demand upon the terms of exchange in international trade appear to be of little practical importance."[5] It is incorrect to assume, the argument proceeds, that the fall in prices in the United

---

[4] *Ibid.*, p. 414.

[5] *Ibid.*, p. 419. There is no real contradiction in terms here. Ohlin would doubtless agree that, with respect to mechanism-of-adjustment problems, the greater the elasticity of foreign demand, the *more* important is the effect of relatively small changes in the terms of exchange. By "detailed studies," however, Ohlin means statistical studies; and if price elasticities are large, a small error in computing prices will cause serious errors in the results, since the range of actual price change will be small as compared to the probable error of the computation. Hence such studies would be of little practical importance.

States is necessary to bring about a shift in the balance of trade. The shift may be achieved through a rise in incomes in Britain. However, the changes in income cannot prevent the terms of trade from moving a little in favor of England; for the relative price position of British factors and United States factors has changed, i.e., they have fallen in the United States, with the result that terms of trade have become more favorable for England.

The result of the change in the direction of production brought about by the loan will be a change in the relative scarcity of the corresponding factors; viz., factors used in comparatively great quantities in the production of semi-international goods and export goods will be in less demand in the country receiving the loan, and will fall in price in relation to factors much used in home-market industries. This movement corresponds to a similar movement of commodity prices; those of exports and semi-international goods fall compared with home-market goods. Actually, factors of the same kind may be paid more in home-goods industries than in foreign-goods industries, due to immobility of factors. In time, this lack of mobility is to a great extent overcome, and the price of any one factor tends more or less rapidly to become the same in all occupations. There will also be a tendency for the supply of different factors to adjust itself to the new conditions of demand. Consequently, the relative prices of the factors of production, and hence relative commodity prices, will tend to recede toward their position before the borrowing started.

Ohlin gives three reasons why prices of home goods will rise relatively to export goods in the borrowing country. Factors are not likely to be obtained from export industries which are giving them up (short-run immobility). To obtain these factors, expanding industries will therefore have to bid up their prices. Although export prices need not rise, the home-market prices will rise relatively to them because the prices in the expanding industries tend to run ahead of costs (assuming some rigidity of costs), with a consequent rise in profits.

According to Ohlin, it is entirely conceivable that there will be no rise in the average prices in the export industries of the borrowing country during the period of borrowing, since, because of factor immobility, there is no necessary bidding up of the factors used by the export industries. Buying power in England may rise considerably in connection with a change in domestic price levels and aggregate money incomes without any tendency, or only a weak one, for its export prices to rise. Buying power may similarly decline in the United States without its export prices tending to fall. It is not impossible for England's export prices to fall relative to those of the United States. The outcome depends upon the direction of the new demand in England compared with the withdrawn demand in the United States. There is no justification for assuming that a noticeable change of the terms of trade in favor of England is the normal or probable outcome either in the early or later stages of the borrowing period. The readjustment of production and trade may proceed under the stimulus of changes in demand and changes in sectional price levels and incomes, such as will leave the terms of trade undisturbed.

In brief, the shift in demand from the United States factors regarded as a whole to English factors which the borrowing implies need not enhance the scarcity of the various productive factors used in England's export industries compared with those used in the United States. The extent to which the terms of trade vary, when they do vary, under the influence of a movement of capital depends upon the circumstances already touched upon, e.g., the mobility of labor between different trades and places, and other reactions of factor supply and elasticity of demand. How closely prices will return in the long run to the old position will depend upon the character of the supply reactions.[6]

The developments in the capital export country (the United States) are considered to be:

1. Both a primary and secondary contraction of credit.
2. Increase of output in export industries.
3. Decrease in demand for domestic goods.
4. Increased output of semi-international goods in comparison with consumption of them, part being exported.
5. A fall in incomes.
6. Difficulty of downward wage adjustment because of wage rigidities.
7. Reduced buying power resulting from reduced production and reduced incomes, tending to lower commodity imports.

[6] *Ibid.*, pp. 420-431.

8. Business losses arising from immobility and stickiness of wages and costs.

9. A rise in interest rates and an inflow of short-term capital, particularly if the decline in income fails substantially to reduce imports.

10. A strong possibility of losses from unemployment which may exceed losses from worsened terms of trade.

11. Further diverse secondary effects depending upon the structure of the economy (e.g., increasing, decreasing, or constant cost industries, time lags, etc.).

In concluding his discussion of the mechanism of adjustment to an international movement of capital, Ohlin stresses the role played by the direction of demand for international goods. If the borrowing country buys much more from the lending country and not so much more of its own goods as a result of the loan, and if the lending country buys less from the borrowing country than it would have bought and not so much of its own, then the demand for the lending country's goods may increase, and that for the borrowing country's decrease, with the result that the terms of trade may shift in favor of the lending country. On the other hand, if the borrowing country buys less import goods from the lending country than the latter would have done itself, then the shift of demand away from the lender's factors of production is a double one, and the terms of trade will move still more in favor of the borrowing country.

The fundamental forces which operate to adjust the balance of trade to new international capital movements are therefore said to be:

1. As a result of borrowing, there occurs a direct and indirect increase in buying power in the borrowing country, which is used to buy more international goods, whereas the lending country buys less of them than before.

2. Higher prices of home market and semi-international goods in the borrowing country, and lower ones in the lending country, compared with prices of international goods, cause a shift of demand to international goods in the borrowing country and from them in the lending country.

3. Supply curves for export goods may be raised in the borrowing country and lowered in the lending country.

Ohlin's formulation provides a useful stepping stone for the further development of balance-of-payments theory. The super-structure has obviously been erected with considerable care for logical consistency. It needs some adaptation, however, to modern terminology.

Ohlin's use of the terms "primary" and "secondary" credit expansions is not that customarily used today. Money incomes, he emphasizes, are increased by an amount much larger than the amount borrowed; for each time the money passes from hand to hand, incomes are increased—by way of the multiplier—and this means an increase in demand. But Ohlin does not differentiate between purely financial purchases and those that create income. The term "purchasing power" is ambiguous; customarily it refers to what one can obtain for a unit of money, or the quantity of purchases people can make per unit of time. Ohlin's use of the term suggests that he means effective demand. But since he does not define the term, it is at times difficult to know exactly what he means. For instance, if a country such as England borrows balances from abroad, its banking system will show an expansion in domestic means of payment in the form of additional deposit liabilities equal to the amount of the loan at the same time that the borrowers' balance sheets show an increase of the same amount in their domestic means of payment in the form of the same bank deposits. The expansion of domestic deposits (plus bank notes) resulting from the purchase by English banks of the dollar exchange, sold to them by the English borrowers, is commonly known in the literature as the primary expansion. It is, of course, not operative in the mechanism until it is actually spent. If the primary expansion is accompanied by an increase in the reserve ratio, then a "secondary expansion" may occur through an expansion of domestic loans by the banks. Consider, however, the presentation by Ohlin. In the aggregate, individuals in country A (England) borrow $100 million from country B (the United States).[7] Borrowers in England want to use $30 million to buy American goods "and a like amount to purchase more of A's (England's) own export goods (machinery and textiles)."[8] Consequently, England's trade balance is made $60 million more passive, and 60 percent of the borrowed capital goes to

[7] Cf. *ibid.*, pp. 409-415.
[8] *Ibid.*, p. 409.

pay for the import surplus. The remaining $40 million is exchanged
at the central bank for currency of country A (England). It is in this
way that borrowers in England obtain buying power in the form of
their own currency. The central bank increases its reserves and increases its deposits.[9]

To call, as Ohlin does, the exchange of foreign reserves into
domestic deposits an increase of credit is a curious usage of terms;
for it implies a secondary expansion, whereas it is only part of the
primary expansion. "Such an increase in credit and buying power,"
writes Ohlin, "must tend to affect the prices of various sorts of commodities and industrial agents. Directly and indirectly it also tends to
increase imports, while keeping back exports."[10] For example, if the
monthly rate of borrowing is $10 million, and $6 million is used at
once by borrowers to purchase foreign goods, the remaining $4 million
is sold to the central bank for pounds sterling. It is this $4 million
transfer into pounds which Ohlin calls an increase in "credit," whereas
it is merely part of the primary expansion of means of payment. The
$6 million plus "the inflation of credit" of $4 million he calls the
primary increase in buying power, with the $4 million, exchanged
into pounds, being used to buy home goods, raising money incomes,
and hence leading to greater purchases of foreign goods.[11]

Ohlin's secondary increase is the effect of the multiplier, i.e., the
additional increase in incomes at home resulting from the injection
of the $4 million into circulation.

His tertiary effect is the result of a change in credit policy by the
banks, i.e., a loosening of credit by the banks because of an increase
in reserves, in this case the $4 million deposited with them by those
who have borrowed abroad. When the English banks wish to expand
credit domestically upon the basis of their increased dollar assets,
they will find it necessary to transfer some of their assets into gold to
support their credit expansion. There appears to be no good reason for
assuming, however, that the banks will typically not import gold until
after the credit expansion has taken place. Ohlin, as noted, insists

[9] Whether these transactions take place through intermediaries, such as private
banks, is immaterial.

[10] Ohlin, *op. cit.*, p. 412.

[11] *Ibid.*, pp. 412-413.

that the expansion of credit *causes* the gold to flow in, and not vice versa. But under certain circumstances (e.g., when exchange risk is being considered), they may wish to turn their dollar accounts into gold immediately upon acquiring them.

For the sake of consistency, Ohlin should have had four stages rather than three.

1. The combination of money used directly to buy from abroad, *plus* the domestic deposits arising from the sale of sight bills to the banks (the latter being the $4 million of domestic deposits, which Ohlin calls the "inflation of credit"), should for purposes of clarity be considered as the primary expansion of means of payment. If the banks are discounting "future" or "time" bills, then the banks do not have ownership of these bills but are lending funds on the long bills as security. The banks, in effect, are increasing their loans and securities, and this is part of the secondary expansion.

2. By virtue of the multiplier effect, the domestic expenditure of primary means of payment (i.e., the $4 million) increases national income by more than this amount. But the multiplier is a converging series with a finite sum, whereas in the above problem we are discussing a specified unit of time; i.e., we are asking by how much total income will be in excess of the primary domestic expenditure *per* month. This cannot be determined without reference to the entire monetary and fiscal expenditure policy of the government, say, per year. One must be careful to differentiate clearly among the different values for the multiplier when its influence is confined to only one month, to a year, or to an indefinitely long period during which its converging series of induced expenditures approaches its limit.

3. The secondary expansion of the banking system results from increased reserves; there is an increased willingness of the banks to grant credit (derivative deposits) and to lower interest rates. Here Ohlin's assumption appears to be that an increase in foreign exchange is used as increased reserves. This has been true for Sweden, but not for other countries. It has never been true in the United States. In the United States or England, central bank reserves have customarily consisted of gold holdings and notes. In England, prior to 1914, commercial banks would not have significant holdings of foreign bills.

After 1919 the Banque de France did hold foreign exchange as part of its reserve. Ordinarily, when this was the case, the country in question was on an exchange standard. Ohlin's particular assumption, and the alleged practice of bringing gold movements in through the back door, are occasioned by the practice of Sweden. They are not the rule.

4. There ought, for consistency, to be a fourth stage of expansion in Ohlin's presentation, an expansion which would include the multiplier effect of the derivative deposits.

Some further clarifications in Ohlin's analysis appear to be required. Suppose a country such as Australia borrows in England. Some of Australia's imports are likely to be purchased through Australian supply houses, introducing an intermediate stage in the process of adjustment. For, if some of the funds are spent in Australia, a time lag intervenes between the loan and the subsequent month-by-month functioning of the mechanism. How is equilibrium finally reached? At first, according to Ohlin, 6,000,000 units of foreign currency are used to buy foreign goods, 4,000,000 units remain for domestic expenditure, and there follow the attendant derivative deposits and multiplier effects. Somehow these 4,000,000 units also get exchanged for foreign goods, but it is not explained just how. What if there is an excessive tendency to accumulate foreign exchange or a tendency to import in excess of the borrowing? Would there be, for each month, an acquisition of foreign exchange equal to the inflow of imports? One could not tell from Ohlin's presentation. What would bring about the final adjustment so that the balance of payments is in equilibrium if the balance of commodities is not?

At a minimum, the excess of borrowing over the import balance is equal to the increase in deposits. Payments abroad manifestly draw down these foreign deposits; but the net effect is an increase in domestic liquidity, and an expansion in the borrowing country occurs. In the lending country, however, there has, *ceteris paribus*, been a contraction of means of payment and this reduces its purchases from abroad. An equilibrating influence thus occurs in both countries.

Ohlin's formulation of the mechanism of adjustment to a movement of international capital under stable exchanges is in several respects different from Viner's; and since there has been much confusion over these two positions, it will be well to state briefly that of Viner.[12] Viner's primary and secondary expansion refers only to the increase in means of payment; it does not refer to effective expenditures. Nor does it refer to multiplier effects. Multiplier effects are dealt with by Viner through the "final purchase velocity" concept. He considered the significant point to be whether a commodity is taken out of the market in the period under consideration. Therefore the final purchase velocity depends upon the unit of time assumed to be appropriate for the analysis; the longer the period of time, the greater the number of final purchases. But there is no difference in principle here between Viner's use of the final-purchase-velocity concept and Ohlin's multiplier concept.

Viner's position on the mechanism of adjustment to an international movement of capital may be outlined as follows:

1. Loans are made by England to Canadians who exchange their sterling for Canadian bank balances.

2. There follows a direct primary increase of bank deposits in Canada *and* of outside reserves of Canadian banks.[13]

3. The level of costs and prices rises in Canada because of the primary expansion of bank deposits and notes.

4. After a lag, secondary expansion occurs based on an increased bank-reserve ratio, exerting further upward pressure on costs and prices.

5. As a result of both primary and secondary expansion, incomes and expenditures increase, the aggregate increase depending upon the length of time considered and the prevailing final purchase velocity.

6. The increase in costs, prices, incomes, and expenditures in Canada, combined with differential cost-price relationships adverse to export industries and favorable to importers (and perhaps to a lesser degree favorable to domestic industries), increase Canadian imports

---

[12] Cf. Jacob Viner, *Canada's Balance of International Indebtedness, 1900-1913*, 1924, Part II; *Studies in the Theory of International Trade*, 1937, pp. 413-426.

[13] Canadian banks had no legal reserve requirements. They treated their English and United States foreign reserves as their domestic reserves, but it is hard to say in what sense they regarded them as reserves. The important thing to notice here is that the deposits are a liability of the Canadian banks and the foreign reserves are assets; i.e., the deposits increase *simultaneously* with reserves.

and discourage Canadian exports, thus tending to develop the equilibrating import balance of commodity and service trade. Within the framework of traditional gold-standard mechanism theory, contributions which have been made since the publication of Ohlin's *Interregional and International Trade* and Viner's *Studies* have been confined to the "superstructure" of the analysis. The most important of these contributions have dealt with the role of short-term capital movements in the balancing process.[14] It is understandable that relatively little more has been done within this framework in view of the drastic changes which have occurred in our economic conditions and institutional environment in recent years.

Ohlin has gone so far as to argue that the "all too static" neo-Keynesian theory of income changes and payment balances, "hailed a few years ago as a great advance, represents a step backwards."[15] In commenting on the relation between past and recent developments, he concedes that changes in employment were not sufficiently considered in the analysis of the mechanism of international payments in the 1920's and the early 1930's. But it is untrue, he maintains, that relative changes in national incomes arising from other causes were either overlooked or neglected. He states that the reasoning in terms of changes in national incomes is neither adequate nor well suited to an analysis of the influence of inflationary and deflationary policies on the balances of payments. Pursuing his more traditional approach, he notes that while an inflationary pressure exists, the total volume of purchases at existing prices tends to exceed the national income and turns *directly* to foreign goods. Purchases financed by excessive credit, the argument continues, are not made as a result of an earlier influence of inflationary policy on national income. Such policy "exerts a pressure *at the same time* on the volume of exports and imports and

[14] See, e.g., F. W. Paish, "Banking Policy and the Balance of International Payments," *Economica*, November, 1936, pp. 402-422; J. C. Gilbert, "The Mechanism of Interregional Redistributions of Money," *Review of Economic Studies*, Vol. V, 1937-1938, pp. 187 ff.; United Nations, *International Capital Movements during the Inter-War Period*, 1949; Arthur I. Bloomfield, *Capital Imports and the American Balance of Payments 1934-39*, 1949. The works of these writers are, of course, not confined to gold-standard conditions.

[15] Cf. the comments by Ohlin and Viner in *National Policy for Economic Welfare at Home and Abroad*, ed. Robert Lekachman, 1955, pp. 214, 232-233. See also Ohlin's discussion in his controversy with Keynes over the German reparations problem in *Economic Journal*, Vol. XXXIX, 1929.

on domestic prices and incomes."[16] Ohlin and Viner are not in disagreement on this issue; Viner emphasizes the importance of monetary income analysis during periods of inflation, whereas Ohlin uses such terms as "purchasing power" or "liquidity" to explain the same phenomenon. There remains an important problem to integrate these concepts with traditional mechanism theory in a way which would show under what monetary conditions balance-of-payments equilibrium or disequilibrium would be likely to emerge.

POSTULATES OF TRADITIONAL THEORY: FLUCTUATING EXCHANGE RATES

The arguments and conclusions which dominate present-day economic thought, both theoretical and practical, on the balancing process under fluctuating exchange rates stem, for the most part, from an article written by Taussig in 1917.[17] His important contribution was formulated upon the following assumptions.

1. Commodity trade, and nothing else, enters into the accounts of the two countries prior to the disturbance.

2. The balance of trade is in equilibrium before the disturbance.

3. The premium on specie corresponds to the real depreciation of paper currency.

4. The quantity of money in the country undergoing depreciation remains constant.

Taussig introduced a disturbance in the form of a large and continued series of loans from England to the United States. He then traced the following sequence of events.

1. The demand for United States dollars rises in London, lowering the value of the pound in terms of dollars; sterling falls in New York or the dollar appreciates in terms of the pound.

[16] Ohlin, in National Policy for Economic Welfare at Home and Abroad, p. 214.
[17] F. W. Taussig, "International Trade under Depreciated Paper. A Contribution to Theory," Quarterly Journal of Economics, Vol XXXI, 1917, pp. 380-403. Cf. also J. H. Hollander, "International Trade under Depreciated Paper: A Criticism," Quarterly Journal of Economics, Vol. XXXIII, 1918, pp. 678-690; F. W. Taussig, "A Rejoinder," Quarterly Journal of Economics, Vol. XXXIII, 1918, pp. 691-692; F. D. Graham, "International Trade under Depreciated Paper. The United States, 1862-79," Quarterly Journal of Economics, Vol. XXXVI, 1922.

2. The gold premium (in terms of United States dollars) falls as compared with the general price level.

3. Imports from England into the United States are obtained at lower prices in terms of the dollar.

4. United States imports from England increase.

5. Imports from the United States into England can be obtained only at higher prices in terms of the pound, at lower prices in terms of the dollar.

6. United States exports to England decrease.

7. The increase in United States imports and the decrease in United States exports restore equilibrium in the balance of trade in the sense that it becomes compatible with the transfer of long-term capital from England to the United States.

8. The general level of prices is lower in the United States (higher in England) and the pound-dollar rate is on a new level.

9. Money incomes remain the same in the United States and England, while real incomes rise in the United States and fall in England; general level of prices is lower in the United States and higher in England, but the terms of trade shift in favor of the United States.

Taussig was interested in comparing the mechanism of adjustment under depreciated paper with that of gold-standard conditions.[18] He concluded that the "real" effects are the same as under the gold standard, though the direction of movement of money prices is different; for the loans from England to the United States result in higher real incomes in the United States and lower real incomes in England, but this is brought about through a fall in money prices in the United States relative to money incomes, and a rise in money prices in England relative to money incomes.[19]

In his original article, Taussig maintained that all prices in the United States would be lower because of the appreciation of the dollar relative to the pound. On the basis of his assumptions this conclusion would appear to be correct, since the decline in import and export prices relative to domestic prices would lead to some substitution of import and export products for domestic goods, resulting in

[18] F. W. Taussig, *International Trade*, 1933, pp. 337-338.
[19] *Ibid.*, pp. 397, 398.

some decline of domestic prices. This emphasis upon the direction in which people spend their money was a contribution of the first rank. However, Taussig assumed that a constant quantity of money means constant money income and constant rates of payment for productive services, and consequently unchanged costs of production. This does not necessarily follow from his assumptions, since the redistribution of money incomes and money expenditures is more than likely to have some effect upon the rates of remuneration and hence upon money costs and incomes.

Concerning the direction of expenditures, Taussig further points out that a currency expansion need not necessarily improve the terms of trade of a country. It would have no such effect unless it influenced the prices of export commodities more than the prices of other things —domestic prices and money wages—"it has confused and irregular effects depending on the individuals into whose hands the added money first comes and the directions in which they spend it."[20] Here Taussig seems to anticipate the "income elasticity of demand" concept. But he did not present a clear statement that shifts in demand could bring about equilibrium without price changes. The "shifts in demand" part of the mechanism referred to by Ohlin or Viner consists of changes in aggregate expenditures, such as those which Taussig introduces by his expansion of paper money, and the effect of such shifts depends on the direction taken by the new expenditures. Taussig recognizes, of course, that the direction of the increased expenditures resulting from his type of disturbance affects the outcome of the disturbance; but his argument stops short of presenting an entirely satisfactory solution. On the whole, Taussig's imperfections are not of major significance insofar as his development of the international mechanism under depreciated paper is concerned.

UNWARRANTED GENERALIZATIONS FROM LIMITED ASSUMPTIONS

Within the framework of neo-classical thought, the contribution which Taussig made to the theory of the balancing process under

[20] *Ibid.*, pp. 390, 385-392.

inconvertible paper has remained essentially where he left it for thirty years. He never tired of drawing attention to the limited assumptions upon which his conclusions were based, whereas in our own time these conclusions have often become a stereotype and those persons who draw them seem to have become oblivious to the limited assumptions upon which they are based.[21] According to these assumptions, the monetary situation in both countries is stable. Whatever inflation or deflation there may have been is over: each country has settled down to a fixed monetary supply. It is not the consequences of changes in the volume of money and in prices that are examined, but the characteristics of international trade between countries having different monetary standards, and between which no money can pass. The rate of exchange has settled down to a level conforming to the altered price conditions, and the sums due in London for United States exports are exactly equal in money value, at the above exchange rate, to the sums due in New York for British exports.

These are not the circumstances which economists usually have in mind today when they discuss the mechanism of adjustment under fluctuating exchange rates. Yet the dominant body of theoretical thought appears to be based, consciously or unconsciously, on these assumptions. Taussig presented his analysis in the form of a carefully guarded hypothesis which, he hoped, would be tested and retested by experience. Instead, virtually identical conclusions are now often handed down as principles for action.

Taussig's fundamental conclusions follow from his premises. But his premises represent one important case only, namely, where the quantity of money and velocity remain the same in the two countries. And as is to be expected, his conclusions may or may not be relevant to experience. Different premises would lead to different conclusions. Our own analysis, based on somewhat more general premises, suggests a new answer which serves not to invalidate but rather to supplement the answer formerly regarded as adequate.

---

[21] *Ibid.*, pp. 341-342.

6

Toward a More General
Mechanism Theory

THE conclusions which dominate present-day economic thought, both theoretical and practical, on the mechanism of adjustment under inconvertible paper stem directly from Taussig's analysis. They have been applied to the balancing process under conditions both of fluctuating exchange rates and of managed flexibility. Taussig's formulation was essentially correct, though it is only one important equilibrium case of many alternative equilibrium and disequilibrium cases which may be formulated under various sets of assumptions. The important fact is that all these cases lend themselves to useful generalization.

THE "NORMAL" CONDITION

Assume that two countries A and B have inconvertible paper currencies in terms of gold but convertible in terms of one another. Country A makes a series of large loans to country B. Assume further that country A raises the loans through taxation at home and that the two countries maintain a stable flow of total domestic expenditures. The sequence of events is customarily presented as follows:

1. Country A raises the loans at home through taxes in terms of its own currency.

2. Country A buys foreign exchange of country B, i.e., from exchange dealers, who, in turn, use the currency to buy bills of exporters in country A.

3. Currency of country A falls in terms of currency B; i.e., more units of currency A are now required to purchase one unit of currency B.

4. Foreign-exchange dealers in A will build up balances in B. While this may be done, in part, through gold shipments (if available), the latter are usually omitted from the analysis.

5. There is no fixed limit to the extent of depreciation of currency A in terms of currency B.

6. International prices rise in country A in response to the shift in the exchange rate, freely competitive internationally traded commodities rising in price in terms of its own currency by virtually the same extent as its exchange rate falls.

7. Costs do not rise at first in country A, while selling prices of internationally traded goods have risen, resulting in immediate windfall capital gains to dealers in exports, and to other holders of internationally traded goods and assets.

8. The favorable cost-price relationship in country A with respect to exportable commodities leads to a shift of resources from domestic goods to exports, expanding the volume of exports from country A to country B.

9. The rise in price of exports and imports in country A in terms of its own currency will, in all probability, lead to some substitution by its citizens of domestic goods which have not, as yet, risen in price for international goods. This has the effect of liberating more exportable goods for the foreign market and, if possible,[1] of increasing the production of import substitutes, both forces normally improving the trade account of country A with respect to country B.

---

[1] Under conditions of full employment this could only be achieved through an increase in the supply of resources and/or an increase in productivity, e.g., by way of an increase in the supply of capital and the labor force, improved allocation and efficiency.

10. When the point is reached where exports of country A are equal to its imports plus loans, say per year, then equilibrium is established in its international accounts at a lower exchange rate of currency A in terms of currency B, a higher price level in country A (same expenditures, less goods) as compared to country B (same expenditures, more goods), and, in all probability, a worsening of the terms of trade for country A as compared to country B.

Hence it is maintained that normally devaluation of a country's currency will result in the following:

1. A rise in its export and import prices relative to the prices of its domestic goods
2. An expansion of its production of exportable goods and import substitutes as compared to domestic goods
3. An expansion of its quantum of exports relative to its imports
4. An expansion of its value of exports relative to imports
5. An improvement in its international liquidity position

Reflection and fact seem to suggest that there is no reason for assuming the above conditions or conclusions either to be "normal" or "abnormal" in the sense of corresponding to reality. They represent the phenomenon of exchange depreciation under the assumption of long-run, complete equilibrium analysis. Such analysis assumes, *inter alia*, hypothetical monetary equilibrium. If its results are not to be misapplied—and if the theory is to be made more useful in explaining reality—it must be supplemented with assumptions which correspond more closely to actual equilibrium and disequilibrium conditions.

No conclusions can be drawn about the effects of a phenomenon such as exchange depreciation (or disinflation under stable exchange rates) on the trade balance of a country unless specific assumptions are made about accompanying monetary and fiscal policies which are at least as likely to be inflationary as deflationary or neutral. Hence in the analysis that follows we shall assume the operation of the balancing process under various given expenditure conditions. We shall not necessarily assume a causal relationship between, say, devaluation on the part of any given country and a change in the size of the income flows in that or any other country. It is useful to assume in some cases a simultaneous autonomous (e.g., coincidental) change in exchange rates and income flows, and in others a causal relationship between them. First, we shall establish our analysis on the basis of the former assumption; in later sections, we shall apply it to some causal relations.

MORE GENERAL CONDITIONS

Assume that country A and country B (which may represent all other countries) trade only in goods and services (i.e., no capital flows or gold flows unless otherwise stated), and that their exports and imports are initially in equilibrium. Country A undergoes an inflation relative to country B. As a result, country A experiences an excess demand for the foreign exchange of country B at the prevailing (fixed) rate of exchange. We shall assume that the loss of international reserves leads country A to devalue its currency (or to disinflate under stable exchange rates) approximately to the extent of the relative rise in its prices with respect to currency B. The problem is to determine the probable effects on the balance-of-payments position of country A under the assumption that, after country A has devalued its currency (or disinflated under stable exchange rates), its stream of total domestic expenditure rises (or falls) in greater, the same, or smaller proportion relative to the stream of total domestic expenditure of country B.

To show these effects it will be required to outline the stream-of-total-expenditure approach. It has been formulated as follows:[2] How to procure and maintain a stream of total expenditure adequate to purchase the goods and services which a country can produce with the resources at its command. If the stream of expenditure is too small for that purpose, some of the goods produced cannot be sold at the prices the sellers expected to obtain, and producers suffer losses. These

[2] The *locus classicus* of the theory to make prospective expenditure and the value of prospective production equivalent without inflationary or deflationary developments is Keynes' study, *How to Pay for the War*, 1940. Cf. also Oscar Lange, *Price Flexibility and Employment*, 1945; Milton Friedman, "Lange on Price Flexibility and Employment," *American Economic Review*, September, 1946, pp. 613-631; Don Patinkin, *Money, Interest, and Prices*, 1956, esp. Chaps. xii-xiv.

losses may materialize either through a fall of selling prices or, failing that, in an accumulation of unsalable inventories. This process, referred to as deflation, usually leads to restriction of output and to unemployment. If, on the other hand, the stream of expenditure is too large relative to the goods and services produced, prices and profits rise. This process, referred to as inflation, may be induced either by monetary expansion or by rising costs. The difficult problem is to maintain a stream of total expenditure large enough to avoid deflation, and yet not too large as to cause inflation. Traditional analysis relied on certain forces to end and reverse deflationary and inflationary pressures, forces which under modern conditions often do not prevail.

The issues which are relevant to our purpose may be illustrated in the following terms. Assume a closed economy with the existence of an excess supply (unemployment) of some factor of production. If the price of the factor is flexible downward, the excess supply will cause a fall in its price. The fall in price will stimulate the substitution of this factor for other factors and will lead to a fall in the price of products produced primarily with it, stimulating the substitution of these products for products produced chiefly with other factors. These substitutions may, in turn, cause the prices of other factors and other products to fall. The question is, Under what conditions will the drop in the price of the factor lead to the removal of unemployment? Primarily, these unemployment variations depend upon the monetary effect of such price changes. If the community does not change its desires as to the real quantity of cash balances it wishes to hold, and if the nominal quantity of money remains the same, then an excess supply of cash balances results. The inflationary influence of this excess supply of cash balances prevents the prices of other factors and other products (and hence all prices) from falling as much as the price of the factor initially unemployed and the prices of the products produced primarily with that factor. As long as this situation exists the initial price decline of the factor will be effective in producing a new equilibrium with full employment of the initially unemployed factor. However, if the price decline leads to a reduction in the real quantity of cash balances available relative to the real quantity desired, say, because the nominal quantity of money is reduced by a larger fraction than the fall of prices (interest rates remaining constant), then all prices will be forced to fall by a greater proportion than the fall in the price of the factor, and more unemployment will result than there was initially. If the initial and induced price decline leads to equality between the real quantity of cash balances available relative to the real quantity desired, say, because the nominal quantity of money is reduced by the same fraction as the fall of prices, then no change in the amount of employment will result.

The argument of traditional economic theory, in maintaining that deflation takes care of itself provided costs are not rigid, assumed that the diminution of the stream of total expenditure would not keep pace with the fall of prices. It held that the fall in prices would increase the real purchasing power of the stock of money held by producers and consumers. Producers and consumers, it was assumed, would find that they had more money than they wished to keep and would spend part of it to buy goods and services. A stimulus would thus arise to investment and to consumer expenditure, stemming from increased liquidity, measured as a ratio of the value of the stock of money to the total wealth or annual income. In addition, the theorizing that was developed by the older economists in the classical tradition relied upon the following to end, and reverse, a process of deflation: the stimulus to investment of a low interest rate expected to rise before long; the stimulus to demand of the decline of inventories to below convenient minima; the stimulus to demand of the piling up of unsatisfied wants which occurs during periods of contraction; the stimulus to investment and consumer expenditures of new discoveries and technological improvements; the stimulus to investment and consumer expenditures, as prices fall—particularly raw material prices—and of the expectation that before long they would take an upward trend.[3]

These forces often provided powerful stimuli for expansion. Traditional analysis overlooked the fact, however, that under certain deflationary conditions the banking system might operate in such a way that liquidity would be reduced rather than increased. Producers who

[3] Cf. Jacob Viner, *International Trade and Economic Development*, 1952, pp. 20-21.

reduce their output might repay their bank loans without obtaining an equal volume of new ones. The amount of bank deposits would be reduced and the decline in the available amount of money would keep pace with the diminution of the demand for loans. An important stimulus upon which traditional economic theory relied to keep the stream of total expenditure from falling proportionally with prices would thus fail to operate. Nor would interest rates necessarily fall at the appropriate time. Conditions could grow from bad to worse; bankruptcies might produce a financial panic. Banks would refuse to renew loans which were demanded by producers and thus force them to restrict output. The quantity of money would then diminish more than in proportion to the fall in prices, and output and employment could decrease still further. Traditional economic theory was not sufficiently aware of this tendency of the banks to destroy money, and of the necessity for government control to avoid deflation; it was aware of it, but forgot it in the context of the international adjustment mechanism. It did, however, clearly recognize the need for government control to avoid inflation. Classical doctrine of monetary management and control of private banking was based on the fear that irresponsible use by government or by private banks of the power to create money may lead to an excessive stream of total expenditure.

For an open economy, traditional economic theory relied on even further stimuli to end and reverse a process of national deflation or inflation. If deflationary forces developed, it was assumed that the stream of total expenditure in the rest of the world would remain the same and, with gold-standard conditions, exports would rise relative to imports, providing still another stimulus to domestic expansion. Conversely, inflationary pressures would lead to an outflow of gold and to enforced monetary contraction. Manifestly, such conditions do not exist today. Deflation in a major trading country may bring on deflation in other countries. Inflation in one country no longer brings on the kind of crisis which gold-standard conditions produced. A country that is out of line is not impelled to follow a policy of monetary contraction. On the contrary, though relative inflationary pressures produce the sort of crises which are associated with the loss of foreign reserves, countries now are apt to impose direct controls over their foreign trade and the domestic inflationary pressures may continue unabated.

EXPENDITURE APPROACH AND THE INTERNATIONAL MECHANISM

Theorists who have worked with the stream-of-expenditure approach have not applied the aforementioned generalized analysis from the domestic sphere to that of the balancing process. They usually revert to the "traditional case" in domestic doctrine when turning to problems of international trade. It is assumed that if an underemployed factor is used exclusively to produce export goods, a reduction of its price is bound to increase its employment. If the price is reduced sufficiently, the argument continues, all excess supply of the factor is bound to disappear. In this case, it is claimed, partial-equilibrium analysis, in terms of a downward-sloping demand curve, is applicable and the result is quite independent of the monetary effect. This is not true. The result is independent of the *domestic* monetary effect, but it is not independent of the foreign monetary effect. The situation considered is a particular case of a more general case which must include the monetary effect of the aggregate expenditures of all the countries which make up the demand for the country's exports. Should a country's export prices in terms of foreign currency (or of any factor in terms of its own currency) be lowered, and the substitution and expansion effects be instrumental in bringing about an increase in the production of exportables, and if, *pari passu,* the stream of aggregate expenditures of all the countries which make up the demand for its exports be reduced by greater proportion than the price of these exports, then the world demand for these exports would fall (and/or its volume of unemployment increase). To maintain the volume of exports, their prices would have to drop proportionally with the decline in the stream of total expenditures. To expand them, their prices would have to fall more than proportionally with the decline in the stream of total expenditures.

By extending the stream-of-total-expenditure approach to an international economy under more or less modern conditions, it appears possible to provide guides as to the probable success or failure of alternative mechanism-of-adjustment policies, guides which are in turn related to the causes which brought about the need for adjustment. We shall proceed by dealing with three possible cases in which the effects of devaluation (or disinflation under stable exchange rates) are accompanied by given expenditure conditions. These cases are designed to be exhaustive. Their results will be generalized in the concluding section.

1. Country A (England) and country B (the United States) maintain a stable stream of total domestic expenditure after the devaluation occurs.

Let there be n goods and services entering foreign trade (exports and imports) and denote their prices by $P_1, P_2 \ldots P_n$. Denote the excess demand for each of them by $D_1, D_2 \ldots D_n$, respectively.[4] D's can be positive, negative, or zero. Denote the excess demand for foreign exchange (the import balance) by X. The relation is:

$$X \equiv P_1 D_1 + P_2 D_2 + \ldots + P_n D_n.$$

And this is an identity holding for any values of the P's and D's.

It can be seen directly that, under freely competitive conditions and with the stream of expenditure (*mutatis mutandis*) remaining the same in the two countries, devaluation of A's currency would, in all probability, lead to a drop in its excess demand for the goods and services of country B at the new rate of exchange.[5] This follows because of the higher import prices to country A in terms of A's currency (but no change in its import prices in terms of B's currency, i.e., the P's), and no change in the export prices of A's freely competitive internationally traded goods in terms of B's currency. Consequently, assuming negatively sloped demand and positively sloped supply functions, the algebraic decline in the D's, with no change in the

---

[4] Excess demand here means the total quantity demanded by country A minus the total quantity produced domestically by country A at the given world price (abstracting from transport costs, tariffs, etc.) within a system of general interdependence. And similarly for exports, which are designated by negative D's.

[5] Although under the present assumption of a constant flow of expenditure in both countries the concept of price elasticity might be somewhat applicable, under other assumptions to be made below it is misleading. The entire analysis has therefore been developed without explicit reference to elasticity.

P's, must reduce X, the excess demand for foreign exchange, and improve the balance-of-payments position of country A.[6] It should be noted that the present formulation includes not only an improvement in the balance of payments via reduced imports (a fall in the value of some positive D's) but also an increase in exports (an algebraic fall in the value of some negative D's) and the introduction of new lines into the export market (the algebraic fall of D's which had been zero and now become negative). Accordingly, under the assumption that, after the country suffering from a trade balance engendered by inflation has devalued its currency, both countries maintain a stable stream of total expenditure, we would expect that so long as the degree of devaluation is sufficient, equilibrium would be reestablished in its international accounts. And this is entirely consistent with Taussig's conclusions.

In order to present a frame of reference for our subsequent more general analysis, let us consider case 1 from a different approach, by examining separately the export and import side. Let there be g export goods and services of country A and denote their prices by P_1/A, P_2/A . . . P_g/A, and the quantity exported of each of them by Q_1/A, Q_2/A . . . Q_g/A, respectively. The Q's can be positive or zero. Let the amount of foreign exchange received from exports by country A be Y_A.[7] The relation is:

$$Y_A \equiv P_1/A Q_1/A + P_2/A Q_2/A + . . . + P_g/A Q_g/A$$

or

$$Y_A \equiv \sum_{i=1}^{g} P_A Q_A. \tag{1}$$

Let M_B denote the final means of payment used by country B to discharge its import obligations to country A. Let V be the average velocity, i.e., the number of times M_B flows through the circle from

---

[6] The term "balance of payments" is here used in the specific sense of an excess of immediate claims on abroad over obligations to abroad, or vice versa, which must be liquidated by specie, by surrender of foreign balances, or by agreed deferment.

[7] It is assumed for the purposes of this analysis that all export transactions of country A are made in B currency (i.e., dollars).

importers in country B to exporters in country A and back again. The relation is:

$$M_BV_B = P_1/_AQ_1/_A + P_2/_AQ_2/_A + \ldots + P_g/_AQ_g/_A$$

or

$$M_BV_B = \sum_{i=1}^{g} P_AQ_A. \tag{2}$$

$$\therefore Y_A = M_BV_B = \sum_{i=1}^{g} P_AQ_A. \tag{3}$$

Similarly:

$$Y_B = M_AV_A = \sum_{i=1}^{h} P_BQ_B. \tag{4}$$

Depreciation of the currency of country A would lead to a rise in its prices, i.e., in terms of A's currency of freely competitive internationally traded goods, by approximately the extent of the depreciation. This immediately provides windfall capital gains to exporters and dealers in possession of inventories for export. Further, since costs of domestic inputs do not rise forthwith, the favorable price-cost relationships provide a stimulus for the increased production of exports. It is customarily argued that these two forces lead to an increased output of export goods and to an improvement in the balance-of-payments position of the country in question *on the export side*. This does not follow from the stated assumptions, for since:

$$\sum_{i=1}^{g} P_AQ_A = M_BV_B \tag{2}$$

an increase in the Q_A's with no change in P_A's (in terms of B's currency) could result only from an increase in M_B and/or V_B. But under the assumption that the stream of total expenditure in country B remains the same, there is no reason for assuming an increased M_BV_B. Under present assumptions, the most plausible of many possible hypotheses would be a constant M_BV_B, and in such circumstances higher Q_A's could be accompanied only by lower P_A's, leaving Y_A unchanged.

Increased exports from country A to country B must depend upon the prices of A's exports rising by less than the devaluation of its currency, or upon new or previously domestic goods becoming profitable for export at the new exchange rate.[8] Theoretically, there is therefore no reason to believe that, with the stream of total expenditure remaining the same in the two countries, depreciation of the currency of one of them would necessarily lead to an expansion of its exports of freely competitive internationally traded goods at previously existing world prices. The position, to the contrary, probably stems from a fallacy of composition, the tendency of treating countries as if they were individual firms. If a country is an important exporter of some commodity—and in many cases the proportional contribution of specific countries to the foreign supply of internationally traded goods is high—an increased output of this commodity must lead to a lowering of its world price, if the world stream of total expenditures is assumed to remain the same. Given a fall in the international price of the exports in question, the country with the depreciated currency would procure more foreign receipts from freely (and monopolistically) competitive internationally traded commodities if the foreign substitution and expansion effect for them are more than proportional to their price decline (i.e., if the weighted average elasticity of demand is greater than one). These substitution and expansion effects include the increased exports resulting from decreased quantities supplied by country B at the lowered prices. If domestic commodities which have not risen in price, or have risen in price by a smaller proportion than the devaluation, or new goods previously not produced at all, are now exported, foreign receipts would clearly increase because of the price substitution and the expansion effects.

On the import side, we would expect the higher-priced goods of country B, in terms of A's currency, to have the effect of reducing imports into country A, and thereby reducing the outflow of foreign exchange.

[8] If we consider country A and the rest of the world, A's exports to B could, of course, increase at the expense of third countries (stimulated by improved cost-price relationships at home); but, in all probability, this would lead to a fall in the P's, for it is most unlikely that the exporters of third countries would passively stand by while their proportion of sales in B was being reduced.

To sum up, with the stream of total expenditure remaining the same in the two countries, we would expect devaluation of the currency, *mutatis mutandis*, to improve the foreign-reserve position of the country having devalued through (1) a reduction in imports; (2) an expansion in exports of previously domestic, and new, commodities; (3) an expansion in exports of freely competitive internationally traded commodities with an infinite elasticity of demand, such as gold imports into the United States; (4) an expansion in exports of internationally traded commodities at previously existing world prices at the expense of domestic producers in country B, or at the expense of third countries; and/or (5) an expansion in exports of freely (and monopolistically) competitive internationally traded commodities whose prices have declined, and whose substitution and expansion effects are more than proportional to their price decline. It is possible, however, that the expansion in A's output of export products may so lower their prices in terms of foreign exchange that its total foreign receipts would decline to a greater extent than the reduction in its foreign expenditures, thus failing to improve its balance-of-payments position.

These conclusions are in general conformity with the extant position. The above analysis presents, however, the *deus ex machina* of devaluation and thereby reveals one qualification that deserves particular attention, viz., the important role of flexibility and expansiveness of supply in the balancing process under traditional assumptions. If, after a period of inflation, a country devalues its currency (or disinflates under stable exchange rates), with the stream of total domestic expenditure remaining the same in the "two" countries after devaluation, its export prices in terms of foreign exchange would not remain the same. Generally, they would have to fall. Further, its volume of imports definitely would decline. Hence its balance of payments could be improved without a contraction in the total volume of world trade only if its output of exportable goods and services expands sufficiently to overcome both its own reduction in imports and the decline in the prices of its exports. These considerations suggest a greater importance of supply and price effects than is usually accorded to them in much of the current literature, especially when one considers the remarkable differences in adaptive capacities as regards supply in the United States, western Europe, and the economically less developed nations.

2. Country B (the United States) expands its stream of total domestic expenditure relative to that of country A (England), or country A contracts its stream of total domestic expenditure relative to that of country B.

We shall assume again that, prior to devaluation, country A had undergone an inflation relative to country B. The problem is to determine the probable effects on the balance-of-payments position of country A under the assumption that after the devaluation has occurred, *mutatis mutandis*, country B expands its stream of total domestic expenditure (so that effective demand exceeds the supply of goods and services and prices rise), while country A maintains a stable stream of total domestic expenditure (sufficient to avoid deflation and yet not so great as to cause inflation).

Consider again the relation:

$$X \equiv P_1D_1 + P_2D_2 + \ldots + P_nD_n$$

using the same notations as those of case (1) above. The rise in the price of imports to country A (in terms of its own currency) relative to its constant stream of domestic expenditure produces a negative substitution effect, and a contraction effect, in regard to its imports from country B. This reduction in country A's excess demand for the goods and services of country B (a decline in the D's) stems from two sources: the devaluation of A's currency and the probable rise in some of B's export prices resulting from the expansion in its stream of total expenditure.

The reduction in the volume of A's imports which is associated only with the devaluation would reduce the value of its imports in terms of foreign exchange. This decline in some of the D's, with the P's remaining constant, or falling (in terms of B's currency) because of the decline in the D's, would tend to reduce X (country A's excess demand for foreign exchange), and hence tend to improve its balance-of-payments position.

The reduction in the volume of A's imports which is associated with a rise in the price of some of B's exports, however, would be accompanied by a more than proportional, proportional, or less than proportional decline in A's imports relative to their rise in price; each respectively improves, leaves unchanged, or deteriorates the balance-of-payments position of country A. The net effect of these forces, insofar as an improvement is concerned in country A's balance of payments on the import side, would depend upon whether the decline in the sum of the products of those DP's which are associated with constant or lower P's, or with higher P's but more than proportional declines in the D's, is greater than the sum of the products of those DP's which are associated with P's that have risen in greater proportion than the D's.[9]

In regard to exports, the expansion in the stream of total expenditure of country B would tend to increase the exports of country A to country B to a greater extent than in case 1. This follows for three reasons. First, those freely competitive internationally traded exports of country A which (as a result of the devaluation) rise in price in country A approximately to the extent of the devaluation now could be exported in greater volume to country B because of the expansion in B's stream of total expenditure relative to the stable price of these goods in terms of B's currency. Second, commodities previously sold only in country A, and new items for export, now could be exported to country B in greater volume. And third, the tendency for freely (and monopolistically) competitive internationally traded exports of country A to decline in price (in terms of B's currency) because of their increased output now would be counteracted by

---

[9] If, in order to obtain a rough first approximation, it is assumed that the expansion in the stream of total domestic expenditure has the effect of raising some of B's export prices all in the *same proportion, while the rest remain unchanged,* then the results may be expressed quite simply; for those export prices of country B which are not affected by the expansion in the stream of total expenditure are a constant and may therefore be omitted from the formulation. The value of country A's imports in terms of foreign exchange is reduced, remains the same, or is increased if the ratio of:

The *total* quantity of A's imports prior to devaluation

The *total* quantity of A's imports after devaluation

is greater than, equal to, or less than the ratio of:

The price of B's exports after the expansion in the stream of its total expenditure

The price of B's exports prior to the expansion in the stream of its total expenditure

the increased effective demand for them, resulting from the expansion in the stream of total expenditure of country B. Indeed, this expansion in the stream of total expenditure may raise the prices of some of A's exports in terms of B's currency; where this rise in price is due wholly to the increase in the stream of total expenditure in B, then the volume and value of these exports from A to B would clearly rise. The exports that may decline in value in terms of foreign exchange are "inferior goods" and those freely competitive internationally traded exports of country A whose prices decline but whose volume rises in smaller proportion. The net effect of all these forces, insofar as an improvement is concerned in country A's balance of payments on the export side, would depend upon whether the increase in the sum of the products of those DP's which are associated with constant or rising P's (in terms of B's currency), and those DP's which represent new export items and commodities which were previously sold domestically only, plus those DP's which are associated with lower P's but more than proportional increases in D's, is greater than the sum of the products of those DP's which are associated with P's that have declined (in terms of B's currency) but whose volume has increased in smaller proportion.[10]

Similarly, the analysis could be applied to the situation where country A contracts its stream of total expenditure relative to that of country B. The results are virtually the same as those derived above.

The probability on *a priori* grounds appears to be extremely high that, with a similar degree of devaluation, the foreign-reserve position of country A would be improved to a greater extent in case 2 as compared with case 1. First, the expansion in the stream of total expendi-

---

[10] If, again, in order to obtain a rough first approximation, it is assumed that the devaluation of A's currency has the effect of lowering some of A's export prices all in the *same proportion while the rest remain unchanged* (in terms of B's currency), then the results may be expressed as follows. The value of country A's exports in terms of foreign exchange is increased, remains the same, or is reduced, if the ratio of:

The *total* quantity of A's exports prior to devaluation

The *total* quantity of A's exports after devaluation

is less than, equal to, or greater than, the ratio of:

The price of A's exports that declined (in terms of B's currency) after devaluation

The price of A's exports prior to devaluation

ture of country B would tend to increase its volume and value of imports more than in case 1. The greater the possibility of country A's expanding its supply of exports with a minimum of rising costs and selling prices, the greater will be the improvement in the balance-of-payments position of country A. Second, the rise in some of B's export prices may reduce the volume and value of A's imports (in terms of B's currency) to a greater extent than in case 1.

The expansion in the stream of total expenditure of country B, however, could have the effect of so raising some of its export prices that the country which had devalued its currency would experience a rise in the foreign value of its imports, despite its reduced volume of imports.[11] Hence the greater the extent to which devaluation of A's currency has the effect of increasing the domestic production of export goods which require such higher-cost imports from country B, the greater would be the possible drain on its foreign reserves from this source. The drain may conceivably be large enough to more than offset the additional receipts from expanded exports, thereby deteriorating further the balance-of-payments position of country A.[12]

Yet the probability, on *a priori* grounds, of a further deterioration in country A's balance of payments appears to be small, for it is unlikely that the imports which have risen in price would be so large a fraction of total costs as to counterbalance A's lowered domestic costs (in terms of B's currency). Therefore, the probability appears to be extremely high that the balance-of-payments position of country A will be improved if after devaluation of its currency, *mutatis mutandis*, country B expands its stream of total domestic expenditure relative to that of country A, or country A contracts its stream of total do-

[11] The tendency for the reduction in A's volume of imports to bring about a decline in B's export prices (in terms of B's currency) is weakened by the expansion in the stream of B's total expenditure; i.e., devaluation is unlikely to improve the terms of trade of country A on the import side if country B is undergoing an expansion.

[12] Since country A suffers from a deficit to begin with, an equal percentage rise in its import and export prices would increase its dollar deficit. But in that case a given increase in the physical volume of its exports (or a decline of its imports) would yield (or save) a proportionally larger quantity of foreign exchange, leaving the country's position no worse in real terms. It is true, of course, that the real value of foreign-exchange reserves would be proportionally reduced by the general increase in prices.

mestic expenditure relative to that of country B. Conditions are conceivable, however, in which the contrary may occur.

The above analysis is confined to one period of time, for, obviously, the expansion in B's stream of total expenditure cannot continue indefinitely without inducing an expansion in country A. If it is assumed that in the next period of time the stream of total expenditure of both countries will be stabilized at the new level, then the analysis presented in case 1 may be readily applied. In case 3 we shall consider the situation in which the stream of total expenditure continues to rise, or to fall, in the next period(s) of time, as well as the interdependence of imports and exports.

3. Country A (England) expands its stream of total domestic expenditure relative to that of country B (the United States), or Country B contracts its stream of total domestic expenditure relative to that of country A.

The problem is to determine the probable effects on the balance-of-payments position of country A under the assumption that after its devaluation has occurred, *mutatis mutandis*, country A expands its stream of total domestic expenditure (so that effective demand exceeds the supply of goods and services and prices rise) while country B maintains a stable stream of total domestic expenditure.

Consider again the relation:

$$X \equiv P_1 D_1 + P_2 D_2 + \ldots + P_n D_n$$

using the same notations as those of cases 1 and 2 above.

The rise in the price of imports to country A (in terms of its own currency) resulting only from the devaluation would tend to produce a negative substitution, and a contraction effect, with respect to imports from country B. But, as already observed, the substitution and contraction effects are not dependent upon import prices alone; they are dependent upon the relation between import prices, on the one hand, and the stream of total expenditures and the prices of domestic goods and services, on the other. If the stream of total expenditure of country A rises in substantially smaller proportion than the weighted average percentage increase of import prices (the stream of total expenditure of country B remaining the same), then this would probably produce a reduction in the excess demand for foreign exchange.[13] If the stream of total expenditure rises, however, in substantially greater proportion than the rise in import prices, this would probably produce an increase in the excess demand for foreign exchange. Similarly, the substitution and expansion (or contraction) effects will depend upon the relation between changes in their prices and changes in the stream of total expenditures.

Consider the situation in which the stream of total expenditure of country A rises in substantially smaller proportion than the rise in the weighted average price of its imports and exports expressed in terms of A's currency. This would tend to produce a reduction in A's excess demand for the exchange of country B. Wherever the substitution of domestic goods for imports is immediately possible, without the necessity of extensive plant conversion, the reduction in imports would be virtually instantaneous—if not anticipated. The greater the difference between the unit cost of imports (in terms of A's currency) and the sum of the unit cost of domestic substitutes plus any outlay for conversion, the larger would be the rate of reduction in imports. Given a positive differential between the former and the latter, the reduction in the volume of imports would be greater the longer the period of adjustment available for disinvestment and reinvestment. The effect of the devaluation, under these conditions, is, therefore, to reduce the D's. The reduction in the D's would tend to lower their prices in terms of B's currency; but so long as their price in terms of A's currency rises in substantially greater proportion than the rise in the stream of total expenditure of country

[13] It is conceivable even under the assumptions of this case that the balance-of-payments position of country A could be worsened by the above changes in the exchange rate and the flow of expenditures—for example, if the expenditure effect is greater than the price effect (i.e., if the increase in the total demand for foreign exchange for the purpose of purchasing imports brought about by the increase in the flow of domestic expenditure is greater than the decrease in total demand for foreign exchange for the purpose of purchasing imports brought about by the increase in the prices of imports expressed in terms of domestic currency relatively to the prices of domestic goods). This may result from a condition in which a given percentage rise in the flow of expenditure is much more effective in increasing the volume of imports than is an equal percentage rise in the relative prices of imports in reducing the volume of imports. An equivalent qualification is applicable to the sentence that follows in the text.

A, the volume and value of A's imports would tend to decline.[14]

In regard to exports, the rise in A's stream of total expenditure would tend to check somewhat the expansion of its exports to country B. First, as a result of the devaluation, A's freely competitive internationally traded exports would tend to rise in price approximately to the extent of the devaluation (i.e., not to change price in terms of B's currency). Hence, these exports could not be exported in greater volume to country B (B's stream of total expenditure remaining the same), unless at the expense of producers in country B or in third countries. Because of their increased supply, the resulting tendency for these exports of country A to drop in price would be checked by the increased effective demand for them, and by the rising costs, associated with the expansion in A's stream of total expenditure. Second, commodities previously sold only in country A, and new items for export, might be exported in greater volume at the lowered exchange rate; but, again, the increase in country A's stream of total expenditure would increase the domestic demand for them, and would thereby raise their costs and reduce their competitive advantage in country B. Conceivably, the increased consumption of country A might reduce the availability of some export goods. But the smaller the rise in A's stream of total expenditure relative to the rise in its export prices, and the larger the amount of its underutilized resources, the greater would be the increase in the volume of its exports.[15]

We would expect, therefore, on *a priori* grounds that if, after devaluation, the stream of total expenditure in country A rises in substantially smaller proportion than the rise in the weighted average price of its imports and exports, the volume and value of its imports would fall, and exports rise. A situation might arise, however, where

[14] It is assumed here that production and the stream of total expenditure in country B are maintained by a reallocation of resources and expenditures away from exports and import substitutes and toward production for domestic consumption, an assumption which will presently be qualified.

[15] In order to forestall a perceivable dilemma, A's export prices (in terms of B's currency) would have to fall sufficiently so that its foreign receipts would be increased, but rise (in terms of A's currency) in substantially greater proportion than the rise in the stream of its total expenditure so that its domestic purchases of export goods would not be increased. There would, of course, be some leeway depending upon the degree of underutilization of its resources.

the value of its exports (in terms of foreign exchange) would decline —despite the probable increase in volume—for in numerous instances export prices (in terms of foreign exchange) might fall in greater proportion than the rise in sales.

Let us now consider the developments that would arise if, following devaluation, the stream of total expenditure in country A rises in substantially larger proportion than the rise in the weighted average price of its imports and exports.

Under the assumption of full employment, this case would involve a greater rise in domestic prices than of import prices in terms of A's currency. Hence there would be both an expansion effect and a substitution effect tending toward an increase in the volume and value of imports into country A. Country A's increased demand for B's exports may induce a rise in the prices of some of B's exports in terms of B's currency.[16] The relation

$$X \equiv P_1 D_1 + P_2 D_2 + \ldots + P_n D_n$$

would consequently indicate a rise in A's excess demand for some or all of the goods and services of country B (the D's become algebraically larger) and a rise in some of the P's associated with them. Country A's excess demand for foreign exchange (X) would therefore rise, and an increased volume of imports would be financed by reserves (if available).

The rise in A's domestic prices (induced by the expansion in its stream of total domestic expenditure) relative to the rise in its export

---

[16] Given the "elasticity of substitution" of imports for domestic commodities, the higher the price rise of A's domestic commodities as compared with imports, the larger would be the expansion in the volume of A's imports. The "elasticity of substitution" represents, of course, the technological facility of substituting one factor (input) for another. Precisely, the "elasticity of substitution"

$$\sigma = \frac{\dfrac{a}{b} d\left(\dfrac{b}{a}\right)}{\dfrac{1}{r} dr},$$

where (a, b) is the combination of factors considered along a constant product curve and r the marginal rate of substitution of the factor B for the factor A in the production of commodity X. For a simple proof of this proposition cf. R. G. D. Allen, *Mathematical Analysis for Economists*, 1942, pp. 340-342.

prices would, in turn, tend to produce a contraction in the volume and value of its exports. Given the "elasticity of substitution," the larger the difference between the increase in unit cost of A's domestic commodities and the increase in unit cost of A's freely competitive internationally traded exports plus any outlays for plant conversion, the larger would be the increase in domestic consumption of these exportable commodities. Moreover, the smaller the amount of A's idle resources, the more likely would be the occurrence of these aggravating relative price changes, and hence the greater the probability of a reduction in the volume of A's exports. And so far as concerns their value, it appears highly improbable that a reduction in volume would be offset by a more than proportional rise in their foreign price. The relation

$$X \equiv P_1 D_1 + P_2 D_2 + \ldots + P_n D_n$$

would consequently indicate an algebraic rise in the value of some negative D's and a rise in some of the P's associated with them, the prices of other exports remaining unchanged, or declining somewhat. Hence country A's foreign receipts from freely competitive internationally traded exports would probably decline.

As these exports of country A become more expensive (in terms of B's currency), creditors in country B would increase their demand for some of its domestic commodities which have as yet not risen in price to the extent of the devaluation. This, in turn, would tend to raise their price. The increased foreign demand for them, superimposed upon the increased domestic demand (stemming from the rise in the stream of total expenditure relative to the devaluation), would so tend to raise the price of these domestic commodities that they too would be unable to compete effectively in country B, even at the depreciated exchange rate.

In short, the expansion in the volume and value of country A's imports, and the probable reduction in its exports, would thus tend to reduce A's holdings of foreign exchange. Devaluation of country A's currency, accompanied by a relatively larger expansion in its stream of total domestic expenditure, the stream of domestic expenditure of country B remaining the same, would therefore bring about a further deterioration in the balance of payments of country A. Equilibrium in A's balance of payments could only be restored after its stream of total domestic expenditure relative to that of country B is stabilized at a level compatible with the price relations required for equilibrium.[17]

Similarly, we may apply this analysis to the situation where the stream of total domestic expenditure of country B falls relatively to that of country A following devaluation.

It is apparent from our previous discussion that if the stream of total domestic expenditure in country B contracts in substantially smaller proportion than the devaluation, while the stream of total domestic expenditure in country A remains the same, the volume and value of country A's imports would decline in terms of B's currency. Country A's freely competitive internationally traded exports, however, might so decline in price (in terms of B's currency) as a result of both their increased supply and decreased demand for them that the foreign value of A's exports might fall despite increased volume of sales. If A's freely competitive internationally traded exports decline in price proportionally less (in terms of B's currency) than the decline in B's stream of total domestic expenditure, even the volume of these exports would normally tend to decline at the prevailing prices.[18] The greater the extent to which a country is the principal supplier of certain export commodities, the greater will be the drop in the foreign prices of its exports as the physical volume of these exports increases, or the less will be the rise in the domestic

[17] Since the discussion above is based on the assumption of a simultaneous, autonomous change in exchange rates and income flows, *mutatis mutandis*, country A's balance of payments would deteriorate even to a greater extent were it not to devalue. If we assume, however, that a causal relationship exists between changes in exchange rates and income flows (e.g., that over certain ranges and in certain circumstances changes in exchange rates tend to *bring about* the kind of disequilibrium situations which are discussed in case 3), then clearly it would not necessarily follow that country A's balance would deteriorate even to a greater extent were it not to devalue. Our analysis points out the market conditions under which devaluation would tend to be effective, or ineffective, in dealing with balance of payments crises. Decisions on alternative mechanism-of-adjustment policies would depend, of course, on much broader issues than the presence of autonomous or causal conditions.

[18] Exception to this statement would arise if the commodities sold by country A are little affected by the fall in B's domestic expenditure (and prices), but are greatly affected by the drop in the prices of those commodities themselves.

prices of these exports in terms of its own currency with a given devaluation. As a result, the smaller will be the improvement in the cost-price relationship which provides the incentive to increase the volume of exports. Devaluation under such conditions is likely to reduce the aggregate value of imports and hence the aggregate demand for foreign exchange; but, due to the multiplicity of conflicting influences on the export side, it is very difficult to conclude that devaluation will typically increase the aggregate value of exports and hence the total supply of foreign exchange. There is, in fact, a strong likelihood that the receipts of foreign exchange from exports will decline. The reduction in receipts from exports might, in effect, so exceed the diminution in foreign expenditures for imports that the balance of payments of country A would deteriorate.

If the stream of total domestic expenditure in country B contracts in larger proportion than the devaluation of A's currency, with the result that B's prices of domestic commodities fall by a greater percentage than the fall in both its import prices and export prices, the stream of total domestic expenditure in country A remaining the same, then the volume of A's imports would tend to rise and it is likely that their aggregate value will fall, while the volume and value of its exports would decline. For, regarding imports, the tendency of A's import prices to rise (in terms of its own currency) because of the devaluation would be more than offset by their tendency to fall because of the more than proportional contraction in B's stream of total domestic expenditure. Consequently, country A's domestic prices would now be higher than its import prices, and this would produce price substitution and expansion effects in regard to imports. The change in value of A's imports would depend upon whether physical quantities increase in the same, larger, or smaller proportion than the respective price declines in terms of B's currency. It appears unlikely that, in the short run, the physical quantities generally will increase in larger proportion than the price declines, particularly if country A's imports are used in large volume for the production of *export commodities*; for the *volume* of A's exports would definitely decline. The fall in country B's stream of total domestic expenditure relative to the fall in its import prices (in terms of B's currency) would produce a negative price-substitution effect, and a contraction effect, in regard to its imports from country A. Hence country A would experience a reduction in the volume and value of its exports.

In all of the above cases it is clear that imports and exports are mutually interdependent. It is the relative changes in the stream of total domestic expenditures, and their relation to relative price structures and relative physical volume of transactions requiring mediation through money, that link them one to another. Thus, for example, as illustrated in case 3, the relative expansion in country A's stream of total domestic expenditure and the consequent probable reduction in the value of its exports would bring about a reduction in the value of its imports during the following period. The expansion in A's imports, by reducing A's holdings of foreign exchange, would also bring about a contraction in its imports during the following period. Moreover, exporters in country B aware of the pressure on A's currency would fear exchange restrictions and/or further devaluation and would therefore tend to restrict their exports to country A except insofar as they could find a convenient method of avoiding risk. Consequently, during the following period country A's imports and exports would tend to decline. And while for practical purposes the "elasticity of substitution" of domestic goods for imports is technologically always a relative matter, there may be no economically feasible domestically produced substitutes for the goods (factors) previously imported within the relevant range of output. As a result, declines in production in the industries affected would occur, with resulting unemployment or other uneconomic diversion of resources and a retardation in the rate of economic growth.[19] The effect would, in turn, have an effect upon relative prices, imports, exports, and the stream of total domestic expenditures—all being mutually interdependent.

The mutual interdependence of these forces may be further illustrated with our symbolic formulations:

[19] So far as economics is concerned, the problem of misallocation of resources is different from the problem of unemployment only in degree. For unemployed resources denote the limiting case of misallocation; namely, not only is the ratio of the marginal physical productivities of the respective factors unequal among different firms and industries but also the marginal physical productivity of the unemployed factor is zero.

$$Y_A = M_B V_B = \sum_{i=1}^{g} P_A Q_A$$

$$Y_B = M_A V_A = \sum_{i=1}^{h} P_B Q_B .$$

A contraction in country B's stream of total domestic expenditure (in larger proportion than the devaluation of A's currency) would, in all probability, reduce the amount of its final means of payment (M_B) and the velocity of its final means of payment (V_B).[20] The reduction in $M_B V_B$ would reduce country B's effective demand for A's exports (i.e., the summation of the products of country A's export prices and the quantities associated with them $\left[\sum_{i=1}^{g} P_A Q_A \right]$), thereby lowering country A's foreign receipts from exports (Y_A). In addition, the contraction in country B's stream of total domestic expenditure would have the effect of lowering its export prices and of increasing the quantity of its exports offered for sale at prevailing prices. The larger the decline in the stream of total domestic expenditure of country B relative to the fall in the prices of its imports, in effect, the larger would be country B's reduction in the volume and value of its imports. And the larger the decline in the stream of total domestic expenditure of country B relative to the fall in the prices of its exports, the smaller would be the amount of exportable commodities consumed domestically, and the larger the amount currently offered for sale at prevailing prices. It appears improbable, on *a priori* grounds, that the increased quantities sold to country A would be more than offset, in the short run, by the lowered export prices; and this for two reasons. First, the diminution in country A's holdings of foreign exchange induces direct efforts to restrict imports. Second, in the short run, lower prices for B's exports cannot be expected to have

[20] Since country B here represents the United States, whose currency is generally acceptable, the above relationship is self-evident. If the contraction in the stream of total domestic expenditure occurred in country A (England), however, then the amount of its immediate final means of foreign payments (United States dollars, M_A) would remain virtually unchanged, but the velocity of its final means of foreign payment (V_A) would, in all probability, decline.

a very marked effect upon the expansion of exports to A. Given the stable stream of total domestic expenditure in country A, we would therefore expect its outpayments for imports to decline less rapidly than its receipts from exports. The decline in Y_A would, in other words, tend to be larger than the immediate decline in $M_A V_A$ (assuming country A has some available reserves, or sources from which to replenish such reserves), and hence larger than the decline in Y_B. While country A's expenditures on imports would therefore tend to decline, its receipts from exports would decline still more, further deteriorating its balance-of-payments position.

Therefore, devaluation of country A's currency, accompanied by the stream of total domestic expenditure in country B falling in larger proportion than the fall in its import and export prices, the stream of total domestic expenditure in country A remaining the same, *mutatis mutandis*, would probably further deteriorate A's balance of payments. Moreover, the reduction in Y_A and Y_B would produce a contraction in country A's imports and exports during the following period.[21] As a result of this contraction of A's imports and exports the volume of its production and employment would decline. Substantial changes in relative price structures, and in the relative physical volume of transactions requiring mediation through money, would generally follow. The stream of total domestic expenditure in the respective countries would be altered. Equilibrium in country A's balance of payments could only be restored after the stream of total domestic expenditure in country B, relative to the stream of total domestic expenditure of country A, is stabilized at a level that would be compatible with the price relations required for equilibrium.

A GENERALIZATION OF EQUILIBRIUM AND DISEQUILIBRIUM PRICE RELATIONS

On the basis of its original assumptions, traditional analysis was correct in maintaining that, in all probability, the devaluation of a

[21] For practical purposes, the process is a mixture of more or less continuous adaptation by banking and foreign-exchange institutions and their periodic discontinuous adjustments based on past experience. For analytical purposes, however, the above formulation appears to lend itself well to a form of Robertsonian period analysis, or neo-Wicksellian sequence analysis.

country's currency (or disinflation under stable exchanges) would improve its balance of payments. These assumptions, however, were strictly limited. The conclusions which followed from them were a particular case of a more general case; namely, conclusions based upon the implicit assumption that, in terms of the currency of the country which devalued (or disinflated), international prices (import and export) would rise relatively to all domestic (noninternational) prices. This implicit assumption followed from the explicit assumptions that the quantity of money and velocity (the stream of total domestic expenditures) remained the same in the two countries. Taussig's analysis was therefore substantially correct. When similar conclusions are applied to more general conditions, the reasoning and the conclusions appear erroneous. For the relation between import, export, and domestic prices is, *inter alia*, a determinate of changes in the relative stream of total expenditures in the two countries—as well as of the devaluation. With a given degree of devaluation (or disinflation), it is the relative change as between the two countries in the stream of total expenditures, and the resulting relative change in their stream of final foreign expenditures, which play a direct role in the international mechanism of adjustment. Aside from the traditional case in which international prices rise relatively to domestic prices (i.e., the stream of total domestic expenditure remains the same in the two countries), we may distinguish three other possibilities the joint probability of which is at least equal to that of the traditional case.

First is the case in which international prices rise relatively to domestic prices to a greater extent than in the traditional case (i.e., the stream of total domestic expenditure in the country which has not devalued rises relatively to that of the country which has devalued, or the stream of the total domestic expenditure in the country which has devalued falls relatively to that of the country which has not devalued). Second is the case in which international prices rise in the same proportion as domestic prices (i.e., the stream of total domestic expenditure in the country which has devalued rises in the same proportion as the rise in its import and export prices). Third is the case in which international prices rise in smaller proportion than the rise in domestic prices (i.e., the stream of total domestic expenditure in the country which has devalued rises in greater proportion than the rise in its import and export prices), or in which international prices fall in greater proportion than the fall in domestic prices (i.e., the stream of total domestic expenditure in the country which has not devalued falls in greater proportion than the fall in the export and import prices of the country which has devalued).

In the first case, the balance of payments of the country which has devalued would improve more markedly as compared with the traditional case. In the second, the balance of payments would remain unchanged.[22] In the third, the balance of payments of the country which has devalued would deteriorate still further.

The purpose of balance-of-payments theory of the more or less generalized kind presented in this chapter is to provide a framework within which particular questions can be usefully discussed. The approach is complementary to, rather than a substitute for, other approaches which have been developed.

[22] It is assumed here that if all prices change in the same proportion, there is no tendency for the pattern of expenditures to change as between different goods and services.

Part II

Applications to Economic Development

7

Adjustment Between Industrial and Primary-Producing Countries

MONETARY and fiscal phenomena as well as direct government activities which influence the circular flow of income are essential elements of a satisfactory theory of the international mechanism of adjustment. It was shown in the previous chapter that the explicit recognition of monetary and fiscal factors strengthens the income approach and helps to determine the balancing or imbalancing tendencies of a given disturbance upon the balance of payments. However, in the nineteenth and twentieth centuries, factors other than strictly financial forces have played an important role in assisting or impeding international adjustment. The difference between the long periods of expansion and contraction that occurred in the nineteenth century and the ease or strain in external accounts that they occasioned was probably due less to the behavior of the monetary mechanism than to the circumstances with which the mechanism had to deal.[1] The purpose of this chapter, and subsequent chapters, is to consider some of these "real" circumstances—

[1] Economists appear to be in general agreement on this issue. "I find it hard to believe," writes Professor Hicks, "that the monetary explanation can often have been the whole explanation. . . . A more general, and more convincing, ap-

particularly those related to economic development—and to analyze their probable effects upon the international mechanism in the contemporary world.

THE DEVELOPMENT OF AGRICULTURAL AND INDUSTRIAL PRODUCTION

Certain relations between agricultural and industrial inputs, outputs, and relative prices have a direct bearing upon the operation of the international mechanism of adjustment. We shall first briefly examine these relations and then apply them to short- and long-term problems of international balance and imbalance.[2]

From year to year agricultural output in the aggregate is remarkably stable, whereas industrial output is erratic. In the United States, for example, a single farm firm produces so small an amount of the total output of any agricultural product that it is impossible for it to exert an appreciable effect on price by restricting output. Hence, in attempting to maintain relatively stable incomes, American farmers stay in practically full production as prices decline. That is, the supply function for agricultural products is highly inelastic. Production inputs in American agriculture in the aggregate are even more stable from year to year than agricultural output. The supply prices of most inputs used in agricultural production are sufficiently flexible downward to permit their continuous employment and the maintenance of output. The relative stability of agricultural output has thus been mutually dependent upon the comparatively atomistic structure of agricultural markets on the selling side (apart from government interference), on the one hand, and upon the relative

---

proach would be to assume that both sources of instability are, at least potentially, at work—that monetary instability, of the kind we have just considered, is superimposed upon the real instability." J. R. Hicks, *A Contribution to the Theory of the Trade Cycle*, 1950, p. 153. For a similar position, cf. Joan Robinson, *The Rate of Interest and Other Essays*, 1952, p. 77.

[2] The statistical data on which the presentation that follows is based has been assembled in Table 1. For background information the reader may wish to consult the following: Theodore W. Schultz, *The Economic Organization of Agriculture*, 1953, Chap. XI; *Agriculture in an Unstable Economy*, 1945; D. Gale Johnson, "The Nature of the Supply Function for Agricultural Products," *American Economic Review*, September, 1950, pp. 537-564; and J. K. Galbraith and J. D. Black, "The Maintenance of Agricultural Production during Depression: The Explanations Reviewed," *Journal of Political Economy*, June, 1938, pp. 305-325.

inelasticity of the supply functions of agricultural inputs, on the other hand. As a result, a reduced demand for farm products has a far greater impact upon price and farm incomes than upon volume of output. Conversely, an enlarged demand raises farm prices, but the output response is usually slow and small.

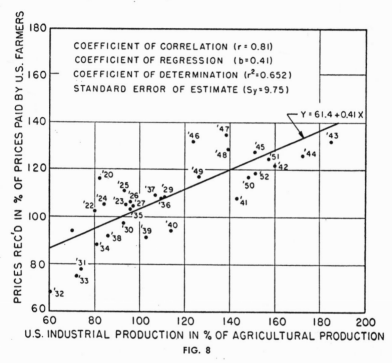

COEFFICIENT OF CORRELATION (r = 0.81)
COEFFICIENT OF REGRESSION   (b = 0.41)
COEFFICIENT OF DETERMINATION (r² = 0.652)
STANDARD ERROR OF ESTIMATE (Sy = 9.75)

$Y = 61.4 + 0.41 X$

FIG. 8

Fluctuations in demand for industrial products, however, drastically affect the rate of industrial output. This phenomenon, in turn, appears to be mutually dependent upon the relatively monopolistic and oligopolistic structure of the markets of industrial products on the selling side, and upon the comparatively elastic supply functions of many industrial inputs in the short run.

Rising levels of industrial output, however, expand the domestic demand for virtually all farm products while their production remains relatively unchanged. An increased output of industrial goods relative to the output of agricultural goods, therefore, raises farm prices relative to industrial prices. It can be seen from Fig. 8 that generally

TABLE 1. Indexes of U.S. Industrial and Agricultural Production, Prices Received and Paid by Farmers, Percent Industrial of Agricultural Production, Percent Prices Received of Prices Paid by Farmers (1935-1939 = 100)

Year	(Physical Volume) Industrial Production[a]				Agricultural Production[b] (Physical Volume)	Industrial Production in % of Agricultural Production	Prices Rec'd by Farmers[c]	Prices Paid by Farmers[d]	Prices Rec'd in % of Prices Paid by Farmers
	Manufactures			Minerals	Total				
	Total	Durable	Nondurable						
1920	75	93	60	83	92	82	198	171	116
1921	58	53	57	66	83	70	116	124	94
1922	73	81	67	71	91	80	122	120	102
1923	88	103	72	98	94	94	133	127	105
1924	82	95	69	89	98	84	134	128	105
1925	90	107	76	92	97	93	146	131	111
1926	96	114	79	100	100	96	136	128	106
1927	95	107	83	100	98	97	132	127	104
1928	99	117	85	99	102	97	139	129	108
1929	110	132	93	107	99	111	138	128	108
1930	91	98	84	93	98	93	117	121	97
1931	75	67	79	80	102	74	81	104	78
1932	58	41	70	67	96	60	61	90	68
1933	69	54	79	76	96	72	65	87	75
1934	75	65	81	80	93	81	84	96	88
1935	87	83	90	86	91	96	102	99	103
1936	103	108	100	99	94	110	107	99	108
1937	113	122	106	112	106	107	114	105	109
1938	89	78	95	97	103	86	91	99	92
1939	109	109	109	106	106	103	89	98	91

Year									
1940	125	139	115	117	110	114	93	99	94
1941	162	201	142	125	113	143	115	106	108
1942	199	279	158	129	124	160	148	121	122
1943	239	360	176	132	129	185	179	136	132
1944	235	353	171	140	137	172	183	145	126
1945	203	274	166	137	134	151	193	151	128
1946	170	192	165	134	136	124	219	166	132
1947	187	220	172	149	135	138	257	191	135
1948	192	225	177	155	137	139	266	207	129
1949	176	202	168	135	138	126	233	200	117
1950	200	237	187	148	135	148	239	204	117
1951	220	272	194	164	140	157	280	225	129
1952	219	280	189	160	145	151	267	230	116
1953	237	319	196	163	146	162	239	224	107
1954	219	282	192	156	146	150	231	225	102
1955	245	319	209	171	152	161	219	225	97
1956	252	334	212	182	153	165	218	228	96
1957	252	336	214	180	152	166	224	236	95

a Data for 1920-1952 from *Federal Reserve Bulletin*, June, 1953, p. 643. Data for 1953-1957 converted to 1935-1939 base; cf. *ibid.*, June, 1958, p. 694.

b Data for 1920-1952 from *Farm Income Situation*, Bureau of Agricultural Economics, U.S. Department of Agriculture, December, 1944, p. 1; December, 1946, p. 12; December, 1952—January, 1953, p. 16. Data for 1953-1957 converted to 1935-1939 base; cf. *Agricultural Outlook Charts*, Bureau of Agricultural Economics, U.S. Department of Agriculture, November, 1956, p. 93; November, 1957, p. 71.

c Data for 1920-1952 from *Agricultural Outlook Charts*, October, 1952, p. 6. Figure for 1952 has been checked with data presented in *Agricultural Prices*, Bureau of Agricultural Economics, U.S. Department of Agriculture, October, 1956, p. 45; Data for 1953-1957 converted to 1935-1939 base; cf. *ibid.*, and *Statistical Abstract of United States*, 1958, U. S. Bureau of Census, Department of Commerce, p. 631.

d Includes taxes, interest, and wages; cf. *Agricultural Prices*, Bureau of Agricultural Economics, U.S. Department of Agriculture, January, 1950, p. 43; October, 1956, p. 45; and *Statistical Abstract of United States*, 1958, U.S. Bureau of Census, Department of Commerce, p. 631. Data converted to 1935-1939 base.

for the period 1920-1952 the ratio of prices received as a percent of prices paid by farmers varies directly with the ratio of industrial output as a percent of agricultural output.

The low elasticity of demand and supply for farm products and the *violent* shifts in demand and supply schedules greatly increase the year-to-year instability of farm prices and farm incomes.[3] For all

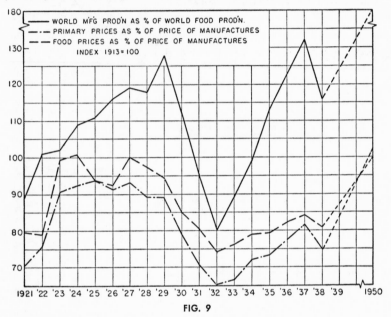

FIG. 9

these reasons the real income of farmers normally tends to rise when industrial output increases relatively to agricultural output, and to fall when industrial output decreases relatively to agricultural output.

The aforementioned relationships between the industrial and agri-

[3] It can be easily shown that, given low price elasticities, shifts in demand need not even be very large to create large changes in prices. Designate the demand schedule by $X = P^{-a}Y^{\beta}$, the supply schedule by $X = P^{\gamma}$. Then $P^{\gamma} = P^{-a}Y^{\beta}$ or $P^{\gamma+a} = Y^{\beta}$ Thus $P = Y^{\frac{\beta}{\gamma+a}}$ and $\dfrac{d \log P}{d \log Y} = \dfrac{\beta}{\gamma+a} =$ elasticity of price with respect to changes in income. If $\gamma = 0$ or almost so, and $\beta > a$, then elasticity of price with respect to income will exceed unity; i.e. the decline in price would be greater than the decline in income. I have benefited from discussion with D. Gale Johnson on this point. Cf. his "Stabilization of International Commodity Prices," in *Policies to Combat Depression*, 1956, pp. 358-360.

cultural segments of the American economy may throw light on the mechanism of adjustment between predominantly industrial and agricultural countries, for they apply to the structure of world industrial and agricultural production, and to world prices of agricultural and industrial products.

World agricultural production is also remarkably stable in the aggregate, whereas world industrial production is erratic. Further, as can be seen from Fig. 9, roughly the ratio of world food (and/or primary product) prices as a percent of world manufacturing prices

TABLE 2. Indexes of World Manufacturing and Food Production, Prices of Primary Products and Manufactures, Percent Manufacturing of Food Production, Percent Prices of Primary Products of Manufactures, 1921-1950

	1	2	3	4	5	6
	World Mfg. Production (1913=100) (Excluding U.S.S.R.)[a]	World Food Production (1913=100) (Excluding U.S.S.R.)[a]	World Mfg. Production as Percent of World Food Production (1913=100)	Prices (in Gold) of Primary Products (1913=100)[a]	Prices (in Gold) of Manufactures (1913=100)[a]	Prices of Primary Products as Percent of Prices of Mfrs. (1913=100)
1921	85.5	96	89	131.2	186	70.5
1922	104.8	104	101	122.2	161	75.9
1923	109.9	108	102	142.2	157	90.6
1924	116.3	107	109	141.4	153	92.4
1925	125.4	113	111	149.0	159	93.7
1926	129.9	112	116	142.2	156	91.2
1927	138.9	117	119	135.8	146	93.0
1928	144.4	122	118	132.0	148	89.2
1929	154.8	121	128	126.2	142	88.9
1930	135.5	121	112	104.6	133	78.6
1931	116.7	123	95	78.2	111	70.5
1932	100.0	125	80	58.6	90	65.1
1933	112.9	127	89	53.2	80	66.5
1934	125.3	126	99	51.2	71	72.1
1935	138.8	124	113	49.8	68	73.2
1936	157.4	128	123	52.4	68	77.1
1937	172.6	131	132	58.6	72	81.4
1938	154.5	133	116	53.8	72	74.7
1950	250.3	139	180	124.4	122	102.0

[a] W. A. Lewis, "World Production Prices and Trade 1870-1960," *Manchester School of Economic and Social Studies*, May, 1952, pp. 106-107, 117-118. Columns 3 and 6 were computed by the author for this study.

varies directly with the ratio of world manufacturing production as a percent of world food (and/or primary) production.

Hence the available information suggests that the relationships previously noted in the structure of American industrial and agricultural production, and in their relative prices, hold generally for the relationships in the structure of world industrial and agricultural production, and in their relative prices. And, as the United States has been the world's major industrial producer since World War I, one should expect changes in the ratio of world prices received to world prices paid by predominantly agricultural (and/or primary) producing countries to vary not only directly with changes in the ratio of *world* industrial to world agricultural production, but also with changes in the ratio of *American* industrial to agricultural production. This interdependence of the world situation with that of the United States is of comparatively recent origin and is particularly striking during periods of rapid business expansion or contraction. The impact of American industrial expansion or contraction on domestic and world primary-product prices is usually sharp and practically instantaneous. A rise in the level of United States industrial production relative to the level of its primary production, and/or relative to the level of world primary production, usually results in a rise of world primary prices *relative to United States industrial prices, and conversely.*[4]

[4] These relationships may be readily observed from the data contained in Tables 1 and 2, on pages 158-159 and 161, respectively. Cf. also *Relative Prices of Exports and Imports of Under-developed Countries*, 1949, pp. 28-33. For example, between November, 1948, and October, 1949, United States industrial production fell about 17 percent, while its agricultural production remained virtually unchanged. Declines in industrial production were also registered in several countries abroad, but the major impact upon relative world prices doubtless stemmed from the United States recession. Despite the American agricultural support program, the index of prices received by American farmers during this period fell about 12 percent, and world prices of wheat, corn, cotton, cocoa, cottonseed, lead, zinc, rubber, and copper fell precipitously. The prices of manufactured goods exported from the United States, on the other hand, scarcely changed. The experiences associated with the Korean War furnish even more spectacular illustrations. On a base of 1948=100, the terms of trade of Latin America improved from an index of 99.6 in 1949 to one of 115.8 in 1950, and declined to approximately 103.2 in 1952. Economic Commission for Latin America, *Economic Survey for Latin America, 1951-52*, 1953, p. 169. Cf. also United Nations, Commission on International Commodity Trade, *Commodity Survey, 1957*, 1958. The data in Table 1 shows that from 1953-1957 the ratio of prices

INDUSTRIAL PRODUCTION, PRIMARY PRODUCTION, AND THE INTERNATIONAL MECHANISM

Let us now examine how the development of industrial and primary structures of production, violent shifts in demand, and resulting relative price changes affect the trade relations between countries which are exporters primarily of manufactures and capital equipment, and those which are exporters primarily of primary products. To be sure, forms of disequilibria come up in such varying shapes in different countries at different times that it would be impossible and of no particular purpose to pursue all the variations of the analysis. What follows is a broad statement of the basic principles within the framework which we have developed.

Assume country A to be an exporter chiefly of primary products and country B primarily of manufactures. Assume further that country A and country B trade only in goods and services, and that their exports and imports are initially in equilibrium. Country A undergoes an inflation relative to country B. As a result, country A experiences an excess demand for the foreign exchange of country B at the prevailing (fixed) rate of exchange. We shall assume that the loss of international reserves leads country A to depreciate its currency (or to disinflate under stable exchange rates) approximately to the extent of the relative rise in its prices with respect to currency B. The problem is to determine how the probable effects on the balance-of-payments position of a country exporting primarily agricultural products would differ from those of a country with more balanced exports under the assumption that, after country A has devalued its currency, its stream of total domestic expenditure rises (or falls) in greater, the same, or smaller proportion relative to the stream of total domestic expenditure of industrial country B.[5] We shall

---

received as a percentage of prices paid by farmers gradually fell; and this was a consequence of the necessary adjustment to the war and postwar expansion of agricultural output.

[5] In the analysis under discussion we do not necessarily assume a causal relationship between devaluation on the part of any given country and a change in size of the income flow in that or any other country. It is useful to assume here a simultaneous, autonomous (i.e., coincidental) change in exchange rates and income flows.

first present the conditions which lead to international balance, and then those which lead to international imbalance.

1. The balance of payments of the primary-producing country not only would improve more than it would under the traditional case of devaluation, but, in addition, would improve to a greater extent than an equivalent devaluation would improve the balance of payments of a country whose exports were not principally primary products, if the stream of total domestic expenditure of the comparatively industrial country B rises relatively to the stream of total domestic expenditure of the primary-producing country A. First, the rise in the stream of total domestic expenditure of industrial country B, relative to that of the primary country A, would bring about a greater equilibrating rise in the international prices of country A (i.e., its export and import prices) relative to the prices of the domestically produced and consumed products of country A, as compared with the traditional case of devaluation, when the stream of total domestic expenditure is assumed to remain the same in the two countries. Second, the rise in the stream of total domestic expenditure of the industrial country B relative to that of the primary country A would, because of the short-term supply and demand conditions of industrial as compared to agricultural production, lead to a rise in agricultural as compared to industrial prices. This would mean, in effect, an assured improvement in terms of trade for country A, and an additional factor which would tend to improve its balance of payments to a greater extent than a comparable devaluation would tend to improve the balance of payments of a more industrialized country.

As can be seen from Fig. 10, the devaluations of primary-producing countries in September, 1949, which were followed by a relative rise in income in the United States, improved their balance of payments to a greater extent than the devaluations of more industrialized countries.[6]

[6] A conceivable qualification to the above argument would be the case in which the primary-goods-producing country is a large importer of materials manufactured chiefly from primary products (e.g., textiles) or a large importer of *particular* manufactures whose prices rise with an expansion in income relative to the general price index of manufactures and also to that of primary products. In this instance the terms of trade will not move in favor of the primary-goods-producing country and its balance of payments might conceivably deteriorate.

2. The balance of payments of the agricultural or primary-producing country would, at best, tend to remain unchanged if, after its devaluation, income in country B remaining the same, its domestic prices rise in the same proportion as its export and import prices. For there would be no relative price effects to expand the volume of exports or to reduce the volume of imports. Moreover, the more predominant is primary production in a country, the less likely it is to suffer from overt mass unemployment. A rise in its stream of total domestic expenditure is therefore more likely to produce inflationary pressures (e.g., as a result of industrialization brought about by credit expansion). Hence, again, a difference may arise between the effects of an equivalent devaluation by either a primary-producing country or an underdeveloped country, as compared with a more developed one. Particularly in an underdeveloped country, the rise in the stream of total domestic expenditure is likely to increase quickly the level of domestic consumption, without having much effect on the level of production, and thereby to reduce the available amount of goods for export and deteriorating its balance of payments.[7] The balance of payments of the agricultural or primary-producing country would tend to deteriorate still further if, after its depreciation, (a) its *domestic* prices rise in greater proportion than the rise in its import and export prices, or (b) the domestic prices of country B (which has not depreciated) fall in greater proportion than the fall in the export and import prices of the agricultural country A. In either case domestic prices in country A rise *relative* to its import and export prices after its depreciation. In the first case, country A suffers from domestic inflationary pressures vis-à-vis country B, brought about by a rise in its domestic expenditure (with no change in domestic expenditure in country B), and therefore its domestic prices rise relatively to its international prices. In the second case, country A suffers from external deflationary pressures. The deflation in industrial country B vis-à-vis country A leads to a fall in country A's domestic prices in smaller proportion than the fall in its import and export prices. Under

[7] We should allow for the possibility that a primary-goods-producing country may have large inventories of its major crops which could for a time make the supply of these commodities highly elastic, thus postponing the full impact of the price and income effects.

Changes in the Direction of Trade Since the Devaluations, as Measured by the Ratio of Trade with the United States to Trade with the United Kingdom. Ratios of Values in the

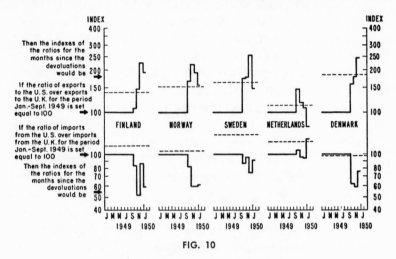

FIG. 10

The charts in Fig. 10 show for each of a number of the devaluing countries an index of its exports to the United States relative to its exports to the United Kingdom, and an index of its imports from the United States relative to its imports from the United Kingdom. For the United Kingdom chart, trade with the United States is compared with trade with the sterling area. The ratios were determined from the national currency values of exports and imports as reported by each devaluing country. The ratio of trade with the United States to trade with the United Kingdom was used as a basis of the charts on the assumption that changes in trade with the United States were representative of changes in trade with all nondevaluing countries and that changes in trade with the United Kingdom were representative of changes in trade with all the devaluing countries.

From September, 1949, to January, 1950, for most of the devaluing countries import prices rose about 10 percent, and for many of the countries export and domestic prices either remained stable or rose much less. The rise in import prices was less than the depreciation of the currencies of the countries concerned, very much less than their depreciation relative to the dollar, and less than their average depreciation relative to the countries from which they normally buy their imports. (See *International Financial Statistics*, January, 1950.) While export prices (mostly unit values) tended to be stable or to rise less than import prices, they rose more than import prices in such primary-producing countries as Australia and Norway. They rose about 20 percent in Australia and 30 percent in Norway. On the other hand, the export-price indexes of the United Kingdom, Belgium, and France at first fell a little and then remained stable. According to our analysis, given the relative rise in national income in the United States after the devaluation, a rise in the export-price indexes of these primary-producing countries relative to the export-price indexes of more industrialized countries was to be expected.

Many factors other than the devaluations, of course, affected these price series. It is noteworthy, however, that with the outbreak of war in Korea and the accelerated relative

National Currencies of Reporting Countries Expressed as Indexes on the Base January-September 1949=100. Broken Line Shows the Index for 1948. Logarithmic Scale.

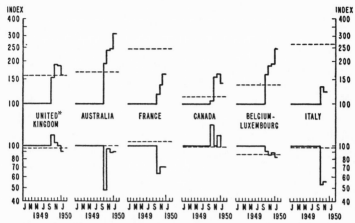

*FOR THE UNITED KINGDOM THE RATIOS MEASURE EXPORTS TO THE U. S. OVER EXPORTS TO THE OUTER STERLING AREA AND IMPORTS FROM THE U. S. OVER IMPORTS FROM THE OUTER STERLING AREA

FIG. 10 (Continued)

Source: International Monetary Fund, International Financial Statistics, April, 1950. For detailed information on the effects of the September, 1949, devaluations, cf. also ibid., January, 1950; Barend A. de Vries, "Immediate Effects of Devaluation on Prices of Raw Materials," Staff Papers, International Monetary Fund, September, 1950, pp. 238-253; J. J. Polak, "Contribution of the September 1949 Devaluations for the Solution of Europe's Dollar Problem," ibid., September, 1951, pp. 1-32; R. F. Harrod, The Dollar, 1954.

rise in national income in the United States, the export-price indexes of the primary-producing countries rose more markedly relative to the export-price indexes of the more industrialized countries. The comparative stability of the export-price indexes of the United Kingdom, Belgium, and France (in their national currencies) also is to be expected, for an important objective of the devaluations was to reduce the existing disequilibria in relative price structures.

These experiences are entirely consistent with the theoretical analysis presented in these studies.

such circumstances it is apparent that the balance of payments of the country which devalued would deteriorate still further.[8] There is another force which operates here to aggravate the difficulties. Because of the structure of industrial as compared with primary

[8] This discussion, of course, is not based on the traditional assumptions of mechanism-of-adjustment theory. It is an application of our more "general" theory which may be applied to short-term as well as long-term disequilibrium conditions. Here, in effect, it pertains to short-term disequilibrium conditions.

production, the deflation in industrial country B relative to the primary-goods-producing country A would lead to a deterioration in A's terms of trade. Consequently, the balance of payments of either a primary-goods-producing country or an underdeveloped country would, in these cases, tend to deteriorate not only to a greater extent than in the traditional case of depreciation (in which it was assumed that the flow of income in both, or all, countries considered was constant), but, in addition, to a greater extent than an equivalent depreciation would deteriorate the balance of payments of a country whose exports were not principally primary products.

FACTOR ALLOCATION AND INTERNATIONAL IMBALANCE

In traditional mechanism-of-adjustment analysis it is assumed that the depreciation of a country's currency (or monetary contraction under stable exchange rates) would bring about a rise in its export and import prices relative to domestic prices, and this, in turn, would tend to reduce the proportion of its resources devoted to the production of domestic goods and to increase the proportion used in the production of exports and of import substitutes. It is assumed, also, that the appreciation (or monetary expansion under stable exchange rates) of a country's currency would bring about a fall in its export and import prices relative to domestic prices, and this would tend to increase the proportion of its resources devoted to the production of domestic goods and to reduce the proportion used in the production of exports and of import substitutes. When factor markets operate in this way, the reallocation of resources plays an important role in assisting countries to attain international balance. But when they do not, strong limiting forces work against the attainment of international balance. In practice, the factor markets often do not operate in an equilibrating way; and this is particularly true in many primary-producing countries and in underdeveloped areas.

The annual wage income per hired farm worker in many countries has characteristically been *lower* than the annual wage income per industrial worker, after adjustments are made for changes in living costs.[9] Consequently, when a country which exports chiefly primary products depreciates its currency, and hence its export (primary goods) prices rise relatively to its domestic (e.g., some protected industrial) prices, and when the money income per person engaged in primary production rises relative to the money income per person engaged in industry, the absolute difference in earnings between them would still tend to discourage the migration of labor into primary production. Higher primary-goods prices and higher money incomes in primary production may, in effect, render it financially feasible for some people to move *out* of agriculture (whereas it may not have been financially feasible to do so heretofore) and thereby to *reduce* the proportion of labor resources devoted to agriculture.[10] Further, because of the overall steadiness of primary production, and because the output response of major primary-goods crops is slow and small, a relative rise in primary-goods prices (with the stream of total domestic expenditure after depreciation remaining the same) probably would not induce a larger proportion of *labor* resources into agricul-

[9] Cf. Theodore W. Schultz, *Production and Welfare of Agriculture*, 1949, pp. 64-82, and *Economic Organization of Agriculture*, p. 123. It is extremely difficult to obtain satisfactory comparisons between the level of "earnings" of persons engaged in agriculture and those engaged in industry. Cf. *Studies in Income and Wealth*, Vol. 15, 1950, Conference on Research in Income and Wealth, 1952. But for the period between World Wars I and II, there appears to be little doubt that, for most Western countries, the annual wage and real income of persons *employed* in agriculture was substantially lower than that of persons *employed* in industry. With respect to real income, this is strongly suggested by the fact that the proportion of the working population engaged in agriculture has been declining secularly, say, from about 1890 to 1948, in Great Britain, the United States, Germany, Canada, Switzerland, Australia, France, Sweden, and Italy. In the United States, ". . . by the end of World War II most of the differences in labor returns had disappeared, except for the southern states, most of Missouri, and an area immediately north of the Ohio River. Transfer of labor out of agriculture in the non-southern areas has continued, and the income differential sufficient to induce the movement is a relatively small one. However, in the south (and the other areas noted), the income differential that is associated with the current rate of outmovement is a very large one, of the order of $500 to $1,000 a year of labor." D. Gale Johnson, "Agricultural Price Policy and International Trade," *Essays in International Finance*, 1954, p. 21.

[10] Thus, the remarkable migration out of agriculture in the United States since 1940 took place as farm prices doubled and the income of agriculture per person virtually trebled. This rise in income per person engaged in agriculture was larger than the rise in income per person engaged in industry.

ture.[11] It would, however, become more feasible and more profitable to devote as large a proportion of labor resources as possible to produce previously imported products and/or import substitutes.

We may conclude that if country A is an exporter chiefly of primary products (with significant opportunities in secondary and tertiary industries) and an importer primarily of finished manufactures and capital equipment, devaluation of its currency (with the circular flow of income remaining the same in the two countries after devaluation) is *unlikely* to increase substantially the proportion of its labor resources devoted to primary production, i.e., to exports. Similarly, if after A's devaluation the circular flow of income in country B rises relatively to that of country A, it appears more likely that the increased output of primary products, i.e., exports (if any), by country A would occur through an increased proportion of *capital* (if available) devoted to primary production rather than an increased proportion of labor devoted to primary production. In any event, the greater the rise in import prices facing the country that has devalued, the more likely is an increased proportion of its resources—labor as well as capital—to migrate to industries producing products which were previously imported and/or goods which are import substitutes.

Conversely, if the currency of the primary-producing country appreciated, say, because foreign lenders were investing capital in the country, it should not be assumed *a priori* that a fall in the country's international prices (import and export) relative to its domestic prices would tend to reduce the proportion of its resources devoted to the production of primary (export) goods and of import substitutes, and to increase the proportion used in the production of domestic goods. To be sure, if such a reallocation of resources occurred, it would tend to reduce exports and to increase imports, thereby assisting the attain-

[11] The high instability of yields in farming suggests the hypothesis that production *inputs* in agriculture might be even more stable from year to year than agricultural *output* itself. Recent experience of the United States confirms this hypothesis. "Variations in total inputs from year to year in agriculture, measured in terms of the change from the preceding year, corrected for the slow upward drift that has taken place, *averaged about 1 per cent* per year from 1910 to 1950. Gross farm production fluctuated on the average four times as much, although it is also one of the more stable variables in our economy." Schultz, *Economic Organization of Agriculture*, p. 210.

ment of international balance through transfer of the loans in the form of goods. But an examination of the data for several countries demonstrates that when farm prices decline relatively to all other prices, the production inputs in agriculture in the aggregate—and particularly the inputs of farm labor—remain extraordinarily stable. This stability of agricultural inputs during periods of falling farm prices relative to other prices is no less striking in primary-producing countries (and in underdeveloped areas) than it is in the more industrial countries, such as the United States. In fact, the smaller the industrial segment of an economy, the less is the scope for factor adjustment (or maladjustment) with respect to the international mechanism. For the smaller the amount of commercial inputs (e.g., wage labor, motor vehicles, lime and fertilizer, etc.), the smaller would be the extent of input contraction.

In a rich industrial country, such as the United States, if farm prices relative to other prices become extremely adverse, farmers can and do contract their operations. Such contraction—however rare—occurs in the commercial class of inputs. In poorer countries (primary-goods-producing or underdeveloped) cost-reducing adjustments are far less possible. Relative declines in farm prices during periods of economic contraction characteristically *increase* the proportion of labor inputs devoted to agriculture. The relevant case (in our own analysis) would be the one in which, after devaluation, the weighted average price of the primary-goods country's exports (in terms of domestic currency) falls in greater proportion than the fall in its domestic prices. Such circumstances occurred in New Zealand during the successive depreciations of 1929-1933.[12] With mass unemployment in New Zealand industry (associated with the decline in domestic expenditures resulting from reduced agricultural exports), one would expect on *a*

[12] By January, 1931, the exchange rate had depreciated by about 10 percent; it was devalued in January, 1933, by another 20 percent. The fall in export prices came first and was caused by external depression. With respect to migration, from 1911 to 1926 the percentage of rural population in New Zealand declined steadily from 49.27 to 40.62, but remained virtually constant from 1926 to 1936. Cf. *New Zealand Official Year Books.* In the United States, during 1932, when farm prices were the lowest they had been in thirty years, there was *a net movement of people to farms,* temporarily reversing a preceding forty-year trend. Cf. *Farm Population Estimates, 1910-1942,* U.S. Department of Agriculture, Bureau of Agricultural Economics, November, 1942, p. 2.

priori grounds that the availability of some employment in primary production, at a level of *absolute* earnings higher than the relief obtainable by unemployed industrial workers, would at the least retard the migration of labor from agriculture and would thereby *prevent* a reduction in the proportion of labor devoted to agriculture. In analyzing the effects of the New Zealand depreciations upon the allocation of resources under such circumstances, G. H. Brown was understandably unable to find statistical verification of the generally accepted erroneous position. He writes:

> According to our theoretical analysis, the marked fall in the foreign demand for export commodities should have led to a *reduction* in the proportion of resources devoted to the production of these commodities. . . . In New Zealand the major exports being agricultural and pastoral products; and home-market products mainly services or manufactured articles, we should expect on theoretical grounds to see a *decrease* in the proportion of population engaged in farming and an increase in the proportion engaged in manufacturing.[13]

Under the aforementioned conditions, one would expect on theoretical grounds that the proportion of labor devoted to agriculture would *increase* rather than decrease, despite the marked fall in the foreign demand for primary exports and the relative decline of primary product and factor prices as compared with those of domestic industry. It is therefore not at all surprising that "this aspect of the theoretical model [was] not verified by [Brown's] findings."[14] In effect, between 1929 and 1933 there was a strong retardation to the exodus of the excess population from agriculture.[15]

Similarly, if a country which exports chiefly primary products

[13] Cf. G. H. Brown, "The International Economic Position of New Zealand," *Journal of Business of the University of Chicago*, April, 1946, pp. 137, 143.
[14] *Ibid.*, p. 143.
[15] For the most part, it was a matter of the small farmowner staying on his land and being relieved of mortgage interest. In addition, there was a large increase in productivity—primarily the result of previous mechanization and fertilization, but also of the acceptance of practices of grassland management, i.e., change in technology. For a detailed account of these developments, see the forthcoming book by J. B. Condliffe, *The Welfare State in New Zealand*, Chap. I. Cf. *New Zealand Official Year Books*, 1929-1933. Similarly, the percentage of workers engaged in American agriculture in 1929 amounted to 24; in 1932 and 1933 the percentage was 29. Calculated from U.S. Department of Agriculture,

devalues, and then its domestic income flow increases in substantially greater proportion than the rise in its export and import prices, the proportion of its labor resources devoted to *exports* would, in all probability, *decline*.[16] The inflationary pressures would probably have the effect of increasing the amount of resources devoted to agriculture; however, this is not likely to yield much more exports in the short run but rather a larger volume of goods for domestic consumption. The smaller the nonprimary segment of the economy, the less likely would be the shift out of primary production, despite the relative rise in domestic as compared with export prices. And the greater the marginal rate of substitution of exportable primary products for domestic goods on the part of domestic consumers, the less likely is the country to devote a larger proportion of its resources to exports. Under the postulated inflationary assumptions, it appears most unlikely that a primary-producing country would experience an equilibrating shift in the allocation of its resources which would help restore international balance. The reallocation of resources is likely to be perverse; and this would tend to produce either more violent fluctuations in the prices of the smaller volume of exports and imports which would be traded (if international balance were to be restored through the operation of the price mechanism) or the imposition of more direct trade controls with an abridgment of the pricing mechanism.

The conclusions above are not inconsistent with classical resource-allocation theory. In traditional mechanism-of-adjustment analysis, the discussion of the effects of relative variations in export, import, and domestic prices upon the allocation of resources relates to long-term competitive conditions under the hypothetical assumption of monetary equilibrium. Our discussion has dealt with imperfectly competitive conditions and unemployment under the assumptions of monetary disequilibrium and relative changes in aggregate money

---

Bureau of Agricultural Economics, *Farm Labor*, February, 1950, p. 9; U.S. Department of Labor, "Employment in agriculture as a percentage of total civilian employed," *Handbook of Labor Statistics*, 1950 ed., pp. 5, 35.

[16] This shows the importance of the income approach for the analysis of *factor allocation* and international balance and imbalance, an approach which has been terribly neglected. Research along these lines is long overdue.

income. The errors in mechanism theory with respect to resource allocation lie not in classical theory, but in the unguarded application of its conclusions to conditions to which it was not meant to apply. For it can easily be shown that it is possible to integrate, and to generalize, resource-allocation analysis under imperfectly competitive assumptions with that under competitive long-term equilibrium assumptions.

Let us consider the case of a country undergoing a sustained period of prosperity and whose product and factor prices are freely competitive. Under such conditions, real earnings for identical services rendered in different occupations would, in the long run, tend to approximate equality. Assume that these conditions are realized and that a sharp reduction then occurs in the demand for the country's primary-goods exports (e.g., because of an expansion in agricultural production abroad owing to postwar reconstruction). If exports and imports of the country which experienced the decline in agricultural exports are maintained in equilibrium by way of an equivalent shift in expenditures away from imports (e.g., away from imports of manufactured goods) to import-substitutes produced domestically, the decline in aggregate demand for primary products in this country would result in a fall in primary product and factor prices.[17] But with mobility of persons between agriculture and industry assumed in the

---

[17] It was shown in Chapter 6 that the customary assumptions with respect to such equilibration of exports and imports, and the attendant equilibration between domestic production and consumption are only warranted for long-run competitive conditions under (hypothetical) monetary equilibrium. Under short-run assumptions, or contemporary conditions, it would, of course, be erroneous to assume that such equilibration occurs. Certain disequilibrating relationships between the balance of payments and the level of economic activity were discussed in Chapter 6. Cf. also Svend Laursen and Lloyd A. Metzler, "Flexible Exchange Rates and the Theory of Employment," *Review of Economics and Statistics*, November, 1950, pp. 285 *et seq;* W. H. White, "The Employment-insulating Advantages of Flexible Exchanges: A Comment on Professors Laursen and Metzler," and the authors' "Reply," *loc. cit.*, May, 1954; A. C. Harberger, "Currency Depreciation, Income, and the Balance of Trade," *Journal of Political Economy*, February, 1950, esp. pp. 57-58; Harry G. Johnson, "The Transfer Problem and Exchange Stability," *loc. cit.*, June, 1956, pp. 212-225; "Increasing Productivity, Income Price Trends and the Trade Balance," *Economic Journal*, September, 1954, pp. 471-485; and the contributions by A. C. L. Day, J. Spraos, and I. F. Pearce in the May, 1954, and May, 1955, issues of *Economica*. For a general discussion of factor movements and trade, cf. J. E. Meade, *Trade and Welfare*, 1955, pp. 319-472.

traditional literature, the relative fall in real earnings in agriculture would tend to bring about a migration of labor (and other transferable inputs) from agriculture to industry, and thereby to remove significant differences in real returns in the two occupations. Similarly, a relative expansion in the demand for agricultural products would tend to raise agricultural prices and real earnings, leading to the migration of labor from industry to agriculture—and thereby to a new equilibrium in relative factor and product prices. It is the availability of a higher absolute level of real earnings in one occupation as compared with another which provides an incentive to migration, not variations in *relative* earnings. Since classical analysis assumed approximate equality in the level of earnings (i.e., a fair degree of equality in the total pecuniary and nonpecuniary advantage between competing occupations) before introducing a disturbance, a shift in the relative level of earnings is, in effect, equivalent to a shift in the level of absolute earnings. But as already observed, under conditions of unemployment and/or imperfectly competitive factor markets, such equality does not necessarily prevail. Properly expressed in terms of the absolute level of earnings, the classical position as to the effects of variations in relative product and factor prices upon the movement of resources remains intact; and, barring noneconomic impediments to movement, holds quite generally under imperfectly competitive and short-term conditions as well as under those postulated in competitive long-term equilibrium analysis.

The aforementioned conclusions are particularly relevant to reasonably long periods of full employment, for under such circumstances the prospects of steady employment in industry provide strong incentives to the migration of labor out of primary production. Discrepancies in the absolute level of earnings therefore tend to be reduced in areas which are accessible to industrial centers. Here conditions in the relevant factor markets begin to approximate those postulated in classical theory and play their appropriate role in the international mechanism of adjustment between primary-producing and industrial countries. The greater the degree of factor mobility, the greater will be the elasticity of supply for primary commodities and the smaller will be the shifts in the terms of trade necessary to make the mechanism of adjustment operate. Under these conditions the important question is that of the rates of change of outputs and demand for primary and industrial goods in response to changes in relative prices and incomes. The experience of the United States over the past 15 years and that of the non-Communist world since World War II suggests that under conditions of moderately flexible prices and incomes and internal mobility of resources, primary-goods-producing countries would not have serious mechanism-of-adjustment problems so long as they are able to control domestic inflations and so long as industrial countries are able to check domestic deflations.[18] When resources are fully utilized and industrial expansion is progressing at a more rapid rate than is the expansion of primary-goods production, there appears to be a long-run tendency for the terms of trade between industrial and primary goods to remain reasonably stable.[19] Under such conditions primary-producing countries may therefore expect to gain from increased output of their products.[20]

[18] In this respect, the domestic experience of the United States between 1942-1952 is suggestive. The index of prices received as a percent of prices paid by U.S. farmers remained quite stable during this period (cf. Table 1, pp. 158-159). To be sure, these were "brimful" employment years for American agriculture, with agricultural exports rising from $738 million, or 20 percent of total exports, in 1939 to $2.9 billion, or 34 percent of total exports, in 1945, and reaching a postwar peak of $4 billion in 1951. Cf. *United States Farm Products in Foreign Trade,* U.S. Department of Agriculture, Foreign Agricultural Service, Statistical Bulletin No. 112; and *Foreign Agricultural Trade of the United States,* U.S. Department of Agriculture, U.S. Agricultural Service, November, 1955, and March, 1956. While terms of trade were hence maintained at abnormally high levels in favor of agriculture, the period does illustrate the tendency of the terms of trade to remain reasonably stable when conditions in the relevant factor markets begin to approximate those postulated in classical theory. Given the necessary adjustment in United States agricultural production and prices, the need of which began to be strongly felt after 1952, and should the conditions postulated in the text prevail, we would expect the terms of trade to stabilize at a somewhat lower level and fluctuate thereafter within a moderate range.

[19] For the world as a whole, the real price of raw materials was about the same in 1872 and 1913. During this period, industrial production increased at a cumulative rate of somewhat less than 4 percent per year and food production at a cumulative rate of somewhat less than 2 percent per year. The assumption underlying our reasoning is that future industrial and primary production of the non-Communist world will not be significantly dissimilar from these magnitudes. It is probably unnecessary to point out that fluctuations in the price of food and raw materials may differ.

[20] The more balanced and the more diversified the economic development of primary-goods-producing countries, the larger will be the domestic consumption

The long-term outlook for primary-producing countries, as they are affected by the operation of the international mechanism of adjustment, thus appears optimistic so long as reasonably full employment can be maintained throughout the major part of the non-Communist trading world. Present indications are that the areas of analysis which will be most relevant for the conditions of world trade during the coming decades are those which deal with long-term economic expansion interrupted by brief though perhaps severe recessions originating in the major industrial countries.

---

of primary products. This tendency would help to reduce the violent downward fluctuations in terms of trade, for it would make the prices of primary products less vulnerable to decline during periods of business contraction in industrial countries. This problem is further discussed in Chapter 10, where trade relations of primary-producing countries whose exports consist mainly of agricultural products other than rubber are contrasted with those whose exports consist mainly of mineral products and rubber. The need for continued United States adjustment of agricultural production is also stressed therein. For additional information and projections which appear to be consistent with our theoretical position, the reader may wish to consult the following: Report of the President's Materials Policy Commission, *Resources for Freedom*, 1952, Vol. I, Chaps. 1-6, and Vol. II, Chap. 1; see esp. p. 5, where it is assumed "that the raw materials will be freely available at approximately the prices prevailing during 1950, abstracting from inflation and deflation in the general price level." Professor E. S. Mason, a member of the Paley Commission, has expressed the opinion that U.S. requirements for agricultural materials are likely to be satisfied over the next two or three decades at little or no increase in real costs. Concerning minerals, he believes that if resources were relatively free to flow to lowest cost sources, the known and inferred reserves in the underdeveloped areas of the world are large enough and of sufficiently high grade to meet the free-world requirements for at least the next 25 years at no increase in real costs. "Raw Materials, Rearmament, and Economic Development," *Quarterly Journal of Economics*, August, 1952, p. 332. See also Henry G. Aubrey, "The Long-Term Future of United States Imports and Its Implications for Primary Producing Countries," *American Economic Review*, May, 1955, pp. 270-287, esp. p. 278; James P. Cavin, "Projections in Agriculture," in *Long Range Economic Projections* (Studies in Income and Wealth, Vol. 16), 1954, esp. pp. 128-129; and Theodore W. Schultz, *Economic Prospects for Primary Products*, 1957 (mimeographed).

8

Differential Rates of
Productivity Growth and
International Imbalance

IF ONLY because of its sheer economic weight, the
economy of the United States plays a key role in the mid-twentieth-
century trading world. Though the widespread use of the term
"dollar shortage" is of fairly recent origin, the persistent export balance
of the United States, of which the dollar shortage is the monetary
manifestation, is clearly a long-term phenomenon. The mechanism
of adjustment *qua* mechanism is monetary, but the fundamental
variables which it is expected to adjust are real variables that may be
unresponsive to the monetary pressures of the mechanism over long
periods of time. This unresponsiveness may be the result of dynamic
forces, such as long-term economic development, which maintain
persistent pressures opposite to those of the adjusting mechanism.

In order to determine the nature of these persistent pressures, we
shall present and evaluate a series of hypotheses designed to explain
long-term international imbalance. By testing these hypotheses with

domestic and international trade data, we shall attempt to determine which of these forces apply generally and which apply only to individual cases; which forces are structural, resulting from growth and change; and which are institutional, resulting from abnormal conditions and ill-advised policies. The conclusions which follow from this analysis help to resolve the relative importance of the structural and institutional factors currently operating in a balancing or imbalancing direction, and to suggest the consequences of alternative policies in dealing with them.

DIFFERENTIAL RATES OF PRODUCTIVITY GROWTH[1]

It is generally maintained that over the past few decades technological progress in the United States has exceeded that in other parts of the Western world, with the result that she has led in increasing productivity. Even though no other obstacles had stood in the way of the effective functioning of the mechanism of adjustment, this continuing relative reduction in real costs of production within the United States would have offset the inflationary price and income effects of the export balance which is an essential part of the adjusting mechanism. This offsetting influence, so the argument runs, was the more marked because the very industries in which the United States was making the greatest technological improvements were those

[1] This phenomenon has been stressed by many economists as a fundamental cause of long-term international imbalance of western Europe vis-à-vis the United States. Cf. John H. Williams, *Economic Stability in the Modern World*, 1952, esp. pp. 9–15; J. R. Hicks, "An Inaugural Lecture," *Oxford Economic Papers*, n.s., June, 1953, pp. 121-135. For more general treatments, cf. Charles P. Kindleberger, *The Dollar Shortage*, 1950, Chaps. 7 and 8; and T. Balogh, *The Dollar Crisis: Causes and Cure*, 1950.

More recent information and analysis appears to confirm the position developed below, which first appeared in a somewhat different form, in the August, 1955, issue of the *Quarterly Journal of Economics*. Cf., in particular, G. D. A. MacDougall, "Does Productivity Rise Faster in the United States?" *Review of Economics and Statistics*, May, 1956, pp. 155–76; and E. M. Bernstein, "American Productivity and the Dollar Payments Problem," *Review of Economics and Statistics*, May, 1955, pp. 101-109. Cf. also F. Seton, "Productivity, Trade Balance and International Structure," *Economic Journal*, December, 1956, pp. 676-693; E. J. Mishan, "The Long-run Dollar Problem: A Comment," *Oxford Economic Papers*, n.s., June, 1955, esp. pp. 217-220; C. P. Kindleberger, "The Dollar Shortage Re-Revisited," *American Economic Review*, June, 1958, pp. 388-395.

which were highly competitive with many important export commodities of leading industrial countries abroad, export commodities which were greatly dependent upon the American market. Had technological improvement in the United States proceeded at a more even rate between industries, and had a similarly even rate of progress occurred abroad, either deflation of prices and wages abroad or a devaluation of some foreign currencies, as called for by the theory of the mechanism of adjustment, would have been more effective in preventing the balance-of-trade disequilibrium. In other words, had rates of technological improvement been more uniform as between industries in the United States and abroad, appropriate degrees of devaluation or deflation sufficient to keep up with the greater rate of technological progress in the United States might have worked along the lines of comparative advantage.

THE CASE OF UNIFORMITY

Professor Hicks has presented a very useful analytical frame of reference for dealing with this problem.[2] The substance of his position (with insignificant modifications) may be summarized as follows. Consider two countries, A and B, which are trading together and which are such that productivity in A is increasing uniformly more rapidly than productivity in B. To simplify exposition, Hicks assumes initially that productivity in A is increasing uniformly among industries and steadily through time, while that in B remains constant. Since disparity in the rate of growth in productivity between different countries is considered to be a persistent phenomenon, there can be no state of equilibrium. The problem concerns the nature of long-term adjustments to such an enduring disturbance.

Let us begin from a position in which the balance of payments between the two countries is somehow in balance. We shall exclude the possibility of gold production or capital transfers as means of long-term adjustment, and abstract from changes in productivity (cost) induced by changes in the scale of output. Assume further that money incomes in B remain the same, while those in A rise to the full extent

[2] Hicks, *op. cit.*

of the rise in productivity. Then the real effects of the development are most unlikely to be harmful to B. The uniform increase in productivity in A would tend to lower costs and prices of A products, but this effect would be wiped out by the rise in A incomes, so that the prices of A products would be unchanged. The prices of B products would also be unchanged. Consequently, B would buy neither more nor less from A than before. But A income has risen; and with all prices the same, this would probably cause A's demand for B exports and A's demand for A exportables to rise. The balance of payments would consequently turn in B's favor. This, however, would be inconsistent with long-term balance. Professor Hicks therefore states that if the balance of payments is not to turn in B's favor but to remain in balance (as it must in the accounting sense), the rise in A incomes must be less than the rise in productivity.[3] If A incomes rise by less than the rise in productivity, there will be some reduction in the prices of A exports. Thus money income in B can remain constant, and the prices of B products can remain constant; nevertheless, the balance of payments can remain balanced, while B gets her imports from A more cheaply than before. The real income of the B population must therefore be improved. So far as the real effects are concerned, a uniform increase in productivity in A is almost certain to affect B advantageously.

However, the monetary effects may be entirely different. In practice one would expect that employers in country A would receive the initial gains from increased productivity. The net reduction in money costs, resulting from the introduction of more productive methods, would in time be followed by lower prices. Employers would be compelled to raise wages, at least to some extent, because either their employees or they achieved greater productivity. There would thus be some increases in money incomes in A. In country B, prices of products and factors and money income remain unchanged. It is therefore certain that B would buy more (at lower prices) from A than before. Commodity terms of trade move in B's favor. But the double factoral terms of trade move in favor of A because the relative value of A factors as compared to B factors has risen; and hence

[3] The validity and relevance of this proposition will be discussed below.

more units of B factors are exchanged per unit of A factor. If the double factoral terms of trade move strongly in favor of A, then the level of money incomes in B will be unable to remain unchanged (i.e., they will tend to fall), unless the money incomes in A are rising rapidly. It was assumed above that A incomes do, in fact, rise sufficiently rapidly; but there is no automatic mechanism which will assure this effect. While one would expect some increase in money incomes in A, in consequence of the rise in A productivity, it would be unlikely (in the absence of extraneous factors, such as a large volume of investment or capital-intensive inventions) that this increase would be sufficient to prevent deflationary pressures in B. Assuming a stable rate of exchange between A's and B's currency, a rapid rate of increase in productivity in A relative to that in B would probably bring about a deflationary effect in B. There will thus be some appropriate rate of increase in A incomes (less, but perhaps not much less, than the rate of increase in productivity) which will keep trade between the two countries in balance, even though the level of B incomes remains in money terms completely unchanged. *If* A incomes do rise at this appropriate rate, then there need be no deflation in B, while B is benefited by better commodity terms of trade.

Hence, when the rate of growth in productivity is more or less uniformly distributed among all industries, and is higher in one country than in another, then the country with the less rapid rate of growth may encounter monetary difficulties; but *if* these can be overcome, some part of the gain of the more progressive country will go to the less progressive one and no mechanism-of-adjustment difficulties need arise.

THE CASE OF NONUNIFORMITY

But if the rate of growth in productivity is not uniformly distributed, structural as well as monetary difficulties are likely to arise. Consider, for example, a uniform improvement in productivity in A's export industries, but no improvement in other A industries, and none at all in country B. Then, if money incomes remain the same in both countries, A export prices must fall while B export prices remain the same. The quantity of A exports to B must increase, but since their prices are reduced, it is uncertain whether their total value will rise. In the long run (and we are here discussing long-run conditions), they probably will rise. Similarly, there is not much reason why the value of B exports to A should rise substantially (Hicks says not at all), since B export prices and A money incomes remain the same, and A export prices fall. The rise in A real incomes would probably tend to increase B exports to A somewhat. Accordingly, with suitable demand conditions in B and A, it appears possible that trade will continue to balance at unchanged money incomes in both countries. Double factoral terms of trade will remain unchanged and commodity terms will improve for B.

Hence, when the improvement is concentrated upon goods which A exports, and when A money incomes remain the same, the general level of factor prices must remain the same; consequently, country B shares fully in the improvement through the lower export prices of A. These circumstances are least likely to lead to monetary difficulties in B; they are least favorable to the progressive, improving country A and most favorable to B.

Consider now the situation when the improvement is concentrated upon those A industries (not exports) which compete most closely with imports from B. In this case, not only will the double factoral terms of trade turn against B (creating the same monetary difficulties as in the case of uniformity), but the commodity terms will also turn against B, and this will tend to bring about a lower level of its real income. Assume that money incomes in both countries remain constant. Owing to the improvement, the prices of A products which compete with B exports will fall. A's demand for B exports will decline. This development would be enough to cause a deficit in B's balance of payments, for there is no reason why B's demand for A exports should be affected. In order to maintain a trade balance there must be a rise in A incomes relative to B incomes. Further, since there has been no improvement in productivity in A's export industries, the rise in A incomes implies a rise in the prices of A exports. This tendency, plus the competitive pressure upon B exporters to lower their prices, must turn the commodity terms of trade against B.[4]

Thus, concludes Hicks, an improvement in A productivity that is concentrated upon those A industries which compete most closely with B exports must make B worse off—regardless of the course of money incomes and irrespective of the type of international monetary arrangements. This conclusion is theoretically correct on the basis of the postulated assumptions.

For the analysis of historical and contemporary experience with respect to international imbalance, a determination of the type of improvements made by the respective countries is therefore a primary requisite. Hicks states that the case of uniform improvements is not applicable to the problem of long-term external imbalance of western European countries vis-à-vis the United States. His explanation of the long-term "dollar-shortage" problem runs as follows.

During the nineteenth century, differential rates of growth in productivity were mainly concentrated in the export fields on both sides of the Atlantic, though the average rate of such progress probably varied among different countries. The general characteristic of British-American trade, for example, was an exchange of the products of American farms for those of British factories. The high productivity of American manufacturing began very early. But British manufacturers were able to compete with Americans on the basis of lower wages. Similarly, the high wages in the United States did not prevent Britain from importing American farm products advantageously to herself, because the exceedingly high productivity of American agriculture kept American farm products cheap. Such mutually advantageous trade continued to grow as balanced improvements were concentrated in the British and American export fields; the rate of progress was even enough to insure a continuing gain to both sides. Under these conditions there was small probability of serious balance-of-payments strains.

---

[4] Hicks does not discuss the possibility that B will shift to production of A-type goods, export these, and import B export-type goods, and that the new commodity terms will be favorable to B. Nor does he deal with the question as to why should B not substitute B export and B domestic for A export commodities. The probability that the rise in A real incomes would tend to increase B exports to A also is not considered.

The time came, however, when the rate of growth in productivity in Britain fell behind that in America. This, in itself, might have caused monetary difficulties. These difficulties were manageable so long as the disparity in the rate of progress remained small, but they became more serious as the disparity became wider. Between World Wars I and II the rate of growth in productivity in the United States was more rapid than in the industrial countries of Europe, including Britain. Hicks states that in the first phase of the dollar shortage (i.e., in the early 1920's) the difficulties which arose were almost exclusively monetary. British industry found it difficult to compete with American industry because British wages (under the restored gold standard) remained fixed in terms of dollars; but the productivity of agriculture (in North America and elsewhere) was still increasing so rapidly that a moderate devaluation would have restored Britain's earning power without imposing more than a very temporary sacrifice upon the British consumer. He argues that it was therefore correct to think of the British-American mechanism-of-adjustment problems in the early 1920's in monetary terms.

Since then, we are told, the British (and western European) situation has become more difficult mainly because the rate of growth in productivity in American agriculture has slowed down. In addition, improvements in American industry have been concentrated upon products which compete most closely with imports from Britain (and western Europe). Consequently, the monetary adjustments needed to keep trade in balance under contemporary conditions may require a fall in the dollar value of British wages in order to keep British manufactures competitive with American manufactures. Britain, moreover, can no longer count upon the real sacrifice involved being temporary or slight, for she can no longer rely upon the increased productivity of American (and other) agricultural suppliers. The situation therefore requires a fall in British wages in terms of British imports, or a rise in the prices of British imports relative to British wages. And the problems involved in attempting to implement policies which lower the level of real wages render the process of international adjustment extremely difficult.

Britain, we are reminded, has for long been unable to pay for her raw materials and foodstuffs by exporting directly to the dollar area. Hicks says that for this the United States tariff must bear some part of the blame; but since Britain has encountered similar difficulties in selling manufactures in Canada as in the United States, "it is clear that the increasing productivity of American industry must be regarded as mainly responsible."[5] He sums up his position as follows:

It is true that the forms in which the dollar problem has actually appeared have constantly tempted us to regard it as something much less deep-rooted. In the nineteen-twenties it was entangled with war debts; in the nineteen-thirties with world depression and the flight of capital before Hitler; in the nineteen-forties with war damage, more war debts, and the Cold War in international trade. A special explanation of the difficulties which were being experienced by *European countries* in setting their dollar debts could always be found. But the continuance of the same consequence, the same dollar shortage, as the result of these various "causes," has by now become very striking. That there is some *general* influence underlying these particular manifestations can now no longer be doubted. It is hard to see that there is any other general force which would account for what has been happening than the disparity in growth of productivity which we have been discussing.[6]

THE RECORD EXAMINED

The available evidence does not lend support to the view that disparity in the rate of growth in productivity has been the general force which provides a satisfactory explanation of "the long-run dollar problem," so far as mechanism-of-adjustment strains or balance-of-payments difficulties are concerned. The compounded annual rate of growth in productivity per man-hour in manufacturing during the period 1920-1938 appears to have been "about the same" in the United States and in most industrial countries of western Europe—with the *exception of Britain*. Considering the notorious pitfalls inherent in working with productivity figures, and especially as regards their comparability between different countries, our statistical estimates are

[5] Hicks, *op. cit.*, p. 132.
[6] *Ibid.*, p. 131. The discussion runs in terms of *general* "dollar shortage" and not in terms of a British "dollar shortage." These are, of course, logically quite different problems, for no one has ever disputed that in a three-area world, with A and B competitive as to exports, B can suffer from more rapid technological improvement in A. Moreover, there need be no decline in the level of real wages in B if productivity is rising in both countries.

presented as first approximations. They do reveal, however, that United States productivity in manufacturing did *not* rise substantially faster than that of most European industrial countries. As can be seen from Table 3, roughly the compounded annual rate of growth in the United States, the Netherlands, and Sweden was 3.5 percent; in France it was around 3 percent. The figure of 2.5 percent for Germany and 3 percent for Japan is probably an underestimate; it omits large-scale military expenditures. Compared with most western

TABLE 3.   Compounded Annual Rate of Growth in Productivity per Man-Hour in Manufacturing, 1920-1938

| Country | Selected Years—In Percentages | | | |
	1 1920-1938	2 1924-1928	3 1929-1933	4 1934-1938
United States[a]	3½	2¾	− 1¾	7½
United Kingdom[b]	2½	2	− ¾	4
France[c]	3	n.a.	n.a.	3½
Germany[d]	2½	n.s.	2½	n.s.
Netherlands[e]	3½	2½	3	4½
Sweden[f]	3½	2¼	3	2¼
Canada[g]	2¾	2	¼	5
Japan[h]	3	6	4½	n.s.
Australia[i]	2¼	3	−2	2

[a] Based on Solomon Fabricant, *Employment in Manufacturing, 1899-1937* (New York: Nat. Bur. of Econ. Res., Inc., 1942), pp. 230, 331; Colin Clark, *Conditions of Economic Progress* (London: Macmillan and Co., Ltd., 1951), pp. 271, 275, 279.

[b] *Census of Production of the United Kingdom*, London Board of Trade, 1908-1948.

[c] Clark, *loc. cit.* In France a census of production was taken in 1861-1865, and not again till 1930. The figure cited is therefore a very rough estimate. (n.a.: not available.)

[d] *Statistisches Jahrbuch für das Deutsche Reich*, Internationalen Übersichten (Berlin, 1938), Vol. 57, p. 58. (n.s.: not satisfactory.)

[e] *Ibid.* Data for Netherlands reduced by 6 percent to exclude mining.

[f] Clark, *loc. cit.*

[g] *Canada Year Book*, Canada Dominion Bureau of Statistics, Department of Trade and Commerce, 1870-1939.

[h] *Statistisches Jahrbuch für das Deutsche Reich.* Data for Japan from 1931 estimated from the Mitsubishi Economic Research Bureau, August, 1939. William W. Lockwood, in his careful study of *The Economic Development of Japan* (New Jersey: Princeton University Press, 1954), pp. 122-171, finds ". . . support for the conclusion that the average tendency in Japanese manufacturing was for gross output per worker to double during the interwar period."

[i] Clark, *loc. cit.*

European industrial countries, Britain definitely lagged behind. The compounded annual rate of growth in productivity per man-hour in British manufacturing during the same period was 2.5 percent. Britain's experience lends itself to careful case study; it does not necessarily lend itself to generalization.[7]

During the depression of 1929-1933, the differential rates of growth in productivity per man-hour in manufacturing actually worked in an equilibrating direction with respect to the international mechanism of adjustment. The United States suffered from a negative compounded annual rate of growth of −1.75 percent, a lower figure than that of any western European country. The higher rates of growth in productivity abroad must have worked in the direction of lowering export prices of those countries and thereby improving their competitive position. For obvious reasons this was not a powerful factor at the time. But it is noteworthy that while the rate of growth in manufacturing in the Netherlands and Sweden was 3 percent, in Germany 2.5 percent, and in Japan 4.5 percent, that of Britain was −0.75 percent. From 1934 to 1938, on the other hand, the compounded annual rate of growth in productivity per man-hour in American manufacturing was 7.5 percent, in Canada 5 percent, in the Netherlands 4.5 percent, in Britain 4 percent, and in France 3.5 percent.

[7] Case studies dealing with Britain's economic development seem to confirm this conclusion. Our data with respect to Britain's comparative productivity growth have been checked against the information contained in the following studies: Walther Hoffmann, "The Growth of Industrial Production in Great Britain: A Quantitative Study," *Economic History Review*, 2nd ser., Vol. II, No. 2, 1949, pp. 162-180; *Wachstum und Wachstumformen der Englischen Industriewirtschaft von 1700 bis zur Gegenwart*, 1940, esp. pp. 261-284, for a useful series of comprehensive summary tables and graphs; L. Rostas, *Comparative Productivity in British and American Industry*, 1948, pp. 27-49, 76-93, 97-248; A. E. Kahn, *Great Britain in the World Economy*, 1946, particularly pp. 141-142, 185; Werner Schlote, *Entwicklung und Strukturwandlungen des englischen Aussenhandels von 1700 bis zur Gegenwart*, 1938. Cf. also Simon Kuznets, *Economic Change*, 1953, pp. 253-277; and E. A. G. Robinson, "Changing Structure of the British Economy," *Economic Journal*, September, 1954, pp. 444-461. Relative growth in productivity per labor unit is, of course, not decisive unless labor is the only cost, but it does provide a first approximation, which appears to be confirmed by the other quantitative and qualitative information contained in these studies and by the information cited below. It must be kept in mind, however, that there are obvious limitations of product-per-labor-unit data as criteria of trends of double-factoral terms of trade, to say nothing of competitive ability. Aside from quality and design changes, shifts in tastes, etc., there is the whole field of cost or input items not covered by wages or labor-unit costs.

This disparity in the rate of productivity growth in manufacturing occurred at the very time that the United States was moving toward equilibrium in its international accounts!

If differential rates of growth in *overall* manufacturing productivity do not appear to have been an important *general* cause of long-term international imbalance, were improvements (as Professor Hicks maintains) so concentrated in export industries on both sides of the Atlantic that this was the chief cause of the difficulty? While detailed research on this problem is long overdue, and while it is impossible on the basis of the available information to reach a categorical conclusion, our analysis of the evidence suggests a partially affirmative but mainly negative reply.

The hypotheses seem plausible that countries are most likely to make their improvements in the production of products which they already make relatively well, and that it is these things which will most readily find an export market. Improvements, says Hicks, will therefore be concentrated in the export fields,[8] and in earlier periods this probably occurred in Britain.[9] In time, one would expect that some younger countries which were formerly customers of the older ones, but which possess the necessary natural resources for home production of the things they used to import, will acquire the necessary skill, adapt techniques to suit their needs, organize production according to new methods, and make improvements in industries which compete closely with the imports from the more developed countries. To some extent this certainly happened in the United

[8] Hicks, *op. cit.*, p. 129.

[9] Hicks presents his argument in a general form. Economic historians appear to agree with it insofar as it applies to Britain. Cf. A. D. Gayer, W. W. Rostow, A. J. Schwartz, and I. Frank, *The Growth and Fluctuation of the British Economy*, 1953, Vol. II, pp. 647-658; W. W. Rostow, *British Economy of the Nineteenth Century*, 1948, Chaps. I and II; T. S. Ashton, *The Industrial Revolution*, 1760-1830, 1948, esp. the discussion of interdependent factors in the fall of real costs, "The Standard of Life of the Workers in England, 1790-1830," and "The Tasks of Economic History," *Journal of Economic History*, Supplement IX, 1949, pp. 25-28. For other countries one must consider the reverse hypothesis: progress may be most rapid in more backward industries (and countries) once they begin to import accumulated know-how from most advanced countries, since the latter can progress only through innovations (i.e., they cannot profitably imitate). For data on average rate of growth of real G. N. P. in 29 countries between 1945-1954, see John H. Adler, "World Economic Growth—Retrospect and Prospects," *Review of Economics and Statistics*, August, 1956, p. 274.

States. And it is of course true that in the latter half of the nineteenth century vast areas in the United States were brought into cultivation and became a source of cheap agricultural exports. But is it true, as Hicks contends, that before the 1920's American improvements were concentrated mainly in the production of agricultural exports and since then improvements have seriously lagged behind in the production of these products? Is there any evidence to show that, generally speaking, improvements in the United States have not been quite evenly spread among the production of domestic, export, and import-substitute products?

Excellent work has recently been done in an attempt to measure the rate of change in productivity in American agriculture.[10] The evidence reveals remarkable progress rather than decline in the rate of productivity growth between 1920 and 1950. The increase in the ratio of farm outputs per unit of input during this period is presented in Table 4. Taking 1946-1948 input prices for weighting the various inputs, one finds that a unit of input in 1950 resulted in 53 percent more agricultural production than in 1910. In 1950 (or 1948) the output of American agricultural production was 75 percent larger than in 1910, and only 14 percent more inputs were required to produce this expansion.[11] Virtually all the improvement took place since 1923; and when it is averaged over the 27-year period 1923-1950, it represents an average increase of 2 percent per year.[12]

The contention is unwarranted that from the early 1920's (until

[10] Cf. Theodore W. Schultz, *The Economic Organization of Agriculture*, 1953, Chaps. 7 and 8; John W. Kendrick, "National Productivity and Its Long-Term Projection," in *Long-Range Economic Projection* (Studies in Income and Wealth, Vol. 16), 1954, esp. pp. 88-93.

[11] Schultz, *op. cit.*, p. 120.

[12] *Ibid.*, pp. 99-145. Cf. also U.S. Department of Agriculture, Bureau of Agricultural Economics, *Farm Income Situation*, July-September, 1951, Tables 1, 11, 12. New and better production techniques were mainly responsible for the advance in efficiency. Labor was withdrawn and cheaper inputs were added. Farm production expenses on the operation of vehicles (less hired labor) amounted to about $7 million in 1910, and $2073 million in 1950, a 296-fold increase; seed purchased increased tenfold; fertilizer and lime, 551 percent. It has been estimated that the federal and state governments allocated about $32 million for agricultural research in 1937 and about $106 million in 1951. This progress in research and the resulting increase in the production of new techniques were quite continuous. The returns to our society were very large. Land did not become a limitational factor, responsible for historical diminishing returns. In effect, it

TABLE 4. Increase in the Ratio of Farm Outputs to Inputs, United States, 1910-1950

(1910-1914 = 100)

Year	Farm Output per Unit of Input[a]	Year	Farm Output per Unit of Input[a]
1910	100	1931	117
1911	98	1932	117
1912	106	1933	111
1913	95	1934	99
1914	101	1935	119
1915	102	1936	105
1916	96	1937	130
1917	104	1938	125
1918	101	1939	126
1919	99	1940	130
1920	102	1941	138
1921	92	1942	152
1922	102	1943	147
1923	104	1944	151
1924	106	1945	149
1925	108	1946	153
1926	111	1947	146
1927	108	1948	158
1928	112	1949	153
1929	111	1950	153
1930	106		

SOURCE: T. W. Schultz, *The Economic Organization of Agriculture* (New York: McGraw-Hill, 1953), p. 122.

[a] Inputs weighted by 1946-1948 prices.

the early 1950's) there was a decline in the rate of productivity in American agriculture, and that this was an important factor contributing to the long-term dollar shortage.

Whether or not improvements in American industry were concentrated upon the production of products which compete most closely with European imports is a problem more difficult to resolve. Goods that might be classified as domestic, import-substitute, or export products were continuously undergoing change. Without

was demonstrated that there is no general *historical* "law" of diminishng returns to inputs used on agricultural land, so long as there is persistent and large-scale technological progress.

specific knowledge to the contrary, one would expect that, owing to the well-balanced resource structure of the United States, and the greater importance of the domestic as compared with the foreign market, improvements would have been distributed quite uniformly as between the production of domestic, export, and import-substitute products. Within each one of these categories, however, one would expect some industries to lead in the rate of growth, then to slacken (occasionally to take a further rise), and, in time, to be overtaken by others whose period of rapid growth was just beginning. The available evidence, inadequate and tentative as it may be, appears to confirm this hypothesis. Table 5 summarizes the average rate of percentage increase during five-year periods of the volume of productive activity in various industries (domestic, export, and import substitute) in the United States, Great Britain, Belgium, Germany, and France.

TABLE 5.   Average Rate of Percentage Increase During Five-Year Periods Shown by Indices of the Volume of Productive Activity in Various Industries in the United States, Great Britain, Belgium, Germany, and France

Country and Nature of Series	Period Covered	Average Rate of % Increase During 1st Half	During 2nd Half	Relative Decrease in Rate (3—4 as % of 3)
1	2	3	4	5
United States				
1. Wheat crops	1866-1924	20.4	7.3	64.2
2. Corn crops	1866-1924	17.7	6.7	62.1
3. Potato crops	1866-1924	17.6	11.5	34.7
4. Cotton Crops	1866-1924	24.2	5.6	76.9
5. Anthracite-coal shipments	1825-1924	70.8	16.3	77.0
6. Bituminous-coal output	1840-1924	62.9	33.9	46.1
7. Crude-petroleum output	1860-1924	70.5	51.4	27.1
8. Pig-iron production	1856-1924	46.7	29.4	37.0
9. Crude-steel production	1866-1924	157.7	46.2	70.7
10. Portland-cement output	1880-1924	337.4	90.0	26.7
11. Cotton consumption, domestic mills	1871-1924	30.4	19.0	37.5
12. Raw-silk imports	1866-1924	66.0	41.8	63.3
13. Locomotives produced, Baldwin Locomotive Works	1836-1923	47.9	22.3	53.4

TABLE 5 (Continued)

Country and Nature of Series	Period Covered	Average Rate of % Increase During 1st Half	During 2nd Half	Relative Decrease in Rate (3 − 4 as % of 3)
1	2	3	4	5
Great Britain				
14. Coal output	1856-1913	16.2	10.4	35.8
15. Pig-iron production	1856-1913	15.4	4.0	74.0
16. Raw-steel output	1876-1913	39.3	20.4	48.1
17. Tonnage of ships cleared, all ports	1816-1913	24.8	18.9	23.8
18. Raw-cotton imports	1781-1913	35.4	11.1	68.6
19. Tea consumption[a]	1810-1919	14.8	12.6	14.9
Belgium				
20. Coal output	1831-1913	25.6	6.9	73.0
21. Pig-iron output	1851-1913	18.8	21.6	14.9[b]
22. Steel (crude) output	1881-1913	58.9	46.8	20.5
23. Zinc production	1846-1913	29.0	14.5	50.0
Germany				
24. Wheat crops	1881-1913	14.7	6.7	54.4
25. Coal output	1861-1913	28.6	25.7	10.1
26. Pig-iron consumption	1861-1913	36.7	25.5	30.5
27. Steel output	1881-1913	73.8	67.8	8.1
28. Zinc (crude) production	1846-1913	24.7	10.5	57.5
29. Raw-cotton consumption[c]	1836-1910	43.5	22.8	47.6
France				
30. Wheat crops	1825-1913	7.8	2.0	74.4
31. Coal output	1811-1913	29.6	15.9	46.3
32. Petroleum consumption	1866-1913	57.9	26.6	54.1
33. Pig-iron output	1825-1913	24.3	16.8	30.9
34. Steel output	1871-1913	47.3	35.4	25.2

SOURCE: Simon Kuznets, *Economic Change* (New York: Norton & Co., 1953), from Table, p. 256. The results were obtained by taking the volume of output or consumption for an industry, averaging it for nine years (or seven where the data were short at the end of the series) centered around the year ending with o or 5, and dividing one average by the preceding. The percentage rate of increase or decrease by five-year periods was thus obtained. To see whether the general tendency was to decline, rise, or remain stable, the entire period covered by each series was divided into halves, and an average percentage rate of increase for each half obtained. Of 35 series, only one showed an increase in the average percentage rate of increase.

[a] Ten-year averages until 1854.
[b] Increase.
[c] Ten-year averages through the whole period.

During the first half of the periods covered, the rate of growth in activity in selected industries in the United States was generally much higher than in Britain. But during the second half of the periods covered, the rate of expansion in the United States industries was greatly reduced as compared with the other countries.[13] During both the first and the second half of the periods covered, with the exception of the remarkable rates of growth in the output of cement and steel, the average percentage rate of increase in the volume of productive activity in domestic and export industries, such as bituminous coal, pig iron, crude petroleum, anthracite coal, cotton, and wheat, were not dissimilar to the average rate of percentage increase in the import-competing industries, such as cotton and silk manufactures. While variation in output change exceeded variation in efficiency change, virtually every industry in the United States showed an upward trend in efficiency.[14]

As can be seen from Table 5, even before World War I Britain was unable to maintain her rate of growth in output of such industries as coal, iron, and steel, as compared with the rate of growth either in the United States or in Belgium, Germany, and France. She was lagging behind practically all the rapidly industrializing countries of the world. World War I and its aftermath did not improve this trend. We have observed that during the period 1920 to 1938 the compound annual rate of growth in productivity per man-hour in

---

[13] The spectacular rates of growth between 1866 and 1888 and the very high rates between 1894 and 1914 help to explain the much higher level of per capita real income the United States attained, as compared with the industrial countries of Europe, before World War I, and has maintained at a compound (though irregular) rate thereafter. As already observed, between World Wars I and II the rate of growth per man-hour in manufacturing was not greatly dissimilar in the United States and in most industrial countries of Europe. Professor Kuznets' data show that from 1869 to 1888 the United States national income increased at a rate of almost 39 percent per quinquennium, and per capita income increased at a rate of about 23 percent per quinquennium. From 1869 to 1938 the national income increased at a rate of about 19 percent per quinquennium, while the per capita income increased at an 8.5 percent rate. Computed from Simon Kuznets, *National Income: A Summary and Findings*, 1946, Table 10, p. 32.

[14] For an informative survey, cf. Solomon Fabricant, *Economic Progress and Economic Change*, 1954, pp. 3-18, and the list of relevant National Bureau of Economic Research publications cited on pp. 85-88; and by the same author, *Notes on Efficiency and Size, with Particular Reference to the United States*, 1957 (mimeographed). A good selected bibliography may be found in Rostas, *op. cit.*, pp. 249-259.

manufacturing in Britain amounted to about 2.5 percent, while in the United States it was about 3.5 percent.[15] In British manufacturing, mining, building, and public utilities, over the 30-year period from 1907 to 1937, the increase in output per man-hour amounted to 65 percent and in output per wage earner to 47 percent.[16] In the same period the increase in the United States amounted to 133 percent in output per man-hour and to 71 percent in output per wage earner.[17] The rate of increase in productivity in terms of man-hours was thus nearly twice as high in the United States as in Britain. Over the 30-year period, the average compound rate of increase amounted to 1.7 percent per man-hour per year in Britain, and to 2.9 percent per man-hour per year in the United States.[18]

TABLE 6. Average Compound Percentage Rate of Annual Increase in per Man-Hour Productivity in United Kingdom and United States Industry as a Whole, 1907-1937 (1907=100)

	United Kingdom	United States
1907-1937	1.7	2.9
1909-1924	1.4	2.8
1924-1937	2.1	3.0

SOURCE: Adapted from L. Rostas, *Comparative Productivity in British and American Industry* (Cambridge: Cambridge University Press, 1948), p. 42.

Similarly, between 1908 and 1936-1937 output increased somewhat over 40 percent per man-hour and about 30 percent per head in British agriculture; in the comparable period of 1909 to 1937 the increase of productivity in American agriculture amounted to about 66 percent per man-hour and to about 58 percent per head.[19] The rate of increase per head per year was a little over 2 percent in the United States, and only 1 percent in Britain.[20] Between 1937 and 1944 there was a further 18 percent increase in output per head (and perhaps a little less per man-hour) in American agriculture, while in Britain the wartime increase per man-hour has been estimated at 13 percent.[21]

[15] Cf. Table 3.
[16] Rostas, *op. cit.*, p. 42.
[17] *Ibid.*
[18] The results are summarized in Table 6.
[19] Rostas, *op. cit.*, p. 79.
[20] *Ibid.*
[21] *Ibid.*

Data relating to productivity comparisons in individual industries reveal the same tendency, with practically all the British export industries lagging behind comparable industries in the United States. From 1909 to 1939 British output per man-hour in the cotton industry increased by only 46 percent, while in the United States output per man-hour more than doubled;[22] in the woolen industry British output per man-hour increased 26-35 percent, while in the United States output per man-hour increased 78 percent.[23] The rate of increase was substantially greater in United States steel rolling, vehicles, chemicals, mining, tobacco, clothing, food and drink, etc. There was in fact no single main-industry group in which the rate of increase in output per man-hour in the United States was smaller than in Britain.[24]

HYPOTHESIS REJECTED

However, the rate of increase in output in the United States as compared with Britain between World Wars I and II does not suggest that improvements were concentrated in American import-competing industries. If one compares United States output per worker with British output per worker in similar industries before World War II, one gets the impression that not only has improvement in American efficiency tended to rise persistently but it has also tended to rise in all sectors of the economy. The ratio of United States to British output per worker in different industries and the corresponding ratio of United States to British exports is presented in Table 7.

If, as one would expect, industrial improvements in the United States and in Britain were reflected in the relative output per worker in comparable industries, then the fact that United States output per worker before World War II was greater than the British in domestic, export, and import-substitute industries suggests that American improvements were not concentrated particularly in the import-competing fields. United States output per worker was more than twice the British in the production of such products as electric lamps, mining,

[22] *Ibid.*, Appendix 9, p. 136.
[23] *Ibid.*, Appendix 10, p. 144.
[24] *Ibid.*, p. 46; Appendixes 1-37, pp. 97-248.

TABLE 7. Ratio of United States to British Output per Worker and
United States to British Exports in Selected Industries[a]

Industry	Output per worker U.S. : U.K.	Exports U.S. : U.K.
Electric lamps	5.4	0.94
Tin cans	5.25	3.0
Pig iron	3.6	5.1
Wireless receiving sets and valves	3.5	7.6
Motor cars	3.1	4.3
Biscuits	3.1	0.23
Matches	3.1	0.09
Rubber tires	2.7	0.74
Soap	2.7	0.35
Machinery	2.7	1.5
Glass containers	2.4	3.5
Paper	2.2	1.0
Beer	2.0	0.056
Linoleum, oilcloth, etc.	1.9	0.34
Coke	1.9	0.19
Hosiery	1.8	0.30
Cigarettes	1.7	0.47
Rayon weaving	1.5	0.20
Cotton spinning and weaving	1.5	0.11
Leather footwear	1.4	0.32
Rayon making	1.4	0.091
Woolen and worsted	1.35	0.004
Men's and boys' outer clothing, wool	1.25	0.044
Margarine	1.2	0.031
Cement	1.1	0.091

SOURCES: L. Rostas, *Comparative Productivity in British and American Industry*
(Cambridge; Cambridge University Press, 1948), p. 42; G. D. A. MacDougall,
"British and American Exports: A Study Suggested by the Theory of Comparative
Costs, Part I," *Economic Journal*, December, 1951 p. 700. Before World War II,
American weekly wages in manufacturing were roughly double the British. Mac-
Dougall has shown that where American output per worker was more than twice
the British, the United States had in general the bulk of the export market
(electric lamps, biscuits, matches, rubber tires, and soap being exceptions); while
for products where it was less than twice as high, the bulk of the market was
held by Britain. *Ibid.*, p. 698.

[a] For 1935, 1937, or 1939 in each country with minor exceptions. Rostas
suggests the following rough relative productivities per worker, U.S. : U.K., in
certain nonmanufacturing sectors: mining, 4.15; communications, 2.7; electricity,
1.9; gas, 1.7; distribution, 1.5; building, 1.15; commercial and other services,
1.0; transport of goods, 1.0. *Op. cit.*, p. 89; cf. MacDougall, *op. cit.*, p. 709.

tin cans, pig iron, radios, motor cars, biscuits, matches, rubber tires, soap, machinery, glass containers, and paper. It was less than or equal to 1.5 times the British in the production of woolens and worsted, cotton spinning and weaving, rayon weaving, men's and boys' outer clothing of wool, and leather footwear. It was about the same in the production of cement, building, commercial services, and transport.[25] The figures suggest that American efficiency has been relatively greater than the British in the capital-intensive (and other) industries which have been able to take especial advantage of mass-scale production and distribution methods at home, and which have probably also benefited from enlarged markets abroad. Many of these industries have competed successfully within the British market and in third countries; but they surely cannot be differentiated as United States import-competing industries. Those that can (e.g., woolens and worsted, cotton spinning and weaving) manifestly were not ahead of most other American industries in efficiency growth. In the strictly domestic fields (e.g., building and commercial services), American and British productivity appears to have been about the same. Apparently British balance-of-payments difficulties cannot be attributed primarily to a tendency for American improvements to be concentrated in import-competing industries.[26] Britain generally lagged behind in productivity growth not only as compared with the United States but also as compared with the leading industrial countries of western Europe.

THE CHANGING STRUCTURE OF WORLD TRADE
AND INTERNATIONAL IMBALANCE

Britain's declining position in world trade was doubtless interrelated with the aforementioned widening gaps in industrial efficiency. It is therefore not surprising to find that explanations of long-term

[25] Cf. Table 7.
[26] For data on the extent of American capital-intensive type of imports see Wassily Leontief, "Domestic Production and Foreign Trade; The American Capital Position Re-examined," *Proceedings of the American Philosophical Society*, September, 1953, pp. 332-349; and the comments thereon by Gottfried Haberler, "A Survey of International Trade Theory," International Finance Section, Princeton University, 1955, pp. 22-25.

international imbalance which are expressed in terms of differential rates of change in productivity are usually "reinforced" with material dealing with "the changing structure of world trade." It appears doubtful, however, whether the long-term imbalance of Britain—and particularly any such tendency of western Europe as a whole—vis-à-vis America can be explained in such terms.

As was to be expected, from 1899 to 1937 Britain's relative share in world trade decreased by a greater amount than that of any other country. It dropped from 32.5 percent to 22.4 percent.[27] Britain's exports to North America amounted to 10.3 percent of her total exports in 1900, while her exports to Europe amounted to 41 percent. In 1910 her exports to North America amounted to 12.7 percent and those to Europe to 34.9 percent. In 1929 the ratios were 11.7 percent and 34.7 percent respectively. By 1936 British exports to North America still amounted to 11.9 percent of her total exports and those to Europe to 35.8 percent.[28] Similarly, the long-term trend shows that Britain's export position deteriorated in terms of all industrial countries and not only in terms of North America. British exports of finished manufactured goods to the United States rose steadily from about £5.5 million in 1827-1830 to £31.9 million in 1927-1929. But of her total exports to the United States, 93.2 percent were finished manufactured goods in 1827-1830, whereas only 67.5 percent were these goods in 1909-1913, a decline of 25.7 percentage points. Of her exports to "industrial Europe," finished manufactures amounted to 83.4 percent in 1827-1830 and 60.5 percent in 1909-1913, a decline of about 22.9 percentage points. British exports of finished manufactured goods to all industrial countries amounted to 86.9 percent of her total exports in 1827-1830 and 61.9 percent in 1909-1913.[29] None of the other industrial countries of Europe fared as badly. Indeed, from 1899 to 1937 the percentage share in world trade of Sweden, Belgium, and Germany actually rose somewhat and those of Switzerland and Italy fell slightly, but that of Britain fell 10.1 and that of France 9.4

[27] Cf. Table 8.
[28] Cf. W. Schlote, *British Overseas Trade from 1700 to the 1930's*, trans. W. O. Henderson and W. H. Chaloner, 1953, pp. 159-160.
[29] Cf. Table 9.

TABLE 8. Changes in World Share and Structure of Trade of 11 Countries, 1899, 1937, 1950

| | | Share in World Trade | Structure of Trade | | | | |
			Expanding	Stable	Declining	N.C.	Total
U.S.A.	1899	11.2	23.4	54.1	21.7	0.8	100
	1937	19.6	58.8	32.4	8.5	0.3	100
	Change	+ 8.4	+35.4	−21.7	−13.2	− 0.5	0
	1950	29.1	52.4	32.1	13.5	2.0	100
	Change	+ 9.5	− 6.4	− .3	+ 5.0	+ 1.7	0
United Kingdom	1899	32.5	17.7	18.6	62.9	0.8	100
	1937	22.4	31.2	25.0	43.6	0.2	100
	Change	−10.1	+13.5	+ 6.4	−19.3	− 0.6	0
	1950	25.0	43.0	24.8	31.6	0.4	100
	Change	+ 2.6	+11.8	− 0.2	−12.0	+ 0.2	0
France	1899	15.8	5.8	31.0	62.8	0.4	100
	1937	6.4	27.9	36.1	35.8	0.2	100
	Change	− 9.4	+22.1	+ 5.1	−27.0	− 0.2	0
	1950	10.2	34.0	27.4	38.3	0.6	100
	Change	+ 3.8	+ 6.1	− 8.7	+ 2.5	+ 0.4	0
Germany	1899	22.2	11.2	45.8	42.5	0.3	100
	1937	22.4	35.3	46.1	18.4	0.1	100
	Change	+ 0.2	+24.1	+ 0.3	−24.1	+ 0.1	0
	1950	7.1	43.5	44.3	12.1	0.3	100
	Change	−15.3	+ 8.2	− 1.8	− 6.3	− 0.1	0
Belgium	1899	5.6	13.6	49.2	35.5	1.7	100
	1937	5.9	35.0	41.3	23.7	—	100
	Change	+ 0.3	+21.4	− 7.9	−11.8	− 1.7	0
	1950	5.8	33.6	37.1	29.2	—	100
	Change	− 0.1	− 1.4	− 4.2	+ 5.5	—	0
Sweden	1899	1.0	46.2	45.4	8.1	0.2	100
	1937	2.5	49.2	40.8	10.0	0.0	100
	Change	+ 1.5	+ 2.9	− 4.6	+ 1.9	− 0.2	0
	1950	2.7	42.1	40.8	15.9	1.0	100
	Change	+ 0.2	− 7.1	—	+ 5.9	+ 1.0	0
Canada	1899	0.3	9.3	57.8	22.6	10.3	100
	1937	5.0	14.9	75.4	9.6	0.1	100
	Change	+ 4.7	+ 5.6	+17.6	−13.0	−10.2	0
	1950	6.1	11.2	80.3	8.1	0.2	100
	Change	+ 1.1	− 3.7	+ 4.9	− 1.5	+ 0.1	0

TABLE 8 (Continued)

		Share in World Trade	Structure of Trade				
			Expanding	Stable	Declining	N.C.	Total
Switzerland	1899	3.9	73.6	25.9	0.6	—	100
	1937	2.9	21.9	50.6	27.5	—	100
	Change	− 1.0	− 51.7	+ 24.7	+ 26.9	—	0
	1950	4.0	29.8	50.8	19.2	—	100
	Change	+ 1.1	+ 7.9	+ 0.2	− 8.3	—	0
Japan	1899	1.5	0.1	25.3	72.8	1.8	100
	1937	7.2	13.3	18.4	68.0	0.3	100
	Change	+ 5.7	+ 13.2	− 6.9	− 4.8	− 1.5	0
	1950	3.3	16.6	21.8	61.4	0.2	100
	Change	− 3.9	+ 3.3	+ 3.4	− 6.6	− 0.1	0
Italy	1899	3.7	1.6	14.7	83.6	—	100
	1937	3.6	23.6	17.6	58.7	—	100
	Change	− 0.1	+ 22.0	+ 2.9	− 24.9	—	0
	1950	3.8	26.1	15.6	58.1	0.2	100
	Change	+ 0.2	+ 2.5	− 2.0	− 0.6	—	0
India	1899	2.3	0.0	30.8	68.9	0.3	100
	1937	2.1	5.2	22.2	72.2	0.4	100
	Change	− 0.2	+ 5.2	− 8.6	+ 3.3	+ 0.1	0
	1950	2.9	.6	9.3	89.7	0.4	100
	Change	+ .8	− 4.6	− 12.9	+ 17.5	0.0	0
World	1899	—	13.4	33.2	52.8	0.6	100
	1937	—	34.8	35.7	29.3	0.2	100
	Change	—	+ 21.4	+ 2.5	− 23.5	− 0.4	0
	1950	—	39.1	33.3	26.8	0.8	100
	Change	—	+ 4.3	− 2.4	− 2.5	+ .6	0

SOURCE: Calculated from data presented in H. Tyszynski, "World Trade in Manufactured Commodities, 1899-1950," *Manchester School of Economics and Social Studies*, September, 1951, pp. 277-281. Because of rounding, percentage totals do not always equal 100.

percentage points. Canada, on the other hand, gained 4.7; Japan, 5.7; and the United States, 8.4 percentage points.[30]

HYPOTHESIS REJECTED

The drastic decline in Britain's share of world trade cannot be explained directly in terms of the changing structure of world trade, if

[30] Cf. Table 8.

Table 9. Exports of Britain's Home Products to Industrial Countries by Commodity Groups, 1827-1929

Commodity Group	In £1,000,000						Percent					
	1827-1830	1854-1857	1877-1879	1898-1901	1909-1913	1927-1929[a]	1827-1830	1854-1857	1877-1879	1898-1901	1909-1913	1927-1929[a]
Exports to industrial Europe												
Foodstuffs	1.0	1.6	2.8	3.0	5.3	6.9	10.6	5.8	5.1	4.2	4.9	5.2
Raw materials[a]	0.2	3.9	7.3	19.3	27.8	46.3	2.3	14.2	13.3	27.7	25.5	34.7
Finished manufactured goods	7.8	20.3	41.2	42.4	65.8	80.3	83.4	74.7	74.8	60.9	60.5	60.1
Unclassified	0.3	1.3	3.7	4.9	10.0	—	3.7	5.3	6.8	7.2	9.1	—
Total	9.3	27.1	55.0	69.6	108.9	133.5	100	100	100	100	100	100
Exports to the United States												
Foodstuffs	—	0.3	0.1	0.7	2.2	1.9	—	1.5	0.6	3.9	7.5	4.1
Raw materials	—	1.1	2.1	2.2	5.5	12.1	—	5.5	12.3	12.4	18.6	26.4
Finished manufactured goods	5.5	17.9	14.2	14.1	20.0	31.9	93.2	89.9	83.0	79.2	67.5	69.5
Unclassified	0.4	0.6	0.7	0.8	1.9	—	6.8	5.1	4.1	4.5	6.4	—
Total	5.9	19.9	17.1	17.8	29.6	45.9	100	100	100	100	100	100
Exports to all industrial countries												
Finished manufactured goods	13.3	38.2	55.4	56.5	85.8	112.2	86.9	81.1	76.9	64.6	61.9	62.5
Raw materials and foodstuffs[a]	1.9	8.8	16.7	30.9	52.7	67.2	13.1	18.9	23.1	35.4	38.1	37.5
Total	—	—	—	—	—	—	100	100	100	100	100	100
Exports to all agrarian countries												
Finished manufactured goods	20.3	54.6	111.3	149.7	259.8	450.8	93.3	90.0	91.0	83.2	82.1	83.3
Total exports	37.0	107.7	194.4	267.3	455.0	720.7						

Source: Werner Schlote, *Entwicklung und Strukturwandlungen des englischen Aussenhandels von 1700 bis zur Gegenwart* (Jena: Gustav Fisher, 1938), p. 92.
[a] Excluding Eire.

TABLE 10. Change in Share of World Trade in Expanding, Stable, and Declining Industry Groups of 11 Countries, 1899-1937

	By Group No.	U.K.	U.S.A.	France	Germany	Belgium	Italy	Sweden	Switzer- land	Canada	India	Japan
Expanding groups												
Motor vehicles, etc.	10	− 6.6	22.5	−15.8	− 9.4	− 2.7	6.1	0.6	−0.4	3.2	—	1.8
Industrial equipment	6	−18.1	7.2	− 4.5	10.2	− 3.7	3.8	−0.2	0.8	0.8	−0.08	2.7
Iron and steel	1	−29.4	9.5	3.0	4.3	7.8	0.5	−1.3	0.09	1.0	1.1	3.2
Electric goods	7	−10.7	− 3.0	2.1	10.7	− 3.4	−0.6	3.8	−7.1	1.9	—	3.8
Total expanding groups		−22.9	13.6	1.7	4.0	0.3	2.0	0.2	−0.3	1.9	0.3	2.7
Stable groups												
Miscellaneous material	5	− 2.1	− 6.2	−11.9	−11.6	− 1.1	−0.7	5.5	−0.06	22.7	−1.8	3.4
Nonferrous metals	2	− 2.1	−20.6	− 8.5	− 6.8	6.5	0.3	1.1	2.4	28.4	2.0	−2.6
Chemicals	3	− 5.4	4.1	− 2.2	3.1	3.1	0.02	0.3	2.9	2.4	−1.1	1.6
Agricultural equipment	8	−22.7	2.1	− 1.2	15.4	0.5	0.5	−1.5	−0.2	2.7	—	0.3
Met. manufacturers, NCS	14	− 6.8	1.2	− 7.4	9.6	− 2.5	0.8	1.4	0.5	1.3	−0.02	4.2
Books, films, etc.	15	6.9	13.9	−16.9	−13.9	1.5	−0.2	0.3	−0.07	1.6	0.2	6.8
Nonmetalliferous	4	4.4	8.0	−10.4	5.0	−13.1	1.7	−2.0	0.2	0.3	0.13	5.8
Total stable groups		− 2.6	− 0.4	− 8.2	− 1.8	1.4	0.1	1.5	1.0	10.0	−0.8	2.6
Declining groups												
Drinks and tobacco	11	26.9	− 2.8	−22.2	− 7.1	5.4	−3.8	0.04	−0.3	8.6	−0.15	1.4
Railways, ships, etc.	9	−27.9	− 3.4	0.3	19.3	− 1.9	0.3	6.9	−0.2	0.6	−0.03	5.9
Miscellaneous mfg.	16	3.8	2.8	−11.1	− 5.2	− 0.8	−0.04	−0.5	−0.3	0.4	0.12	11.0
Apparel	13	− 1.6	5.4	−27.1	−10.4	1.7	3.7	0.5	1.6	4.7	0.2	21.3
Textiles	12	− 8.8	1.0	− 8.2	4.2	3.9	1.6	0.2	−0.4	0.2	3.42	16.8
Total declining groups		− 5.4	1.0	−11.0	− 3.8	1.0	1.3	0.7	−2.3	1.5	−2.3	14.7

SOURCE: H. Tyszynski, "World Trade in Manufactured Commodities," *Manchester School of Economic and Social Studies*, September, 1951. Calculated from Tables I–V, pp. 276-282; cf. also Table XI, p. 290.

203

TABLE 11. Change in Share of World Trade in Expanding, Stable, and Declining Industry Groups of 11 Countries, 1937-1950

	By Group No.	U.K.	U.S.A.	France	Germany[a]	Belgium	Italy	Sweden	Switzer-land	Canada	India	Japan
Expanding groups												
Motor vehicles, etc.	10	17.0	− 2.8	2.6	− 7.4	−1.1	−3.9	−0.1	−0.3	− 2.6	−6.0	−1.4
Industrial equipment	6	4.1	11.3	2.9	−21.6	0.6	−1.0	3.2	2.5	0.1	−3.3	−1.9
Iron and steel	1	3.6	2.3	8.4	− 8.2	0.6	0.7	−2.0	0.06	1.6	−0.7	1.2
Electric goods	7	11.2	7.3	4.8	−23.8	0.6	1.6	−0.5	2.3	0.5	—	−2.9
Total expanding groups		7.4	5.8	3.1	−14.8	−1.0	—	−0.4	1.3	0.4	0.1	−1.3
Stable groups												
Miscellaneous material	5	− 0.5	5.3	1.2	−17.9	−1.9	−0.3	2.7	0.3	15.8	2.0	−3.2
Nonferrous metals	2	− 4.2	− 9.3	1.3	− 1.7	−0.7	0.2	−0.1	2.9	0.8	−0.8	4.6
Chemicals	3	0.6	20.1	0.2	−24.3	1.7	−0.5	0.2	2.2	2.0	−1.9	2.4
Agricultural equipment	8	7.1	− 2.6	1.1	− 8.5	−0.2	0.7	−1.5	0.05	4.3	—	−0.26
Met. manufacturers, NCS	14	7.0	10.6	5.5	−29.1	0.5	0.7	0.4	6.5	0.4	−1.1	−1.8
Books, films, etc.	15	3.0	12.4	2.2	−19.0	1.4	0.8	0.2	2.3	0.7	−2.0	−2.6
Nonmetalliferous	4	5.9	10.4	5.7	−21.3	−4.4	−1.3	−0.32	—	8.4	−3.3	−3.1
Total stable groups		3.0	10.2	2.0	−19.4	−0.4	—	0.5	2.1	4.1	−0.5	−1.5
Declining groups												
Drinks and tobacco	11	− 9.2	7.4	5.6	− 3.1	0.4	−4.2	0.16	2.5	1.2	−8.3	−1.7
Railways, ships, etc.	9	3.7	13.4	3.4	−25.8	−2.6	2.7	2.8	0.5	4.2	−1.3	−2.2
Miscellaneous mfg.	16	14.3	7.2	6.4	−24.8	—	−0.1	0.6	2.4	−0.3	−3.9	−6.2
Apparel	13	7.9	16.0	10.6	−20.0	2.7	—	0.3	1.0	3.2	−6.6	−16.1
Textiles	12	− 8.4	7.2	7.5	− 6.6	−0.1	1.8	−0.03	−0.3	0.1	6.6	−10.0
Total declining groups		− 3.8	5.8	6.8	−10.9	1.6	1.0	8.0	3.0	0.2	4.5	−9.1

SOURCE: Calculated from data presented in H. Tyszynski, "World Trade in Manufactured Commodities," *Manchester School of Economic and Social Studies*, September, 1951, pp. 276-282.
[a] West Germany.

by that is meant her failure to concentrate on expanding industries, for Britain lost ground in the stable and declining industries as well as in the expanding ones.[31] She was unable to keep pace with the manufactured products of the expanding industrial nations, and she was unable to retain her competitive position with respect to them in the stable and declining fields as well. It was not the case that Britain's share of world trade in each one of these industry groups remained about the same, while the industries in which she concentrated her production declined in importance. By subtracting a country's share of world trade in the expanding, stable, and declining industries in 1899 from its share in 1937, one can estimate the share of world trade gained or lost by selected countries in each group of industries. This information is summarized in Table 10. In the expanding industries Britain lost ground in each group. However, had she retained in 1937 the share of trade in the iron and steel and engineering industries that she held in 1899, her share of world trade would have fallen only from 32.5 percent to 31.3 percent, instead of to 22.4 percent.[32] Each of the three countries which gained most in its relative importance in world trade—the United States, Japan, and Canada—advanced by means of improving its competitive position in different groups of industries. The American advance was mainly in the expanding industries, that of Canada in the stable ones, and that of Japan in the declining groups. Other countries, such as Germany, gained somewhat in the expanding industries, Belgium in the declining and expanding ones, Italy in all three groups, Switzerland in the stable ones, Sweden and India in the declining industries. France, on the other hand, lost ground in all three industry groups, despite the fact that she experienced a sharp movement from the declining toward the expanding industries.

As can be seen from Table 10, the United States forged ahead in the expanding fields; her share of world trade rose substantially in motor vehicles, in iron and steel, and in industrial equipment. Japan

[31] Cf. Table 10.
[32] Cf. H. Tyszynski, "World Trade in Manufactured Commodities, 1899-1950," *Manchester School of Economics and Social Studies*, September, 1951, pp. 291-292.

and Canada gained in each group of the expanding fields. Britain lost ground in each group. Germany made striking gains in industrial and electrical goods, Belgium in iron and steel, and Sweden in electrical goods. In the stable fields, the United States was unable to maintain her relative position, falling behind in nonferrous metals, but gaining in films. Canada improved her relative position most strikingly in these fields, with nonferrous metals and paper leading her advance. Japan also gained in virtually every one of the expanding groups, and Belgium increased her share substantially in nonferrous metals. Britain lost ground in the stable fields as a whole, and heavily in agricultural equipment—precisely the field in which Germany had the greatest gain. In the fields of declining importance in world trade, Japan and Canada made gains in every group. Japan's greatest gains were in apparel, textiles, and miscellaneous consumer goods. Britain lost ground heavily in the declining industries, particularly in railways and ships and in textiles.

Because of Britain's early economic development, and of the predominant share of the declining industries in the structure of her trade and economy in the nineteenth century, adaptation to the changing pattern of world trade was made more difficult in all fields.[33] In some of the expanding industries Britain showed very rapid domestic growth. This was especially true during the 1920's and 1930's in power, automobiles, electrical machinery, rayon, and chemicals. The proportion of Britain's trade accounted for by the expanding industries increased from 17.7 percent of her total trade in 1899 to 31.2 percent in 1937.[34] While this was a significant shift, it was smaller than the shift of world trade as a whole in these industries.[35] Unfortunately, the extent of the British adjustment was insufficient to relieve her from contraction of export income. Not only was there a world shift toward those industries in which British exports were at all times less important, but in addition there was a decreasing

[33] At the turn of the twentieth century, 62.9 percent of Britain's total exports were in the declining fields. Cf. Table 8.

[34] Cf. Table 8.

[35] Table 8. The difficulty of making frequent and costly shifts of this kind has constituted the most important practical factor in Britain's structural problem. Throughout the period, Britain had shifted resources to relatively new industries, but she had not shifted them on a sufficiently large scale.

importance of exports in each individual British industry.[36] The decline in exports was quite general; it revealed, in part, the world's greater competitive power as compared with that of Britain. The rapid rise of British imports of the new manufactured products told the same story. The underlying trade position was moving against Britain steadily throughout the interwar period; and it had begun much earlier.

After World War II, there was a dramatic reversal of the interwar trend both in productivity and in trade. But some of the long-term forces in the developing structure of world trade seem to have reappeared. In 1946, industrial output per head and manufacturing output per head were perhaps 3 percent lower than the average of the years 1935-1938.[37] Between 1946 and 1950 both increased at the annual rate of 5 percent and 6 percent respectively.[38] The striking fact is not only that the rate of productivity increase appears to have been higher during the postwar years than in the interwar period but also that virtually all industries showed improvements.[39] Moreover, the development of productivity in British industry over the postwar period compares favorably with progress in American industry. In the United States, output per man-hour in manufacturing in 1950 "was about 20% higher than in 1939, and the rate of increase over the postwar years was not substantially different from that in the United Kingdom."[40] Hence, looking beyond the immediate period of recon-

[36] Cf. A. Maizels' discussion of C. T. Saunders' paper, "Consumption of Raw Materials in the United Kingdom: 1851-1950," *Journal of the Royal Statistical Society*, Series A (general), Vol. CXV, Part III, 1952, pp. 313-354, particularly p. 322; R. S. Sayers, review of A. E. Kahn, *Great Britain in the World Economy*, in *Economic History Review*, 2nd series, Vol. I, No. 1, 1948, p. 73.

[37] L. Rostas, "Changes in the Productivity of British Industry, 1945-1950," *Economic Journal*, March, 1952, p. 22.

[38] *Loc. cit.*

[39] On a base of 1948=100, output per head in steel wire improved from 90 in 1935 to 128 in 1951. However, output per head in coal, iron founderies, and nonferrous metals showed rather smaller increases. In various branches of textiles, productivity either improved little (e.g., cotton and rayon weaving) or actually declined (e.g., cotton spinning and doubling). *Loc. cit.*

[40] *Loc. cit.* and MacDougall, *The World Dollar Problem*, p. 131. In the postwar period, productivity per man-hour in manufacturing actually rose faster in western Europe as a whole than in the United States until 1951 and at least as fast thereafter. The same was true of individual countries, but there appeared some tendency for the United Kingdom to lag behind. On a base of 1951=100, the figures for 1955 were as follows: United States, 113; United Kingdom, 110; Netherlands, 116; Italy, 127; France, 119; Austria, 120; W. Germany, 124.

struction and "transition," differential rates of change in productivity over the postwar years do not appear to have been important contributing factors to Britain's long-term balance-of-payments difficulties.[41]

The volume of world trade greatly increased after World War II, and the volume of world trade in manufactures rose at an unprecedented rate. Britain made prodigious efforts to expand her exports; yet her share of world trade from 1937 to 1950 increased by only 2.6 percentage points.[42] Her share of world trade in manufactures rose from 19.1 percent in 1937 to 20.2 percent in 1951, but it fell back to 19.0 percent in 1952,[43] despite the fact that Germany and Japan had not yet returned as strong competitors in world markets. The trend is even more apparent if we examine the trade in world manufactures of the following group of seven countries: Britain, Western Germany, France, Belgium, Sweden, Switzerland, and Italy. These countries conducted 50.4 percent of world trade in manufactures in 1937, only 46.0 percent in 1951, and 43.6 percent in 1952.[44] The share

[41] The fact that American weekly wages in manufacturing, which were about twice the British before World War II, were about 3½ times as high in 1951 suggests that despite any changes in relative productivity that may have occurred during the war, such changes, when translated into relative money prices, probably were not an important cause of Britain's external strains. An index of relative United States to British export prices seems to be consistent with this view:

U.S. : U.K.	Relative Export Prices
1934-1938	0.84
1937	0.79
1948	1.06

Cf. G. D. A. MacDougall, "British and American Exports: A Study Suggested by the Theory of Comparative Costs, Part II," Economic Journal, September, 1952, p. 501. For some relevant arguments to the effect that the real post-World War II background has generally not involved deflation, but only relative degrees of inflation, cf. Svend Laursen, "Productivity, Wages, and the Balance of Payments," Review of Economics and Statistics, May, 1955, pp. 101-109. Since World War II, prices have risen faster in a substantial majority of other countries than they have in the U.S. Cf. I.M.F. International Financial Statistics.

[42] Cf. Table 8.

[43] Cf. Austin Robinson, "The Future of British Imports," The Three Banks Review, March, 1953, p. 8. Britain's share of world trade in manufactures (excl. of Soviet bloc), had declined to approximately 16 percent in 1956. Calculated from G.A.T.T., International Trade 1956, 1957, p. 43, and Bd. of Trade, Report on Overseas Trade, Vol. viii, 1957, p. 1.

[44] Robinson, op. cit.

of the United States, on the other hand, rose from 16.6 percent in 1937 to 28.0 percent in 1952[45] and her share in *total* world trade rose 9.5 percentage points from 1937 to 1950.[46] Canada also made substantial gains. Hence the long-term structural changes in the pattern of world trade had reappeared. But these structural changes in world trade did not operate against Britain's virtual attainment of international balance. It is not the *changing share* in world trade but the *changing absolute volume* of a country's trade that may assist or impede its international adjustment. There is no direct relationship between a country's share in world trade and its balance-of-payments situation. France increased her share of world trade by 3.8 percentage points between 1937 and 1950; she suffered from serious balance-of-payments crises. India improved her share somewhat; she did not suffer from balance-of-payments crises. Belgium's share declined slightly; her balance-of-payments position was strong. Regarding the longer trend, Switzerland's share in world trade declined from 1899 to 1937; she did not suffer from international imbalance. Britain's share declined steadily after the 1870's; yet her external position was not weak before World War I. Insofar as the mechanism of adjustment is concerned, the important thing was not that Britain's share of world trade (and particularly her share of world trade in manufactures) was declining, for it was a declining share of a rapidly *growing* trade. World trade in manufactures, for example, increased threefold between 1880 and 1913.[47] The absolute volume of Britain's trade grew rapidly and this *assisted* the operation of the international mechanism of adjustment.

Britain, France, and Germany were responsible for 60-65 percent of world trade in manufactures in 1913.[48] Between World Wars I and II, the volume of world trade in manufactures never appreciably exceeded that of 1913; the peak of 1926-1930 was hardly above the 1913 level; the average of 1931-1935 was only 76 percent of 1913; and the average of 1936-1938 was 92 percent.[49] The fact that the share of

[45] *Loc. cit.*
[46] Cf. Table 8, which also contains data that follows in text.
[47] Cf. Folke Hilgerdt, *Industrialization and Foreign Trade*, 1945, p. 157.
[48] Cf. Robinson, *loc. cit.*, p. 57.
[49] *Loc. cit.*

Britain in particular was declining markedly within this *reduced total* was the significant factor in impeding her international adjustment. The external strains of the 1930's were in considerable part the result of the need of European countries (especially Britain and France) to adapt themselves to this changing situation. It is probably for this reason (and on the implicit assumption that the volume of world trade in manufactures in the postwar era would either continue to decline or remain the same) that much emphasis has been placed upon the need of European countries to expand their *share* of world trade in order to solve their postwar balance-of-payments problems. In the case of Britain, as a result of wartime and postwar changes in assets and earning position, she was confronted with the necessity of increasing her exports of manufactures by 50 to 100 percent if she was to balance her payments. However, Britain's share in world trade hardly changed between 1937 and 1952; yet her balance of payments by 1952 practically reached equilibrium. As a result of the expansion in the volume of world trade (and particularly in the volume of world trade in manufactures), Britain was able to expand her exports almost 75 percent without the necessity of increasing her *share* in the total.[50] The changing structure of world trade therefore does not in any *direct* sense explain, nor is it responsible for, long-term international imbalance. It is not through changes in the share of world trade but through changes in relative cost structures, price levels, price structures, income levels, and exchange rates that international balance or imbalance may emerge.

CONCLUSIONS

To sum up, differential rates of growth in productivity do not provide a satisfactory general explanation of long-term international

[50] On a base of 1937=100, the volume of world trade in manufactures rose to 170 in 1952. Britain's share of the total remained about the same. It is noteworthy that during this period Britain made remarkable progress in the expanding fields. Her share of world trade in this division rose 7.4 percentage points, while that of the United States rose only 5.8 percent. Britain's share in the stable fields also rose, while her share in the declining fields fell. The United States made her greatest gains in the stable and declining industries. Calculated from Tyszynski, *op. cit.*, pp. 276-286. Obviously, if Britain is not going to increase its *total* output on the same relative scale as, say, the United States and Germany, its share of world trade is likely to decline.

imbalance. A hypothesis expressed in such terms, and designed to explain "the" long-term imbalance of western European countries as a whole vis-à-vis the United States, appears to be refuted by the facts. The disparity in the overall rates of increase of productivity in manufacturing between the United States and the industrial countries of western Europe was shown to be surprisingly small. The only exception was the case of Britain. Theoretically, differential rates of change in productivity *can* cause balance-of-payments difficulties. A more rapid rate of productivity growth in the United States, as compared with Britain, may lead to a decline in United States export prices and, given a lag in the rise of American money incomes, bring about an increase in United States exports over imports. This might force Britain to reduce her export prices relative to American export prices if she is to maintain her trade in balance (or be compelled to lose reserves). The lower the United States price and income elasticities for British imports and the higher the British price and income elasticities for United States imports (the level of money income remaining the same, and the level of real income rising, *mutatis mutandis*, in each country), the more likely are such conditions to prevail. If such conditions were to prevail, Britain would, in effect, tend to suffer from real as well as monetary balance-of-payments difficulties.[51] On the basis of the evidence, it seems probable that at certain times during the interwar period Britain did so suffer. The record of the postwar years, however, suggests that differential rates of productivity growth were not an important factor in Britain's balance-of-payments difficulties. Under conditions of reasonably full employment and a high volume of world trade, price and income elasticities appear

---

[51] Hicks has maintained that under such conditions the country in question (Britain) would not suffer from real (as compared with monetary) balance-of-payments difficulties. *Op. cit.*, pp. 122-124. This seems to me questionable on theoretical grounds. On occasion, Hicks is prone to argue as if stability conditions either in the domestic or in the international sphere could be used to "prove" that a system possesses stable properties because one assumes (as he does) that in capitalist reality the economic system does not explode. Hicks used this device in *Value and Capital*, 1939, and *The Trade Cycle*, 1950, but it is particularly misleading in the field of mechanism-of-adjustment theory. Schumpeter observed that a long-run theoretical system may be explosive while the corresponding reality is not, and a long-run theoretical system may be stable while the corresponding reality is not. J. A. Schumpeter, *History of Economic Analysis*, 1952, p. 1180, n. 22.

to be fairly high in the long run.[52] Under such conditions, differential rates of productivity change are most unlikely to cause international imbalance; the higher the average annual rate of increase of productivity in each country, the greater the flexibility and ease of domestic adjustment to changes in international balances.

Differential rates of change of productivity in the United States, as compared with the industrial countries of western Europe—expressed in terms of American improvements being concentrated on the production of products which compete most closely with those from Europe, as compared with improvements being concentrated on the production of American agricultural and other export products— also do not provide a satisfactory general explanation of long-term international imbalance, so far as mechanism-of-adjustment difficulties are concerned. While theoretically such conditions could produce monetary as well as real mechanism-of-adjustment strains, the available evidence suggests that such conditions did not prevail during the interwar period.

Nor does the changing structure of world trade provide us with a satisfactory explanation of "the" long-term international imbalance of western European industrial countries vis-à-vis the United States. The evidence suggests that before World War II, changes which countries experienced in their relative shares of world trade, and the resulting balance-of-payments strains that this may have occasioned, were not so much due to the structural shifts in world demand for exports as to the ability of each country to compete in world markets for individual groups of commodities. These two forces were not necessarily related, though in the case of Britain an *indirect* relationship probably prevailed. The sheer weight of her early resource allocation in fields which were declining in world trade must have made the problem of adjustment extremely difficult.

Differential rates of productivity growth (either quite uniformly or otherwise distributed) and the changing pattern of world trade therefore probably played an important role in the long-term imbalance of Britain vis-à-vis the United States. But her situation in many respects

[52] For a select bibliography on materials dealing with these issues, see the present writer's "A Note on Demand Elasticities, Income Elasticities, and Foreign Trade Multipliers," *Nordisk Tidsscrift for Teknisk Okonomi*, October, 1953, pp. 39-55.

was quite unique.[53] The root of the difficulty appears to have centered in Britain's relatively lower rate of productivity growth with respect to virtually all industrial countries under conditions of arrested growth in world trade of manufactures during the 1920's, and the actual decline of world trade in manufactures during the 1930's. Britain therefore encountered monetary as well as real balance-of-payments difficulties. It appears to have been erroneous to regard her external strains in the 1920's in monetary terms—the contrary position of Hicks and Keynes notwithstanding. The overvaluation of the pound in 1925 had devastating effects precisely because it was superimposed upon a relatively weak industrial structure. It was the painful task of long-term adjustment to the aforementioned factors which explains, in part, why Britain had difficulty in selling her goods in Canada, the United States, and nearly all industrial countries. It seems not to have been "the increasing productivity of American industry [which] must be regarded as mainly responsible."

High average annual increases of productivity in Britain over the first decade following World War II and expansion in the volume of world trade in manufactures greatly helped to bring about virtual equilibration in her international accounts. The experience of this and earlier periods suggests that a country's *average increase* in productivity and its *absolute volume* of world trade may be more important in assisting (or impeding) the mechanism of adjustment in equilibrating (or disequilibrating) the real variables that require adjustment than the relative rates of change in productivity among countries or their respective share of world trade.

There appear to be no *structural* forces which have been operating *abroad* during the interwar period that provide a satisfactory *general* explanation of long-term imbalance of the industrial countries of western Europe vis-à-vis the United States. In Chapter 10 we shall examine whether such forces have been, or are currently, operating in the United States; and if so, to what extent they have been the result of fundamental processes of economic development, and to what extent they have been the result of abnormal conditions and/or ill-advised policies.

---

[53] In Chapter 9 we discuss in greater detail the relation between Britain's economic development and her long-term international imbalance.

9

Economic Growth and

International Equilibrium

DURING the century preceding World War I the industrialization of Britain and of a number of other European countries, which, like her, were at first comparatively favored by an abundance of natural resources, followed a somewhat common pattern. While theoretical analysis does not (and cannot) neatly fit this complex process of economic development, several fundamental forces appear to have been operating which lend themselves to systematic theoretical formulation and application to the problem of long-term international balance and imbalance. Even such fundamental forces are merely facets of a system of interdependent factors (economic as well as noneconomic) in the general process of economic growth. Hence our objective here must be a modest and tentative one. We shall endeavor to show how certain economic forces have influenced the operation of the international mechanism under different conditions of economic development. These forces may affect the balancing process favorably or unfavorably depending upon circumstances. It is therefore necessary to specify a schema of possible *modi operandi* that would focus attention upon the kinds of circumstances to watch and upon the nature of the effects which they produce.[1]

HYPOTHESIS

The quality of the factors, their geographic location, the resource base, and the resource structure of a country strongly affect its pattern of international trade and payments during economic growth. With respect to the overall trade balance, imports and exports may develop at about the same rate; imports may expand relatively to exports; or exports may rise relatively to imports. The conditions that determine which of these three results occur and the manner in which they are brought about are key factors in assisting or impeding the balancing process. Different conditions and different policy measures of one country, in effect, induce different conditions and different policy measures among its trading partners.

Changes in technical innovations, in training, in the accumulation of capital, in scale of plant, and in demographic developments continually alter the structure of the pattern of costs; changes in national incomes and tastes continually alter the pattern of demand. The hypothesis which we wish to test is whether the law of "comparative cost" and/or "comparative income," operating dynamically through time, from country to country—and hence registering all these influences—provides an important force in assisting or impeding the attainment of international balance under different conditions of economic development. Systematic and detailed research on this problem is long over-due. Our task here is to present briefly the relevant ex-

[1] I have found the following publications suggestive for a framework to relate the problems of economic growth to the international balancing process: Joseph A. Schumpeter, "Theoretical Problems of Economic Growth," *Journal of Economic History*, Supplement VII, 1947, pp. 1-10; Joseph J. Spengler, "Theories of Socio-Economic Growth," *Problems in the Study of Economic Growth*, 1947, pp. 47-111; A. K. Cairncross, *Home and Foreign Investment, 1870-1913*, 1953; Brinley Thomas, *Migration and Economic Growth*, 1954; Joan Robinson, *The Accumulation of Capital*, 1956, Bk. II; Simon Kuznets, *Toward a Theory of Economic Growth*, 1956; Harvey Leibenstein, *Economic Backwardness and Economic Growth*, 1957; and Arthur Smithies, "Economic Fluctuations and Growth," *Econometrica*, January, 1957, pp. 1-52, and sources cited therein.

perience of Britain, Western Europe, and the United States in this particular regard and to examine the generalizations that emerge within a theoretical framework that may be useful in explaining some of the most important relations between economic development and international balance and imbalance.[2]

RECORD EXAMINED: BRITAIN'S INTERNAL AND EXTERNAL BALANCE, 1780's-1850's

After Britain's Industrial Revolution had been under way for several decades, her growing need for foodstuffs and industrial raw materials to feed her expanding population and growing manufacturing industries was reflected in her balance of trade. It is now considered to be clear that in real values Britain was a net importing country throughout the period 1798-1853.[3] Her import surpluses did not begin with the freer trade policies which were launched in the 1840's, but in fact preceded them by many decades. In terms of current values, the best available estimates show that in only four years did Britain have an excess of exports over imports in visible trade during this period. Apparently her invisible credits, the net receipts from the services rendered by shipping, business, insurance, and banking agencies, from the savings of colonial officials and technical experts serving overseas, and, as the volume of foreign investments grew, from interest and dividends on capital placed abroad, made up the proceeds to meet the deficit in Britain's visible trade.[4] Foreigners were also willing to hold substantial amounts of sterling as reserves,

[2] "Economic analysis," writes Joan Robinson, "requires to be supplemented by a kind of comparative historical anthropology which is still in its infancy as a scientific study. Meanwhile economic analysis has by no means completed its own task of clarifying the consequences, and the proximate causes, of differences in, and changes in the rate of accumulation." Op. cit., p. 56. These observations apply even more forcefully to the broader context of economic development and its impact on international balance and imbalance.

[3] Cf. Albert H. Imlah, "The Terms of Trade of the United Kingdom, 1798-1913," Journal of Economic History, November, 1950, pp. 186-188.

[4] The important role of invisible credits is stressed by Imlah, "Real Values in British Foreign Trade," Ibid., November, 1948, p. 149. A characteristic neo-Marxist interpretation is given by Rosa Luxemburg, The Accumulation of Capital, 1951, Section Three.

which they may have earned by way of an excess of exports over imports to Britain.[5]

While the volume of imports and exports did not increase at equal rates throughout the period, the average annual percentage rate of change from 1793 to 1847 was very close: the volume of total imports rose 3.2 percent per year and the volume of total exports rose 3.4 percent per year.[6] If we exclude the war years of 1793-1815, we find that from 1815 to 1847 the volume of total imports rose 3.6 percent per year, while the volume of total exports rose only 2.8 percent per year. The balanced rate of growth between imports and exports for the period as a whole (with the absolute value of imports exceeding that of exports) was a stabilizing force in the international mechanism. As the economy developed, Britain's rate of economic growth was held in check by domestic and foreign conditions: at home by the relatively limited resource base; abroad by the extent of the market.[7]

From 1781 to 1913 the rate of growth of Britain's industrial output measured in terms of the average percentage increase per year was, according to Hoffmann, approximately 2.8.[8] From 1820 to 1860 it was

[5] Cf. R. C. O. Matthews, "The Trade Cycle in Great Britain, 1790-1850," *Oxford Economic Papers*, February, 1954, pp. 24-25; and *A Study in Trade-Cycle History: Economic Fluctuations in Great Britain, 1833-42*, 1954, pp. 75-83.

[6] These figures and the ones that immediately follow are given in Table 12.

[7] J. R. Hicks, "An Inaugural Lecture," *Oxford Economic Papers*, n.s., June, 1953, p. 129: "Though the division of labour will be limited in Adam Smith's famous phrase, by the extent of the market—or, as we should say, by the inelasticity of foreign demand—such relative inelasticity of foreign demand is at this stage a stabilizing factor. It prevents the advancing countries from advancing too rapidly in relation to the rest, and thus from upsetting the international equilibrium." For indication of the limitational nature of Britain's population-resource base at existing levels of technology, see Brinley Thomas, "Migration and the Rhythm of Economic Growth, 1830-1913," *Manchester School of Economic and Social Studies*, September, 1951, pp. 215-272; *Migration and Economic Growth, op. cit.*, Part III, *passim*, p. 224: "The evolution of the Atlantic community could be described in terms of two frontiers—the ever-widening frontier of surplus population in the Old World and the moving frontier of economic opportunity in the New."

[8] Walther G. Hoffmann, *British Industry, 1700-1950*, trans. W. O. Henderson and W. H. Chaloner, 1955, Part A, Vol. III, esp. pp. 34-35, 45-57; "The Growth of Industrial Production in Great Britain: A Quantitative Study," *Economic History Review*, 2nd series, Vol. II, No. 2, 1949, pp. 165-168. Hoffmann's index for the period 1700 to 1780 is "0.7 or 0.8." The growth of foreign trade during this period also was slow and steady, somewhat over one percent per year. Cf. Werner Schlote, *British Overseas Trade from 1700 to the 1930's*, trans. W. O. Henderson and W. H. Chaloner, 1953, p. 43; and F. J. Fisher, "London's Export Trade in the Early Seventeenth Century," *Economic History Review*, 2nd series,

TABLE 12. Average Annual Percentage Rate of Change in Britain's Population, Production, Prices, Foreign Trade, and Financial Instruments, 1793-1847

	1793-1815	1815-1847	1793-1847
Population of England and Wales	1.5 (1801-1815)	1.4	1.4 (1801-1847)
Production			
Hoffmann's index of consumers' goods production	1.9	3.2	2.7
Hoffmann's index of producers' goods production	2.3	4.3	3.5
Hoffmann's index of total production	2.0	3.5	2.9
Kondratieff's index of textile production	2.7	5.2	4.5
Production of coal	1.6 (1803-1815)	3.4 (1816-1846)	2.6 (1803-1847)
Production of iron	4.4 (1796-1818)	6.5 (1818-1847)	5.6 (1796-1847)
Prices			
Index of prices of imported commodities	1.7	−2.8	−1.0
Index of prices of domestic commodities	1.8	−1.1	0.1
Gazette price of wheat	2.2	−1.4	0.1
Price of British pig iron	0.8	−1.5	−0.5
Price of Sunderland coal	1.6	−1.9	−0.6
Price of cotton piece goods' exports	—	−4.5	—
Price of raw cotton, including duty	−0.5	−4.7	−3.0
Foreign Trade			
Volume of domestic exports	3.8	3.8	3.8
Volume of total imports	2.6	3.6	3.2

	(1807-1815)		(1807-1847)
Volume of total exports	4.1	2.8	3.4
Volume of domestic exports	1.4	0.8	0.9
Volume of exports of cotton manufactures	10.6	5.1	7.3
Consumption of raw cotton	5.5	6.3	6.0
Volume of exports of woolen manufactures	1.6	2.4	2.1
Volume of exports of iron, hardware, and cutlery	1.6	5.6	3.9
Quantity of wheat imports	4.1	5.6	5.0
Volume of reëxports	—	0.3	—
Finance	(1795-1815)		(1795-1847)
Bills and notes discounted at the Bank of England	8.1	-2.6	1.4
Yield on 3 percent consols	0.8	-1.1	-0.4
Total public and private advances by the Bank of England	5.7	-3.9	-0.2
	(1795-1815)	(1815-1846)	(1795-1846)
Bank of England notes in circulation	3.9	-0.8	1.1
Bullion in the Bank of England	0.3	3.2	2.1

SOURCE: A. D. Gayer, W. W. Rostow, A. J. Schwartz, and I. Frank, *The Growth and Fluctuation of the British Economy*, 1790-1850, 1953, p. 625. For critical review articles of this work, and of some of the estimates cited in it, cf. R. C. O. Matthews, "The Trade Cycle in Great Britain, 1790-1850," *Oxford Economic Papers*, February, 1954; J. F. Wright, "An Index of the Output of British Industry Since 1700," *Journal of Economic History*, September, 1956, pp. 356-364; and P. Deane, "Professor Hoffmann on the Growth of British Industry," *Economic Journal*, September, 1956, pp. 493-500. At best, the indices of production and trade are to be taken as first approximations.

as high as 3 percent; but in the years immediately preceding World War I it was only about 1 percent.[9] Such rapid and changing rates of economic growth had striking effects on, and were interdependent with, Britain's international specialization; it affected the structure, the terms, the volume, and the direction of her foreign trade.[10]

The rapid industrial expansion which occurred in the 1780's continued to center in manufactured consumption goods, primarily textiles.[11] At first coal was in short supply, but soon its output increased.[12] The output of iron and bar iron grew rapidly.[13] Exports of coal and iron rose though textiles were considerably more dependent

---

Vol. III, 1950, esp. p. 159; "Commercial Trends and Policy in Sixteenth-Century England," *ibid.*, Vol. X, 1940, p. 95; and Lawrence Stone, "Elizabethan Overseas Trade," *ibid.*, Vol. II, 1949, p. 50, for interesting studies on the comparative stability of earlier English foreign trade.

[9] Hoffmann, "The Growth of Industrial Production in Great Britain . . . ," *op. cit.*, p. 178.

[10] For convincing evidence that Britain's gradual social, political, and economic developement from the 1550's to the 1780's was a necessary condition for the more rapid industrial expansion which occurred in the late eighteenth and nineteenth centuries, cf. T. S. Ashton, *An Economic History of England: The 18th Century,* 1955, esp. Chaps. II, III, and IV, which are full of relevant fact and wisdom on this subject; and John U. Nef, *The Rise of the British Coal Industry,* 1932, Vol. II, pp. 3-134, 319-330. "If the origin of industrial capitalism is to be explained," writes Nef, "as it surely must be, by a concatenation of causes, it is especially important to search for them in this [the earlier] period," p. 320, *passim.* What marks off the economic history of Great Britain in this period from that of her continental neighbors is both the extent of general economic development— with striking investment in so-called "social capital"—and the difference in the kind of industry which developed. English agriculture also obtained a new technological base during these centuries and this served as an essential prelude to the industrial revolution. Consequently, at the beginning of the eighteenth century the economic structure of England was predominantly self-sufficient. Exports were based on the utilization of plentiful indigenous resources. Down to 1730 England was an exporter rather than an importer of grain. Imports consisted primarily of manufactures and produce of other climates. The ratio of retained imports to net national income was only about 5 percent. Approximately 70 percent of the gainfully employed population was engaged in agriculture; perhaps 40 percent of the gross national product was derived from it. Cf. E. A. G. Robinson, "The Changing Structure of the British Economy," *Economic Journal,* September, 1954, pp. 444-458. As the eighteenth century evolved, industrial advance became most marked in the producers' goods industries: in the means of transport, the output of coal, iron, copper, cotton and woolen yarn, and other semifinished products.

[11] Ashton, *op. cit.,* pp. 94 ff.; A. D. Gayer, *et al., The Growth and Fluctuation of British Economy,* Vol. II, pp. 648-652.

[12] Nef, *op. cit.,* Vol. I, pp. 19-20, 165.

[13] Gayer, *et al., op. cit.,* Vol. I, p. 194.

upon the external market.[14] From the 1780's to the 1850's, textiles were the major item of British export; and they were matched by an expanding demand for raw materials and food imports. The importance of all this for our analysis rests in the fact that Britain's resource endowments, economic growth, and foreign trade were in reasonably good balance.

The increasing domestic supply of coal and iron, the emerging entrepreneurial-labor milieu, the growing home and foreign markets, the expanding demand for imports of abundantly available cotton, wool, and flax—all, in effect, were interrelated in enabling Britain to acquire a very satisfactory industrial complex for the kind of economic development and foreign trade that she undertook.[15]

From 1795 to 1815, British wartime expenditures involved considerable capital outflow and this produced an "abnormal" expansion of exports. On a base of 1880 = 100, the volume of domestic exports rose from an index of 3.4 in 1789 to 7.4 in 1815; the volume of net imports, though larger than exports in every year, rose but little from an index of 6.7 to 7.6. From 1816 to 1825, however, the import-volume index more than doubled, rising from an index of 6.1 to 12.6, whereas the export-volume index increased only from an index of 6.3 to 8.3. During this period the gross barter terms of trade (the ratio of import-volume index to export-volume index) thus rose from an index of 97 to 152. Thereafter, from 1826 to 1846, the import-volume index rose from 10.2 to 21.7, the export-volume index from 7.2 to 23.3. Practically throughout the period of 1815 to 1850, in volume terms, Britain was more of an importing country than an exporting country, even more so when compared with the later period of 1850

---

[14] "After 1782," observes Ashton, "almost every statistical series of production shows a sharp upward turn. More than half the growth in the shipments of coal and the mining of copper, more than three-quarters of the increase of broadcloths, four-fifths of that of printed cloth, and nine-tenths of the exports of cotton goods were concentrated in the last eighteen years of the century. After 1782 Englishmen turned, more than at any previous period, to the development of resources at home." *Op. cit.*, pp. 125-126 and Statistical Appendix, pp. 239-254.

[15] The secular trends in Britain's production, population, trade, and finance are summarized in Tables 13 and 14. For a discussion of the emerging entrepreneurial-labor milieu, cf. Reinhard Bendix, *Work and Authority in Industry*, 1956, Chap. II, entitled, "Entrepreneurial Ideologies in the Early Phase of Industrialization: The Case of England."

TABLE 13. Secular Movements in British Foreign Trade: Weighted Average Change Per Month from Cycle to Cycle

(In Percentages)

Volume of total exports (1793-1846)	+0.27
Volume of reëxports (1793-1848)	+0.16
Volume of domestic exports (1793-1847)	+0.30
Volume of exports of domestic mfrs. (1816-1847)	+0.36
Volume of exports of domestic raw materials (1816-1850)	+0.45
Volume of exports of domestic foodstuffs (1816-1848)	−0.05
Volume of exports of cotton mfrs. (1793-1847)	+0.58
Volume of exports of woolen mfrs. (1793-1848)	+0.15
Volume of exports of iron, hardware, and cutlery (1795-1848)	+0.33
Volume of exports of brass and copper mfrs. (1819-1854)	+0.34
Volume of total imports (1793-1850)	+0.27
Quantity of raw cotton imports (1791-1846)	+0.47
Quantity of raw wool imports (1791-1847)	+0.47
Quantity of flax imports (1806-1851)	+0.29
Quantity of hemp and jute imports (1805-1852)	+0.09
Quantity of fir timber imports (1789-1839)	+0.18
Quantity of wheat imports (1795-1848)	+0.26
Quantity of raw sugar imports (1795-1850)	+0.17

SOURCE: Adapted from tables in A. D. Gayer, et al., The Growth and Fluctuation of British Economy, Vol. II, pp. 722-731.

to 1870.[16] All the indices of the rate of growth of production and trade were higher during this peaceful period of 1815-1850 than during the Napoleonic Wars.[17] Technological progress and expansion

[16] Cf. tables in Imlah, "The Terms of Trade of the United Kingdom, 1798-1913," op. cit., May, 1950, pp. 177-182.

[17] Gayer, et al., op. cit., Vol. II, pp. 623-658. The authors show that ". . . major expansion of British industrial plant took place in the second (1815-1850) and not in the first (1790-1815) secular period." P. 646. During the war years, total production (including the output of war goods) increased approximately 2 percent per year and the population grew by 1.5 per cent per year. The trend of food prices was upward, and though the same was true of the skilled-man's income and of the semiskilled and the laborer's wage, there was strain on resources, and that, together with variations in the yield of crops, probably reduced the real earnings of domestic workers and of many unskilled laborers from the 1790's to the close of the Napoleonic Wars. Ibid., p. 955. Cf. T. S. Ashton, "The Standard of Life of the Workers in England, 1790-1830," Journal of Economic History, Supplement IX, 1949, pp. 19-38; W. W. Rostow, British Economy of the Nineteenth Century, 1947, pp. 13-14; and Sidney and Beatrice Webb, English Poor Law History: Part II—The Last Hundred Years, 1929, pp. 4-7. The thesis that epochs of peace, rather than war, fundamentally have been responsible for economic (as well as noneconomic) progress is developed by John U. Nef in War and Human Progress, 1952, cf. esp. Chap. XV, "The Industrial Revolution Reconsidered."

TABLE 14. Secular Movements in British Foreign Trade: Weighted
Average Change per Month from Cycle to Cycle
(In Percentages)

Value of total exports (1803-1848)	+0.07
Value of reëxports (1803-1850)	+0.07
Value of domestic exports (1803-1848)	+0.08
Value of exports of domestic mfrs. (1817-1848)	+0.11
Value of exports of domestic raw materials (1816-1850)	+0.35ᵃ
Value of exports of domestic foodstuffs (1816-1848)	−0.24
Value of exports of cotton mfrs. (1816-1846)	+0.12
Value of exports of woolen mfrs. (1817-1848)	+0.03
Value of exports of iron, hardware, and cutlery (1797-1803, 1817-1848)	+0.26
Value of exports of brass and copper mfrs. (1816-1851)	+0.22
Value of total imports (1804-1850)	+0.14
Balance of trade (1802-1850)	+0.07
Gross barter terms of trade (1789-1850)	
Volume of exports divided by volume of imports	+0.02
Net barter terms of trade (1802-1847)	
Import prices divided by export prices	+0.14

SOURCE: Adapted from tables in A. D. Gayer, et al., *The Growth and Fluctuation of British Economy*, Vol. II, pp. 722-731.
ᵃ Largely minerals.

were the principal features of the era: domestic investment increased rapidly, real costs fell, and the volume of production rose at an unprecedented rate.

DISADVANTAGE IN AGRICULTURE

Though Britain was well endowed with key industrial raw materials for her economic growth, she was relatively poor in agricultural resources. The accelerated expansion of the coal and iron industries, for example, can be related directly to the growing requirements of domestic railway construction in the 1830's and 1840's.[18] Between 1815 and 1847 the production of coal rose 3.4 percent per year and the production of iron 6.5 percent per year. The price of coal fell on the average 1.9 percent per year and the price of iron 1.5 percent per year. The price of wheat, on the other hand, *rose relatively* to the

[18] Gayer, et al., op. cit., Vol. II, p. 650; C. R. Fay, *Round About Industrial Britain, 1830-1860*, 1952, pp. 81-98.

price of coal and iron; it fell on the average 1.4 percent per year. However, the production of wheat rose at a much *slower* pace than that of coal or iron, indicating that relative changes in costs were making it comparatively unprofitable for British agriculture to expand crop production.[19] For short-term intervals, as demand rose and costs increased, the domestic price of wheat also rose.[20] In the 1820's and 1830's, Britain's imports of grains increased, though they fluctuated violently.[21] The home price of wheat rose from 55.3 shillings per quarter in 1829–1836 to 64.3 shillings per quarter in 1837-1841.[22] Wheat imports for consumption increased from 57.5 thousand metric tons to over 385 thousand metric tons during the same period.[23] Home production failed to meet the expanding demand. Even when the home price of wheat was rising, increased costs of production checked the growth in output. Britain's disadvantage in producing crops such as wheat was made abundantly clear by the very rapid increase in imports which occurred after the drop in duty in 1846.[24] By the beginning of the 1850's, imports of wheat had reached 20 percent of Britain's production, and eventually they exceeded domestic output.[25] Diminishing returns in the production of grains appear to have manifested themselves in two ways. First, there was a tendency toward reduced output per unit of input as production expanded and natural resources of lower quality were brought into use. This, however, was not of major significance. Technological advance apparently offset somewhat the deterioration in the quality of marginal agricultural resources as rising output pressed on available land. Much more important was the second impact of diminishing returns: it had the effect of restricting the expansion of crops whose output could be increased only at sharply increasing costs. *The tendency toward historical diminishing returns revealed itself not so much in absolute*

[19] Cf. Table 12; and Schlote, *op. cit.*, pp. 60-62.
[20] Gayer, *et al.*, *op. cit.*, p. 826, *passim*.
[21] *Ibid.*, p. 758.
[22] Schlote, *op. cit.*, p. 61.
[23] *Loc. cit.*
[24] Net wheat and wheat flour imports (in 1,000 quarters) amounted to 2291.1 in 1846, 4366.4 in 1847, 2986.6 in 1848, 4660.1 in 1849, and 4691.8 in 1850. Gayer, *et al.*, *op. cit.*, Vol. I, p. 307.
[25] Schlote, *op. cit.*, p. 62.

lower efficiency but in relatively lower expansion of output. For Britain, in other words, the relative mechanization of industry had made further expansion of agriculture less profitable than that of manufacturing.

COMPOSITION OF IMPORTS

From the Napoleonic Wars till the mid-nineteenth century, in absolute terms, Britain's imports of foodstuffs increased continually. After the 1840's their relative share showed a marked increase as compared with raw materials and finished goods. The composition of Britain's imports, expressed as a percentage of total volume, is shown in Table 15.

TABLE 15. Composition of Britain's Total Imports, 1814-1850
(In Percentages)

Year	Finished Goods	Raw Materials	Foodstuffs
1814	11.3	48.1	40.6
1825	8.3	66.9	24.8
1840	5.6	66.9	27.5
1850	7.1	59.2	33.7

SOURCE: A. D. Gayer, *et al.*, *The Growth and Fluctuation of the British Economy*, Vol. II, p. 785.

The decade after 1814 depicts postwar adjustment. Foodstuffs as a percentage of Britain's total imports fell, but this merely reflected a decline in the import of colonial goods for reëxport to the continent. The tendency for food imports to rise thereafter is to be expected in view of the predominantly industrial character of Britain's development from 1814 to 1850. It is to be accounted for mainly by the increasing relative volume of imports of grain, meat, tea, and sugar.[26]

Britain's total home production of foodstuffs reached a level in the 1850's which was seldom surpassed before World War II. The production of crops actually declined in the second half of the nineteenth century, clearly attesting to Britain's comparative advantage in other fields.

[26] Gayer, *op. cit.*, Vol. II, pp. 784-796, *passim.*

The growth and composition of Britain's imports of raw materials also have been determined primarily by its changing "comparative advantage" and "comparative mechanization," which, in turn, have been affected by the country's technological development, its resource structure and base. From 1814 to 1825 the relative increase in imports of raw materials was not due to any specific change in industrial demand, but was for the most part an indication of the aforementioned decline in imports of colonial foodstuffs for reëxport. From 1825 to 1840, however, the proportion of raw-material imports remained remarkably stable. The percentage decline from 1840 to 1850 manifestly was interrelated with the proportional growth in imports of foodstuffs; nonetheless, it suggests that Britain was at this time comparatively better able to draw upon her domestic resources for raw materials than for foodstuffs. With respect to some important raw materials, such as coal, iron, and other minerals, Britain was endowed sufficiently well to provide both for her own expanding industries and to increase her exports. In the aggregate, the absolute volume of her raw-material imports rose during the first half of the nineteenth century and, in effect, was closely correlated with the level of industrial production.[27] Britain's comparative advantage lay not only in the manufacture of consumers' goods and the production of key minerals, it lay also in the reëxport of raw materials. Her commercial expertise in this reëxport trade made an important contribution to her balance of payments and to the economic development of western Europe. The British Isles became a kind of "free port," with earnings derived from the growing reëxport trade contributing substantially to meeting Britain's deficit on current account.[28]

[27] The close correlation between the index of net import volume of raw materials and the index of industrial production from 1814 to 1933 is shown in Schlote, *op. cit.*, p. 56. Cf. also C. T. Saunders, "Consumption of Raw Materials in the United Kingdom: 1851-1950," *Journal of the Royal Statistical Society*, Series A (General), Vol. CXV, Part III, 1952, p. 334, where it is shown that since 1913 a combined index of raw-material consumption lagged behind the index of industrial production. On a base 1907-1913=100, the index of raw-material consumption rose from 29 for the period 1851-1856 to 97 for the period 1902-1906; the index of industrial production rose only from 31 to 90. However, from 1909-1913 to 1948-1950, the index of industrial production rose from 100 to 222, whereas the combined index of raw-material consumption rose only from 100 to 149. Apparently since 1913 Britain has required a smaller amount of raw-material inputs per unit of industrial output.

[28] Schlote, *op. cit.*, Statistical Appendix, pp. 127-130.

Rising levels of income of larger sections of Britain's population resulted in an expansion and diversification of her imports. The importation of finished manufactures increased steadily from the 1830's and in relation to total imports grew from about the 1840's.[29] Similarly, the *proportion* of "luxury" foodstuffs declined and the proportion of mass-consumed foodstuffs increased. These developments were gradual and quite continuous. But they too showed up markedly with the spread of Britain's mechanization and the rise in real incomes during the period of fundamental tariff reforms between 1842 and 1860. They were especially accelerated after the completion of her free-trade policy.

COMPOSITION OF EXPORTS

The *modi operandi* of Britain's economic development and balance of payments may be further checked with respect to exports. In the first half of the nineteenth century, no less than 75 percent of Britain's home-produced exports were manufactured articles; at times the figure was as high as 87 percent. Generally, "finished goods" constituted over 80 percent of the volume and about 90 percent of the value of total domestic exports.[30] Britain, as we have noted, was at this time mainly a textile economy; in the 1820's, textiles made up 78 percent of her exports of finished manufactured home products.[31] Between 1814 and 1817, foodstuffs (including livestock) constituted 17.5 percent of total home-produced exports; but the proportion fell rapidly. By 1838-1840, it amounted to only 5.4 percent of the total. Raw materials, on the other hand, constituted 3.7 percent of the volume and 1.7 percent of the value of home-produced exports in 1814. But these proportions rose throughout the period. By 1850, they amounted to 8.1 percent of the volume and 5.8 percent of the value of home-produced exports.[32] The upward secular trend in the volume and value series of home-produced raw-material exports was actually

[29] *Ibid.*, p. 68; and Table 15, p. 225, above.
[30] Schlote, *op. cit.*, p. 71.
[31] *Ibid.*, p. 74. Nonferrous metal goods, chemicals, pottery, and porcelain, as well as leather goods, furs, and skins, were represented in Britain's list of manufactured exports during this period.
[32] *Ibid.*, pp. 124-125. Among the major items were such products as coal, pig iron, tin, copper, wool, salt, and alum.

steeper than that for finished goods or for total domestic exports.[33]
The secular decline in the relative importance of Britain's exports
of foodstuffs between 1814 and 1850 and the relative rise in exports
of finished manufactures and raw materials again demonstrate the
predominantly industrial character of Britain's development during
this period. The relative rise in her exports of industrial raw materials
confirms the proposition that Britain was relatively well endowed
with some of the most important raw materials required for the kind
of economic development which she pursued.[34]

TERMS OF TRADE

The intensive economic development of Britain during the first half
of the nineteenth century was to be matched only by the extensive
economic development of the United States, and both forces strongly
influenced the terms of trade. On a base of 1880 = 100, Britain's
export-price index fell from 430.4 in 1798 to 277.9 in 1818, and to
102.2 in 1850. The import-price index rose from 193.6 in 1798 to

[33] *Ibid.*, p. 71; and see Fig. 11, p. 229, below.

[34] In the main, Britain had to rely on her own resources for her rapid economic
development. The capital required was created by the act of domestic investment,
probably through the plowing back of profits by merchants and manufacturers,
with substantial contributions from the nobility and gentry. To a large extent
the increased labor required in manufacturing, collieries, transportation, etc., was
provided by the natural increase in population. "The north of England triumphed
over the south," writes Cairncross, "mainly by superior fertility (and not, as we
used to be taught, by attracting migrants)." *Op. cit.*, p. 79. But there was, of
course, some exodus from agriculture and from domestic services which assisted
the process of economic growth. Britain's economic development is no exception to
the general rule that it is home resources and domestic materials which must
chiefly be relied upon to effect industrialization, simply because so much real
capital is immovable in international trade. This theme is developed by Norman
S. Buchanan in *International Investment and Domestic Welfare*, 1945, p. 19 ff.,
and Norman S. Buchanan and Howard S. Ellis, *Approaches to Economic Development*, 1955, Parts I and II. Cf. also W. Arthur Lewis, *The Theory of Economic
Growth*, 1955, pp. 225-283; and E. A. G. Robinson, "The Changing Structure of
the British Economy," *op. cit.*, pp. 445-446 and p. 458: The approximate ratio
of Britain's retained imports to net national income at factor cost in 1812-1820
still was only 12 percent. However, by 1820-1830 the economic structure of
Britain was beginning to alter. Exports were composed now of about 50 percent
of indigenous products of the United Kingdom and manufactures made from
them. Imports of materials were about 60 percent of total imports, out of which
textile materials, mainly cotton, accounted for about 24 percent. Foreign supplies
of food represented approximately one-seventh of total supplies.

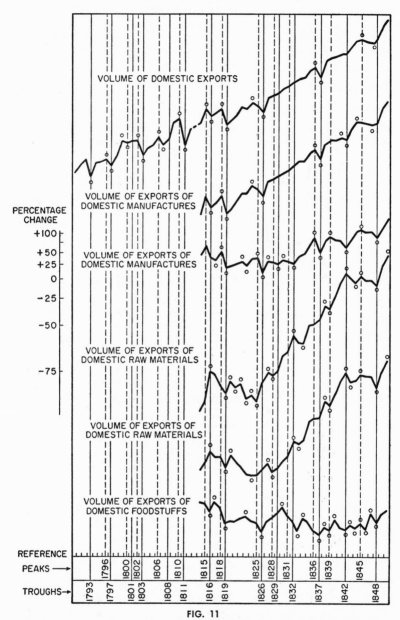

FIG. 11

Source: A. D. Gayer, et al., *The Growth and Fluctuation of the British Economy*, Vol. II, Oxford: The Clarendon Press, 1953, p. 744.

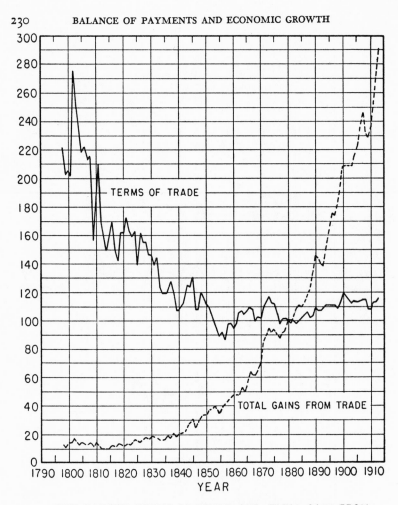

NET BARTER TERMS OF TRADE AND TOTAL GAIN FROM
TRADE OF THE UNITED KINGDOM, 1798-1913

FIG. 12

196.8 in 1818, but fell thereafter to 91.0 in 1850. Britain's net barter terms of trade (export-price index over import-price index) therefore fell throughout the period; the ratio declined from 222.3 in 1798 to 141.2 in 1818, and to 112.3 in 1850.[35]

[35] See Fig. 12 constructed from data in Imlah, "The Terms of Trade of the United Kingdom, 1798-1913," *op. cit.*, pp. 177-182.

A ratio between price indices over so many years may be expected roughly to reflect indices of productivity, though in effect it reflects all the forces operating on a country's economy. Since in the early stages of Britain's economic development major emphasis was placed upon consumer-goods exports, one would therefore expect that as Britain developed her comparative cost advantage in cottons and woolens, the price of textile exports would be sensitive to changes in productivity relative to money wages on the one hand, and to changes in raw cotton and wool prices on the other.

The tremendous decline in Britain's export prices from 1798 to 1850 can be attributed primarily to the rapid application of cost-reducing machine methods of manufacture in the major export industries.[36] In no export industry did prices fall more rapidly than in cottons, where the new techniques were most extensively applied. From 1816-1818 to 1849-1851, export prices of cottons fell 72 percent. In the woolen industry, mechanization was somewhat less thorough; export prices fell 63 percent. Other industries, which were less mechanized, reduced their prices by less.[37]

The decline in export prices resulted also from extensive development in the growth of cotton in the United States during the 1820's and 1830's. However, cotton costs were only about 20 percent of the total cost of finished fabrics.[38] Since the price of finished fabrics fell by much more than 20 percent, the decline in Britain's textile prices must be accounted for principally by the technological revolution.[39]

[36] The index of money wages in the textile trades indicates a slow decline from 1807 to 1831 and a gradual rise from 1831 to 1850. Secularly, money wages were fairly stable from 1815 to 1850. But the cost of living index dropped sharply; hence real wages rose by perhaps as much as 50 percent during the period. (See Kondratieff's index of money wages in the textile industry and Tucker's index of money wages, the cost of living, and real wages of London artisan's in Gayer, et al., op. cit., Vol. II, pp. 950-953).

[37] See Imlah, "The Terms of Trade of the United Kingdom, 1798-1913," op. cit., pp. 183-184.

[38] Cf. E. Baines, History of the Cotton Manufacture, 1835, p. 353.

[39] "The decline in cotton export prices," writes Rostow, "resulted mainly from the interaction of two long-period developments: the fall in the costs of growing, transporting, and cleaning raw cotton, especially in the United States; and the rising productivity of manufacture in England. . . . The net downward effect on the terms of trade of the movement of cotton export prices down to 1830 must be accounted principally a consequence of the technological revolution. This conclusion in no way alters the basic interdependence of the technological revolutions

In neither America nor Europe at this time were improvements and mechanization in food production on a scale to match the growth in textiles. Though diminishing marginal productivity in agriculture, for a given resource complex, was more than offset by historical increasing returns brought about by the expanding supply of resources and improving techniques, the price of foodstuffs (particularly wheat) fell slowly from 1820 to 1850. As people moved into new agricultural lands in America, labor became relatively scarce, its earnings rose and this probably prevented agricultural foodstuff prices from falling by as much as the price of cotton. These factors contribute somewhat to an explanation of the fall in Britain's net barter terms of trade. But, primarily, the explanation lies in the enormous expansion and technical improvements which took place in her major export industries. With increasing productivity, comparatively stable money wages, and rising real wages on the one hand, and with growing demand for her manufactures on the other, the fall in Britain's export prices was a reflection of the improvement in her single factoral terms of trade.[40]

The fall in Britain's net barter terms of trade produced no balance-of-payments difficulties. As regards gains from trade, Britain's export-gain-from-trade index rose from 8 in 1798 to 10 in 1818, and to 35 in 1850.[41] The greatest gain was actually made when Britain's *export prices* were falling most rapidly (i.e., from 1818 to 1850). Britain's total-gain-from-trade index rose from 12 in 1798 to 13 in 1818, and to 33 in 1850. Deterioration in net barter terms of trade was, under the prevailing circumstances, clearly consistent with improvement in national welfare.

---

in manufacture and cotton growth." W. W. Rostow, "The Historical Analysis of the Terms of Trade," *Economic History Review*, 2nd series, Vol. IV, No. 1, 1951, p. 59 and pp. 61-62.

[40] The relationship which is most relevant to a discussion of changes in the absolute standard of living of a country as affected by foreign trade is the *single* factoral terms of trade, which is a ratio of "interchange" between units of domestic productive power and the volume of imports. It is probably unnecessary to point out that the single factoral terms of trade may improve concurrently for both (all) trading countries as their productivity rises. See D. H. Robertson, "The Terms of Trade," *International Social Science Bulletin*, Spring, 1951, pp. 28-33; and William H. Fink, *Ratios of International Exchange and Their Relation to National Welfare and Advantage*, unpublished Ph.D. dissertation, 1954, Chaps. 3 and 4.

[41] Imlah, "The Terms of Trade of the United Kingdom, 1798-1913," *op. cit.*, pp. 177-182. See Fig. 12, p. 230, above.

Intensive and extensive improvements in export industries were beginning to be made among virtually all the trading countries of the world. Just as the developing structure of Britain's exports and imports was at this time complementary with her needs and resources, so was it complementary with the needs and resources of the newly developing countries in Europe and abroad.

BRITAIN'S PIVOTAL POSITION

The United Kingdom was emerging as the nucleus of a wider community of nations whose economies were undergoing dynamic transformation. Propelled by domestic changes in comparative productivity, Britain's economic development at the end of the first half of the nineteenth century was contingent upon freer trade for its further rapid industrialization. Mechanization had stimulated the need for freer trade; freer trade, in turn, became a requisite for increased mechanization. Had Britain remained more protectionist and more self-sufficient, she also would have remained less mechanized and less prosperous. The operation of free trade furnished labor and capital with strong incentives to migrate toward industry and helped liberate resources for capital formation. By adopting free trade, Britain made herself dependent on food in the interests of her own national prosperity as well as that of world trade and development. Once the course was launched, the emerging pattern of her trade and payments became inextricably linked with the form of her economic growth.

The spread of mechanization in British industry, coupled with the innovating force of free trade, generated a complementary movement of labor and capital from England to the "young" underdeveloped countries.[42] John Stuart Mill referred to this evolving "larger community" as the Anglo-Saxon economic sphere which comprised the colonial settlements overseas and the United States. He, and other

[42] For suggestive discussions on this issue see Brinley Thomas, *Migration and Economic Growth*, *op. cit.*, pp. 1-25; and Ragnar Nurkse, "International Investment Today in the Light of Nineteenth Century Experience," *Economic Journal*, December, 1954, pp. 744-758; "A New Look at the Dollar Problem and the U.S. Balance of Payments," *Economica Internazionale*, February, 1954, pp. 52-58; and *Problems of Capital Formation in Underdeveloped Countries*, 1953, pp. 24-29, 79-107.

classical theorists, did not regard foreign trade with the colonies as foreign trade at all; it was considered an appendage to domestic trade. When the classical economists dealt with the theory of international trade, they appeared to have in mind the commerce between England and the "old" countries outside the British "economic sphere." In such cases it was perhaps not too unrealistic to assume the absence of international flows of labor and capital, for the predominant flows were to the rich lands of recent settlement.

Nonetheless, the aforementioned assumptions suggest that, at least to some outstanding writers of the period, the balancing process between Britain and the "underdeveloped areas" was not considered a problem. The complementary movement of labor and capital from Britain to its "economic sphere," which emerged on a large scale for the first time in the 1840's and 1850's, contributed much to the comparatively smooth functioning of the international mechanism and gave some credence to the classical assumptions themselves.[43]

Migration provided the United States with additional manpower and demand for the investment boom of the 1850's. This upsurge of economic activity, spearheaded by railway development, was dependent not only on favorable American conditions and displaced European labor, but also on British capital. British foreign investments supplemented American savings and thereby assisted the absorption of Europe's redundant workers into the growing economy of the United States. The recurrent excess of savings over domestic investment in Britain on the one hand, and the excess of investment over domestic savings in the regions of recent settlement on the other, were an integral part of the evolving process of economic development. Mechanization and free trade in Britain, probably with an increased rate of investment as a percentage of national income,

[43] The number of migrants to America, which had been 20,000 in 1843, reached 220,000 in 1851. Of the 2,093,000 who landed in America from Europe between 1849 and 1854, 80 percent came from Ireland and Germany. For the most part, they were driven out by population pressure, by the transformation of agriculture, and by free trade. The revolution in transport had by 1852 so reduced the cost of passage that the fare from Liverpool to New York had dropped to approximately £2 per person, and this for the first time made migration to America possible on mass scale. Cf. Brinley Thomas, *Migration and Economic Growth*, op. cit., pp. 95-96.

brought about an increased rate of growth in income. This higher rate of growth in income appears to have generated a level of savings that periodically could not be invested at home. The transfer of excess savings abroad reduced potential domestic deflationary pressures and increased effective demand for British exports. This transfer enabled Britain to achieve a more regular rate of internal economic growth and, interdependently, played a fundamental role in the equilibration of international accounts. It is the interdependence of all these forces and especially the role of savings in excess of domestic investment, and investment in excess of domestic savings, in the international balancing process that deserves particular attention.

The impact of Britain's mechanization and free trade brought about an international redistribution of the factors of production. Those persons engaged in sectors of British (or German) agriculture which had been adversely affected by these developments found an outlet in migration. They either left, or were driven out, by the force of agricultural famine and free trade; by the related pressure of increased mechanization in manufacturing which had raised real wages, generally, and consequently which had rendered their occupations in agriculture relatively uneconomic; and by the growth in numbers which had encountered difficulty in being absorbed at the higher wage rates into the manufacturing industries. Furthermore, periodic diminishing returns on British investment at home reduced the rate of new investment and, consequently, increased the amount of unemployment. Both factors, related as they were, brought on spasms of foreign investment and emigration.

The men who came to America transported western tastes, experience, and techniques. Many of them were skilled and enterprising people. In an important sense, they served as the business medium and catalytic agent in Anglo-American economic growth. If they helped to produce American goods for the British market, they also increased the demand for British exports.

Later in the century, as the flow of migrants increased and provided a pool of cheap labor, a corps of driving American entrepreneurs, imbued with the spirit of innovation and mechanization, and a small elite of highly skilled machine-tool makers brought about a marked increase in the "productivity of labor" by incorporating their efficiency into the machines. The process of comparative mechanization, free trade, and the migration of labor and capital at first contributed to international economic balance, but it carried with it—on both sides of the Atlantic—potential seeds of international economic imbalance. The time-sequence of economic development from country to country (and the adjustment or lack of adjustment to it) was a key factor in the evolution of the balancing process in the second half of the nineteenth century. International economic balance in one institutional context gradually developed into international economic imbalance in another. But much of this anticipates the forces which were just beginning to emerge in the middle of the nineteenth century.

TIME SEQUENCE OF ECONOMIC GROWTH AND TRADE PATTERN

The pattern of trade that developed in the second half of the nineteenth century was closely connected with Britain's continued economic growth and her pivotal role in world trade. This role influenced and was in turn influenced by (1) the diffusion of economic development in "Industrial Europe" during the 1850's and 1860's;[44]

[44] Following Schlote (*op. cit.*, p. 81), we include the following countries in the category, "Industrial Europe": Germany, the Netherlands, Belgium, Luxemburg, Switzerland, Austria-Hungary (or after 1918 the Succession States), France, and Italy. The diffusion of economic development among these countries may be illustrated by the historical and geographical spread of business cycles. In 1792-1793, 1799-1800, 1810-1811, and 1815-1816, Britain experienced brief but, on occasion, sharp crises. Primarily they were of the financial, speculative, inventory, postwar-reconstruction sort, sometimes aggravated by bad harvests or the cessation of war expenditures. They did not bring about mass unemployment or a great contraction of output. Cf. Gayer, *et. al.*, *op. cit.*, Vol. I, p. 117. Few, if any, foreign countries were affected directly by these crises. But during the recession of 1825-1826, France was so affected; and in 1839 France, Belgium, and the United States were affected; in 1847 France, Belgium, the United States, and Holland; in 1857 all these countries were affected, and Germany as well, but only slightly; and in 1866 they all felt the impact of the British slump and Germany was affected fully. *Ibid.*, pp. 203-205, 297, 333-336. See also J. A. Schumpeter, *Business Cycles*, 1939, Vol. I, pp. 220-383. It was during the 1850's and 1860's that the spread of economic development among the countries of Industrial Europe became striking.

(2) the extension of economic development into primarily agricultural countries from the 1880's to World War I;[45] and (3) the emergence of the United States as the world's greatest economic power. In considering this historical sequence we are examining merely one facet of a complex, comprehensive problem, viz., the way in which a key industrial country affects the commercial relations of other countries which are less economically developed, and how the development of the latter, in turn, affects less developed economies, all in a system of interdependence under changing conditions. Special factors, of course, have operated in each country. Political, geographical, social, cultural, and accidental considerations have always played an important role in trading contacts. These factors, however, generally appear to have influenced the rate of change in the composition and direction of trade, but not the direction of these fundamental changes themselves.

Britain's rate of growth in industrial production continued at an uninterrupted pace in the 1850's and 1860's.[46] Finished goods constituted approximately 90 percent of the volume (and value) of total domestic exports. As changing comparative costs and incomes influenced the movement of resources toward manufactures, a decisive shift occurred in the proportion of imports of foodstuffs, raw materials, and finished goods. The proportion of imported foodstuffs expanded rapidly and the proportion of raw materials declined. From 1845 to 1880, foodstuffs, as a proportion of net imports, increased from 20 to

---

[45] From the 1880's to the outbreak of World War I, Italy, Austria-Hungary, Russia, Spain, Portugal, the Balkans, Switzerland, Sweden, Canada, Greece, Brazil, Argentina, China, Japan, Mexico, and Cuba were influenced by the economic development of the more industrial countries and made important strides in their own development. For a good discussion of this diffusion of economic development to primary producing countries, cf. A. Sartorius von Waltershausen, *Die Entstehung der Weltwirtschaft*, 1931, pp. 407-627. The problem is discussed under the heading of "Der Ausbau der Weltwirtschaft bis zum Weltkrieg (1880-1914)" ("The Development of the World Economy up to the World War"). See particularly the discussion on Russia, pp. 318, 357-358, 360, 603; Italy, pp. 355, 591-598; Spain and Portugal, pp. 362-363; Switzerland, p. 350; Sweden, p. 367; Japan, pp. 631-632; and Austria-Hungary, pp. 346-347.

[46] See Hoffmann, *British Industry*, 1700-1950, *op. cit.*, pp. 307-330; *Wachstum und Wachstumformen der Englischen Industriewirtschaft von 1700 bis zur Gegenwart*, 1940, pp. 261-284.

45 percent; raw materials dropped from about 75 to 35 percent; finished goods rose from 5 to 20 percent of total net imports.[47]

The first country to undergo the Industrial Revolution, Britain became dependant at an early stage upon large imports of foodstuffs and raw materials from regions whose climate and resource structure probably gave them an absolute advantage in the production of these goods. Britain's imports came for the most part from India, China, Africa, the Baltic, the northern countries, Russia, central and southern Europe, the West Indies, and America.[48] The gradual economic development of European countries and, later, the United States enabled them to expand their exports of foodstuffs and raw materials to Britain. For, as they progressed in their economic development, their comparative cost advantage at first became marked in these fields. During the 1850's, Britain's combined imports from Industrial Europe and the United States consisted of 85 to 90 percent foodstuffs and raw materials and only 10 to 15 percent manufactured goods.[49] During 1854-1857, 35.6 percent of Britain's imports from Industrial Europe were foodstuffs, 29.4 percent were raw materials, and 22.4 percent finished manufactured goods (12.6 percent were unclassified).[50] The United States, at this time, exported chiefly raw

[47] Schlote, op. cit., Statistical Appendix, pp. 131-132. By 1850 the ratio of retained imports to net national income had risen to about 18 percent; in 1870 the figure was 28 percent and in 1880, 33 percent. By 1851 the proportion of the occupied population engaged in agriculture had fallen to approximately 21 percent; the proportion engaged in manufacturing had risen to about 33.5 percent, a figure which was not exceeded until 1951. Between 1850 and 1870, Britain had become a country of high specialization, with a high import ratio and a great dependence on manufactured exports, especially textile exports. But the main sources of food were still in her own agriculture: home agricultural produce accounted for about 82 percent of total supplies of the main staple foodstuffs. Nonetheless, Britain's dependence on indigenous raw materials and home food supplies was diminishing; she was rapidly adjusting her economy to a world market made accessible by new and improved means of transport. Cf. E. A. G. Robinson, op. cit., pp. 447-450.

[48] Figures on the value and geographical distribution of British foreign trade during the eighteenth century are given in Sir Charles Whitworth's folio volume, *State of the Trade of Great Britain in its Imports and Exports, Progressively from the Year 1697, 1776.* Cf. also Eli F. Heckscher, "Mercantilism, Baltic Trade, and the Mercantilists," *Economic History Review*, 2nd series, Vol. III, No. 2, 1950, pp. 219-228.

[49] Schlote, op. cit., Table 33, p. 85. Typographical errors have been corrected on the basis of data cited in the original German edition (cf. p. 91).

[50] *Ibid.*

materials, such as cotton and tobacco. Foodstuffs accounted for only one-fifth of United States total merchandise exports between 1851 and 1860.[51] For the period 1854-1857, 67.4 percent of Britain's imports from the United States were raw materials, 24.0 percent were foodstuffs, and 1.3 percent finished manufactured goods (7.3 percent were unclassified).[52]

Between 1854-1857 and 1877-1879, Britain's imports of foodstuffs from Industrial Europe rose from 35 to 38.7 percent of her total imports from that region; raw materials dropped from 29.4 to 13.4 percent, whereas finished manufactured goods rose sharply from 22.4 to 40.8 percent.[53] The rapid economic development of Industrial Europe in the 1850's and 1860's which made this expansion of manufactured exports possible, in turn, began to affect the composition of Industrial Europe's imports of foodstuffs, raw materials, and manufactures. As these countries obtained comparative cost advantages in manufactures, advantages which were usually associated with rising real wages and increasing mechanization in both agriculture and industry, they expanded their imports of foodstuffs and raw materials from countries whose resources were either generally better suited for primary production and/or from countries which were, as yet, at a lower stage of economic development.

With the expansion of railway transport into the interior of the United States and to the West Coast in the 1870's and 1880's, the United States became principally an exporter of foodstuffs. From 1860 to 1880, United States exports of crude foodstuffs increased more than twenty-fold.[54] By 1876-1880, crude foodstuffs and manufactured foodstuffs together constituted over one-half of United States total exports.[55] To a considerable extent the abundant supply of American cereals, flour, meat, etc., began to determine price movements and adjustments of production in Europe. Britain's imports of foodstuffs as a percentage of total imports from the United States rose from 24.0

[51] U.S. Department of Commerce, *Historical Statistics of the United States, 1789-1945,* 1949, pp. 246-247.
[52] Schlote, *op. cit.,* Table 33, p. 85.
[53] *Ibid.*
[54] From $12 million to $266 million.
[55] U.S. Department of Commerce, *op. cit.,* pp. 246-247.

percent in 1854-1857 to 51.3 percent in 1877-1879. Raw materials, on
the other hand, dropped from 67.4 percent to 37.2 percent, and
finished manufactured goods rose from 1.3 percent to 3.4 percent.[56]
Industrial Europe also increased its imports of foodstuffs and raw
materials from the United States and from other countries which, in
turn, were undergoing economic development in the 1880's and 1890's,
countries which at this time were improving their comparative advantage in primary production.[57]

Foremost among the industrial countries of Europe, Germany
began to rely increasingly upon net imports from such countries as the
Balkans and from "regions of more recent settlement" on other continents.[58] Its rapid industrialization during the last three decades of
the nineteenth century witnessed a characteristic drop in death rates,
a large rise in population, and an increased demand for food and raw
material imports. Germany's agricultural output increased rapidly
from the 1880's to 1914. But its population increased 50 percent during the same period.[59] In 1890 Germany had an export surplus to the
United States; by 1900 this had become a large import surplus. In
addition, Germany had developed large import surpluses with Argentina, Australia, Brazil, Egypt, India, and the Netherlands Indies.[60]

[56] Schlote, *op. cit.*, Table 33, p. 85.

[57] For example, the excess of commodity imports over exports of "Industrial
Europe" with Argentina, Australia, Brazil, and India increased from £14 million
in 1880 to £40 million in 1890, to £58 million in 1900, and to £115 million in
1910. Industrial Europe was able to pay for this growing volume of primary imports
through its positive trade balance with Britain, its growth in income from investments and other invisible services, the direct positive trade balance of Italy and
Austria with the United States, and through its indirect earnings from non-In-
dustrial Europe which also had a positive trade balance with the United States. See
S. B. Saul, "Britain and World Trade, 1870-1914," *Economic History Review*, 2nd
series, Vol VII, No. 1, 1954, Table IV, p. 57, and p. 58. For a discussion on the
changing structure of Germany's foreign trade, cf. Von Waltershausen, *op. cit.*, pp.
338-340, 571-574; France, pp. 584-591; and Belgium-Holland, pp. 605-669.

[58] League of Nations, *The Network of World Trade*, 1942, p. 84. "Other
regions of recent settlement" include South Africa, Canada, Newfoundland and
Greenland, Argentina, Paraguay, and Uruguay, and Oceania.

[59] Von Waltershausen, *op. cit.*, pp. 338-340, 571-575. Despite the marked rise
in German agricultural production, Germany's food imports from the Balkans,
the Ukraine, Holland, Denmark, and Austria-Hungary increased sharply. Germany's
population increased from approximately 45 million in 1880 to 67.8 million in
1914.

[60] League of Nations, *op. cit.*, p. 84.

Though Germany's resources were more balanced than those of Britain, and she was thus better suited to expand the domestic output of food, her emerging comparative advantage lay primarily in industrial production.[61] Output per unit of input rose in agriculture, but it rose even more in manufacturing. The number of persons per thousand of population engaged in agriculture dropped from 42.5 in 1882 to 28.6 in 1907, while the number in industry rose from 35.5 to 42.8. By 1913 one-sixth of Germany's food came from abroad.[62]

The volume and value of primary imports rose not only in absolute terms but as a percentage of total imports. Foodstuffs and raw materials constituted 81.5 percent of Germany's total imports in 1907 and 83.6 percent in 1913. Finished products fell from 15.9 percent of total imports in 1907 to 13.7 percent in 1913. The composition of Germany's exports did not change significantly during this period. However, because of the more rapid pace of Germany's mechanization, as compared to that of other central European countries, she developed import balances of primary products from practically all the tropical countries and export balances with almost all European countries. The composition of Germany's exports, as an annual average for 1911-1913, was as follows: foodstuffs, 11.3 percent; raw materials, 21.7 percent; manufactured goods, 67 percent. Generally speaking, this structure of exports became typical for a manufacturing country; the pattern slowly emerged in Belgium, Holland, France,

---

[61] Germany was so well endowed with raw materials that Frenchmen found it profitable to invest in her nonferrous-metals industries: in zinc, lead, copper, and silver. In the first half of the nineteenth century, Germany lacked the engineering skill, the venture capital, and the financial institutions to develop these industries. France, on the other hand, was deficient in such key minerals. French investment in German nonferrous-metals industries was therefore channeled to supply the French market with them, and the men who made the investments were generally either metal manufacturers or traders. In the second half of the nineteenth century, major technological innovations occurred in the heavy industries (and others) that also relied extensively on power minerals and the basic metals. Germany was well endowed for such industrialization; France much less so. It was precisely in such heavy industries that France lagged behind and Germany forged ahead. See Rondo E. Cameron, "Some French Contributions to the Industrial Development of Germany, 1840-1870," *Journal of Economic History*, September, 1956, esp. pp. 281-284; 311-316; and J. H. Clapham, *The Economic Development of France and Germany, 1815-1914*, 1951, pp. 278-281 *et seq.*

[62] Von Waltershausen, *op. cit.*, pp. 571-574.

Italy, and Switzerland.[63] As a country mechanized and real wages increased, the "opportunity cost" or "comparative cost" of producing agricultural products usually rose and that of producing manufactures declined. It therefore turned to less industrialized countries—in Europe, America, or in the tropics—to obtain imports of primary products. These imports were paid for either directly by exports to the underdeveloped areas or indirectly by exports to other industrialized countries which, in turn, exported manufactured consumption goods and other products to them. With some exceptions, the greatest expansion of trade occurred, as would be expected, among the industrial countries themselves.

The chronological and geographical sequence of economic development in the nineteenth century had the effect of spreading improvements in the export industries of all countries which were swept into the trading orbit. As regards Industrial Europe, economic development in primary production was a requisite for the expansion of output and the release of resources for the production of manufactures. With greater industrialization abroad, improvements in manufactures became necessary in order to compete with other industrializing countries for primary products. Less developed regions in turn had to improve their efficiency in primary production if they were to expand their imports of manufactures. Such overall improvements in single factoral terms of trade may have eased the balancing process, but for the equilibration of international trade accounts at high levels of exports and imports a high volume of foreign investment remained a primary requisite. Income effects and price effects appear not to have been strong enough to consummate equilibrium in international balances of payments.

COMPOSITION AND DIRECTION OF TRADE

The relative self-sufficiency of the United States, from the 1860's to the 1890's, was not a destabilizing factor at this time. On the contrary, the great expansion of American output enabled the United States to rely primarily on domestic sources of supply for primary products.

[63] Von Waltershausen, *op. cit.*, pp. 584-598, 609-619.

Consequently, she did not have to compete with Britain and Industrial Europe for primary products on other continents. The greater the amount of primary products which the United States (and Industrial Europe) were able to supply from domestic sources, the smaller was the pressure on them to compete with Britain in exporting manufactures to pay for primary imports. Undoubtedly this cushioned the process of adjustment.

Technological improvements and changing demands nonetheless kept altering the relation between a country's economic development, fixed investments, and resource base on the one hand, and the direction and composition of its trade on the other. While Britain admitted virtually all goods duty-free, countries undergoing industrialization (e. g., Industrial Europe, the United States, and Japan) erected tariff barriers against British imports. These tariff barriers often were imposed for the express purpose of industrialization and were designed to restrict imports of British manufactured goods. From the middle of the nineteenth century to the outbreak of World War I, Britian's exports of all home products to agricultural countries had increased five-fold; her exports to industrial countries had increased only three-fold.[64] The proportion of Britain's exports of all home products going to agricultural countries had increased from 56 percent to 70 percent, whereas the proportion going to industrial countries had decreased from 44 percent to 30 percent.[65] Britain's manufactured goods showed a considerable decline as a proportion of her total exports. In the 1850's, finished manufactured goods constituted approximately 85 percent of Britain's exports of home products by·volume, and 86 percent by value; before World War I they constituted 75 percent by volume and 76 percent by value.[66] Moreover, the proportion of manufactured goods (as compared with raw materials and foodstuffs) exported to all industrial countries during this period fell from 81 percent to 62 percent, whereas the proportion exported

---

[64] See Table 9, p. 202. In absolute terms, British exports of finished manufactured goods to all industrial countries amounted to approximately £38 million in 1854-1857 and to £86 million in 1909-1913; whereas British exports of finished manufactured goods to all agrarian countries amounted to approximately £55 million in 1854-1857 and to £260 million in 1909-1913.

[65] Schlote, op. cit., Table 31, p. 82.

[66] Ibid., Table 24, p. 71.

to all agricultural countries fell only from 90 percent to 82 percent.[67] Further, the share of Britain's exports of *all home products* (and of manufactures) going to the United States fell more rapidly than the share going to Industrial Europe.[68] At the same time the proportion of Britain's exports of raw materials (especially coal to Industrial Europe and wool and metals to the United States) rose markedly.[69]

On the other hand, finished manufactured goods as a proportion of Britain's *imports* increased considerably. They amounted to 7 percent of total imports in the 1850's and 20 percent in 1913.[70] This relative expansion in the demand for manufactured imports is to be explained primarily by the rise in national production and real income per capita on the one hand, and by the nature of Britain's growth and resource-structure on the other.[71] By 1880, Britain's imports from all indus-trial countries consisted of about 25 percent manufactures and 75 percent primary products. At the outbreak of World War I the figure for manufactures stood at 38 percent and primary products at 62 percent. Of Britain's imports from Industrial Europe at this

[67] See Table 9, p. 202, above.

[68] *Ibid.*, and Schlote, *op. cit.*, Table 31, p. 82.

[69] Table 9, p. 202, above.

[70] Based on Schlote, *op. cit.*, Statistical Appendix, Table 8, pp. 131-133. Textiles, leather, leather goods, furs and skins, iron, and steel products, machinery, chemi-cals, and paper products composed the main United Kingdom imports of finished manufactured goods. *Ibid.*, Table B, pp. 144-147.

[71] On a base of 1800=100, it has been estimated that British average real in-comes rose from an index of 193 in 1851 to 405 in 1902. See Phyllis Deane, "The Industrial Revolution and Economic Growth: The Evidence of Early British National Income Estimates," *Economic Development and Cultural Change*, January, 1957, p. 171. Real wages in Britain were perhaps 70 to 80 percent higher in 1900-1910 than they had been in the 1850's. Cf. Schlote, *op. cit.*, pp. 65-66. For data on United Kingdom net national income from 1860-1953, see Simon Kuznets, "Quantitative Aspects of the Economic Growth of Nations," *Economic Development and Cultural Change*, October, 1956, Table 1, pp. 53-55. Cf. also James B. Jefferys and Dorothy Walters, "National Income and Expenditure of the United Kingdom, 1870-1952," *Income and Wealth*, Series V, 1956, Table III, p. 14. Considering the resource endowment and development of the United Kingdom, France, and Germany, one can probably explain the nature of Britain's manufactured imports from France and Germany on economic grounds similar to those discussed in the text: France continued to specialize in the production of luxury commodities requiring large proportions of skill, design, and individuality relative to the value of raw materials; whereas Germany specialized more and more in heavy industries requiring large proportions of power minerals, basic metals, and unskilled labor relative to the value of skilled technicians.

time, 56 percent constituted manufactured goods; of her imports from the United States only 13 percent constituted manufactured goods.[72]

In the second half of the nineteenth century the relative share of Britain's sales to Europe and the United States declined. The share going to other continents, such as Africa, Asia, and Australia, steadily increased. On the other hand, the share of Britain's purchases from Europe increased while that from the United States declined.[73]

A process of fundamental change took place in the nature of Britain's imports. After the 1890's, imports of chemicals, machinery, iron, and steel gained in importance. The proportion of imported raw materials to be used in the manufacture of producer goods increased in comparison with the proportion to be used in the manufacture of consumer goods.[74] This tendency appears strikingly if we compare the periods immediately before and after World War I. As Britain's production of capital goods, consumer durables, and paper products increased, her imports of rubber, mineral oils, copper, and raw materials for making paper rose sharply. Since the turn of the twentieth century, Britain's motor industry, electrical engineering, and paper-making trades have grown at a remarkable pace. Many of the raw materials required for these expanding industries either were not produced in Britain or were produced in inadequate amounts. Between

---

[72] Schlote, op. cit., Table 33, p. 85 and p. 87.

[73] Ibid., Table 31, p. 82, and Statistical Appendix, Table 19, pp. 157-160.

[74] By 1913 Britain had become dependent upon imports for about seven-eighths of its raw-material supplies (apart from coal) and for over half of its food. The proportion of the population engaged in agriculture had fallen to 8 percent. In 1857-1863, Britain could depend on her own wool supplies for 58 percent of her needs; by 1907-1913 the figure had fallen to 22 percent. In 1857-1863 she could supply all her needs of lead, 88 percent of her needs of tin and 71 percent of her needs of copper. By 1907-1913, Britain supplied only 11 percent of her lead, 21 percent of her tin, and 1 percent of her copper. From 1870 to 1914, Britain's share of total world trade fell from 40 to 27 percent; her exports of manufactures from 32 to 14 percent of the world total. Moreover, British manufactured exports as a percentage of total British exports fell from 91 to 78 percent and textiles from 56 to 34 percent. On the other hand, Britain's metal engineering exports rose steadily; by 1917 they constituted 27 percent of total British exports. Britain was increasingly becoming dependent upon her ability to export engineering goods, and in this field she did not enjoy the predominance she had for over a hundred years in textiles. See C. T. Saunders, op. cit., pp. 336-338, and E. A. G. Robinson, op. cit., pp. 450-451, 460.

1903-1913 and 1927-1929, Britain's *net* imports of these materials increased by £56 million; at the same time her total raw-material imports increased by only £52 million. Imports of textile raw materials actually fell in absolute terms during this period.[75] Before World War I, textile raw-material imports accounted for over 40 percent of Britain's net imports. This proportion fell continually between World Wars I and II; in effect, Britain's exports of textiles also declined in absolute terms.[76] Britain suffered not only from the fact that her most important manufactures—textiles—faced a reduced demand and were less competitive in world markets, but also from the fact that she was not as well supplied domestically, as were other industrial countries, with raw materials required to produce the "new goods" which were increasing in world demand. A new relationship had therefore developed between Britain's resource structure, economic development, accumulated capital, and foreign trade which required major readjustments. The future state of Britain's international accounts would depend largely on the rate of possible development of newer consumer durable and capital goods industries.

DEVELOPMENT AND DECLINE OF A TRADE PATTERN

The long-term strains in international trade and payments which had emerged after World War I were closely associated with the pattern of economic growth which Britain and Industrial Europe had pursued in the nineteenth century on the one hand, and with the general characteristics of United States economic development after the 1880's on the other.

The pattern of economic growth which Britain and Industrial Europe had pursued brought about a network of trade balances which was uniquely associated with that development. The changing *composition* of trade and the emerging *direction* of trade balances were not unrelated. However, for the most part, they were the result of different sets of causes.

The changing *composition* of trade was, as we have observed, the result of fundamental shifts in comparative cost structures and effec-

[75] Schlote, *op. cit.*, Tables 13 and 14, pp. 57-58.
[76] *Ibid.*, Tables 26 and 27, pp. 73-74.

tive demands of the respective countries, shifts which were strongly affected by the process of economic growth. They were so affected through the operation of two important forces. First, the opening of freer trade adjusted market prices of products which were charged to consumers within each trading country so that they would approximately correspond to the marginal importance of these products to consumers in each country. This process did not depend upon any *shift* of productive resources in the industrial or primary-producing countries. It depended upon the condition that the ratio of, for example, say, textile prices to food prices charged to consumers in Britain, Industrial Europe, or regions of more recent settlement equal the ratio of the marginal satisfaction of textiles to the marginal satisfaction of food to consumers in the same country, and that goods exchange freely between the countries at this same price ratio. When these conditions prevail, the attendant result may be called "optimization of trade." The closer countries moved toward freer trade in the latter half of the nineteenth century, the more closely were these conditions fulfilled. Secondly, in Britain and Industrial Europe the process of economic growth shifted resources, in percentage terms, from the relatively unprofitable production of food and raw materials to the more profitable production of manufactures. Similarly, regions of more recent settlement expanded their production of primary products. Complete adjustment of production among trading countries depends upon the condition that the market price offered to producers of each product in each country correspond to the cost of production of each product in each country. This condition tends to be fulfilled if the ratio of, for example, textiles to food received by producers in each country is equal to the ratio of the marginal (social) cost of textiles to food in the same country, and if the goods are freely tradable at this same price ratio. When these conditions prevail the attendant result may be called "maximization of production." For the important members of the network of world trade in the latter half of the nineteenth century, these conditions were more closely fulfilled than at any previous time in history.[77]

[77] These statements clearly do not imply comparable gains from free trade among participants, much less so the equalization of factor prices. The key influence of freer trade was to stimulate innovation, compelling greater mobility and forcing changes in supply functions and demand functions. Freer trade may

The evolving *direction* of trade balances was the joint product of historical, political, and economic forces. Historically, Britain has been a principal supplier of manufactured consumption goods to tropical countries. The trade of Latin America, tropical Asia, Africa, China, and other continental Asiatic countries developed primarily as a result of the inflow of European capital and the exchange of foodstuffs, raw materials, and exotic products of these countries against European manufactured goods. Inasmuch as most tropical countries were poor, they concentrated their expenditures on low-priced, manufactured consumption goods which British industry was well suited to supply. Many tropical countries in effect developed large import balances with Britain. India was quite typical; she bought more than 80 percent of her imports from Britain in the 1870's.[78] Britain supplied India with cotton piece goods, metal manufactures, and other industrial products. India, in turn, owing to the widespread demand for her exports, developed export balances with Continental Europe, the United States, and various other parts of the world. As Britain became ever more dependent on foreign foodstuffs and raw materials, her investors and traders found it more profitable to invest capital and to establish widespread trade connections in North and South America, in Australia and New Zealand, in Argentina and other regions of recent

---

have had beneficial "spread effects" as well as harmful "dampening effects," but neither *a priori* reasoning nor empirical evidence warrant Myrdal's generalization that the "normal result of unhampered trade between two countries, of which one is industrialized and the other underdeveloped, is the initiation of a cumulative process towards the impoverishment and stagnation of the latter." Gunnar Myrdal, *Economic Theory and Under-developed Regions*, 1957, p. 99. In terms of absolute levels of real national product and real product per capita, most—though probably not all—of the participants gained. Nonetheless, the international inequality of income distribution increased. It is an open question, however, whether or not such inequality would have increased even to a greater extent without freer trade. Cf. the statistical record and discussion in Simon Kuznets, "Quantitative Aspects of Economic Growth of Nations," *Economic Development and Cultural Change*, July, 1957, Table 7, pp. 18-19, Table 14, pp. 28-31, Appendix Table 2, pp. 68-74, and Table 4, pp. 82-95; *Ibid.*, October, 1956, Table 2, p. 13, pp. 19-29, and Appendix, pp. 52-94; Kuznets, *Toward a Theory of Economic Growth, op. cit.*, Statistical Appendix, Table 7, p. 142. Cf. also Folke Hilgerdt, "Uses and Limitations of International Trade in Overcoming Inequalities in World Distribution of Population and Resources," World Population Conference, 1954 (mimeographed); and James E. Meade, *Trade and Welfare*, 1955, pp. 52-65, and *Problems of Economic Union*, 1953, Chaps. 1 and 3.

[78] See League of Nations, *op. cit.*, p. 59; and S. B. Saul, *op. cit.*, esp. pp. 64-66.

settlement. Britain became their principal supplier of manufactures. These regions supplied her with an increasing proportion of cereals, meat, butter, and other products of the temperate zones. With increasing receipts from foreign investments and invisibles from these regions, Britain developed import surpluses with them and with the United States as well.[79]

The economic development of Britain thus produced export surpluses with the tropics, and import surpluses with Continental Europe, the United States, and the regions of recent settlement. Institutional factors played an important role in the development of the direction of these trade balances. Nevertheless, the further one traces the chronological sequence of economic development back to the Industrial Revolution, the closer seems to become the relationship between the economic development of an area or country in question and the emergence of its import surpluses from areas or countries at lower stages of economic development. Important exceptions to this pattern can be cited. Staggered patterns of export-import relations between specific creditor-debtor countries arose, but generally the process appears to emerge. It is not inconsistent with *a priori* reasoning, though it does not necessarily follow from it.

In the case of Britain, the early start in economic development, her singular suitability to supply the foreign demand of less developed areas, the rapid improvement in her single factoral terms of trade, the comparatively small capacity of British industry in the aggregate to absorb capital (after the railroads had been built and before the util-

[79] But as we shall discuss presently, Britain's imports did not expand sufficiently to consummate balance in her international accounts. British investments in Europe after 1870 were small. Before that time, British investments were concentrated on the bonds of foreign governments, either in Europe or in the Near East, and contributed far less to economic development than they did subsequently. From 1870-1913, Britain invested abroad (mainly to regions of recent settlement) approximately two-fifths of her savings or one-twentieth of her national income. By 1913 her foreign investments were equal to nearly four-ninths of her home investments. They represented more than one-third of all European foreign investments and their returns amounted to approximately one-tenth of her national income. See Cairncross, *op. cit.*, Chaps. 1, 6, and 7; United Nations, *International Capital Movements during the Inter-War Period*, 1949, p. 2; H. Feis, *Europe, The World's Banker, 1870-1914*, 1930, esp. pp. 23, 51, 75; and the graph on the location of British, French, and German long-term international investments in 1914, J. B. Condliffe, *The Commerce of Nations*, 1950, p. 327, and the relevant discussion on pp. 282-357.

ity industries became large), the growth in her invisible exports, her military and diplomatic prestige, the political and personal ties with many regions of recent settlement—all contributed first, to expand British foreign investment and then, to utilize the proceeds from foreign investment on further investment and for merchandise import surpluses.

All these forces operated in a setting of mutual support and causation under ever changing c<nbsp>nditions of cumulative growth. In the case of the tropics we have an illustration of the proposition that there is no "structural" economic reason why a more developed economy should necessarily have a merchandise import balance with any specific less developed economy. Britain's export balance with the tropics continued into the early 1930's. They were associated with the factors listed above, particularly with Britain's suitability and adaptability to meet virtually all the foreign demands of the tropics and with the especially widespread demand for the goods of the tropics in Continental Europe. However, in the latter 1930's, Britain also developed import surpluses with the tropics.[80]

The evolution of Britain's economic structure toward ever more manufactures and away from primary production, and the rising level of incomes associated with it, undoubtedly assisted the mechanism of transfer of the import surpluses both from the viewpoint of multilateral adjustment with Continental Europe and from the viewpoint of debtor-creditor adjustment with the United States and with regions of recent settlement. To the extent that Britain's foreign investments were made on the basis of higher marginal efficiency of capital abroad than at home, the *overall* size of her merchandise import balance was the result, *inter alia*, of market-directed forces of economic growth. But in a multilateral trading world, with no tied loans, this does not necessarily imply import surpluses with specific countries in which foreign loans are made. Decisions to make investments abroad usually are made by different people and for different reasons than decisions to import from abroad.[81] There appears to be

[80] League of Nations, *op. cit.*, p. 90.
[81] Professor W. Arthur Lewis has stressed that capital tends to flow toward places where new rich natural resources can be fairly easily opened up, such as regions of fertile soil, oil, coal, or ores, and away from places where resources are

no fundamental structural reason why more developed countries should, in all cases, have import surpluses from less developed ones, or conversely. In the case of Britain, however, the aforementioned institutional, political, and commercial policy forces became so causally interrelated with the cumulative economic and financial forces, that decisions to invest abroad and decisions leading to merchandise import surpluses from Continental Europe, the United States, and the regions of recent settlement were rendered quite consistent with one another. In effect, the evolution of Britain's balance of payments on current account disclosed certain unique features which do not appear to conform to our current *equilibrium* theory of the mechanism of adjustment.

If the balancing process had been operating in accordance with current theoretical explanations, Britain's imports from time to time during this extended period should have been much larger than they actually were. How otherwise explain the fact that for so many years Britain was able to maintain an active balance on current account which did not generate sufficiently strong changes in the direction of investment, and in relative incomes and prices to reverse this balance; or persistently to maintain a net export of capital *along with* an excess of total imports over exports of goods *plus* services? It is well known that during the entire period of 1870 to 1913 Britain had an excess of imports over exports in merchandise trade, and an excess of exports over imports in invisibles. But with the exception of the years 1871 to 1874 and 1911 to 1913, the excess of imports in merchandise trade exceeded the excess of exports in invisibles.[82] This passive balance in goods plus services was more than offset by the large inflow of interest on foreign investments, rendering the balance

---

already highly capitalized, and where new resources are much less abundant. "This," he rightly states, "is not the same as saying that a country becomes a capital exporter when it needs to import raw materials or food." *Op. cit.*, pp. 249-250. A good deal of Britain's foreign investment in the nineteenth century was channeled wherever money could be made. It would undoubtedly be agreed, however, that many opportunities to make relatively profitable investments abroad were connected, directly or indirectly, with her growing demand for imports.

[82] Computed from data to be found in Cairncross, *op. cit.*, Table 40, p. 180; derived by adding total shipping earnings and other invisibles (column 1 and 3) and subtracting from this total the excess of merchandise imports (column 4).

on current account active throughout the period. Clearly from the customary income-generating point of view the effects of the net inflow of interest were not those generally ascribed to an inflow of specie stemming from an excess of exports over imports in goods and services; for otherwise, the active balance on current account would have tended to oscilliate about an equilibrium level. Research on the different effects of an active balance in merchandise trade, invisibles, and interest from foreign investments is long overdue. The issues involved in the British experience, however, were more fundamental. Professor Taussig had observed that on occasion the balancing process seemed to operate too rapidly for the facts to be fully in accord with the price-specie-flow mechanism. It has often been suggested that the difficulty lay in the neglect of income effects. But in so far as Britain's current account is concerned, for at least four decades before World War I the international mechanism appears to have worked either too slowly or not in the "equilibrating" direction to be explained in terms of income effects and/or price effects.

Britain's net export of capital was, of course, equal to the excess balance on current account, adjusted for net export or import of bullion and specie.[83] As regards the balancing process, these international loans are usually treated as a branch of equilibrium mechanism theory. The evidence suggests, however, that the process whereby international accounts were cleared cannot be explained satisfactorily in such equili-

[83] For the years before 1914 the estimated balances of payments on current account, adjusted for trade in bullion and specie and, hence, including changes in foreign capital in Britain as well as changes in British capital abroad, were as follows:

	U.K. net export of capital in £ million, annual averages	U.K. net export of capital in $ billion (1947-1955 prices), annual averages
1871-1877	35.6	0.3
1878-1886	31.2	0.3
1887-1895	51.4	0.6
1896-1904	20.8	0.3
1905-1913	134.5	1.6

Computed from Cairncross' estimates, *ibid.*; the figures in the second column have been raised to 1947-1955 prices (U.K. Board of Trade wholesale price indices) and converted into dollars at the average exchange rate for 1947-1955. Cf. G.D.A. MacDougall, *The World Dollar Problem*, 1957, Appendix XII A, p. 533.

brium terms. It must, in addition, be explained in terms of a cumulative process, inter-related with periods of relative expansion and contraction, setting into operation forces which *simultaneously* induced (and were induced by) changes in relative costs, prices, and incomes, as well as changes in savings and plans to invest both at home and abroad.

The cumulative process between 1860 and 1914 centered in capital accumulation and population growth, improvement in productivity and extension of the market—advance in national incomes. British capital per employed person more than doubled; its quality improved.[84] On the average, the population of the United Kingdom per decade rose 11.2 percent; national product, 26.1 percent; product per capita, 13.4 percent. Satisfactory as these rates of growth may have been, the national product and product per capita of Germany, Japan, Sweden, and Canada increased at a more rapid rate. Even more spectacular was the rate of growth of the United States; indeed, this was the most outstanding characteristic of the period. From 1869 to 1908, on the average, its population rose per decade 22.5 percent; national product, 56.5 percent; product per capita, 27.7 percent.[85] In the United Kingdom domestic gross capital formation was approximately 10 percent of gross national product; in the United States, 21 percent.[86]

Although productivity in British manufacturing kept increasing, the demand for capital at home did not rise rapidly after the mid-1870's. By 1875 most of Britain's main-line railways had been built and further railway expansion required smaller amounts of new equipment. The demand for industrial capital in British manufacturing was still relatively small, its total stock was less than that of the railways.[87] Domestic net capital formation amounted to 8.7 per-

[84] See E. H. Phelps Brown and B. Weber, "Accumulation, Productivity and Distribution in the British Economy, 1870-1938," *Economic Journal*, June, 1953, p. 281. D. H. Robertson has commented on the difficulty of drawing a clear line between changes in quality and changes in quantity of fixed capital. Cf. *Utility and All That*, 1952, pp. 127-130.

[85] Kuznets, *Toward a Theory of Economic Growth*, *op. cit.*, Statistical Appendix, Table 7, pp. 142-144. The comparable rates of growth in Canada during the period 1870-1919 were 18.6 percent; 46.1 percent; and 23.0 percent, respectively.

[86] *Ibid.*, Table 10, pp. 153, 155.

[87] Cairncross, *op. cit.*, p. 8.

cent of net national product in the 1870's, 7.4 percent in the 1880's, and 7.9 percent in the 1890's.[88] The ratio of Britain's reproducible capital to annual national income was as high as 4.6 in 1865. It was approximately 5.3 in 1875, and 5.5 in 1885.[89] Given such relatively high capital-output ratios, coupled with Britain's unbalanced resource structure and limited resource base on the one hand, and the consistently high marginal efficiency of capital in the regions of recent settlement on the other, Britain's investors were nearly always able to find profitable outlets for their savings whenever the marginal efficiency of capital at home tended to decline. The demand for British savings and the yield on British capital were settled not only by the outlets in British industry, but also by the opportunities to invest in other countries, especially in the United States, Canada, Australia (including Ceylon), Argentina, and Brazil. Foreign investment was never as high as domestic net investment (except in 1913), but it was frequently half as large. Extensive loans were made in the regions of recent settlement without outrunning the exceptional advantages to invest. As soon as one area appeared to be yielding diminishing returns, another would be opened up, while investment in the first was absorbed in preparation for the next advance. It was a fortuitous historical circumstance that Britain was able to invest much of her excess savings abroad whenever plans to invest at home declined relative to the level of total savings. A cumulative process of

[88] Kuznets, *Toward a Theory of Economic Growth*, *op. cit.*, Statistical Appendix, Table 10, p. 155. For the United States the percentages were 13.9, 13.8, and 14.6, respectively. The early increase in British capital was one of the chief sources of its economic progress, and the continued rise in national output and population after the 1870's, in turn, increased the demand for capital at home, probably to a large extent by way of a broadly interpreted multiplier-acceleration process. Structural maladjustments and adjustments with divergences between the behavior "of the construction and consumption trades" were, of course, also very important in the Victorian era. Cf. D. H. Robertson, A *Study of Industrial Fluctuation* (1915), 1948, New Introduction, p. xii, and pp. 125, 187-188, 211. For a comparison and appraisal of some recent variants of the acceleration principle, including the contributions of Samuelson, Harrod, Domar, and Hicks, cf. William Fellner, "The Rate of Growth and Capital Coefficients," *Long-Range Economic Projections, Studies in Income and Wealth*, Vol. 16, National Bureau of Economic Research 1954, pp. 287-298.

[89] Kuznets, *Toward a Theory of Economic Growth*, *op. cit.*, Table 11, p. 156. In the United States the ratio in 1879 was 2.8; in 1889, 3.0.

foreign lending was set into motion, not a smooth but a continuous process.

According to Hoffmann's figures, the period between 1851 and 1871 was marked by an abnormally small increase in the national wages bill as compared with the growth in the net value of industrial output.[90] Real wages apparently lagged behind the increase in productivity and profits and savings formed a comparatively high proportion of the national income. The savings were predominantly invested at home.[91] Domestic industrial output was not only maintained at high levels but grew at an annual rate of 2 to 3 percent.[92]

Around 1870, however, an important interrelated phenomenon occurred in Britain: a turning point from a high to a lower rate of capital formation and from a high to a relatively low rate of increase of industrial output.[93] From 1865 to 1875 physical industrial capital per head rose by as much as 35 percent,[94] but the rate of growth of industrial output had already begun to decline.[95] It seems that a disparity developed between the growth in physical capacity to produce of some major industries and the growth of the current output of their mines and factories. Industries had expanded production capac-

---

[90] Hoffmann, British Industry, 1700-1950, op. cit., p. 55.

[91] Cairncross states that British foreign investment did not assume formidable proportions until after 1870. Yearly figures are not available for the period before 1866. Estimates for the latter 1860's show that it amounted to approximately £20 million a year. Cf. Cairncross, op. cit., p. 205, and Paul H. Douglas, "An Estimate of the Growth of Capital in the United Kingdom, 1865-1909," Journal of Economic and Business History, August, 1930, p. 680.

[92] Hoffmann, British Industry, 1700-1950, op. cit., p. 31.

[93] Ibid., p. 55 n.

[94] It rose only 14 percent between 1875-1885, 6 percent between 1885-1895, and 7 percent between 1895-1905. Based on Douglas, op. cit., p. 680.

[95] "Between the middle of the 1860's and the outbreak of the First World War," notes Hoffmann, "there were certain rhythmical fluctuations in the rate of growth of output, but the general trend was one of declining rate of expansion of industrial output." British Industry, 1700-1950, op. cit., p. 55. It rose by less than 2 percent per year. Ibid., p. 31. The rate of growth of exports also declined from an annual average percentage increase of 5.3 between 1840-1860, and 4.4 between 1860-1870, to 2.1 between 1870-1890, and 0.7 between 1890-1900. Schlote, op. cit., p. 42. Similarly, British manufactured exports grew at approximately 4.8 percent per year from 1852-1872 and only 2.1 percent per year from 1876-1910. Cf. W. A. Lewis and P. J. O'Leary, "Secular Swings in Production and Trade, 1870-1913," Manchester School of Economics and Social Studies, May, 1955, p. 122.

ity beyond the need of current operations.[96] Profits as a *percentage of national income* were lower in 1872, and nearly so in 1873, than in any other year during the period 1871 to 1913.[97] Savings as a percentage of national income reached a major peak between 1872 and 1874, a peak which was not surpassed in the pre-World War I era.[98]

As the rate of growth of industrial output declined in the early 1870's relative to the rate of growth of production capacity, the net export of capital greatly increased.[99] In effect, an examination of the data for the period 1870 to 1895 reveals that in practically every year when the volume of domestic investment fell or remained the same, the volume of foreign investment rose.[100] Both in absolute terms and as a percentage of net national product, Britain's foreign investment and home investment moved in opposite directions over the long period.[101] Recurring declines in the marginal efficiency of capital

[96] E.g., the value of machinery retained for home use increased nearly 40 percent between 1870 and 1873, and the number of cotton spindles increased approximately 400 percent. See Cairncross, *op. cit.*, Table 37, p. 117. Concerning industrial fluctuations during the entire period from about 1870 till 1914, D. H. Robertson observed that the collapse of investment was essentially due "to a temporary saturation with instrumental goods." *A Study of Industrial Fluctuation*, New Introduction, p. xiii. He wrote in 1915: "Although therefore a country may be actually increasing both its current consumption and even its accumulation of consumable goods, it may still be engaged in over-investment," p. 180. Such cyclical overinvestment occurred in the boom of the early 1870's, in 1883, 1890, and 1900-1901, pp. 181, 240. Evidence presented before the Royal Commission of 1886 affirmed overdevelopment of fixed capital in almost every large British industry. Cf. Rostow, *British Economy of the Nineteenth Century, op. cit.*, esp. pp. 74-89.

[97] See A. R. Prest, "National Income of the United Kingdom, 1870-1946," *Economic Journal,* March, 1948, pp. 58-59.

[98] Hoffmann, *British Industry, 1700-1950, op. cit.*, p. 55.

[99] The net export of capital rose from £28.1 million in 1870 to £76.4 million in 1872 and amounted to £63.4 million in 1873. Cf. Cairncross, *op. cit.*, Table 40, p. 180. Home ingot consumption of iron and steel actually fell from 1871 to 1874. *Ibid.*, Table 36, p. 165.

[100] Cf. Brinley Thomas, *Migration and Economic Growth, op. cit.*, Tables 100 and 101, Statistical Appendix, pp. 290-291. The series are based on estimates by Cairncross and Douglas. See also Thomas, *ibid.*, Chaps. VII, XI.

[101] During the decade 1870-1879, domestic net capital formation amounted to 8.7 percent of net national product and foreign investment to 4.7 percent of net national product. Domestic net capital formation declined during the decade 1880-1889 to 7.4 percent of net national product, and foreign investment rose to 5.8 percent of net national product. During the decade 1890-1899, domestic net capital formation rose to 7.9 percent of net national product, and foreign investment declined to 3.6 percent of net national product. I would not have been

schedule at home impelled investors to seek better opportunities for the supply of their savings abroad.[102]

As regards the demand for savings, throughout the period 1870 to 1913 foreign investment offered higher returns than most home investment, and the difference in returns turned out to be more than sufficient to compensate for extra risk. In the years 1870-1880 the average yield on all foreign bonds was 5.5 percent and other foreign securities nearly 7 percent. The average yield on British consols during this period was 3.2 percent. After 1880, yields on colonial and foreign investments were generally higher than those at home. From 1900 to 1910, foreign investments paid an average yield of 5.2 percent compared with an average yield of about 3.5 percent on home securities generally, and approximately 3 percent on consols.[103]

---

able to reach this conclusion but for the statistical work of E. H. Phelps Brown, Handfield-Jones, A. K. Cairncross, A. H. Imlah, A. R. Prest, and J. H. Lenfant. Their data have been brought together by Simon Kuznets in, "International Differences in Capital Formation and Financing," *Capital Formation and Economic Growth*, 1956, Table I-3, p. 62 and Table II-4, p. 70.

[102] It is only an *apparent* paradox also to find a high positive correlation between the years of maximum capital exports (as measured by the ratio of foreign investment to net national income): 1872, 1881, 1890, 1907, 1913, and the peak years of cyclical prosperity: 1873, 1883, 1890, 1907, 1913. (Cf. Rostow, *British Economy of the Nineteenth Century, op. cit.*, p. 33; Prest, *op. cit.*, pp. 58-59; Cairncross, *op. cit.*, p. 180.) For during each peak in the business cycle there was a maximum absolute share of profits, rent, and interest; and hence an extraordinarily large volume of savings for both domestic and foreign investment. In most of these peak cyclical years the expected marginal efficiency of capital at home was probably already leveling off or declining; but even if it were still rising, the *level of earnings* on investments made at home was in any event generally lower than the level of earnings on investments made abroad. This phenomenon is discussed below.

[103] See Sir Arthur Salter, "Foreign Investment," Princeton University, *Essays in International Finance*, February, 1951, pp. 2, 5; Royal Institute of International Affairs, *The Problem of Foreign Investment* 1937, *passim*; Cairncross, *op. cit.*, pp. 226-235; Sir George Paish, "Great Britain's Capital Investments in Other Lands," *Journal of Royal Statistical Society*, September, 1909, pp. 465-480. Paish has estimated that in 1907-1908 British foreign investment in copper mines yielded 13.2 percent, diamonds and other stones 30.5 percent, gold 9.3 percent, silver, lead, and zinc 8 percent, tin 5 percent, nitrate 15 percent, rubber 8.2 percent, tea and coffee 8.4 percent, canals and docks 19.6 percent, banks 13.6 percent. Foreign investments in coal and iron ore, however, yielded only 3.9 percent, railways between 3.9 and 4.7 percent, electric lighting and power 4.2 percent. *Ibid.*, p. 475. Yields on British consols between 1871-1874 were: yearly low 3.27, high 3.28; between 1886-1890, yearly low 2.61, high 2.98; 1905-1913, yearly low 2.78, high 3.41. Yields on "best five American

One can infer from the evidence that, *inter alia*, the growth of do-mestic investment as a percentage of net national product periodic-ally generated a rate of growth in income which, in turn, generated a rate of growth in savings (as a percentage of net national product) larger than that of planned investment; and, at the going or antici-pated rates of return, these excess savings could be invested more profitably overseas.

The importance of this phenomenon as regards the international mechanism of adjustment rests in the fact that, so far as Britain was concerned, it was the same set of domestic forces that often, on the one hand, brought about a reduction in the volume of domestic in-vestment and, on the other, provided the incentives for an expansion in the volume of foreign investment, migration, and exports. The growth in Britain's capital stock would lower the marginal efficiency schedule of investment, as insufficient innovations were introduced to raise it. The returns on capital and expected returns on new invest-ment would thus decline, the growth process be interrupted, full capacity supply be in excess of the total demand for the net national product, output would fall, and labor become unemployed. Concur-rently, with higher levels of return on investment abroad, the decline in the marginal efficiency of investment schedule at home would bring on spasms of foreign lending.

As to depression in British agriculture during the 1880's, this too manifested a discrepancy between short-term and long-term economic growth. The higher returns on capital abroad were themselves re-lated to Britain's continued economic development. *In toto*, the ex-pansion of her imports was probably more important than foreign lending in facilitating the growth of underdeveloped regions. But these two forces clearly worked hand in hand. In an important sense

---

railroad bonds" (i.e., lowest yielding) between 1871-1874 were: yearly low 6.66, high 6.90; between 1886-1890, yearly low 3.82, high 4.01; 1905-1913, yearly low 3.57, high 4.07. Cf. J. Stafford, "The Future of the Rate of Interest," *The Manchester School of Economic and Social Studies*, No. 2, 1937, p. 137; and F. R. Macaulay, *The Movements of Interest Rates, Bond Yields and Stock Prices in the United States Since 1856*, 1936, pp. A 111-A 112. For "American stock yields, 1871-1937," see U.S. Department of Commerce, *Historical Statistics of the United States, op. cit.*, pp. 206-207. Cf. also William Fellner, *Trends and Cycles in Economic Activity*, 1956, Appendix, pp. 396-400.

Britain's foreign investments were induced by her own growth. Profits depended on large markets, and the mass market for primary products was exports to Britain and to the other industrial countries of Europe. The higher marginal productivity of capital overseas was therefore related to this growth of effective demand, as well as to the external economies and technical complementarities in the underdeveloped regions, complementarities which themselves were a function of the foreign investments. It ought to be a commonplace but is nowadays a matter of dispute that Britain's economic growth and foreign investments helped raise the efficiency of primary-producing countries. Surely the higher return on *capital* in these regions was indicative of its comparative efficiency in producing foodstuffs and raw materials overseas; and this increasing efficiency had an important bearing on British migration and agriculture. For as the marginal efficiency schedule of capital at home declined and the number of jobless increased, foreign investment rose and more men left Britain to carry out the work of the new growth for which British capital was wanted.[104] The emigration left houses empty in Britain and rents fell. Soon the decline in demand for housing hit the building industry. Builders, in addition, were faced with worse terms of credit since investors reduced their purchases of house property and bought foreign bonds. The railways and public utilities similarly were adversely affected; they too were closely dependent upon the rate of growth of population and of cities. The decline of agricultural prices, however, raised real wages of the employed, especially those catering to the enlarged export market, which was induced by the increased foreign loans. But at the same time, falling agricultural prices and some reduced domestic effective demand brought distress to British agriculture. Agricultural workers would not move to towns in large numbers where job opportunities were scarce and insecure. Hence they migrated overseas.[105]

[104] Brinley Thomas, *Migration and Economic Growth*, *op. cit.*, Appendix 4, Table 100, p. 290.

[105] The percentage of unemployed appears to have varied with the index of home investment. It was approximately 5 percent in 1880 and 10 percent in 1886. The index volume of British home investment fell from 64 in 1880 to 55 in 1887 and as a percentage of the trend from 106 to 78. On the other hand, capital exports as a percentage of total British investment rose from 4.8 in 1880 to 39.5 in 1887. Real wages of industrial workers never rose faster than in this period. There was some emigration to the towns but the combined force of "depression"

British agriculture was compelled to reorganize and in the process its productivity greatly increased. As the prices of agricultural imports continued to fall relative to money wages, and productivity and real wages in non agricultural production rose more rapidly than those in agriculture, the pressure to economize on labor in agriculture became more powerful.[106] The (efficient) contraction of British agriculture as a proportion of national income freed a comparatively larger proportion of savings for capital formation both at home and abroad. It thereby contributed to long-term economic growth.[107]

But it does not appear to be true, as we have been taught, that Britain's foreign lending increased substantially when the terms of trade moved in favor of the primary-producing countries. The most recently compiled indices on terms of trade suggest that Britain's heavy foreign lending did not occur when primary prices were un-

---

in British agriculture and unemployment in the housing industry, combined with foreign loans and expansion abroad, resulted in a tremendous rural exodus. See Cairncross, *op. cit.*, Fig. 17, p. 199; Brinley Thomas, *Migration and Economic Growth*, *op. cit.*, Appendix 4, Table 100, p. 290; and E. H. Phelps Brown and S. V. Hopkins, "The Course of Wage Rates in Five Countries, 1860-1939," *Oxford Economic Papers*, June, 1950, p. 276.

[106] The number of persons occupied in British agriculture fell from approximately 3.5 million in 1851 to 2.6 million in 1881 and to 2.2 million in 1901; and as a percentage of the total from 27.6 to 16.3 and to 11.9, respectively. Between 1870 and 1910 the wheat-producing area of England fell by over one-half. The total value of agricultural incomes fell from £201 million in 1870-1876 to a low of £135 million in 1894-1903 and rose thereafter to £162 million in 1911-1913. Agricultural incomes as a percentage of national income fell from 20.2 in 1867-1869 to 15.4 in 1877-1885 and to 7.1 in 1911-1913. The contraction of tillage to best soils, technical improvements, increase in the proportion of capital to other inputs, expansion of livestock, dairy, and fruit production—all helped to raise productivity. Output per worker rose from an index of 100 in 1867-1869 to 108 in 1877-1885 to 119 in 1894-1903, and to 124 in 1911-1913. But the index of output per worker in manufacturing and mining was uniformly higher; it had risen to 132 during the same period. Cf. E. M. Ojala, *Agriculture and Economic Progress*, 1952, Tables XLIX, LI-A, LV, pp. 129, 135, 153, and Appendix.

[107] The process of adjustment was costly and, in retrospect, it has been argued that the government may have paid insufficient attention to the continued improvement of agriculture, just as in recent years its protection has been excessive not only in Britain and the United States, but in most of western Europe. Cf. E. A. G. Robinson, "Agriculture's Place in the National Economy," and E. F. Nash, "The Sources of Our Food Supplies" (papers given at the conference entitled *Agriculture in the British Economy*, 1957, pp. 21-45, 47-58); and see "Organization for European Economic Coöperation," *Agricultural Policies in Europe and North America* 1956, esp. Chaps. 4, 5, 9, 18, and 21.

usually high, or rising, relative to the prices of manufactures. If we examine the three periods (see Table 16) when large overseas investments occurred, in 1871-1874, 1886-1890, and 1905-1913, we find that in the first two periods Britain's import-price index was reasonably stable, while its export-price index on the whole was rising. In the third period, Britain's import-price index and its export-price index were generally rising, but export prices were rising more rapidly than import prices. Thus in each period of high overseas lending

TABLE 16. Terms of Trade of the United Kingdom During Periods of High Foreign Lending

Year	1 Export-Price Index of U. K. Produce and Manufactures (1880=100)	2 Import- Price Index (1880=100)	3ᵃ Terms of Trade (1880=100)	4 Net Export of Capital (in £ million)
1871	118.0	107.9	109.4	53.4
1872	130.6	115.6	113.0	76.4
1873	135.2	115.4	117.2	63.4
1874	127.7	112.8	113.2	49.5
1886	83.6	80.1	104.4	61.5
1887	83.4	78.4	106.4	67.1
1888	82.9	81.0	102.3	75.2
1889	84.6	82.1	103.0	70.5
1890	88.3	80.9	109.1	85.6
1905	84.0	74.6	112.6	59.1
1906	89.0	77.8	114.4	97.6
1907	93.4	81.3	114.9	132.7
1908	89.8	78.3	114.7	127.4
1909	86.5	79.1	109.4	102.9
1910	90.2	83.6	107.9	135.5
1911	91.8	81.5	112.6	171.3
1912	93.4	83.0	112.5	186.2
1913	96.9	83.4	116.2	198.2

SOURCES: Columns 1, 2, 3: A. H. Imlah, unpublished revised series. Published series in "The Terms of Trade of the United Kingdom, 1798-1913," *Journal of Economic History*, May, 1950, pp. 177-182. Column 4: Cairncross, *Home and Foreign Investment, 1870-1913*, 1953, Table 40, p. 180.
ᵃ Column 1 divided by column 2.

Britain's terms of trade improved and primary prices remained compartively stable. These results are not surprising, for foreign investors would not be adverse to expanding their loans in primary-producing countries when the prices of such products remained stable while productivity and output increased. On the other hand, the enlarged effective demand for British exports—induced by large foreign loans— would tend to raise British export prices.

CONSUMMATION OF A TRADE PATTERN AND EMERGENCE OF INTERNATIONAL DISEQUILIBRIUM

From about 1900 to 1914, Britain's rate of economic growth sharply declined. Industrial productivity, real income per head of the working population, and net national income per capita registered small advance.[108] At about the beginning of this period, a fundamental change had occurred in Britain's pattern of domestic and foreign investments and in the structure of her foreign trade.

The volume of domestic investment had risen gradually from 1890 until 1899 and, as had been customary, the net export of capital declined.[109] But on this occasion it fell drastically and, what is more significant, a change had taken place:The reduction in foreign lending in the early 1900's no longer had the effect of raising the volume of investment at home.

By the turn of the century the British economy had definitely lost its preëminence as the manufacturing center of the world.[110] In 1870,

[108] Output per worker in mining and manufacturing and real income per worker rose approximately one-third from 1860 to 1890; then there was little progress in productivity or real income from 1900 to 1914. During this latter period, net national income per capita rose less than 1 percent per year. See E. H. Phelps Brown and S. J. Handfield-Jones, "The Climacteric of the 1890's: A Study in the Expanding Economy," *Oxford Economic Papers*, October, 1952, pp. 266-307, esp. p. 271; and Jefferys and Walters, *op. cit.*, p. 14. A break in the long-term trend of industrial growth first appeared, as we have seen, about 1870. Cf. D. J. Coppock, "The Climacteric of the 1890's: A Critical Note," *Manchester School of Economic and Social Studies*, January, 1956, pp. 3-22.

[109] Thomas, *Migration and Economic Growth, op. cit.*, p. 290; Cairncross, *op. cit., p.* 180.

[110] Marshall noted in 1903 the loss by Britain of the industrial leadership she had had 60 years before. He wisely observed that it was not inevitable that she should have lost so much. The greatness and rapidity of her loss, he maintained,

Britain's share of world manfacturing production was approximately 32 percent and that of the United States 23 percent. By 1896-1900, Britain's share had fallen to 19.5 percent and the United States' share had risen to 30.1 percent.[111] It was in this same period that a transformation had taken place in the structure of Britain's trade. Up to 1873, two-thirds of Britain's trade consisted of an exchange of manufactured goods for food and raw materials. By 1894-1903, this form of interchange had fallen to one-third. One-quarter of Britain's total trade had become an exchange of manufactures for manufactures, and invisibles financed another quarter of her total imports.[112]

From about the end of the 1890's until the outbreak of World War I, there seems to have been no clear relationship between fluctuations in Britain's home and foreign investment. Foreign lending assumed an independent cumulative tendency. Certainly from 1902 to 1913, foreign investment kept rising while home investment experienced considerable fluctuation. During this period, the boom in foreign lending and migration induced an expansion in exports, and the percentage distribution of manufactures against raw materials and food rose to 42.2 per cent, at the same time commodity imports against invisibles dropped to 15.1 percent. But this proved to be a short-term check on an intractable trend.[113]

---

was partly due to the very prosperity which followed the adoption of free trade. The combination of advantages that she had enjoyed in those years encouraged "the belief that an Englishman could expect to obtain a much larger real income and to live much more luxuriously than anybody else, at all events in an old country; and that if he chose to shorten his hours of work and take things easily, he could afford to do it." See "Memorandum on the Fiscal Policy of International Trade," *Official Papers of Alfred Marshall* (1903), 1926, Section L. The decline in the enterprising spirit of business leaders and workers was both an effect and a cause of Britain's lower rate of economic growth. For an interesting discussion of changes in entrepreneurship in Britain, cf. Bert F. Hoselitz, "Entrepreneurship and Capital Formation in France and Britain since 1700," *Capital Formation and Economic Growth*, National Bureau of Economic Research, 1955, esp. pp. 330-337; and David S. Landes, "Entrepreneurship in Advanced Industrial Countries: The Anglo-German Rivalry," *Entrepreneurship and Economic Growth*, Harvard University Research Center in Entrepreneurial History, November, 1954.

[111] League of Nations, *Industrialization and Foreign Trade*, 1945, p. 13.

[112] See A. O. Hirschman, *National Power and the Structure of Foreign Trade*, 1945, p. 145.

[113] By 1925-1929, the percentages had fallen back to their 1890-1903 levels; the percentage distribution of manufactures against raw materials and food

The cumulative growth of Britain's balance of capital credit abroad before World War I yielded interest and dividends which, together with receipts from the excess of exports over imports of manufactures and invisibles, were sufficiently large not only to pay for Britain's excess of imports over exports of food and raw materials, but also to expand the volume of her foreign loans.[114] It was this accumulating balance of capital credit abroad, and receipts therefrom, which explains how concurrently Britain was able to maintain a net export of capital and an excess of imports over exports of goods *plus* services. Manifestly, differences in the stock of capital relative to other resources—larger in Britain as compared with the United States and the regions of recent settlement—coupled with insufficient countervailing inventions, were of so large a magnitude and long-run in nature that neither were differentials in rates of return on capital removed nor changes in relative incomes to reduce the flow of investment generated.

Britain's foreign lending therefore was not a phenomenon which can be dealt with in terms of "short-run" or characteristically "long-run" *equilibrium mechanism-of-adjustment* theory. Nor did it operate according to such tenets. But it did provide, in effect, a most important stabilizing factor both for Britain's internal economic growth and for international economic equilibrium. Although foreign lending somewhat intensified periods of boom, it dampened the severity of British depressions and the intensity of their international propagation. Hence it helped Britain to maintain a high level of exports rather than to suffer from mass unemployment and to maintain a high level of imports rather than to spread severe depressions. One cannot overemphasize the fact, however, that this operation of foreign

---

amounted to 35.4 and commodity imports against invisibles 23.1. *Ibid.* Britain's share of world manufacturing production in 1926-1929 was 9.4 percent and that of the United States 42.2 percent. League of Nations, *Industrialization and Foreign Trade, op. cit.,* p. 13.

[114] Britain's accumulating balance of credit abroad grew from approximately £236 million in 1851 to £774 million in 1871, to £1998 million in 1891, and to £3975 million in 1913. Her annual net balance of interest and dividends was never as large as £100 million before 1897; it was equal to £200 million in 1913. Cf. Imlah, "British Balance of Payments and Export of Capital, 1816-1913," *Economic History Review,* 2nd series, Vol. V, No. 2, 1952, Statistical Appendix, pp. 234-239.

lending as an internal and external "automatic" stabilizer, assisting economic growth or restraining decline, was largely the product of historical circumstance: the higher marginal value product of capital abroad than at home, which was permitted to work itself out not with unmixed effects in a liberal political environment.[115]

Once the pattern of Britain's investments, interest and dividend returns, and export and import surpluses became established, it sparked a chain reaction. Britain's excess of imports over exports from Industrial Europe, we noted, helped finance Industrial Europe's excess of imports over exports from countries at a lower stage of economic development. As Industrial Europe mechanized and developed comparative cost and income advantages in manufactures, it began to depend upon Russia, the Balkans, the United States, and regions of recent settlement for its imports of primary products. This general pattern, an excess of imports over exports by more developed economies from less developed ones, greatly contributed to the comparatively smooth functioning of the balancing process. But the economic growth of the United States broke the sequence of this development. At the very time when Britain was consummating her pivotal position in the network of world trade, the United States had grown in economic power to replace her in that position. Herein, we shall endeavor to show, lies an important source of the international balance-of-payments disequilibrium which occurred during much of the first half of the twentieth century and, if left unchecked, will persist into the second. If that be the case, have the forces of international economic disequilibrium emanating from the United States been primarily of an

---

[115] Leland H. Jenks observed that, even with respect to the third quarter of the nineteenth century, British foreign investments had "fostered the growth of a rentier governing class, whose economic interests lay outside the community in which they lived and exerted influence." See his *Migration of British Capital to 1875*, 1927, p. 334. Given the alternatives open to her, it was virtually impossible for Britain to adjust quickly enough to the rapidly changing economic conditions which in part her own development had fostered. The race was never simply the classical one between diminishing returns and technical improvement. The penalty which Britain had to pay for industrial leadership also lay in the race between mobility and "wrong" specialization. Although these two races were interrelated, the latter became more and more difficult as Britain's rate of economic growth declined.

institutional or structural nature? Do theory and fact support the conclusion of chronic dollar shortage? The following analysis suggests
that the forces have been primarily of an institutional nature; they
have been associated with and aggravated by weighty structural and
cyclical factors, but the world dollar problem is *not* chronic.

10

Economic Growth and

International Disequilibrium

.

EVEN prior to the turn of the twentieth century the system of multilateral trade had assumed the general pattern that evolved in the years before World War I and during the interwar period.[1] The direction of trade balances was such that at the outbreak of World War II the United Kingdom had an excess of imports over exports from Industrial Europe, the United States, the regions of recent settlement, and the tropics. Industrial Europe, in turn, had an excess of imports over exports from the United States, the regions of recent settlement, and the tropics. Had the United States followed her predecessors in this sequence of economic development, she would long since have developed an excess of imports over exports from the regions of recent settlement and the tropics. The direction of trade balances would then have appeared as shown in Fig. 13.

[1] Cf. League of Nations, *The Network of World Trade*, 1942, pp. 78, 90; Robert L. Sammons, *Survey of Current Business*, 1948; and S. B. Saul, "Britain and World Trade, 1870-1914," *Economic History Review*, 2nd series, Vol. VII, No. 1, 1954, esp. p. 61. However, Britain ran a surplus with the tropics in 1910 and 1928; the surplus had turned deficit by 1938.

The United States represents the only case of divergence between this schematic or theoretical pattern of trade balances and the recorded facts of experience up to 1938; despite the important changes which had occurred during and after World War II, by 1951 this pattern had shown strong signs of reappearance. But it must be kept

EXCESS OF IMPORTS OVER EXPORTS $M > X$		EXCESS OF EXPORTS OVER IMPORTS $X > M$		
TRADE OF / TRADE WITH	A BRITAIN	B INDUSTRIAL EUROPE	C UNITED STATES	D REGIONS OF RECENT SETTLEMENT	E TROPICS
A BRITAIN	/////	$X > M$	$X > M$	$X > M$	$X > M$
B INDUSTRIAL EUROPE	$M > X$	/////	$X > M$	$X > M$	$X > M$
C UNITED STATES	$M > X$	$M > X$	/////	$X > M$	$X > M$
D REGIONS OF RECENT SETTLEMENT	$M > X$	$M > X$	$M > X$	/////	$X > M$
E TROPICS	$M > X$	$M > X$	$M > X$	$M > X$	/////

FIG. 13   Economic Growth and Pattern of Trade Balances

in mind that although the United States had developed an import surplus with the tropics, she had not done so with the regions of recent settlement.[2]

[2] The data for 1951 and thereafter are, of course, not entirely comparable to those of 1938, but the general pattern appears to reveal the same form, with further evolutionary changes manifesting the relative growth and decline among participants. But the changes incident to the full emergence of the United States to the pivotal position in the system cannot be overemphasized. For data on the network of international balances in 1938, 1949-1952, and 1955, see United Nations, World Economic Survey, 1956, 1957, Tables 7-11, pp. 29-34, and 38-39; W. S. Woytinsky and E. S. Woytinsky, World Commerce and Governments, pp. 86, 96-103, 112; and Herbert B. Woolley, "On the Elaboration of a System of

Needless to say, had the United States developed an import surplus with the regions of recent settlement, she would have become an importer of food and raw materials to an extent far exceeding anything so far experienced. She might then have provided the foreign exchange through her purchase of primary products to finance the sale of her growing "surpluses" of industrial goods. Her persistent export balance with its consequent "dollar shortage" may then have been a phenomenon of minor and temporary importance, if it had developed at all. But powerful economic and political forces intervened which prevented the United States from fitting into this development sequence. For an explanation of them, a glance at the salient features of the evolution of the United States balance of payments is a primary requisite.

FACTUAL BACKGROUND: UNITED STATES TRADE BALANCE, 1870's–1950's

In America, as in Britain, balance-of-payments developments were inextricably linked with the longer term cumulative forces of econ-

International Transaction Accounts," *Problems in the International Comparison of Economic Accounts*, Studies in Income and Wealth, Vol. 20, National Bureau of Economic Research, pp. 270-272; "Study of Structure of World Trade and Payments," *Foreign Economic Policy*, Hearings Before the Subcommittee on Foreign Economic Policy, 84th Congress, 1st Session, 1955, esp. Table 2, p. 220, and Fig. 1, p. 221. The grouping of countries is somewhat different in the study by the United Nations, in the ones by Woolley, and the League of Nations. The study by the United Nations groups together the trade of the United States and Canada, and deals with primary-producing countries which export mainly mineral products and rubber and those which export mainly agricultural products other than rubber. Woolley also groups together the trade of the United States and Canada and deals with the trade of "Latin America" and "other countries" rather than that of the "regions of recent settlement" and the "tropics." Hence Woolley's data for 1951 show that the United States and Canada *combined* had an excess of exports over imports with "Latin America" and with "other countries." However, if we use the original League of Nations' classification, we find that the United States had an excess of imports over exports with the *tropics* in that year; imports amounted to $5042 million and exports $4701 million. (Calculated from Bureau of the Census, *Quarterly Summary of Foreign Commerce of the United States*, May, 1951, pp. 2-3.) On the basis of similar classification, the results appear to be generally comparable and consistent with one another. By the early 1950's, settlements within the non-Communist trading world had again reverted to something closely akin to the prewar pattern. The important changes that emerged will be referred to below.

omic growth and the shorter term forces of the international mechanism of adjustment. As regards the longer term, from 1870 until 1910 productivity per worker and real wages in American agriculture increased at least as much as in industry. Total farm employment consequently rose rather than fell as it had done in Britain.[3] Until about the turn of the century, the American comparative advantage in primary production vis-à-vis Britain and Industrial Europe became ever

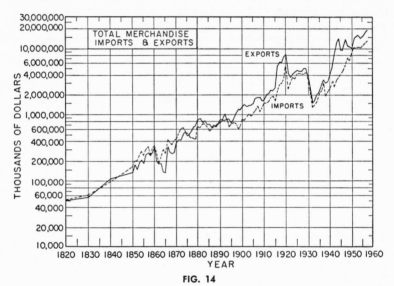

FIG. 14

more pronounced as European industrial growth continued and as American transportation costs and transatlantic freight rates declined. It can be seen from Figs. 14, 15, and 16 that the period beginning around 1875 marks an important turning point in the structure of the United States balance of payments.[4] From 1821 to 1874 (with

[3] Average agricultural income of American gainful agricultural workers as a percentage of the corresponding national average income rose during this period and particularly so from 1880 to 1914, whereas in England it fell. Cf. E. M. Ojala, *Agriculture and Economic Progress*, 1952, p. 134. For data on productivity per worker in American agriculture and total farm employment, see T. W. Schultz, *Agriculture in an Unstable Economy*, 1945, p. 86.

[4] Figs. 14-16 are based on the following sources: U.S. Department of Commerce, *Historical Statistics of the United States, 1789-1945*, 1949, pp. 246-247; *Statistical Abstract of the United States*, 1956, 1956, p. 909, and *Statistical Abstract of the United States*, 1957, 1957, p. 899, for data covering the period

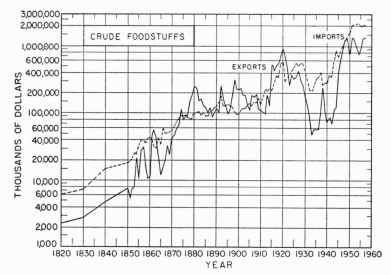

FIG. 15

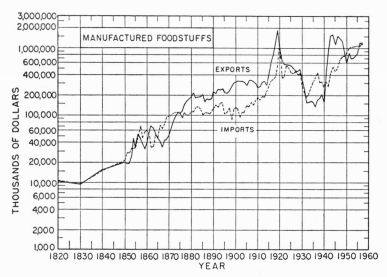

FIG. 16

the exception of the three years 1861, 1862, 1863), the United States had an excess of imports over exports of crude foodstuffs. But in 1874 our trade in crude foodstuffs turned from a passive to an active balance and, from 1877 until 1887 these exports exceeded imports each year. Similarly, in most years from 1820 to 1875, and without exception in the last decade, the United States had an excess of imports over exports of manufactured foodstuffs. But in 1876 our trade in manufactured foodstuffs also turned from a passive to an active balance. United States total merchandise trade turned active in 1874 and, although 1875 was an exception, from then on it too remained active until 1887. Indeed, for the entire period 1874 till 1895 the active trade balance in crude foodstuffs, manufactured foodstuffs, and crude materials not only provided proceeds to pay for the excess of imports over exports of semimanufactures and finished manufactures, but it also contributed to the net outpayment of interest on foreign investments in the United States, tourist expenditures abroad, freight charges on shipping, and immigrant remittances.[5] This shift

---

1946-1956; and U.S. Department of Commerce, Bureau of Foreign Commerce, World Trade Information Service, Part 3, No. 58-6, February, 1958, p. 3, and Ibid. No. 58-8, March, 1958, p. 2, for data covering 1957. Export data, unless otherwise stated, are exports of all United States "merchandise" shipped from the United States customs area, with the exception of supplies destined for United States Armed Forces abroad for their own use. In addition to commercial trade, by definition, the data on "merchandise trade" include relief, economic aid, and shipments of military equipment and supplies exported by the Department of Defense under the Mutual Defense Assistance and Mutual Security programs. Import data cover foreign merchandise received in the United States customs area; they are "general imports" through 1932 and imports for consumption thereafter. For more detailed explanatory notes see sources cited above and ibid., Part 3, No. 58-5, February, 1958, p. 2. Following are some of the important and typical commodities included in each of the economic classes shown on the charts— crude materials: crude petroleum, crude rubber; crude foodstuffs: grains, coffee; manufactured foodstuffs: prepared fruits, sugar; semimanufactures: steel plates, wood pulp; finished manufactures: electrical machinery, nonferrous manufactures.

[5] For the period as a whole (1874-1895), the United States active trade balance amounted to almost $2.5 billion and the net growth of foreign investments in the country to about $1 billion. The interest charge on foreign investments, on the other hand, has been estimated at $1.87 billion, tourist expenditures abroad $770 million, net freight charges $560 million, and immigrant remittances $440 million. These debits and credits were balanced by exports of gold amounting to $112 million. Errors and omissions accounted for $35 million. Cf. U.S. Department of Commerce, "Balance of Payments of the United States, 1919-1953," Survey of Current Business, July, 1954, p. 14; Charles J. Bullock, John H. Williams, and Rufus S. Tucker, "The Balance of Trade of the United States," Review of Economic Statistics, July, 1919, pp. 215-266, and esp. pp. 223-232.

from a passive to an active balance in total merchandise trade and its commodity composition reflects, *inter alia*, the transition which America made from a net "capital inflow" to a net "capital outflow" position under conditions of rapid economic development in primary production.[6]

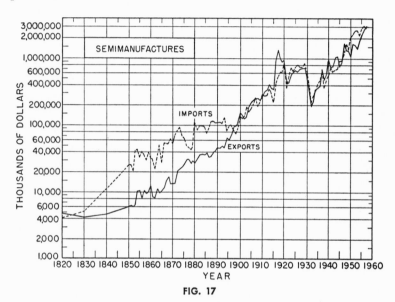

FIG. 17

As regards the shorter term, the effects of the panic of 1873 and the depression that followed accelerated the transition. The policy designed to achieve specie resumption by 1879 contributed to the deflationary adjustment. For as domestic prices, national production, money wages, and real wages declined, the United States' cost, price, and income structures were so readjusted relative to those of the rest of the world that her merchandise trade balance turned from an excess of imports amounting to approximately $137 million in 1873 to an excess of exports amounting to approximately $244 million in 1878.[7] The immediate transition from a passive to an active trade

[6] I.e., if we compare the period 1850-1873 with the period 1874-1895, we find that the United States reversed its position from a *net* inflow to a net outflow of the volume of the following combined transactions: long-term foreign investments, private remittances, and interest charges. *Ibid.*

[7] U.S. Department of Commerce, *Historical Statistics of the United States, 1789-1945, op. cit.*, p. 246

balance was achieved by way of a reduction in imports and an expansion in exports; but primarily by a reduction in imports, for exports actually fell in 1875 and were still below their 1874 level in 1876. American imports in fact dropped precipitously relative to exports during the worst depression years. Foreign trade therefore provided a stabilizing factor to domestic economic activity; but only at the expense of the outside world.

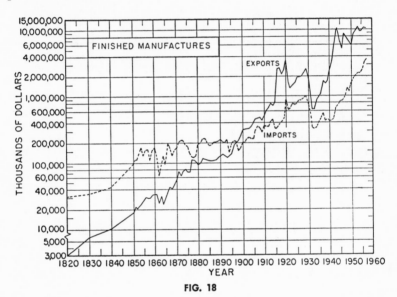

FIG. 18

Manufacturing production, as we have seen, was also rising rapidly in the United States during the second half of the nineteenth century and, as a consequence, it can be observed from Figs. 17 and 18 that the period beginning around 1896 marks another important turning point in the structure of its balance of payments. In 1897, for the first time since the 1830's, semimanufactures turned from a passive to an active balance. In 1898, finished manufactures did the same—a new occurrence in American history. The excess of total merchandise exports over imports increased remarkably. For the entire period, 1896-1914, the United States total active balance of merchandise trade grew to a magnitude of over $9 billion. Net foreign investments in the country increased by about $1 billion; whereas net interest on foreign investments, net tourist expenditures abroad, and immigrant remittances amounted to between $2.8 billion and $3.4 billion each. Net freight charges advanced to $640 million and other miscellaneous services to around $570 million.[8]

The growth in America's capacity to produce manufactures was a prime factor in enabling the balancing process under gold-standard conditions to transfer such large interest, service, and unilateral pay-

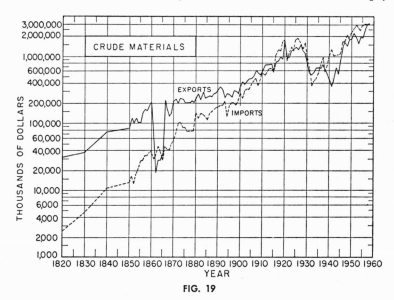

FIG. 19

ments in the form of goods without causing serious strain on the domestic economy. In effect, it was during this period that the demand for dollars by foreigners to pay for their imports of goods and services from the United States, plus their capital outflow, began to exceed the supply of dollars made available to them by the United States through its imports of goods and services, plus their capital inflow. In order to settle the American balance, foreigners shipped $174 million of gold to the United States.

Britain's balance of payments required major adjustment as a re-

[8] U.S. Department of Commerce, "Balance of Payments of the United States, 1919-1953," *op. cit.*, p. 14; and Bullock, Williams, and Tucker, *op. cit.*, p. 232.

sult of these developments. In the United States, the increase in population and real income raised the effective demand for crude foodstuffs. From 1898 to 1914, this demand was met primarily through an expansion in domestic production, a small rise in imports, and a sharp drop in exports. Consequently, Britain had to turn to other sources of supply for her wheat and meat. For the most part, she turned to Canada, Australia, and Argentina. As these countries developed, however, they much increased their demand for American manufactures. The United States increased its imports from them of such goods as hides and wool, timber products, and minerals; but she provided them with practically no market for some of their other key primary exports, e.g., grain and meat. The United States therefore developed large export surpluses with these regions of recent settlement. Another outstanding feature of this period was the enlarged active trade balance of the United States with Industrial Europe. Britain, on the other hand, had developed import surpluses with Canada and Argentina and was rapidly increasing her imports from Australia. Significantly, these countries had required only minor multilateral settlement of their international accounts in the early 1880's. Now, they had to expand greatly their net exports to Britain and other third countries in order to settle their deficits with the United States. To the extent that Britain did not sufficiently reduce her import surplus with the United States, her exports to India and the newly developing countries of Asia and Africa began to contribute more and more to the balancing of her international accounts. In these markets, as in the regions of recent settlement, her exports of manufactures faced growing American competition. Thus even before World War I, the economic growth of the United States and the emerging pattern of its trade balances revealed that in the very process of supplanting Britain from her pivotal position in world trade and payments the United States had set into motion strong forces of potential international economic disequilibrium.

The world dollar *problem* periodically has been with us since World War I. For the period July 1, 1914, to December 31, 1918, the American active balance on merchandise trade amounted to a total of $11.8 billion.[9] Until April, 1917, when the United States became a belligerent, foreign countries financed their current account debits with us by borrowing in this country approximately $2.4 billion, by selling around $2 billion of United States securities, and by shipping, net, approximately $1.1 billion of gold. From April, 1917, until the end of the war, our current account surplus was financed in the main by United States government loans to our allies amounting to $7.3 billion.[10]

The years 1919 to 1921 witnessed further abnormal (though after 1919 diminishing) merchandise trade surpluses which were made possible by new loans on the part of our government to foreign countries, augmented by private unilateral remittances, loans, or extensions of short-term credits. These funds proved insufficient to offset our credits on current account; for the three-year period foreign countries shipped to us another $500 million of gold.[11]

During the period 1922 to 1929 the United States active trade balance further declined, but it was still approximately 40 percent above the prewar average. These credits were enlarged by foreign repayments of earlier United States government loans and by foreign remittances of interest and dividends on United States investments abroad. The latter net credits were, of course, in marked contrast to American net

[9] *Ibid.* For the purpose of our analysis, changes in the United States balance on "merchandise trade," and in its economic classes, appear to be a better starting point for analyzing international transactions than changes in the entire balance on current account. After World War II, even in times of peace the current account has recorded large military transfers and expenditures which have been determined chiefly by political and security considerations. These items do not, of course, directly reflect either secular or cyclical changes in underlying economic conditions. Their magnitude has fluctuated widely in the past and may be expected to do so in the future. Whenever possible, they will be dealt with separately; and whenever relevant, data on more inclusive balances will be furnished. A penetrating, summary discussion on characteristics of United States balance-of-payments data is to be found in Walther Lederer, "Major Developments Affecting the United States Balance of International Payments," *Review of Economics and Statistics,* May, 1956, pp. 178-181.

[10] Bullock, Williams, and Tucker, *op. cit.,* pp. 237, 246-247, 251-252; and John H. Williams, "The Balance of International Payments of the United States for the year 1920 with a Statement of the Aggregate Balance July 1, 1914-December 31, 1920," *Review of Economic Statistics,* June, 1921, pp. 169-212, esp. p. 201.

[11] U.S. Department of Commerce, "Balance of Payments of the United States, 1919-1953," *op. cit.,* p. 14.

debits on investment account before the war. Nonetheless, American tourists' expenditures abroad, remittances by immigrants and charitable foundations, and purchases of shipping and insurance services contributed greatly to the foreign supply of dollars. The remaining foreign indebtedness was met mostly by a net outflow of private United States capital either in the form of long-term portfolio investment, or short-term, and other loans which averaged over $500 million a year.[12] However, even this outflow of capital and loans proved insufficient to cover our external claims, and in order to balance their American accounts foreign countries shipped to us another $625 million of gold.

The great depression cut our active trade balance almost in half. United States capital exports were drastically curtailed from a net outflow of $1.5 billion in 1928 to a net inflow of $777 million in 1931. From 1930 to 1933, the total supply of dollars that the United States made available to the rest of the world through its current payments and capital outflow was reduced by two-thirds. Foreign capital reversed its direction from a net inflow of $346 million in 1928 to a net outflow of $1.2 billion in 1931. This was one of the primary ways in which foreign countries met their immediate dollar deficits. Direct foreign exchange and trade controls followed. Practically all American receipts on war debts ceased after 1932 and, despite the curtailment of imports from the United States associated with the decline in foreign production and monetary contraction, the net drain of gold to the United States persisted. The devaluation of the dollar in 1934, combined with the policy of readily importing the precious metals, contributed to yet another tremendous gold inflow, and helped maintain our merchandise export surplus.

From 1934 to 1937 the United States active balance on total merchandise trade was further reduced. The American merchandise, as well as total current account, was in approximate equilibrium between 1935 and 1937, with merchandise imports actually exceeding exports in 1936. But when the recession of 1937-1938 struck, our merchandise imports fell from $3.01 billion in 1937 to $1.95 billion in 1938, whereas our exports declined only from $3.29 billion to $3.06 bil-

---

[12] *Ibid.*

lion.[13] Heavy unemployment, exchange and trade restrictions notwithstanding, gold and dollar reserves again were transferred to the United States; but the enormous drain that occurred throughout this period was primarily the result of political and monetary instability in Europe.[14] By the time World War II broke out, the stock of gold in the United States had risen to over $20 billion—nearly three-quarters of the entire world monetary gold stock.

From 1938 to 1941 the American active balance on merchandise trade amounted to a total of $5.2 billion; her active balance on goods and services to $6.4 billion. Until the advent of lend-lease in 1941, the rest of the world had to finance its large deficit with the United States by very heavy transfer of gold and the sale of dollar assets. Britain, in particular, virtually exhausted her reserves of gold and dollars and sold many of her dollar securities.[15] During the years 1942 to 1945 (inclusive) the United States active balance on merchandise trade amounted to over $30 billion; her active balance on goods and services to over $37 billion. For the entire period of United States participation as an active belligerent, more than 80 percent of total United States merchandise transfers represented lend-lease.[16] In fact,

[13] In order to maintain consistency in the use of data on merchandise trade, these figures are based on U.S. Department of Commerce, *Historical Statistics of the United States, 1789-1945, op. cit.,* p. 246.

[14] See Arthur I. Bloomfield, *Capital Imports and the American Balance of Payments, 1934-39,* 1950, pp. 13-14: "The bulk of the phenomenal rise in foreign short-term assets in the United States was the result of two major disturbing factors that induced a strong desire on the part of foreigners to be liquid in terms of dollars: anticipations of depreciations of foreign currencies *vis-à-vis* the dollar (most important in 1935-37) and, more especially, increasing international political tension (which dominated the situation in 1938-39)."

[15] It is usually assumed that British savings invested abroad before World War II were worth about £4000 million. During the war she sold over £1000 million of these foreign investments and, in addition, accumulated liabilities to countries overseas of about £3000 million. Shortly after the war (March, 1946), she had to borrow $2.75 billion from the United States and $1.25 billion from Canada. Cf. "Washington Negotiations," *Statistical Material presented during the Washington Negotiations,* Sessional Papers, Session 1945-1946, Vol. 21 (Cmd. 6707). Still, in 1938 the official gold reserves of the total sterling area amounted to $3.4 billion, whereas in 1948 the official gold *and* dollar reserves of the total sterling area amounted to only $2.5 billion. See *Federal Reserve Bulletin;* and International Monetary Fund, *International Financial Statistics* (estimates of official dollar holdings are given in the latter publication for November, 1956, p. 19).

[16] See U.S. Department of Commerce, *International Transactions of the United States During the War 1940-45,* prepared under the direction of Robert L. Sammons, 1950, p. 7.

the rest of the world built up its gold and dollar reserves during this period.[17]

The large United States active balance on total merchandise trade continued into the years of postwar reconstruction. From 1946 through 1949, excluding military transfers under aid programs, it amounted to $28.5 billion, or an average of $7.1 billion a year. Foreign countries spent in the United States for American exports of goods *and* services (excluding military transfers under aid programs) $67 billion and for repayments of American loans and unrecorded transactions $4.8 billion. They obtained dollars from the United States through American imports of goods and services of $35.1 billion, American net capital outflow (excluding repayment of loans) and private remittances of $6.2 billion, American government grants, loans, changes in short-term assets abroad, and disbursements of government-subscribed funds by the International Bank and Monetary Fund of $23.4 billion. This left a dollar deficit of $7.1 billion, which foreign countries met by drawing on their own gold and dollar assets.

From 1950 through 1953 the United States active balance on merchandise trade was strikingly reduced; excluding military transfers under aid programs, it amounted to a total of $7.8 billion or an average of $1.95 billion a year. Foreign countries spent in the United States for American exports of goods *and* services (excluding military shipments under aid programs) $67.7 billion and for repayment of loans and unrecorded transactions $3.2 billion. They obtained dollars from the United States through American imports of goods and services of $59.2 billion, American net capital outflow (excluding repayment of loans) and private remittances of $6.3 billion, and American government grants, loans, and changes in short-term assets abroad of $13.2 billion. This provided a dollar *surplus* of $7.8 billion, which was added to foreign gold and dollar assets.[18]

But the mild recession of 1953-1954, the Suez episode, and the recession of 1957-1958 again increased the United States active balance

[17] U.S. Department of Commerce, "Balance of Payments of the United States, 1919-1953," *op. cit.*, p. 15.
[18] *Ibid.*, pp. 10, 13, 15.

in merchandise trade. From 1954 through 1957, excluding military transfers under aid programs, it amounted to $16.7 billion or an average of $4.2 billion a year.[19]

To be sure, estimated gold reserves and dollar holdings of foreign countries and international institutions rose during this period. They rose from $26.4 billion at the end of 1953 to $31.1 billion at the end of 1956, primarily because the United States had more than covered the dollars it received through its current trade surplus by two compensating capital movements: aid to, and investment in, the outside world.[20] Then, during most of 1957, the net outflow of dollars from the United States was sharply reversed. The causes of this reversal were neither simple nor singular, but among them were certainly the events which originated in the Suez episode and undermined confidence in the "sterling area system." There was flight from sterling and the international currency crisis of September, 1957, exposed once again the precarious international liquidity position of the non-Communist world outside the United States.[21]

Since that time the net outflow of American capital has been resumed. Total holdings of gold reserves and liquid dollar assets of foreign countries and international institutions at the end of the first quarter of 1958 were about $200 million higher than before the Suez crisis, and the seasonally adjusted rate of growth of these reserves was not far below the previous peak rate during the second half of 1952.[22]

[19] U.S. Department of Commerce, *World Trade Information Service*, Part 3, No. 58-5 February, 1958, p. 5. In these figures, exports include reëxports.

[20] *Federal Reserve Bulletin*, October, 1955, p. 1195 and May, 1958, p. 621.

[21] Gold and dollar reserves of the non-Communist world outside the United States as a percentage of the foreign visible trade of these countries (i.e., the estimate of world trade—imports plus exports—excluding U.S.S.R., eastern Europe, and China, minus total United States imports and exports) were approximately 30 percent before World War II and less than 20 percent in the 1950's. Cf. International Monetary Fund, *International Financial Statistics*.

[22] *Survey of Current Business*, June, 1958, pp. 9-14. It is noteworthy, however, that the decline in United States seasonally adjusted merchandise imports from an annual rate of $13.8 billion in the first quarter of 1957 to $12.4 billion in the first quarter of 1958 was considerably *more* than in total outpayments. Most important among the outpayment items that increased were military expenditures. The reduction in seasonally adjusted merchandise imports (excluding purchases by military organizations) from the fourth quarter of 1957 to the first quarter of 1958 was 10 percent; the reduction in seasonally adjusted merchandise exports was approximately 11 percent. The foreign gold and dollar accumulations during

Nonetheless it is understandable that most non-Communist countries of the outside world fear that the dollar gap may reappear. They maintain that in 1957–1958, the gap was kept down only because many western countries slowed down their rate of production to keep in step with the slower American pace. True of false, it is generally held that the most pressing economic problem in the international field today is still the problem of dollar shortage.

We are here concerned with one important facet of this problem, viz., the economic forces operating in the United States which have tended to produce balance-of-payments disequilibrium, or "dollar shortage," in the specific sense of an excess of immediate claims on foreign countries over obligations to them, which must be liquidated by specie, by surrender of foreign balances, or by agreed deferment.

UNITED STATES ECONOMIC GROWTH AND INTERNATIONAL DISEQUILIBRIUM

As in the case of Britain, the evolution of the American balance of payments has revealed certain unique features which do not conform to our current explanations of equilibrium mechanism-of-adjustment theory. How otherwise explain the fact that since 1896, virtually without interruption, the United States has been able to maintain an active balance on merchandise trade—and on current account—which did not generate sufficiently strong changes in relative incomes, prices, or the flow of capital to reverse this balance? As early as 1920, eminent economists predicted that our trade balance would be reversed within a decade. The evidence strongly suggests that the process whereby our international accounts were cleared must, in addition to equilibrium balancing theory, be explained in terms of a more or less continuous process which was interrelated with periods of relative expansion and contraction, and which set into operation forces which *simultaneously* induced changes in relative costs, prices,

---

the first quarter of 1958—a period of recession—resulted from a *more rapid reduction in foreign expenditures* in the United States than in United States expenditures abroad. This novel phenomenon may represent a new tendency for the future.

and incomes, as well as changes in planned saving, capacity to produce, and plans to invest both at home and abroad. Many interrelated forces working at home have checked the expansion of American imports relative to exports. Until recently, a deliberate national policy of high tariff and administrative protection; the continental character and climate of the United States; its abundance, richness and variety of natural resources; the great distances from most foreign trading and producing centers; the protection to inland producers by high internal transportation costs; the technical skills of its people; the technological efficiency of its mass-scale production and distribution in manufacturing; the generally well-organized and mechanized agriculture; the nature of its commodity imports—all these factors have tended to limit the expansion of American imports without heavy cost either in the production of domestic substitutes or in the deprivation of important products.

MORE SPECIFIC HYPOTHESES

Granted all this, we submit that during the interwar period one of the most pervasive disequilibrating forces in industry and agriculture, which was not unrelated to the forces mentioned above, has been the relation between the volume and growth in American productive capacity, on the one hand, and the volume and growth in domestic income and demand for final products, on the other. The available evidence shows that "full-capacity output" was in substantial excess of actual output not only during most of the 1920's and 1930's, but even in times of the business-cycle peaks.[23] Since consumption is a more stable (i.e., dependable or predictable) constituent of output

[23] Cf. Bert G. Hickman, "Capacity, Capacity Utilization, and the Acceleration Principle," *Problems of Capital Formation*, Studies in Income and Wealth, Vol. 19, National Bureau of Economic Research 1957, esp. Table 6, pp. 434-435; and Edwin G. Nourse, *America's Capacity to Produce*, 1934, where it is estimated that the American economy entered the Great Depression with an excess capacity of 17 percent, which became inordinately more excessive as the depression deepened. For a discussion of the tortuous theoretical and statistical concept of "capacity" see Hickman, *op. cit.*, pp. 419-423. By the term "full-capacity output" we mean the output that the existing stock of equipment is intended to produce under normal working conditions with respect to hours of work, number of shifts, etc. It corresponds to the usual statistical-engineering notion of full capacity as used by the steel and other industries. "Excess capacity" denotes the difference between full-capacity output and actual output.

·than is investment, the growth of excess capacity over the long pull implies that either the rate of new investment was not large enough and/or the structural adjustments not rapid enough to generate a sufficiently high equilibrium rate of growth in national income.[24]

Recent studies have shown that in the United States, changes in capacity—and by inference fixed investment—were dominated by secular growth.[25] In the case of growing industries, the secular expansion of output gave a relative immunity to cyclical contractions. For in such industries, contractions of production usually did not prevent the expansion of capacity because projects initiated during upswings were carried over a year or two into contractions, and favorable long run expectations encouraged investment even during periods of depressed demand. Hence in the absence of long periods of cyclically depressed demand, the expansion of productive capacity in

[24] In terms of the well-known Harrod-Domar-Fellner models, the warranted or equilibrium rate of growth of income was not achieved. According to a rough estimate for the period 1879-1938, Domar suggests that our real national income should have grown perhaps 3.6 to 4.0 percent per year in order to prevent an excessive accumulation of capital; it grew approximately 3.3 percent per year. See E. D. Domar, "The Problem of Capital Accumulation," *American Economic Review*, December, 1948, p. 783, and "Capital Expansion, Rate of Growth, and Employment," *Econometrica*, April, 1946, p. 141; R. F. Harrod, "An Essay in Dynamic Theory," *Economic Journal*, March, 1939, and *Towards a Dynamic Economics*, 1948; and William Fellner, "The Rate of Growth and Capital Coefficients," *Long-Range Economic Projections*, Studies in Income and Wealth, Vol. 16, 1954, pp. 275-331. The aggregate condition for the equilibrium rate of growth is that at full employment the percentage rate of growth of output times the incremental (i.e., marginal) capital-output ratio be equal to the *ex ante* average propensity to save (i.e., aggregate investment be equal to *ex ante* aggregate saving at full employment). If (V) represents the stock of capital, (O) the full employment rate of output, (t) time, and (a) the *ex ante* average propensity to save, the condition is $\dfrac{\Delta V}{\Delta O} \cdot \dfrac{\Delta O / \Delta t}{O}$ be equal to a; or $\dfrac{\Delta V}{\Delta t}$ (i.e., aggregate investment) be equal to a.O (i.e., *ex ante aggregate* saving). Smithies has shown that the use of these aggregative models may yield large errors in estimating equilibrium rates of growth. Cf. "Economic Fluctuations and Growth," *Econometrica*, January, 1957, p. 24, n. 30. It is probably unnecessary to point out that in the past, economic growth inherently has been an irregular process; technically the essence of the problem of growth is that all parameters become variables. The usefulness of these models, nevertheless, when combined with other forms of analysis, lies in their validity as a device for thinking about the questions they pose and for analyzing how and why the future average rate of growth of income is likely to be different from that of the past.

[25] Cf. Hickman, *op. cit.*, pp. 419-450, esp. pp. 426-429; and Smithies, *op. cit.*, pp. 28-29.

these industries could be regarded as virtually continuous. In a major depression, however, the burden of excess plant and equipment retarded their capacity growth. Industries undergoing secular decline, on the other hand, experienced relatively continuous disinvestment; cyclical expansions of production often failed to press heavily on available capacity or to engender optimistic long-run expectations.

We have had occasion to examine the relatively rapid growth of manufacturing industries in the United States.[26] The increase in capacity of these industries has been associated with the more progressive changes in the complexion of the economy: technological improvement, emergence of new products, growth of cities, relative decline of agriculture, etc. In the process, the American economy tended to generate productive capacity faster than demand. Moreover, the American economy appears to have had a greater tendency to generate excess capacity than other developed countries.

In a dynamic economy, a tendency toward excess capacity intensifies efforts of producers to sell their current products and introduce new ones in order to utilize that capacity. This may help to account for the more pronounced role of salesmanship in the United States than elsewhere. However, when efforts at home fail to achieve a reasonable (i.e., profitable or expected) degree of balance between full-capacity output and domestic demand for final products, producers may intensify efforts to expand sales abroad. The lower the level of domestic demand in relation to full-capacity output, the greater would be the pressure to cut prices and expand exports.[27] If, on the other hand, prices are lowered abroad in order to stimulate sales in the United

---

[26] See Chapter 8.

[27] In the simplest terms, assuming that average variable costs can be met and conditions permit, it would be profitable for them to keep expanding the level of their total sales and output as long as marginal costs are below the point of equilibration with marginal revenue at home and abroad. Actually, the price policies that here apply are primarily those of dynamic oligopolistic market structures. In many cases the relevant price to the exporter is not the current price but the price *after* entry. A rich literature exists on "monopoly" in the field of international trade as it applies to governments but not to private firms. Tariff theory, for instance, is "monopoly theory." Much productive research on oligopoly awaits its application to the kind of international-trade problems raised above. See, e.g., Joe S. Bain, *Barriers to New Competition*, 1956, and sources cited therein; Franco Modigliani, "New Developments on the Oligopoly Front," *Journal of Political Economy*, June, 1958, pp. 215-232.

States and thereby check a deficit, the greater the volume of excess capacity in the United States the more American producers would be inclined to cut prices or petition for import restrictions to meet or counteract foreign competition. Furthermore, in the event of a substantial rise in prices or incomes abroad or at home, a comparatively greater volume of excess capacity in the United States would give American producers an advantage both in regard to early deliveries and costs. In terms of "elasticities," one would say that, *cet. par.*, the tendency of the American economy to generate excess capacity would tend (1) to raise the United States supply elasticity of exports with respect to price increases (lower it with respect to price decreases) vis-à-vis the rest of the world; (2) to lower the United States price elasticity of import demand for foreign price decreases; (3) probably to raise the foreign price elasticity of import demand for American price decreases; (4) to lower the United States income elasticity of import demand for American income increases (raise it for decreases); and (5) to raise the foreign income elasticity of import demand for foreign income increases (probably lower it for decreases).

These factors would all tend to produce dollar shortage. But just as it is essential to analyze the expected effects of changes in domestic developments upon the balance of payments, so it is essential to analyze the *attendant* expected effects of changes in balance of payments upon domestic developments. With respect to the problem at hand, this entails relating the effects of changes in productive capacity to changes in actual production and expenditure at home and abroad, for it is only through changes in relative costs, prices, incomes, and expenditures that export and import surpluses manifest themselves. If American excess capacity has been an important factor contributing to dollar shortage, then it must be shown how it has contributed to the level of actual production in the United States to exceed the level of domestic expenditure ("absorption") and to the level of American exports to exceed imports. Similarly, since a United States export surplus means an import surplus for the rest of the world, it must be shown how American excess capacity has "simultaneously" contributed to the level of domestic expenditure in the relevant rest-of-world compound to exceed the level of production, and to the level of imports to exceed exports, without at the same time bringing about equilibrating gold and/or "accommodating" capital movements. To show how and when such conditions occurred, it will be useful briefly to tie these forces together and to relate them to the pattern of economic growth so that we may compare the evolving conditions in the United States with those required for international economic equilibrium.

AGGREGATE RELATIONSHIPS BETWEEN PRODUCTION AND EXPENDITURE, EXPORTS AND IMPORTS

Disregarding for a moment all capital flows other than foreign investment, the basic relationships may be expressed in this way: A country's realized (*ex post*) consumption (C) is equal to its national production (P) minus domestic investment inclusive of inventories (I_d) plus imports (M) minus exports (X); or

$$C + I_d = P + (M - X) \qquad (1).$$

This is a truistic equation or an identity and is the consequence of nothing but the definition of national production or income. Inasmuch as we are disregarding all capital flows other than foreign investment, here income and production are equal. They usually differ, as is shown below. We assume in the above equation that domestic expenditures on consumption (C) and investment (I_d) include the expenditures on imported consumption and investment goods. It would be difficult otherwise to distinguish statistically between these two categories of domestic expenditures. Hence total domestic expenditure (E) is equal to domestic expenditures on consumption goods (C) plus investment goods (I_d), or

$$E = C + I_d \qquad (2).$$

From equations (1) and (2) we obtain

$$P - E = X - M \qquad (3).$$

It can readily be seen from equation (3) that, if in a certain period of time a country's national production (P) exceeds its domestic expenditure (E), its exports (X) must be greater than its imports

(M); and conversely. As regards the relevant rest-of-world compound, assuming no other trade, the excess of the combined imports over exports $(M - X)$ of these countries must equal the excess of their combined domestic expenditure over domestic production $(E - P)$.

As soon as we expand these equations to include interest and dividends, private unilateral transfers, and government aid (collectively designated by A), the volume of domestic production no longer equals national income. If a country makes aggregate net payments (A), by customary definition its production (P) is larger than national income (Y). Similarly the national income of a country that receives net payments (A) is larger than domestic production.

Hence for a country that makes aggregate net payments (A), such as the United States in the postwar era,

$$Y = P - A \tag{4},$$

and, from equations (3) and (4), we obtain

$$Y + A = E + (X - M) \tag{5}.$$

It can be perceived from equation (5) that whenever the national income of the United States (Y) exceeds domestic expenditure (E), the export surplus $(X - M)$ exceeds the aggregate net payments of private unilateral transfers, interest and dividends, and government aid (A); and conversely. National income includes foreign loans. Therefore the difference between (Y) and (E) or $(X - M)$ and (A) equals the realized (ex post) volume of net foreign investment (I_t), including changes in the stock of monetary gold but excluding those resulting from home production. From equations (3) and (5), we thus obtain

$$P - E = X - M = I_t + A \tag{6}.$$

We shall find it useful to have these relationships expressed in such truistic form so that we may consider the circumstances in which they acquire more substantive meaning.

First let us observe what they do *not* signify. An excess of domestic production over expenditure does not preclude inflation. A country such as the United States may simultaneously experience a rising price level, an excess of production over expenditure, and an excess of exports over imports. The total volume of production, for example, may be greater than domestic real expenditure, but the excess of exports over imports may so reduce the volume of goods at home that effective demand exceeds supply. Nor does an American export surplus, of, for example, $5 billion a year, imply that an equivalent increase in United States expenditure (or a decrease in the relevant rest-of-world compound) would eliminate this surplus. An increase or decrease in expenditure would, *inter alia*, affect the level of production; the net result on the balance of payments would depend upon the comparative effectiveness of all the factors operating in the international mechanism. Moreover, an excess of domestic expenditure over production (excess of imports over exports) certainly does not signify that domestic consumption is larger than production. Since domestic expenditure is equal to domestic investment plus consumption (eq. 2), an excess of expenditure over production means that consumption is less than, equal to, or greater than production if domestic investment is greater than, equal to, or less than the import surplus, respectively (eq. 1). The problems of domestic and international disequilibrium can now be considered in terms of these relationships.

Although identities cannot explain cause and effect relationships, they can be helpful in their exposition once they have been derived from *a priori* reasoning (with the assistance of experience). We have noted that during the interwar period there was much disparity between the volume and growth in American productive capacity, on the one hand, and the volume and growth in income and demand for final products, on the other. For the period, the economy tended to generate excess capacity faster than final demand. The American economy also had a greater tendency to generate excess capacity than other developed countries; i.e., the volume of underutilized capacity was substantially larger at home than abroad.[28]

[28] The above views imply that American saving tended to rise faster than investment. But they do not imply that realized saving as a percentage of net national product was higher in the United States than in the other developed countries. Nor do they imply that productivity per man-hour in the United States rose faster than in the other countries, though the fact that it did rise faster than in Britain is important to our analysis. There was no clear-cut relationship in the United States between the growth in productive capacity and productivity per

These tendencies to generate excess capacity brought about the tendency to generate actual output in excess of demand. On critical occasions, as we shall see, excess capacity in time became more the result than the cause of the rise in full-capacity output relative to actual output. Nonetheless, it was the rise in excess capacity that brought about the tendency toward imbalance between production and expenditure. In effect, as regards the forces working within the United States, the tendency for production to rise faster than domestic expenditure appears to have been the primary cause of the systematic dollar-shortage problem. This tendency was the most important single cause of the persistent, furtive existence of dollar shortage on a small scale and of the periodic occurrence of dollar shortage on a large scale.

The facts of the interwar period appear to be consistent with this view. In order to explain them we shall consider the record in terms of the above equations expressed in the form of expected (*ex ante*) cause and effect relationships. As the mechanism of adjustment *qua* mechanism is a monetary phenomenon, the analysis will be presented in monetary terms.

Consider the relationships: $P - E = X - M = I_f + A$. The direction of causality can take several forms.

Changes in the volume of excess capacity may be the cause more or less simultaneously of an excess of production over anticipated expenditure, an export surplus, and an outflow of capital.[29] On theoreti-

---

man-hour. Productivity appeared to increase as rapidly in the late 1930's as in the 1940's and 1950's, even though productive capacity increased much more rapidly in the latter period. For data on comparative productivity see Chapter 8, above. Statistics on gross private savings as a percentage of gross private income in selected countries are presented in United Nations, *World Economic Survey, 1957, 1958*, pp. 24-27.

[29] In terms of the equations presented above, production (P) and expenditure (E) by definition include domestic investment (I_d) which, in turn, is defined to include inventories. Hence, to be consistent, the reference in the text is to imbalance between production and *anticipated* expenditure. The difference between production (exclusive of the export balance) and anticipated "native" expenditure may result, *inter alia*, in the accumulation of "involuntary" or "unplanned" inventories and in an excess of exports over imports. Once the involuntary inventories are sold, *cet. par.*, by definition (P) and (X) rise to the same extent and hence (*ex post*), $P-E=X-M$. The process of such imbalance is discussed in greater detail below.

cal grounds one would expect that, *cet. par.*, the greater the correspondence between the rate of growth of full-capacity output and actual output, the smaller the likelihood of dollar shortage. If the rate of growth of full-capacity output is larger than that of actual output, the export surplus may be expected to rise; if smaller, to fall. Simultaneously, if the rate of growth of full-capacity output is larger than that of actual output, *cet. par.*, the return on domestic capital and on anticipated new investment may be expected to fall and the volume of foreign investment to rise. These adjusting forces, coupled with differentials in interest rates and variations in exchange rates, would work toward the equilibration of the export surplus $(X - M)$ and the net export of capital $(I_f + A)$ exclusive of any inflow of monetary gold, surrender of foreign balances, or agreed deferment. But they may—or may not—be powerful enough to bring about balance. If they are, a general dollar shortage cannot arise; if they are not, it cannot help but arise.[30]

Regardless of the amount of excess capacity, if the United States government makes foreign loans and renders mutual aid, the attendant excess of exports over imports may tend to induce the excess of production over expenditure. Simultaneously the excess of imports over exports in the capital receiving countries may tend to induce the excess of expenditure over production.[31] *Ex post*, these relationships between production and expenditure by definition would have to prevail in monetary and real terms. The manner in which the real transfer is achieved, however, can radically affect economic fluctuations and growth. Regarding the United States, given its strong tendency to generate excess capacity one would expect *a priori*, a con-

---

[30] I.e., in terms of the above equations, if we exclude from net United States foreign investment (I_f) the inflow of monetary gold to the United States, the surrender of foreign balances by the rest-of-world compound, or agreed deferment, then a dollar shortage, balance, or surplus would develop in the *ex ante* (and *ex post*) sense whenever $(X - M)$ tended to be larger than, equal to, or smaller than $(I_f + A)$, respectively.

[31] This is entirely consistent with healthy economic development. The direction of causality discussed above could occur, e.g., if the monetary and fiscal authorities in the capital-importing countries increased the stream of monetary expenditure only to the extent of the increase in the import surplus plus the expansion (if any) in domestic production, and conversely for the capital-exporting country. Otherwise, the real transfer would in all probability be achieved by way of relative inflation.

siderable range within which the larger the export of capital, the closer the correspondence between the rate of growth of actual and full-capacity output. Hence, the larger would be the export of capital, the smaller the imbalance between domestic production (exclusive of the export balance) and anticipated "native" expenditure, and the smaller the tendency toward dollar shortage. We would therefore expect an enlarged export of capital under these conditions to result in a higher and smoother rate of economic growth and to help bring about international economic equilibrium.[32] The economy could thereby be maintained in a state of healthy "exhilaration," with the actual rate of economic growth approximating the "warranted" or equilibrium rate, and with the (real) net export of capital approximating the difference between production and anticipated expenditure, on the one hand, and the export surplus, on the other. However, if at full employment the increase in domestic expenditure resulting from the export surplus is not sufficiently offset by taxation, effective demand is likely to exceed supply at existing prices.[33] The rate of growth of actual output may then be expected to exceed that of full-capacity output. Ensuing spurts of inflation would, in all probability, reduce the rate of economic growth and lead to fluctuations rather than steady expansion. During the boom, *cet. par.*, one would expect the propensity to spend to exceed the propensity to produce, and this would tend to promote balance-of-payments equilibrium or even a dollar surplus. The reverse tendency during the slump would tend to produce a dollar shortage. The fact that capital exports affect the relation between production and expenditure, as well as exports and imports tends to reduce pressures working toward dollar shortage. In any event, as shown above, these relationships may be expected to

[32] Considering the characteristics of past full-employment and unemployment periods, I believe that high employment (and expectations of high employment) without much dispersion are likely to induce a higher average rate of secular growth than strongly fluctuating periods of employment (and strongly fluctuating expectations).

[33] The principles of the "balanced-budget" theorem may here be applied to the problem of the requisite offset. Cf. Paul A. Samuelson, "The Simple Mathematics of Income Determination," *Essays in Honor of Alvin P. Hansen*, 1948, pp. 140-150; and John G. Gurley, "Fiscal Policies for Full Employment," *Journal of Political Economy*, December, 1952, pp. 525-533, and sources cited therein.

produce an export surplus which is smaller than, equal to, or greater than the outflow of capital, resulting in a dollar surplus, balance, or deficit, respectively.

Secular structural maladjustments and cyclical economic fluctuations may be expected to work, *seriatim*, from an excess of production over anticipated expenditure to an excess of carry-over stocks and inventories, to an excess of exports over imports. We have observed that American agriculture remains at high levels of output during periods of expansion and contraction.[34] For obvious reasons, it is even more difficult to define excess capacity in agriculture than in industry. Yet in practice, acreage-restriction schemes, etc., which attempt to improve the balance between the rate of growth in supply and demand of selected crops at parity-determined prices, in effect, attempt to reduce the full-capacity output of farms. The larger excess capacity in agriculture and the greater immobility of agricultural resources—as well as the higher relative uncertainty of employment in urban areas—the more one would expect to find persistent surpluses of agricultural products. It need hardly be stressed that the higher the parity price supports and the greater their certainty—as well as the more rapid the rise in agricultural productivity—the larger would be the tendency for carry-over stocks to accumulate. With respect to some crops, excess capacity may be the *result* of international disequilibrium rather than its cause. Nonetheless, the greater the imbalance at home (and abroad) between agricultural production and industrial production, on the one hand, and agricultural demand and industrial demand on the other, the higher would be the probability of increased surpluses. If the government succeeds in exporting them by lowering export prices, accepting payment in local currencies, and granting loans and gifts, the real income of the recipient countries would tend to rise. Dollar shortage would not directly develop. But other agricultural-exporting countries certainly would tend to suffer from a deterioration in their balance of payments generally, and, specifically, with the United States. Even more important for all concerned, one would expect the accumulation of surpluses and the anticipation of them

---

[34] See Chapter 7.

in the future to retard the rise in American imports of agricultural products.[35]

SOME RELATED CYCLICAL FACTORS

The direction of causality from the tendency of production to exceed expenditure to an excess of exports over imports is even more pronounced in periods of cyclical contraction than in those of secular maladjustment. From what has already been said, we can summarize the expected cause and effect relationships in terms of Fig. 20. As

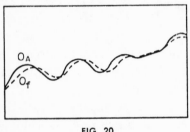

FIG. 20

we are here concerned with influences stemming only from the American economy, in simplest and briefest terms we assume that the increase in United States actual output depends on the increase in domestic effective demand which, in turn, depends on the increase in investment plus the multiplier and "asset" effects on consumption. The rate of growth of full-capacity output (for some relevant range) depends on the proportion of current output that the economy is prepared to devote to increasing output (including improvement of the quality of land, labor, and capital); on the technical effectiveness of investment in increasing output; and on the rate at which existing capacity output is reduced through depreciation and obsolescence. Structural forces such as changes in the composition of demand, output, and investment, as well as technological, fiscal, monetary, and psychological factors would have to be considered. For they are bound to affect relative costs, prices, and profits which in turn affect changes in the available stream of investment opportunities and the induce-

[35] The direction of causality discussed above may be illustrated by way of the equation $P - E = X - M$, considered in terms of *ex ante* cause and effect relationships. If, at parity prices, the production of agricultural products tends to exceed the *commercial* expenditures for them (i.e., exclusive of the "involuntary" accumulation of inventories on the part of private parties), the United States government would be obliged to increase its expenditures on carry-over stocks. *Cet. par.*, the excess of agricultural production (P) over *voluntary* expenditure (E), therefore, would lead to the accumulation of government surpluses and to the excess of exports (X) over imports (M). Once the surpluses are exported, by definition this means that (P) rises commensurately with (X).

ments to use them. All these vital elements of reality, including the influence of trends, would have to be integrated even in a skeleton outline of the process of economic growth and fluctuations.[36]

The solid line in Fig. 20 denotes the behavior of actual output (O_A) and the dotted line that of full-capacity output (O_f).[37] It is assumed, for the most part, that the economy is in a state of fluctuating endogenous growth with each peak and each trough occurring at a higher level of output than the preceding one. This may or may not depend upon trends affecting the fluctuations; it is here assumed that they do. Specifically, it is assumed that the forces of endogenous expansion are linked to those of an upward trend in investment. The intervention of such an upward trend would probably affect expectations of output, consumer expenditures, prices, profits, etc. With the assistance of reasonably effective counter-cyclical policy, it may change the endogenous model from one of fluctuations to one of steady continued expansion.[38] This possibility is depicted in Fig. 20 by superimposing the solid line of actual output on the dotted line of full-capacity output. It corresponds to the equilibrium or warranted rate of growth. Inflationary forces may in turn alter the structure of the economy from one of steady continued expansion to cyclical fluctuations, and this is shown on the right of Fig. 20.

[36] The literature on this subject is voluminous. It awaits detailed integration with international trade theory. Our purpose here is merely to relate some selected key elements to the problem at hand. Cf. the useful discussions and references to the literature in Arthur Smithies, *op. cit.*; Robert A. Gordon, "Investment Behavior and Business Cycles," *Review of Economics and Statistics*, February, 1955, pp. 23-34; and N. Kaldor, "The Relation of Economic Growth and Cyclical Fluctuations," *Economic Journal*, March, 1954, pp. 53-71. Syntheses are to be found in William J. Baumol, *Economic Dynamics: An Introduction*, 1951; and James S. Duesenberry, *Business Cycles and Economic Growth*, 1958.

[37] The volume and changes in capacity are not shown on the diagram. Nor is the depression of the 1930's, which is considered to be an exception when abnormally aggravating factors were at work. We wish to illustrate periods of cyclical expansion in which firms operate above capacity; hence, during the upswing, O_A is drawn to be above O_f. In practice, this of course is true only at the later stages of expansion. By stressing the relations between changes in excess capacity and the export balance, it is not meant to imply that other internal forces may not also produce an export surplus with or without the existence of excess capacity.

[38] Trend influences may offset or reinforce tendencies toward steady growth or persistent exhilaration. In the United States, an upward trend in investment appears most likely to reinforce such tendencies. The greatest danger is that it will bring about persistent inflation, as is noted below in the text.

Consider a position at the bottom of depression (left of Fig. 20) with much excess capacity. As the period of expansion gets under way, one would expect the rate of growth of actual output (O_A) to exceed that of full-capacity output (O_f). This would tend to bring about a more balanced relationship between actual and full-capacity output, an expansion of expenditure in relation to production, and a movement toward balance-of-payments equilibrium. Should the volume of excess capacity nonetheless remain high (not shown on diagram), it would continue to stimulate an export surplus. As the peak of the cycle is reached and actual output begins to decline, plant and equipment in the process of construction would tend to be completed and expanding industries would continue to add to their productive capacity. Hence for a time full-capacity output would continue to rise even after actual output had begun to decline. As depression becomes more severe, one would expect the rate of decline of actual output to exceed that of full-capacity output. Excess capacity would therefore grow and actual expenditure decline relative to output. With the cumulative onslaught of depression—as production, employment, and income fall while inventories rise—excess capacity would tend to retard domestic investment.

It is at this point that the pivotal position of the American economy in the network of world trade must be most closely compared with the position held by Britain before World War I. In the case of Britain, when a disparity developed between the growth of full-capacity output and actual output, the economy found profitable outlets for its excess saving overseas and hence was able to maintain a comparatively high volume of output and trade. In the United States when, among other factors, the growth of domestic investment as a percentage of net national product periodically tended to generate a rate of growth in income and an excess of planned saving over planned domestic investment, there was no foreign outlet for the excess of planned saving over planned domestic investment in the way that was prevalent in Britain before World War I. The returns on domestic capital would thus decline, the growth process be interrupted, full-capacity output be in excess of actual output, actual output be in excess of total demand, production be curtailed, labor become unemployed, and the pressures to expand exports and reduce imports would become overwhelmingly strong.

The sheer weight of American depression would reduce the marginal efficiency of capital in countries closely knit to the American economy. On the other hand, no strong and stable *long-term* tendency to export capital from the United States could be expected. The *comparatively* balanced rate of growth of American factor supplies coupled with technological improvements appear to have checked any secular tendency in the United States toward diminishing returns on capital. Hence, in the interwar period, the "overall" marginal value product of capital in the United States and expectations as to its long-term trend were in all probability higher than in most other industrial countries as well as in many regions of recent settlement and the tropics.

One would consequently expect during periods of depression (and to a smaller degree during a recession) the long-run forces of economic growth, the structural maladjustments, and the cyclical fluctuations to become powerfully linked in bringing about an export surplus and a dollar shortage.

But under such conditions the attempt to maintain a large American export surplus would become abortive, and the direction of causality would probably be reversed. For as foreign gold and liquid dollar reserves were reduced, imports from the United States would have to be curtailed. The value of the American export surplus would therefore tend to decline, although the dollar-shortage problem would tend to become ever more acute. Since the American government could induce an expansion of domestic output and employment by increasing the export surplus *via* a rise in the outflow of capital, it would be surprising indeed if such policies were not adopted. The impact of such policies on economic growth and international economic equilibrium, however, would depend upon their affect upon production and expenditure, on the one hand, and the net outflow of private and government capital on the other.

If United States policies were successful in raising the export surplus, there would be no assurance that domestic consumption plus investment would be increased. A rise in the export surplus accompanied by an equal, or smaller, rise in production would leave domestic consumption plus investment unchanged, or reduced, respectively. If domestic consumption plus investment is to rise, production must rise to a greater extent than the export surplus (eq. 1). Correspondingly, if international economic equilibrium is to be maintained, starting from a position of external balance, an expansion in the difference between production and expenditure, and/or exports and imports, would have to be matched by a corresponding expansion in the outflow of private plus government capital (eq. 6).

Whatever may be the nature of United States policies designed to maintain or increase the export surplus, be they a rise in the price of gold, foreign loans and gifts, or mutual tariff reductions, the average propensity to consume and/or invest would at least have to be raised if the current rate of economic growth were to be increased rather than reduced; and similarly for the capital-receiving countries. Usually the reduction of excess capacity would be an essential prerequisite to generate such forces of domestic recovery, and hence an essential prerequisite for the recovery of countries whose national incomes were substantially dependent upon their trade with the United States.

APPRAISAL OF DISEQUILIBRIUM: HYPOTHESES AND FACTS

To appraise the actual causes of international economic disequilibrium since the United States became the pivotal country in world trade, let us now coördinate the theoretical analysis with the facts of experience.

The singular characteristic of the United States in the multinational sequence of economic growth and pattern of trade balances lies in the fact that the abundance and quality of its resources combined with its high mechanization have enabled the economy to develop without the emergence of a strong comparative disadvantage in any important field of economic activity with the exception of such industries as mining and petroleum. These same factors underlie the favorable returns to capital in the United States, the high productivity per manhour in manufacturing, the structural maladjustments in agriculture, and the combined impact of these forces on international economic disequilibrium.

Incipient tendencies toward dollar shortage appeared before World War I. The evidence on the evolving structure of world trade reveals that Britain was to be critically affected by these developments. It was the remarkable expansion of American net exports of crude foodstuffs and finished manufactures that chiefly accounts for claims on foreign countries being greater than obligations. But the entire inflow of gold from 1896 to 1914 was less than $175 million, an inconsiderable sum in the light of Britain's strong capital-export position. During this period the American export surplus was induced primarily by the net payments to foreign countries of interest and principal on foreign debt, net tourist expenditures abroad, immigrant remittances, and payment for freight and other miscellaneous services. Under conditions of rising productivity in industry and agriculture, the gold standard provided the equilibrating mechanism whereby the merchandise export surplus was maintained in balance with these out-payments. The fact that the United States was able to make such large transfers in the form of goods and, in addition, to acquire net claims on foreign countries without causing serious strain on the domestic economy attests to the healthy economic development of the country. It seems that the net transfer of dollar balances to the rest of the world tended to induce the export surplus, and the operation of both these forces under gold-standard conditions induced an excess of production over expenditure in the United States; and conversely in the relevant rest-of-world compound. It is surprising how well the balancing process worked to maintain international economic equilibrium. American economic expansion, which was reflected in its balance of payments, appears to have contributed much to world economic growth during this period.

Before the United States became a belligerent in World War I, her subsequent allies suffered from a dollar shortage. This was not a dollar shortage caused by normal economic or financial causes. Certainly it did not stem from the United States. If it is agreed that the mechanism of adjustment *qua* mechanism is a monetary phenomenon, then this was not a mechanism-of-adjustment problem. It was caused by a military crisis that brought about a shortage of virtually all physical resources. This shortage was partially alleviated by way of imports from the United States, financed in part by drawing down gold and foreign reserves, selling foreign investments, and foreign borrowing. It thus engendered an excess of British obligations over claims vis-à-vis the United States and manifested itself as a dollar shortage. The years of immediate postwar reconstruction witnessed a similar crisis.

The cause of dollar shortage notwithstanding, the war and its aftermath weakened the economic and financial condition of western Europe and enlarged the industrial capacity of the United States. These factors were to increase the tempo of the long-term process of international economic disequilibrium, especially as it affected the respective positions of Britain and the United States.

As in periods of more recent history, excess capacity in the American economy before World War I facilitated the expansion of output and contributed to the war effort of the allies. During the interwar years, industrial excess capacity fell during cyclical peaks and rose during troughs. Nevertheless, the tendency of productive capacity to grow relative to demand was sufficiently strong to render the volume of excess capacity large throughout the period. This does not imply the notion of secular stagnation. A certain amount of excess capacity is essential to healthy economic growth. It can be one of the most economical ways toward increased productivity, and during the 1920's it probably was.

From 1920 to 1927 the United States witnessed the flowering of a prolonged investment boom. It was followed by a spurt of inflation that culminated in the Great Depression, an inflation characterized by stock exchange speculation, a rise in inventories, and an expansion in output of manufactures and producers' durables. By 1927 the capital-output ratio seems to have caught up with that most profitable for the time. From then until the Great Depression the volume of investment opportunities appears to have fallen, but the inducements to exploit them rose.[39] It was the failure to control inflation and thereby to permit the requisite structural adjustments rather than secular

[39] I have benefited from the work and discussion of my colleague, Professor Robert A. Gordon, on these points. See his studies on "Cyclical Experience in the Interwar Period: The Investment Boom of the 'Twenties,'" *Conference on Business Cycles*, 1951, pp. 163-215; and "Investment Opportunities in the U.S. Before and After World War II," in Erik Lundberg, ed., *"The Business Cycle in the Post-War World*, 1952, pp. 283-310.

stagnation or excess capacity in the late 1920's that accounts in large measure for the severity of the depression that followed.

Yet the evidence shows that American domestic (and total) net capital formation as a percentage of net national product were lower in the decade 1919–1928 than in any previous decade since 1869. American foreign investment as a percentage of net national product was higher than in any previous peacetime decade. But it was erratic and (although often exaggerated) much of it economically mis-directed, being closely related to the needs of neither foreign nor domestic economic development. The rates of growth of national product, population, and product per capita had slowed down, but the period was nevertheless one of rapid economic expansion. In Britain, on the other hand, the rates of growth of national product, popula-tion, and product per capita were extremely low.[40] Also, during the 1920's output per man-hour in American manufacturing generally rose faster than hourly earnings, whereas in Britain hourly earnings in manufacturing rose at least as rapidly as per man-hour productivity.[41]

[40] See Simon Kuznets, *Toward a Theory of Economic Growth*, 1956, Statistical Appendix, Table 7, pp. 142-143 and Table 10, pp. 153-155. United States domestic net capital formation as a percentage of net national product fell from 14.6 percent in 1889-1898 to 8.8 percent in 1919-1928; and foreign investment as a per-centage of net national product rose from 0.2 percent to 1.9 percent. British domestic net capital formation as a percentage of net national product fell from 8.8 percent in 1900-1909 to 5.4 percent in 1924-1930; and foreign investment as a percentage of net national product fell from 14.9 percent to 6.6 percent. E. H. Phelps Brown and B. Weber have shown that between 1870 and 1913 the physical quantity of British capital (other than buildings) per occupied person almost doubled. From 1924 to 1938 it did not on balance rise at all. "The outcome, in the virtual failure to make any increase for fourteen years in industrial equipment per head of the occupied population, was very serious: the more so because it oc-curred even after the virtual abandonment of foreign investment, itself necessary for the development of supplies of food and raw materials for an island conurba-tion." "Accumulation, Productivity and Distribution in the British Economy, 1870-1938," *Economic Journal*, June, 1953, p. 281. Cf. also B. Weber and S. J. Handfield-Jones, "Variations in the Rate of Economic Growth in the U.S.A., 1869-1939," *Oxford Economic Papers*, n.s., June, 1954, pp. 101-131; and Ragnar Nurkse, "The Relation Between Home Investment and External Balance in the Light of British Experience, 1945-1955," *Review of Economics and Statistics*, May, 1956, pp. 132-134.

[41] Cf. U.S. Department of Commerce, *Historical Statistics of the United States*, pp. 66-72, esp. (column D) 124, and (Series D) 213-217. Differential rates of growth in American and British industries are discussed in Chapter 8, above. Cf. also Phelps Brown and S. V. Hopkins, "The Course of Wage Rates in Five Countries, 1860-1939," *Oxford Economic Papers*, June, 1950; and Donald Mac-Dougall, *The World Dollar Problem*, 1957, pp. 74, 81.

As regards agriculture, the United States was able to expand her industrial and primary production without the need of increasing her imports of food and raw materials to the same extent as had the industrial countries of Europe. From 1881–1913 the United States and other countries expanded their manufacturing production at different rates, but the increase in total manufacturing output brought about an approximately proportional increase in the quantum of trade in primary products.[42] If one plots the total volume of world trade in primary products (corrected for price changes) against world manufacturing production (excluding the U.S.S.R.) on a logarithmic scale, the result is almost a straight line. The figures for the 1920's also lie on a straight line, but not the same straight line as those for 1881–1913. The line of the 1920's lies to the right, indicating that an increase of manufacturing production occurred without a corresponding increase of primary imports. The United States, as we had occasion to observe, had increased her manufacturing production rapidly during World War I, whereas other countries were unable to do so. She did not however increase her imports of primary products at the same rate as her output of manufacturing production. It appears reasonable to assume that the straight line relationship which was resumed after World War I, but at a lower level, is to be explained in part by the growth of the comparatively self-sufficient American economy. The evidence for this position is strengthened by the fact that if one uses for manufacturing a series which excludes the United States (and the U.S.S.R.), the result for the entire period 1881–1929 is a single straight line. The data on specific imports suggests the same conclusion.[43] American imports of primary products were confined largely to a small group of items such as natural rubber, wood pulp, crude petroleum and natural gas, nonferrous metals and minerals, complementary agricultural and fisheries products, which together

[42] See W. A. Lewis, "World Production, Prices and Trade, 1870-1960," *Manchester School of Economic and Social Studies*, May, 1952, pp. 111-112; Food and Agricultural Organization of the United Nations, *The State of Food and Agriculture*, 1956, 1956, p. 64 ff.

[43] See tables and overlay chart for Figure 1 in Wassily Leontief, "Domestic Production and Foreign Trade; The American Capital Position Re-examined," *Proceedings of the American Philosophical Society*, September, 1953, pp. 336-341.

formed a relatively insignificant part of the United States total demand for primary products.

The juxtaposition of these forces—particularly the enlarged capital stock per worker in the United States as compared with that of Britain, the enormous natural resource base of America and the strictly limitational one of Britain, the rise in American and the precipitous decline in British foreign investment, the substantial volume of excess capacity in American expanding and in British declining industries—not only generated a higher rate of productivity growth in American manufacturing (relative to earnings) as compared with that of Britain, but further impelled the transformation of world trade and payments. The evidence appears to be consistent with our theoretical analysis as to why the United States was unable to fit into the pattern of previous growth and trade developments. Given her prodigious resource base and its diversification, on the one hand, and the high degree of mechanization of industry and agriculture on the other, the rise in American productivity strengthened her competitive position in world markets without lowering real incomes and, hence, inducing the contraction of output in any important branch of the American economy. As compared with other countries that had undergone rapid industrialization, the United States found it unnecessary to turn to foreign sources for the vast bulk of her raw materials. Strong pressures therefore developed for American production to exceed expenditure and exports to exceed imports.

In Britain unduly strong pressures developed for expenditure to exceed production and imports to exceed exports. Internal and exterternal forces mutually reinforced one another in cumulative causation.. As a result, she suffered from real as well as monetary balance-of-payments difficulties. These difficulties resulted in a specific as well as a more general mild "dollar shortage." Regions of recent settlement and the tropics depended upon an expansion of exports to Britain in order to finance their growing needs for economic development. Through multilateral clearing, a large proportion of their imports in fact came from the United States. But Britain's low rate of productivity and economic growth checked the expansion of her exports as well as imports. In addition, the low level of British investment as a percentage of net national product curtailed the rate of growth of national income and thereby reduced the volume of savings available for foreign investment. It is true that Britain's low rate of economic growth, and the unemployment incident to it, restrained the rise in her import surplus and checked the outflow of foreign reserves. This alleviated the balance-of-payments problem in Britain, but extended it to the regions of recent settlement and the tropics.

The survival of a viable multilateral trading system required the rapid adjustment in Great Britain to changing demands at home and abroad. Her pervasive role in world trade made this a matter of penultimate importance, second only to the primary role which had devolved upon the American economy. The United States had replaced Britain in world trade supremacy, but as yet had not developed a pattern of investment, trade, and payments that could serve as a new moving anchor upon which the evolving network of world trade could be securely built.

Disequilibrating forces thus operated on both sides of the Atlantic. It would be erroneous, however, to consider the period 1922–1929 as one of serious dollar shortage. The net inflow of gold into the United States amounted to $625 million. Industrial excess capacity in the United States does not appear to have been of sufficient magnitude to have rendered it a strong imbalancing factor, as was the case with excess capacity in agriculture. The United States export surplus during this period was induced primarily by the net outflow of United States private capital, tourists' expenditures abroad, remittances by immigrants and charitable foundations, and purchases of shipping and insurance services. Structural maladjustments in agriculture, the slower rise of hourly earnings in manufacturing relative to productivity per man-hour, and cyclical fluctuations also served to maintain the export surplus and to engender a small dollar shortage.

We have shown that in the interwar period differential rates of growth in productivity among the main industrial countries did not provide a satisfactory general explanation of long-term dollar shortage. The disparity in the overall rates of increase of productivity in manufacturing between the United States and other industrial countries, except Britain, was shown to be surprisingly small. Most industrial countries did not suffer from mechanism-of-adjustment strains during the 1920's. Britain was the exceptional case and it would appear that her extremely low rate of growth in productivity combined with her most difficult structural and institutional circumstances propagated some balance-of-payments pressures among countries that were closely linked to the British and United States economies. But in retrospect these were not intractable balance-of-payments problems.

Britain made remarkable progress during the 1920's in some of her new and expanding industries. Underlying imbalancing forces were giving way throughout the world to the progressive and ameliorative forces of economic growth. Had the developed countries been able to sustain their economies in a state of reasonably balanced expansion, the forces of international economic disequilibrium would not have been of major significance. Inflation in the United States, followed by the Great Depression with the attendant monetary contractions and trade restrictions among the major developed countries, were mainly responsible for the resulting internal and external disequilibriums.

The record of the Great Depression too strongly confirms theoretical expectations, for the cyclical factors discussed above were intensified by exceptionally abnormal institutional conditions. The rise in United States domestic investment, particularly during the inflationary spurt before the depression tended to generate a rate of growth in income and an excess of planned saving over planned investment. The disparity between the growth in physical capacity to produce and the growth of current demand and output became acute. As returns on domestic capital declined, the excess of planned saving not only failed to be invested abroad, but the flow of capital was reversed from a net outflow to a net inflow. The growth process was interrupted; excess capacity, unemployment, and inventories grew apace. Abnormally perverse monetary policies along with inflexible cost-price structures aggravated the deflation. Production became more and more excessive relative to expenditure, and the pressures to expand exports and to reduce imports became terribly strong. It was the American economy that primarily generated the ensuing dollar shortage.

As was to be expected, the reduction in the supply of dollars to foreign countries made it impossible for the United States to maintain its large export surplus. Indeed, the active trade balance was cut approximately in half. The devaluation of the dollar in 1934 and adoption of the Reciprocal Trade Agreements Program were intended, among other things, to maintain or expand the export surplus and thereby aid domestic recovery. In part, these measures appear to have achieved this objective, but it is most doubtful whether they contributed to the solution of dollar shortage.[44]

During the period of recovery from 1934 to 1937, actual output rose more rapidly than full-capacity output. By 1937, industrial excess capacity had been reduced to normal levels.[45] Droughts stimulated the importation of crude and manufactured foodstuffs. By 1936–1937 these factors were important in bringing about equilibrium in United States merchandise trade and total current accounts. The effects of the 1937–1938 recession that followed were in conformity with the hypothesis formulated in our analysis: Once more, fluctuations in the American economy resulted in dollar shortage.

From the outbreak of World War II until the advent of lend-lease, and from 1946 through 1949, the dollar-shortage problem was comparable to the experience of World War I and its aftermath. The greater magnitude of the problem, as well as the more complex and diverse political, security, and economic development issues, doubtless contributed to the controversy as to the nature of its causes. But

[44] The devaluation did much harm to the international comity of nations. For a key country in international trade to devalue its currency during a depression in order to improve its domestic and/or external position is fraught with danger. It may also be ineffective: the devaluation may have the effect of so reducing the country's imports, and thereby the national incomes of important trading partners, that the devaluing country's exports may fall rather than rise. Or, the improvement may be at the expense of the rest of the world. The United States export surplus on merchandise account increased in 1934, following the devaluation. Cf. Chapter 6, pp. 140-147 for extended analysis applicable to such situations. A comparison of United States foreign trade in 1934-1935 and 1938-1939 shows that in this interim the relative and absolute increase of United States exports exceeded that of imports. This is the most important criticism that can be legitimately directed against the Reciprocal Trade Agreements Program. Its failure to achieve a more adequate reduction of United States tariffs limited its contribution to the solution of the dollar-shortage problem. The data is presented in my study, *Reciprocal Trade Agreements in the World Economy,* 1948, pp. 27-32.

[45] See Hickman, *op. cit.,* Table 6, pp. 434-435, and Table 10, p. 445.

fundamentally it was again caused by the military crisis and postwar reconstruction that brought about a shortage of practically all physical resources. To the extent that this shortage was alleviated through imports from the United States, financed by drawing down gold and foreign reserves, selling foreign investments, and foreign borrowing, it produced an excess of obligations over claims with the United States and manifested itself as a dollar shortage. It was basically neither a monetary phenomenon nor a mechanism-of-adjustment problem; it did not stem from the United States.

The expansion of American productive capacity during the war enabled her to assist foreign countries during reconstruction to a much greater extent than otherwise would have been possible. But the capital-output ratio had greatly fallen during the war. Productive capacity in the United States was being replaced and increased during the reconstruction period. Capital shortage added tinder to the inflationary forces, aggravated by the accumulation of liquid assets. Aggregate demand exceeded supply and prices rose; the rise in hourly earnings in manufacturing exceeded the increase in productivity. Foreign countries were short of supplies and found it extremely difficult to expand exports. Countries industrializing at an unduly rapid pace experienced an excess of expenditure over production and of imports over exports. This often occasioned specific dollar shortages. But there were no strong pressures working in the United States to promote general dollar shortage. The American export surplus from 1946–1949 was induced primarily by the expansion of United States foreign loans and grants to our friends and allies.

For some industries United States foreign assistance provided markets which otherwise would have been sorely missed. This was particularly true of agriculture. Consequently, following the reconstruction years of 1946–1949, these industries generated production in excess of demand and stimulated an export surplus. Still, from 1950–1953, excluding military transfers, the United States merchandise export surplus amounted to only $1.95 billion a year. The total supply of dollars made available to foreign countries, including government grants, loans, and changes in short-term assets abroad was large enough to enable them to increase their dollar holdings by $7.8 billion. Even the recession of 1953-1954 failed to produce a serious dollar shortage; the United States had maintained a satisfactory balance between the expansion of her export surplus and the outflow of capital. Conditions of economic expansion in the rest of the world also greatly contributed to the maintenance of international equilibrium. Nevertheless, from 1953-1957 the United States active balance in merchandise trade averaged $4.2 billion. True, gold reserves and dollar holdings of foreign countries and international institutions rose during this period. They rose primarily because the United States maintained its aid to, and investment in, the outside world. On the other hand, strong inflationary pressures were at work throughout the postwar period in the vast majority of foreign countries as compared with the United States, and they were most important in bringing about *specific* dollar shortages.[46]

Considering the entire period 1950-1957, the American economy progressed quite satisfactorily and its international accounts were maintained in reasonable balance through the expansion of United States imports of goods and services and the maintenance of a comparatively stable outflow of government and private capital. Unfortunately, the balancing factors were not strong enough to prevent a reversal in American capital flows during the recession of 1957-1958. A brief but sharp reversal occurred from a net outflow to a net inflow of American dollars. This fact, together with the pressures arising from the excess of production over expenditure, tended to call forth a dollar shortage. Confidence in the internal and external stability of the American economy was shaken.

As regards the forces working within the United States, the evidence seems to be consistent with the view that from the 1890's until the 1950's the tendency for American production to rise faster than expenditure was the primary cause of the systematic dollar-shortage problem. During the interwar period, this tendency of American production was the most important single cause of the persistent existence of dollar shortage on a small scale. Whenever serious recessions or depressions occurred, it was the most important cause of dollar shortage on a large scale. However, the tend-

---

[46] See International Monetary Fund, *op. cit.* Cf. also Robert Triffin, *Europe and the Money Muddle*, 1957, pp. 55-70; and G. D. A. MacDougall, *op. cit.*, p. 94.

ency for American production to rise faster than expenditure was primarily the result of *institutional* rather than structural factors. Natural scarcities or secular stagnation were not responsible for these difficulties. Had more effective stabilization policies been successful in controlling spurts of inflation and of achieving a higher rate of growth in national income, the dollar-shortage problem would have been greatly relieved. Abstracting from periods of war and reconstruction, it emerged as a serious and general problem *only* when the rate of growth of actual and full-capacity output failed to be in reasonable balance and/or the outflow of capital to be sustained at a high and stable level. Thus, as postulated, the forces of international economic disequilibrium emanating from the United States have been primarily of an institutional nature; they have been associated with and aggravated by weighty structural and cyclical factors; but the world dollar-shortage problem is not chronic.

PROSPECTS AND CONCLUSION

If our appraisal of international economic equilibrium and disequilibrium is generally correct, some important practical conclusions appear to follow from it. As always, however, the relevance of theoretical conclusions to policy formation is contingent upon certain assumptions as to the political-economic environment and the interdependence of other government policies incident to it. In presenting our conclusions as to the probability of dollar shortage emanating from the United States in the coming decades, its likely affects on developed and newly developing countries, and the need for certain policies, we shall assume that the United States will continue to undergo a mild degree of economic exhilaration. The validity of our conclusions is also based on the following considerations of long-term trends in the United States and of key government policies.

LONG-TERM EQUILIBRATING TRENDS

It is often overlooked that powerful forces have for long been working toward international economic equilibrium in the United States.[47]

[47] Cf. Figs. 14-19, above, regarding this discussion.

Abstracting from the abnormal conditions of World War I and reconstruction, there has been a strong tendency since 1909 for the United States to have an excess of imports over exports of crude foodstuffs. From 1923 to 1958 United States imports had exceeded exports of crude foodstuffs virtually every year, despite depression conditions of the early 1930's. Similarly, since 1915, the American excess of imports over exports of crude materials has been quite general, the only important exceptions being those of the years 1932-1933. More remarkable still has been the long-run trend toward balance of American trade in manufactured foodstuffs and in semifinished manufactures. From 1876 until 1932 the United States exports of manufactured foodstuffs exceeded imports in every year but 1920. However, from 1932 to 1940, the trend was reversed; the United States maintained an annual excess of imports over exports of these products. This trend was gradually resumed after World War II. But from 1953 to 1958 the structural maladjustments in agriculture brought about a rapid expansion of exports of manufactured foodstuffs; at the close of the period exports had about caught up with imports. It appears likely that net imports of these products will continue their upward trend. Further, in most years from 1897 to 1921 United States exports of semifinished manufactures exceeded imports, but from 1922 until 1936 imports exceeded exports every year. This trend has also been resumed since World War II, although in the recession year of 1957 imports and exports of semifinished manufactures were approximately equal. Lastly, since World War II, American exports of finished manufactures have not shown a secular tendency to rise, whereas United States imports of finished manufactures have continued steadily to expand. In *toto*, from 1950 to 1958 United States imports of goods and services furnished foreign countries with approximately 90 percent of their funds to pay for their imports of goods and services from the United States.

HARD CORE OF IMBALANCE

Despite these strong forces working toward international economic equilibrium, there has remained a considerable degree of imbalance in United States total trade. Even under full-employment conditions and reasonably steady economic growth, a hard core of structural imbalance—especially in agriculture—has tended to promote an excess of production over demand, exports over imports, and a dollar shortage. Were it not for the outflow of capital, the evidence appears to be incontrovertible that the American economy would generate a moderate dollar shortage even under conditions of a mild degree of domestic economic exhilaration.[48]

AGRICULTURE

The United States will for long continue to face a relative abundance rather than a relative scarcity of agricultural resources. These conditions will affect the balance of payments and the economic growth of newly developing countries, some in a beneficial, others in a deleterious, way. This is because the benefits of real income which accompany effective economic growth accrue to different regions in proportion to their economic ties with developing industrial centers. The areas that supply products, the demand for which is expanding most rapidly, probably will benefit most. Those that are not equipped to supply such products, or whose resources are poor

---

[48] By projecting ranges of the possible variation in the significant items in the United States balance of payments, MacDougall draws the conclusion that by 1975, under pessimistic assumptions, the United States balance of payments might reach a surplus from structural causes of $16 billion; under optimistic assumptions, a deficit of $4 billion. He writes: "Our range of estimates suggests that a worsening in the rest of the world's balance is more likely than an improvement." *Op. cit.*, p. 237. For his assumptions and careful analysis see Chap. 10. An anticipated United States export surplus approximating the upper pessimistic range means, of course, an anticipated comparable excess of saving over domestic investment in the United States and a comparable excess of investment over domestic saving abroad. Such high surpluses are conceivable, but unless military expenditures are greatly reduced, they seem highly improbable, particularly when one takes into account the impact of balance-of-payments surpluses on domestic production and expenditure. MacDougall's projections and those of other scholars appear to substantiate our theoretical analysis. However, the stress we have placed on the inextricable relationships between internal and external forces necessitates serious qualifications of any statistical projections of foreign trade. Cf. the useful studies by Henry G. Aubrey, *United States Imports and World Trade*, 1957; Don D. Humphrey, *American Imports*, 1955; and J. H. Adler, E. R. Schlesinger, and E. Van Westerborg, *The Pattern of United States Import Trade Since 1923*, 1952; also see the review article by C. P. Kindleberger, "The Dollar Shortage Re-Revisited," *American Economic Review*, June, 1958, pp. 388-395; and W. F. Stolper, "American Imports," *Journal of Economic History*, September, 1956, pp. 382-385.

and insufficiently mobile to adapt to changing demands, are likely to benefit least. In so far as their trade with the United States is concerned, one would expect developing countries that are primarily producers of agricultural products, which are in excess supply in the United States, to fare worse than those that are producers of complementary products, be they in the fields of agriculture, minerals, petroleum or semifinished manufactures.[49] The longer the disequilibrium prevails in American agriculture and the stronger its force, the more will newly developing countries suffer if their industrialization is contingent upon exports of agricultural products which compete with those of the United States.

ROLE OF NATURAL SCARCITIES

In analyzing the sequence of economic growth and the pattern of trade balances, we had occasion to stress the importance of specific factor scarcities and their relation to the structure of costs and prices. The aggregate theories of economic growth, and of the balance of payments, disregarded these considerations. But they must be incorporated into the analysis if it is to have relevance. The question centers about the availability of specific inputs for the continued expansion of aggregate output. Considering the abundance, diversity, and mobility of American resources, one would *not* expect specific input requirements to impede the normal growth trends of the American economy in the foreseeable future. The implicit assumption of constant relative real costs and prices in most aggregate theories of economic growth may be quite satisfactory for certain periods and categories of output in the United States. But it is not a satisfactory assumption for large changes in the composition of output. It is even less applicable to small countries whose foreign trade is a substantial proportion of gross national product, or to newly developing countries with scarce specialized resources whose supply must rapidly be expanded. As regards the relations between economic growth and the

---

[49] For striking confirmation of this position compare the merchandise trade balances of countries exporting mainly agricultural products other than rubber and those exporting mainly minerals and rubber, 1938-1955. United Nations *World Economic Survey, 1956, op. cit.,* pp. 29-39.

balance of payments, this assumption not only is misleading but may be disastrous if applied to actual plans of economic development.

ROLE OF INSTITUTIONAL SCARCITIES

In periods of expansion, institutional scarcities are likely to have a greater impact than natural scarcities on the balance of payments of the United States. Given a period of full employment with reasonably stable prices, changes in labor costs per unit of output (in value terms) can be expected to exert two influences pulling in opposite directions. They change profit margins and thus, *cet. par.*, change the incentives to produce. But the *cet. par.* condition does not hold, for changes in labor costs also tend to change the propensity to consume. It would be fortuitous if these two factors cancelled one another; and yet, the maintenance of full employment depends to some extent on the proportion of full-employment output that would have to be consumed and on the proportion that would have to be invested. Expectations as to future costs, productivity, prices, and profits would in all probability affect the aggregate propensity to consume and invest. If expectations are favorable, it would be most difficult to maintain a stable price level. Trade unions in efficient expanding industries would demand wage increases approximately in line with their expected marginal productivity, and industry would consider itself in a position to meet such demands. Should comparable increases be granted to industries in which productivity is not rising as rapidly, the average increase in wage rates would exceed the average increase in productivity. The stronger the expectation on the part of industry that productivity would keep rising and that the government would not tolerate depressions, the greater would be the tendency to grant wage increases which, in effect, would exceed the increase in productivity. If productivity should not rise sufficiently to cover the increased labor costs, the higher costs per unit of product would be passed on in the form of higher prices.

With such expectations, prices would tend to remain comparatively stable or to rise during recessions. As aggregate supply exceeds aggregate demand, and production falls, firms would operate at increased average unit costs. Trade unions would refuse to accept lower wages in the expectation of an early economic revival. Industry would feel compelled to raise prices in order to cover costs. Nonetheless, firms would operate at reduced capacity. In most instances, they would incur lower profits or suffer losses rather than uselessly strain management-labor relations and/or resort to the presumptively pejorative policy of cutting prices which, it is alleged, might have the effect of "spoiling" future markets. If the expectations of labor and industry are well founded, one would expect them to be realized by the assistance of characteristic government counter-cyclical policies.

Periods of American expansion with relative inflation will in all probability tend to bring about external balance. But as the 1957-1958 experience has shown, recessions with rising prices are likely to have different effects. The decline of American imports, associated first with a substantial decline of industrial production and then with falling incomes is likely to exceed the tendency toward an expansion of imports resulting from the relative rise in domestic prices. It is most doubtful whether the rise in some export prices would sufficiently reduce the volume of exports to offset this effect. The total value of exports may indeed increase. *Barring countervailing forces,* one would therefore expect future American recessions with rising prices to increase the export surplus and to create a dollar shortage. Although on *a priori* grounds, one would expect these tendencies toward dollar shortage to be weaker than those associated with comparable recessions in which prices have fallen, the probability of exceptions is strong and there is need for detailed research on this problem.

COUNTER-CYCLICAL POLICY

As indicated by postwar United States experience, a reasonably successful counter-cyclical policy in the coming decades is likely to have the effect of lowering the marginal (and average) capital-output ratios. In all probability it would increase the rate of output as compared with the interwar period. The product of these two terms

$$\left(\frac{\Delta V}{\Delta O} \cdot \frac{\Delta O}{\Delta t} \right)$$ is equal to the rate of investment. Hence one cannot

state categorically whether the rate of investment under such conditions would be likely to rise or fall. It seems that the reduction of uncertainty stemming from a reasonably successful cycle policy would tend to raise the rate of output sufficiently to counteract any reduction in the capital-output ratio so that the rate of investment would at least tend to remain unchanged; it might even rise. In any event, a lower capital-output ratio and a higher rate of output would operate to reduce the degree (if not the absolute amount) of excess capacity and would consequently reduce the pressures toward dollar shortage. If an upward trend in investment should occur, it seems likely that it would assist in the attainment of steady expansion with the attendant equilibrating effects on the balance of payments.

The control of inflation, however, is likely to be a paramount problem. On the basis of past experience, the American economy is unlikely to be burdened by lack of finance. Even if the Federal Reserve System follows energetic counter-inflationary policies, the probability seems to be greater that the rise in prices would be checked rather than stopped. The smaller the responsibility of the Executive and the Congress to maintain reasonably stable prices, the greater would be the probability that spurts of inflation would be followed by recessions. And the greater the probability of recessions, the stronger would be the pressures for long-term inflationary budgetary policies. No matter how enlightened banking or budgetary policy may be, the one could always be contravened by the ill-advised practices of the other. Furthermore, any projection of undistributed profit ratios of the postwar era suggests that a considerable portion of American economic expansion in the coming decades could be financed from profits. Consequently, unless more powerful financial measures are adopted than heretofore, it seems unlikely that they will be successful in stemming the tide of inflation. In that event, one would expect the long-term forces of general dollar shortage operating in the United States to be greatly moderated if not entirely eliminated. But the objective of continuous expansion would be impeded.

Deserving particular attention is the potential influence of banking policy on internal and external balance under conditions of a mild degree of exhilaration. Under such conditions of economic growth, on occasion the American economy may be expected to generate a mild dollar shortage. By effectively controlling the supply of money at varying interest rates in accordance with the degree of inflationary pressure, banking policy would make a substantial contribution to this domestic objective. At the same time, it could furnish one of the most effective stabilizing elements in the international balancing process. As full-employment aggregate supply tends to exceed aggregate demand, the forces of dollar shortage would become more powerful; simultaneously, monetary policy would become less stringent and the pattern of interest rates would be reduced. One would therefore expect differentials in the rates of interest to stimulate the outflow of private capital and to contribute to financing the export surplus. When full-employment aggregate demand tends to exceed aggregate supply, the forces of dollar shortage would be diminished. Monetary policy would then become more stringent and the pattern of interest rates would be raised. Monetary policy—combined with budgetary policy—could therefore play a vital stabilizing role in stimulating and checking the rate of economic growth at comparatively stable prices and in assisting the equilibration of international accounts.[50]

POLITICAL CRISES

In an age of ideological conflict, seething nationalism, and dynamic industrial change, one cannot but expect the continuous eruption of political crises and military revolutions over the entire globe. David Ricardo made reference to sudden changes in the direction of world

[50] The United States is in a unique position to provide the requisite institutional framework in this field. She alone can apply monetary policy with virtual disregard of the balance of payments. In other countries, a comparatively low rate of interest may cause an outflow of gold and foreign reserves and thereby bring about a balance-of-payments crisis. Conversely, a stringent monetary policy with a comparatively high rate of interest may reduce effective demand and check the rate of economic growth, even though demand may be excessive for the maintenance of balance-of-payments equilibrium. In either case, a dollar shortage would impede steady expansion and/or require structural adjustments. It is practically inconceivable that American balance-of-payments difficulties should adversely affect the economic growth of the United States. Given a high rate of economic growth, an expansion of United States imports is likely to encourage innovation, stimulate the application of capital-intensive techniques, improve resource-use, and further raise the level of real income. For suggestive material on the potential role of monetary policy in assisting the maintenance of international equilibrium see "Dollar Flows and International Financing," *Federal Reserve Bulletin*, March, 1955, pp. 241-248.

trade stemming from similar causes. They distort the established pattern of sources of supply and outlets for demand. In the modern world, the occurrence of such crises is the most certain assumption that can be made. To deal with them often requires access to specific resources; market forces and government regulations must mobilize all available supplies. No matter how complex their causes, there can be no doubt that in the coming decades the United States will be ever more constrained to cope with episodic international crises. Whenever they affect the sources of strategic supplies of our friends and allies, they may be expected to engender a "dollar shortage," for a large part of the strategic requirements will have to be imported from the United States.

It must be amply evident that the causes of dollar shortage, at home and abroad, are neither singular nor lend themselves to generalization. Nevertheless, our analysis of the transition from a pattern of international economic equilibrium to disequilibrium leads to certain definite conclusions. Theory and fact appear to be in accord: Given the strong tendency of the American economy to generate excess capacity, a high and continuous level of United States foreign investment is a necessary, if not sufficient, condition for the achievement of international economic equilibrium. Moreover, it would be of great value for the maintenance of reasonable balance between the rate of growth of actual and full-capacity output. This balance would tend to reduce the pressures working in the United States toward dollar shortage and assist in the gradual removal of structural maladjustments. The actual rate of economic growth could thus be maintained at a level approximating the equilibrium rate, with the net export of capital approximating the difference between production and expenditure, on the one hand, and the export surplus, on the other.

It would also be of great assistance in expanding United States imports. The statistical evidence for the postwar period suggests that the further liberalization of United States commercial policy is likely to improve the balance of payments of many countries, but it cannot be relied upon to solve the problem of international economic disequilibrium. Freer trade improves the quality, but not necessarily the quantity, of resource-use; whether or not it improves the quantity depends upon its effects on average propensities to consume and/or invest. Hence, by improvement of resource-use and relative adjustment of earnings among different occupations, tariff reductions would hasten the removal of structural maladjustments and thereby reduce the pressures generating dollar shortage. The United States must continually adapt its economy toward a position consistent with that of a mature creditor country, but our analysis suggests that for the practical future the interests of the free trading world would be better served if she continued to maintain an export surplus matched by a corresponding outflow of capital. Most foreign countries—and especially the newly developing ones—require dollar-earning and dollar-saving production. By supplementing domestic savings of these developing countries, the United States could make an important contribution toward alleviating this problem; if managed effectively, their rate of economic growth would be increased and balance-of-payments crises restrained.

As we have observed, the success of such policies in the United States and abroad is contingent upon the control of inflation. The postwar record reveals that in the vast majority of foreign countries prices rose more rapidly than in the United States. The analysis suggests the likely continuation of this trend, primarily because their money earnings tend to rise much more rapidly than productivity, rather than their productivity more slowly than that in the United States. Should these forces continue, balance-of-payments disequilibriums would be induced primarily by more rapid rates of inflation in foreign countries than in the United States. The strongest pressures on international imbalance would arise when the United States suffers from depression or serious recession while foreign countries suffer from inflation: For under such conditions American production would exceed expenditure and foreign expenditure exceed production.

The achievement of a reasonably continual high rate of economic growth with international equilibrium is an extremely difficult task. But the task is not greater than the need. Although much progress has been made since World War II in economic doctrine, development of institutions, and practice in these fields, general solutions or rigid formulas cannot provide both true and relevant conclusions on these matters. Hence formal and informal joint working arrangements are indispensable. Joint measures should be required to secure sustained economic growth; joint undertaking of a long-term aid and investment program; joint negotiations for adequate reserves and convertibility; joint accord on a body of economic principles which would meet the need of flexibility in regard to the relative values of currencies through time; and joint agreement on a genuine low-tariff area.

The closely knit relationships between internal and external balance, or imbalance, suggest that for the implementation of such measures the fusion of domestic and international objectives and policies is a primary requisite. In addition, exigencies of national and international crises require wide administrative discretion. In either case, the emergence of the United States as the pivotal country in world trade has thrust upon her responsibility and leadership in these undertakings.

Bibliography

Adler, J. H., "The Post-War Demand for United States Exports," Division of Research and Statistics, Board of Governors of the Federal Reserve System, April, 1945, Appendix A, mimeographed.

Adler, J. H., "United States Import Demand during the Interwar Period," *American Economic Review*, June, 1945.

Adler, J. H., "World Economic Growth—Retrospect and Prospects," *Review of Economics and Statistics*, August, 1956.

Adler, J. H., and Wallich, H. C., *Public Financing in a Developing Country—El Salvador: A Case Study*, Cambridge: Harvard University Press, 1951.

Adler, J. H., *et al.*, *The Pattern of United States Import Trade Since 1923*, New York: Federal Reserve Bank of New York, 1952.

Alai, H., "The Liquidity Crisis Abroad," *American Economic Review*, December, 1947.

Alexander, S. S., "Devaluation versus Import Restrictions," *International Monetary Fund Staff Papers*, April, 1951.

Alexander, S. S., "Effects of a Devaluation on a Trade Balance," *International Monetary Fund Staff Papers*, April, 1952.

Allely, J. S., "Some Aspects of Currency Depreciation," *Canadian Journal of Economics and Political Science*, August, 1939.

Allen, R. G. D., *Mathematical Analysis for Economists*, London: Macmillan and Co., Ltd., 1942.

Allen, R. G. D., *Mathematical Economics*, London: Macmillan and Co., Ltd., 1956.

Allen, William R., "A Note on the Money Income Effects of Devaluation," *Kyklos*, Fasc. 3, 1956.

Angell, James W., *The Theory of International Prices: History, Criticism, and Restatement,* Cambridge: Harvard University Press, 1926.

Arndt, H. W., "The Concept of Liquidity in International Monetary Theory," *Review of Economic Studies,* No. 37, 1947-1948.

Ashton, T. S., *The Industrial Revolution, 1760-1830,* Oxford: Oxford University Press, 1948.

Ashton, T. S., "The Standard of Life of the Workers in England, 1790-1830," *Journal of Economic History,* Supplement Vol. IX, 1949.

Ashton, T. S., *An Economic History of England: The 18th Century,* London: Methuen and Co., 1955.

Atallah, M. K., *The Terms of Trade Between Agricultural and Industrial Products,* Netherlands Economic Institute, Rotterdam, 1958.

Attwood, Thomas, *Prosperity Restored,* London: Baldwin, Cradock, etc., 1817.

Attwood, Thomas, *Observation on Currency, Population and Pauperism,* Birmingham: R. Wrightson, 1818.

Attwood, Thomas, *The Scotch Banker,* 2nd ed., London: James Ridgway, 1832.

Aubrey, Henry G., "The Long-Term Future of United States Imports and Its Implications for Primary Producing Countries," *American Economic Review,* May, 1955.

Aubrey, Henry G., *United States Imports and World Trade,* Oxford: The Clarendon Press, 1957.

Baghot, Walter, *Economic Studies,* London: Longmans, Green and Co., Ltd., 1895.

Bain, Joe S., *Barriers to New Competition,* Cambridge: Harvard University Press, 1956.

Baines, E., *History of the Cotton Manufacture,* London: H. Fisher, R. Fisher, and P. Jackson, 1835.

Baldwin, Robert E., "Equilibrium in International Trade: A Diagrammatic Analysis," *Quarterly Journal of Economics,* November, 1948.

Baldwin, Robert E., "The New Welfare Economics and Gains in International Trade," *Quarterly Journal of Economics,* February, 1952.

Baldwin, Robert E., and Meier, Gerald M., *Economic Development: Theory, History, Policy,* New York: John Wiley & Sons, Inc., 1957.

Balogh, T., "The International Aspects of Full Employment," in *The Economics of Full Employment,* Six Studies in Applied Economics prepared at The Oxford University, Institute of Statistics, Oxford: Basil Blackwell, 1945.

Balogh, T., "Static Models and Current Problems in International Economics," *Oxford Economic Papers,* June, 1949.

Balogh, T., *The Dollar Crisis: Causes and Cure,* Oxford: Basil Blackwell, 1950.

Balogh, T., "The Dollar Crisis Revisited," *Oxford Economic Papers*, September, 1954.

Balogh, T., "Some Theoretical Implications of International Aspects of the United States Recession, 1953/54," *Economic Journal*, December, 1955, pp. 641-653.

Balogh, T., and Streeten, P. P., "Exchange Rates and National Income," *Bulletin*, Oxford University Institute of Statistics, March, 1951.

Balogh, T., and Streeten, P. P., "The Inappropriateness of Simple 'Elasticity' Concepts in the Analysis of International Trade," *Bulletin*, Oxford University Institute of Statistics, March, 1951.

Bastable, Charles F., *The Theory of International Trade with Some of its Applications to Economic Policy*, London and New York: Macmillan and Co., 1887 and 1903.

Bauer, P. T., and Paish, F. W., "The Reduction of Fluctuations in the Incomes of Primary Producers," *Economic Journal*, December, 1952.

Baumol, W. J., *Economic Dynamics: An Introduction*, New York: The Macmillan Co., 1951.

Baumol, W. J., "Acceleration Without Magnification," *American Economic Review*, June, 1956.

Baumol, W. J., "Speculation, Profitability, and Stability," *Review of Economics and Statistics*, August, 1957.

Baumol, W. J., "Analyse Graphique de Modèles de Cycles non Linéaires de Premier Ordre," mimeographed.

Beach, Walter E., "Some Aspects of International Trade Under Monopolistic Competition," in *Explorations in Economics: Notes and Essays Contributed in Honor of F. W. Taussig*, New York: McGraw-Hill Book Co., 1936.

Becker, G. S., "A Note on Multi-Country Trade," *American Economic Review*, September, 1952.

Becker, G. S., and Baumol, W. J., "Classical Monetary Theory: The Outcome of the Discussion," *Economica*, November, 1952.

Beckerman, W., "Price Changes and the Stability of the Balance of Trade," *Economica*, November, 1952.

Beckerman, W., "A Note on Veritable Prices and Foreign Trade Multipliers," *Review of Economic Studies*, No. 55, 1953-1954.

Beckerman, W., "The World Trade Multiplier and the Stability of World Trade, 1938 to 1953," *Econometrica*, July, 1956.

Bell, P. W., *The Sterling Area in the Postwar World*, Oxford: The Clarendon Press, 1956.

Bendix, Reinhard, *Work and Authority in Industry*, New York: John Wiley & Sons, Inc., 1956.

Benham, Frederic, "The Terms of Trade," *Economica*, November, 1940.

Bensusan-Butt, D. M., "A Model of Trade and Accumulation," *American Economic Review*, September, 1954.

Bentham, Jeremy, *Truth versus Ashurst*, 1792, London: T. Moses, 1823.

Bentham, Jeremy, "Defence of Usury," in *Jeremy Bentham's Economic Writings*, W. Stark, ed., London: George Allen & Unwin, Ltd., 1952.

Bernstein, E. M., "Multilateral Trade in an Unbalanced World," *Canadian Journal of Economics and Political Science*, August, 1950.

Bernstein, E. M., "American Productivity and the Dollar Payments Problem," *Review of Economics and Statistics*, May, 1955.

Beveridge, William H., *Full Employment in a Free Society*, New York: W. W. Norton & Co., Inc., 1945.

Bezanson, Anne, "The Early Use of the Term Industrial Revolution," *Quarterly Journal of Economics*, February, 1922.

Bickerdike, C. F., "The Instability of Foreign Exchanges," *Economic Journal*, March, 1920.

Black, J. D., and Galbraith, J. K., "The Maintenance of Agricultural Production during Depression: The Explanations Reviewed," *Journal of Political Economy*, June, 1938.

Blank, John, *Trade Revived*, London, 1659.

Bloch, E., "U.S. Foreign Investment and the Dollar Shortage," *Review of Economics and Statistics*, May, 1953.

Bloomfield, A. I., "The Significance of Outstanding Securities in the International Movement of Capital," *Canadian Journal of Economics and Political Science*, November, 1940.

Bloomfield, A. I., "Operation of the American Exchange Stabilization Fund," *Review of Economics and Statistics*, May, 1944.

Bloomfield, A. I., "Foreign Exchange Rate Theory and Policy," in *The New Economics: Keynes' Influence on Theory and Public Policy*, Seymour E. Harris, ed., New York: Alfred A. Knopf, 1947.

Bloomfield, A. I., "Induced Investment, Overcomplete International Adjustment, and Chronic Dollar Shortage," (with rejoinder by C. P. Kindleberger), *American Economic Review*, September, 1949.

Bloomfield, A. I., *Capital Imports and the American Balance of Payments, 1934-39*, Chicago: University of Chicago Press, 1950.

Bloomfield, A. I., *Speculative and Flight Movements of Capital in Postwar International Finance*, Princeton: Princeton University Press, 1954.

Bourneuf, Alice, "Exchange Practices of the Fund," in *Essays in Honor of Alvin H. Hansen*, New York: W. W. Norton & Co., Inc., 1948.

Bowley, A. L., "The Statistics of Wages in the United Kingdom during the Last Hundred Years," *Journal of the Royal Statistical Society*, December, 1898.

Bowley, Marian, *Nassau Senior and Classical Economics*, London: George Allen & Unwin, Ltd., 1937.

Brems, H., "Foreign Exchange Rates and Monopolistic Competition," *Economic Journal*, June, 1953.

Brems, H., "A Solution of the Keynes-Hicks-Hanson Non-Linear Employment Model," *Quarterly Journal of Economics*, May, 1956.

Brems, H., "The Foreign Trade Accelerator and International Transmission of Growth," *Econometrica*, July, 1956.

Brems, H., "Devaluation, A Marriage of the Elasticity and the Absorption Approaches," *Economic Journal*, March, 1957.

Brems, H., "Employment and Money Wages Under Balanced Foreign Trade," *Econometrica*, April, 1957.

Bresciani-Turroni, C., *Inductive Verification of the Theory of International Payments*, Cairo: Egyptian University Publication, 1932.

Bresciani-Turroni, C., "The Purchasing Power Parity Doctrine," *L'Egypte Contemporaine*, May, 1934.

Bridgman, P. W., *The Logic of Modern Physics*, New York: The Macmillan Co., 1927.

Brisman, S., "Some Reflections on the Theory of Foreign Exchange," in *Economic Essays in Honor of G. Cassel*, London: George Allen & Unwin, Ltd., 1933.

Brofenbrenner, M., "The Keynesian Equations and the Balance of Payments," *Review of Economic Studies*, No. 3, June, 1940.

Brown, A. J., *Industrialization and Trade, the Changing World Pattern and the Position of Britain*, Oxford: Oxford University Press, 1943.

Brown, A. J., "International Equilibrium and National Sovereignty Under Full Employment," *International Affairs*, October, 1949.

Brown, A. J., "Trade Balances and Exchange Stability," in *Oxford Studies in the Price Mechanism*, T. Wilson and P. W. S. Andrews, eds., Oxford: The Clarendon Press, 1951.

Brown, E. H. Phelps, and Handfield-Jones, S. J., "The Climacteric of the 1890's: A Study in the Expanding Economy," *Oxford Economic Papers*, October, 1952.

Brown, E. H. Phelps, and Hopkins, S. V., "The Course of Wage Rates in Five Countries, 1860-1939," *Oxford Economic Papers*, June, 1950.

Brown, E. H. Phelps, and Weber, B., "Accumulation, Productivity and Distribution in the British Economy, 1870-1938," *Economic Journal*, June, 1953.

Brown, George Hay, "The International Economic Position of New Zealand," *Journal of Business of the University of Chicago*, April, 1946.

Brown, W. A., *The International Gold Standard Reinterpreted*, New York: National Bureau of Economic Research, Inc., 1940.

Buchanan, Norman S., *International Investment and Domestic Welfare*, New York: Henry Holt & Co., 1945.

Buchanan, Norman S., and Ellis, Howard S., *Approaches to Eco-*

nomic Development, New York: The Twentieth Century Fund, 1955.

Buchanan, Norman S., and Lutz, F. A., Building the World Economy, New York: The Twentieth Century Fund, 1947.

Buck, P. W., The Politics of Mercantilism, New York: Henry Holt & Co., 1942.

Bullock, Charles J., Williams, John H., and Tucker, Rufus S., "The Balance of Trade of the United States," Review of Economic Statistics, July, 1919.

Burns, Arthur F., Economic Research and the Keynesian Thinking of our Times, New York: National Bureau of Economic Research, Inc., 1946.

Burtle, J. L., and Liepe, W., "Devaluation and the Cost of Living in the United Kingdom," Review of Economic Studies, No. 1, 1949-1950.

Busschau, W. J., "The Case for Increasing the Price of Gold in Terms of All Currencies," South African Journal of Economics, March, 1949.

Cairncross, A. K., Home and Foreign Investment, 1870-1913, Studies in Capital Accumulation, Cambridge: University Press, 1953.

Cairnes, J. E., The Principles of Currency Involved in the Bank Charter Act of 1844, London: 1854.

Cairnes, J. E., Essays in Political Economy, London: Macmillan Co., 1873.

Cairnes, J. E., Some Leading Principles of Political Economy Newly Expounded, New York: Harper & Brothers, 1874.

Cairnes, J. E., The Character and Logical Method of Political Economy, London: Macmillan Co., Ltd., 1888.

Cairns, Huntington, Legal Philosophy from Plato to Hegel, Baltimore: The Johns Hopkins Press, 1949.

Canada Yearbook, Canada Dominion Bureau of Statistics, Department of Trade and Commerce, 1870-1939.

Canning, Rev. Richard, of Ipswich, letter by, in The Christian's Magazine, Vol. iii, 1763.

Cantillon, Richard, Essai sur la nature du commerce en général, London: Macmillan and Co., Ltd., 1931.

Carter, William, England's Interest by Trade Asserted, London, 1671.

Carter, William, A Brief Advertisement to the Merchant and Clothier, London, 1672.

Carter, William, An Abstract of Proceedings to Prevent Exportation of Wool Unmanufactured, London, 1688.

Cary, John, A Discourse on Trade, London: For. T. Osborne, 1717.

Cassady, R., and Upgren, A. R., "International Trade and Devaluation of the Dollar, 1932-34," Quarterly Journal of Economics, May, 1936.

Cavin, James P., "Projections in Agriculture," in Long-Range Economic Projections, Studies in Income and Wealth, Vol. 16, Princeton: Princeton University Press, 1954.

Chamberlin, Edward Hasting, *The Theory of Monopolistic Competition*, Cambridge: Harvard University Press, 1942.

Chang, T. C., "International Comparison of Demand for Imports," *Review of Economic Studies*, No. 2, 1954-1956.

Chang, T. C., "The British Demand for Imports in the Inter-War Period," *Economic Journal*, June, 1946.

Chang, T. C., "World Demand for Exports," *Review of Economics and Statistics*, May, 1948.

Chang, T. C., *Cyclical Movements in the Balance of Payments*, Cambridge: University Press, 1951.

Chang, T. C., and Polak, J. J., *An International Economic System*, Washington: International Monetary Fund, 1949.

Cipolla, Carlo M., *Money, Prices, and Civilization in the Mediterranean World*, Princeton: Princeton University Press, 1956.

Clapham, Sir John H., *The Bank of England, A history*, Cambridge: University Press, 1944.

Clapham, J. H., *An Economic History of Modern Britain*, Cambridge: University Press, 1950-1952.

Clapham, J. H., *The Economic Development of France and Germany, 1815-1914*, 4th ed., Cambridge: University Press, 1951.

Clark, Colin, *Conditions of Economic Progress*, London: Macmillan and Co., Ltd., 1951.

Clark, J. M., and others, *National and International Measures for Full Employment*, New York: United Nations Press, 1949.

Clemence, Richard V., ed., *Readings in Economic Analysis*, Cambridge: Addison-Wesley Press, Inc., 1950.

Committee for Economic Development, *Economic Policy for American Agriculture*, January, 1956.

Conan, A. R., "The Changing Pattern of International Investment in Selected Sterling Countries," *Essays in International Finance*, December, 1956.

Condliffe, John B., *The Commerce of Nations*, New York: W. W. Norton & Co., Inc., 1950.

Condliffe, John B., *The Welfare State in New Zealand*, London: George Allen and Unwin, Ltd., 1959.

Condliffe, John B., *New Zealand in the Making*, rev. ed., London: George Allen and Unwin, Ltd., 1959.

Coppock, D. J., "The Climacteric of the 1890's: A Critical Note," *Manchester School of Economic and Social Studies*, January, 1956.

Cournot, Augustin, *Recherches sur les principes mathematiques de la théorie des richesses*, Paris: Chez Hachette, 1838.

Davenant, Charles, "Discourses on the Public Revenues, and on Trade," *Works*, 5 vols., London: For. R. Horsfield, 1771.

Day, A. C. L., "A Geometrical Demonstration of Stability Conditions in International Trade," *Economia Internazionale*, February, 1954.

Day, A. C. L., *The Future of Sterling*, Oxford: The Clarendon Press, 1954.

Day, A. C. L., *Outline of Monetary Economics*, Oxford: The Clarendon Press, 1957.

Day, A. C. L., "Relative Prices, Expenditure and the Trade Balance; A Note," *Economica*, February, 1954.

de Graff, J., "On Optimum Tariff Structures," *Review of Economic Studies*, No. 1, 1949-1950.

de Vries, Barend A., "Price Elasticities of Demand for U.K. Exports to the United States," derived from the U.S. Tariff Commission's study: "Post-War Imports and Domestic Production of Major Commodities," September, 1949, mimeographed.

de Vries, Barend A., "Immediate Effects of Devaluation on Prices of Raw Materials," *International Monetary Fund Staff Papers*, September, 1950.

Deane, Phyllis, "The Industrial Revolution and Economic Growth: The Evidence of Early British National Income Estimates," *Economic Development and Cultural Change*, January, 1957.

Devons, Ely, "Statistics of United Kingdom Terms of Trade," *The Manchester School of Economic and Social Studies*, September, 1954.

Dicey, A. V., *Lectures on the Relation between Law and Public Opinion in England during the Nineteenth Century*, 2nd ed., London: Macmillan and Co., Ltd., 1914.

Dickens, P. D., "Criteria for Determining the Creditor-Debtor Position of a Country," *Journal of Political Economy*, December, 1939.

Dobb, M. H., *The Works and Correspondence of David Ricardo*, vol. III, Cambridge: University Press, 1951.

Domar, E. D., "Capital Expansion, Rate of Growth, and Employment," *Econometrica*, April, 1946.

Domar, E. D., "The Problem of Capital Accumulation," *American Economic Review*, December, 1948, p. 783.

Domar, E. D., *Essays in the Theory of Economic Growth*, New York: Oxford University Press, 1957.

Dorrance, G. S., "The Income Terms of Trade," *Review of Economic Studies*, No. 1, 1948-1949.

Douglas, Paul H., "An Estimate of the Growth of Capital in the United Kingdom, 1865-1909," *Journal of Economic and Business History*, August, 1930.

Duesenberry, James S., *Income, Saving and the Theory of Consumer Behavior*, Cambridge: Harvard University Press, 1949.

Duesenberry, James S., *Business Cycles and Economic Growth*, New York: McGraw-Hill Book Co., 1958.

Dupriez, Leon H., *Des mouvements économiques généraux,* 2 vols., Louvain: De l'université de Louvain, 1947.

Edgeworth, Francis Y., "The Mathematical Theory of Political Economy," *Nature,* Vol. XL, 1889.

Edgeworth, Francis Y., *Papers Relating to Political Economy,* London: Macmillan and Co., Ltd., 1925.

Edinburgh Review, February, 1811.

Egle, W., "The Spreading of Gold Points as a Means of Controlling the Movement of Foreign Short-Term Balances," *Journal of Political Economy,* December, 1939.

Einzig, Paul, *The Theory of Forward Exchanges,* London: Macmillan and Co., Ltd., 1937.

Elliott, G. A., "Transfer of Means-of-Payments and the Terms of International Trade," *Canadian Journal of Economics and Political Science,* November, 1936.

Elliott, G. A., "The Theory of International Values," *Journal of Political Economy,* February, 1950.

Ellis, Howard S., "The Equilibrium Rate of Exchange," in *Explorations in Economics: Notes and Essays Contributed in Honor of F. W. Taussig,* New York, McGraw-Hill Book Co., 1936.

Ellis, Howard S., *German Monetary Theory, 1905-1933,* Cambridge: Harvard University Press, 1937.

Ellis, Howard S., *Exchange Control in Central Europe,* Cambridge: Harvard University Press, 1941.

Ellis, Howard S., "Can National and International Monetary Policies be Reconciled?" *American Economic Review,* 1944 supplement.

Ellis, Howard S., "The Dollar Shortage in Theory and Fact," *Canadian Journal of Economics and Political Science,* August, 1948.

Ellis, Howard S., *The Economics of Freedom: The Progress and Future of Aid to Europe,* New York: Harper & Brothers, 1950.

Ellis, Howard S., ed., *A Survey of Contemporary Economics,* Philadelphia: The Blakiston Co., 1948.

Ellis, Howard S., and Buchanan, Norman S., *Approaches to Economic Development,* New York: The Twentieth Century Fund, 1955.

Ellis, Howard S., and Metzler, Lloyd A., *Readings in the Theory of International Trade,* Philadelphia: The Blakiston Co., 1949.

Ellsworth, P. T., "A Comparison of International Trade Theories," *American Economic Review,* June, 1940.

Ellsworth, P. T., "Exchange Rates and Exchange Stability," *Review of Economics and Statistics,* February, 1950.

Ellsworth, P. T., "The Structure of American Foreign Trade: A New View Examined," *Review of Economics and Statistics,* August, 1954.

Ellsworth, P. T., "The Terms of Trade Between Primary Producing and Industrial Countries," *Inter-American Economic Affairs*, Vol. X, No. 1, Summer, 1956.

Ellsworth, P. T., *The International Economy*, rev., New York: The Macmillan Co., 1958.

Enke, Stephen, and Salera, Virgil, *International Economics*, 2nd ed., New York: Prentice-Hall, Inc., 1951.

Enthoven, A. C., "Monetary Disequilibria and the Dynamics of Inflation," *Economic Journal*, June, 1956.

Fabricant, Solomon, *Employment in Manufacturing, 1899-1937*, New York: National Bureau of Economic Research, Inc., 1942.

Fabricant, Solomon, *Economic Progress and Economic Change*, 34th Annual Report, New York: National Bureau of Economic Research, Inc., 1954.

Fabricant, Solomon, "Notes on Efficiency and Size, with Particular Reference to the United States," International Economic Association Meetings, Lisbon, 1957, mimeographed.

Familton, R. J., "Balance of Payments Equilibrium and Monetary Policy," *Economic Record*, November, 1954.

Fanno, M., *Normal and Abnormal International Capital Transfers*, Minneapolis: University of Minnesota Press, 1939.

Fay, C. R., *The Corn Laws and Social England*, Cambridge: University Press, 1932.

Fay, C. R., "The Movement Towards Free Trade, 1820-1853," in *The Cambridge History of the British Empire*, Vol. II, *The Growth of the New Empire, 1783-1870*, Cambridge: University Press, 1940, pp. 388-414.

Fay, C. R., *Round About Industrial Britain, 1830-1860*, Toronto: University of Toronto Press, 1952.

Federici, L., "On the Validity of the Principles of the 'Foreign Trade Multiplier' Theory," *Economia Internazionale*, August, 1950.

Feis, H., *Europe, The World's Banker, 1870-1914*, New Haven: Yale University Press, 1930.

Feis H., *Churchill, Roosevelt, Stalin: The War They Waged and the Peace They Sought*. Princeton: Princeton University Press, 1957.

Fellner, William, *Monetary Policies and Full Employment*, Berkeley: University of California Press, 1946.

Fellner, William, "Employment Theory and Business Cycles," *A Survey of Contemporary Economics*, Vol. I, H. S. Ellis, ed., Philadelphia: The Blakiston Co., 1948.

Fellner, William, *Competition Among the Few: Oligopoly and Similar Market Structures*, New York: Alfred A. Knopf, 1949.

Fellner, William, "The Rate of Growth and Capital Coefficients," in

Long-Range Economic Projections, Studies in Income and Wealth, Vol. 16, Princeton: Princeton University Press, 1954.

Fellner, William, *Trends and Cycles in Economic Activity*, New York: Henry Holt & Co., 1956.

Fetter, Frank W., "European Convertibility," *American Economic Review*, May, 1957.

Field, H., "A Note on Exchange Stability," *Review of Economic Studies*, No. 37, 1947-1948.

Fink, William H., *Ratios of International Exchange and Their Relation to National Welfare and Advantage*, unpublished Ph.D. dissertation, Berkeley: University of California, 1954.

Fisher, A. G. B., "Some Essential Factors in the Evaluation of International Trade," *The Manchester School of Economic and Social Studies*, October, 1943.

Fisher, F. J., "Commercial Trends and Policy in Sixteenth-Century England," *Economic History Review*, Vol. X, 1940.

Fisher, F. J., "London's Export Trade in the Early Seventeenth Century," *Economic History Review*, 2nd series, Vol. III, 1950.

Forde, J. S., "Cyclical Fluctuations and the Growth of Discriminatory Alignments in International Trade," *Economic Journal*, March, 1955.

Frankel, S. Herbert, *The Economic Impact on Under-Developed Societies, Essays of International Investment and Social Change*, Oxford: Blackwell, 1953.

Friedman, Milton, "Lange on Price Flexibility and Employment," *American Economic Review*, September, 1946.

Friedman, Milton, "The Case for Flexible Exchange Rates," *Essays in Positive Economics*, Chicago: University of Chicago Press, 1953.

Frisch, Ragnar, "On the Need for Forecasting a Multilateral Balance of Payments," *American Economic Review*, September, 1947.

Galbraith, J. K., and Black, J. D., "The Maintenance of Agricultural Production during Depression: The Explanations Reviewed," *Journal of Political Economy*, June, 1938.

Gambino, A., "Money Supply and Interest Rates in Recent Macro-Economic Conceptions," Banca Nazionale del Lavoro, *Quarterly Review*, September, 1954.

Gardner, Richard N., *Sterling-Dollar Diplomacy*, Oxford: The Clarendon Press, 1956.

Gayer, A. D., Rostow, W. W., Schwartz, A. J., and Frank, I., *The Growth and Fluctuation of the British Economy*, 2 vols., Oxford: The Clarendon Press, 1953.

Gehrels, F., "Multipliers and Elasticities in Foreign-Trade Adjustments," *Journal of Political Economy*, February, 1957.

Gendarme, M., "Le multiplicateur du commerce extérieur," *Revue Économique*, November, 1951.

General Agreement on Tariffs and Trade, *International Trade, 1956,* Geneva: G.A.T.T., 1957.

Gervaise, Isaac, *The System or Theory of the Trade of the World,* with an introduction by J. M. Letiche and a forward by Jacob Viner, Baltimore: The Johns Hopkins Press, 1954.

Giersch, H., "The Acceleration Principle and the Propensity to Import," *International Economic Papers,* No. 4, 1954.

Gilbert, J. C., "The Mechanism of Interregional Redistributions of Money," *Review of Economic Studies,* No. 3, June, 1938.

Gilbert, M., *Currency Depreciation and Monetary Policy,* Philadelphia: University of Pennsylvania Press, 1939.

Gilbert, Milton, and Kravis, Irving, *An International Comparison of National Products and the Purchasing Power of Currencies,* Paris: Organization for European Economic Cooperation, 1954.

Glover, J. B., and Cornell, W. B., *The Development of American Industries,* New York: Prentice-Hall, Inc., 1941.

Goldsmith, Oliver, *The Citizen of the World,* 2 vols., London: J. M. Dent and Co., 1900.

Gordon, R. A., "Cyclical Experience in the Interwar Period: The Investment Boom of the 'Twenties,' " in Universities-National Bureau Committee, *Conference on Business Cycles,* New York: National Bureau of Economic Research, Inc., 1951, pp. 163-215.

Gordon, R. A., "Investment Behavior and Business Cycles," *Review of Economics and Statistics,* February, 1955, pp. 23-34.

Gordon, R. A., "Investment Opportunities in the U.S. Before and After World War II," in *The Business Cycle in the Post-War World,* Erik Lundberg, ed., New York: The Macmillan Co., 1955, pp. 283-310.

Goschen, George J., *The Theory of the Foreign Exchanges,* London: E. Wilson, 1863.

Graham, F. D., "International Trade under Depreciated Paper. The United States, 1862-79," *Quarterly Journal of Economics,* Vol. XXXVI, 1922.

Graham, F. D., "The Theory of International Values Re-examined," *Quarterly Journal of Economics,* November, 1923.

Graham, F. D., "Keynes vs. Hayek on a Commodity Reserve Currency," *Economic Journal,* December, 1944.

Graham, F. D., *The Theory of International Values,* Princeton: Princeton University Press, 1948.

Graham, F. D., "The Cause and Cure of 'Dollar Shortage,' " *Essays in International Finance,* Princeton: Princeton University Press, January, 1949.

Great Britain, Board of Trade, *Board of Trade Journal,* London: HM Stationery Office, various issues.

Great Britain, Board of Trade, *Report on Overseas Trade*, London: HM Stationery Office, monthly.

Great Britain, House of Commons, *Statistical Material Presented during the Washington Negotiations*, Sessional Papers, 1945-1946, Vol. 21, London: H M Stationery Office.

Great Britain, House of Lords, *Report from the Lords Committees on the Poor Laws* (101 of 1817), Sessional Papers of the House of Lords, 1801-1859, Vol. LXXXIV, London: H M Stationery Office, 1817.

Gunasekera, H. A. deS., "The Money Supply and the Balance of Payments in Ceylon," Banca Nazionale de Lavoro, *Quarterly Review*, September, 1954.

Habakkuk, H. J., "Free Trade and Commercial Expansion, 1853-1870," in *The Cambridge History of the British Empire*, Vol. II, *The Growth of the New Empire, 1783-1870*, Cambridge: University Press, 1940, pp. 751-805.

Haberler, G., "The Theory of Comparative Costs Once More," *Quarterly Journal of Economics*, February, 1929.

Haberler, G., "Transfer und Preisbewegung," *Zeitschrift für Nationalokonomie*, January and August, 1930.

Haberler, G., "Die Theorie der komparativen Kosten and ihre Auswertung für de Begrundung des Friehandels," *Weltwirtschaftliches Archiv*, 32, 1930.

Haberler, G., "Some Comments on Professor Hansen's Note," *Review of Economic Statistics*, November, 1944.

Haberler, G., "Dollar Shortage?" in *Foreign Economic Policy for the United States*, Seymour E. Harris, ed., Cambridge: Harvard University Press, 1948.

Haberler, G., "Currency Depreciation and the International Monetary Fund," *ibid*.

Haberler, G., "The Market for Foreign Exchange and the Stability of the Balance of Payments," *Kyklos*, Vol. III, 3, 1949.

Haberler, G., "Some Problems in the Pure Theory of International Trade," *Economic Journal*, June, 1950.

Haberler, G., *The Theory of International Trade with Its Applications to Commercial Policy*, London: William Hodge and Co., Ltd., 1950.

Haberler, G., "Currency Depreciation and the Terms of Trade" in *Wirtschlaftliche Entwicklung and soziale Ordnung*, Ernst Lagler and J. Messner, eds., Vienna: Verlag Herold, 1952.

Haberler, G., *Prosperity and Depression*, 3rd ed., New York: United Nations, 1952.

Haberler, G., "Reflections of the Future of the Bretton Woods System," *American Economic Review, Papers and Proceedings*, May, 1953.

✓Haberler, G., "The Relevance of the Classical Theory under Modern

Conditions," *American Economic Review, Papers and Proceedings*, May, 1954.

Haberler, G., A *Survey of International Trade Theory*, International Finance Section, Princeton: Princeton University Press, 1955.

Haberler, G., "Monetary Factors Affecting Economic Stability," International Economic Association First Congress, Rome, September 6-11, 1956, mimeographed.

Hales, John, "A Discourse of the common weal of this realm of England," ms. 1550, 1st ed., 1581, Elizabeth Lamond, ed., Cambridge, England, 1893.

Hall, N. F., *The Exchange Equalisation Account*, London: Macmillan and Co., Ltd., 1935.

Hall, Walter, A *view of our late and of our future currency*, 1819.

Hamilton, Earl J., "The Role of Monopoly in the Overseas Expansion and Colonial Trade of Europe Before 1800," *American Economic Review*, May, 1948.

Hamilton, Henry, *The English Brass and Copper Industries to 1800*, London: Longmans, Green and Co., Ltd., 1926.

Hamilton, Sir William, ed., *The Works of Thomas Reid*, 3rd ed., Edinburgh: Maclachlan and Stewart, 1852.

Hammond, J. L., and Barbara, *The Rise of Modern Industry*, 3rd ed., London: Methuen and Co., Ltd., 1927.

Hansen, A. H., "A Brief Note on Fundamental Disequilibrium," *Review of Economic Statistics*, November, 1944.

Hansen, A. H., "Fundamental Disequilibrium," in *Foreign Economic Policy for the United States*, Seymour Harris, ed., Cambridge, Harvard University Press, 1948, chap. 20.

Hansen, Bent, A *Study in the Theory of Inflation*, London: George Allen & Unwin, Ltd., 1951.

Harberger, A. C., "Currency Depreciation, Income, and the Balance of Trade," *Journal of Political Economy*, February, 1950.

Harberger, A. C., "Stability of the Structure of Import Trade," *International Monetary Fund*, August, 1950.

Harberger, A. C., "Pitfalls in Mathematical Model-Building," *American Economic Review*, December, 1952.

Harberger, A. C., "A Structural Approach to the Problem of Import Demand," *American Economic Review*, May, 1953.

Harris, Seymour E., *Postwar Economic Problems*, New York: McGraw-Hill Book Co., 1943.

Harris, Seymour E., ed., *Economic Reconstruction*, New York: McGraw-Hill Book Co., 1945.

Harris, Seymour E., *The New Economics*, New York: Alfred A. Knopf, 1947.

Harris, Seymour E., ed., *Foreign Economic Policy for the United States*, Cambridge: Harvard University Press, 1948.

Harrod, R. F., "An Essay in Dynamic Theory," *Economic Journal*, March, 1939.

Harrod, R. F., *International Economics*, London: Nisbet and Co., Ltd., 1939.

Harrod, R. F., "A Review of Oscar Lange's Price Flexibility and Employment," *Economic Journal*, March, 1946.

Harrod, R. F., *Towards a Dynamic Economics*, London: St. Martins, 1948.

Harrod, R. F., *The Dollar*, London: Macmillan and Co., Ltd., 1953.

Hawtrey, R. G., "The Function of Exchange Rates," *Oxford Economic Papers*, June, 1949.

Hawtrey, R. G., "Multiplier Analysis and the Balance of Payments," *Economic Journal*, March, 1950.

Hawtrey, R. G., *The Balance of Payments and the Standard of Living*, London: Royal Institute of International Affairs, 1950.

Hayek, F. A., *Monetary Nationalism and International Stability*, London: Longmans, Green and Co., Ltd., 1937.

Hayek, F. A., "A Commodity Reserve Currency," *Economic Journal*, June-September, 1943.

Hearnshaw, F. J. C., ed., *The Social and Political Ideas of Some Representative Thinkers of the Victorian Age*, London: George G. Harrojo and Co., Ltd., 1933.

Heckscher, Eli F., "The Effect of Foreign Trade on the Distribution of Income," *Ekonomisk Tidskrift*, 21, 1919, in *Readings in the Theory of International Trade*, Philadelphia: American Economic Association, 1949.

Heckscher, Eli F., "Mercantilism, Baltic Trade, and the Mercantilists," *Economic History Review*, 2nd series, Vol. III, No. 2, 1950.

Heckscher, Eli F., *Mercantilism*, 2 vols., rev. ed., trans. by Mandel Shapiro, London: George Allen & Unwin, Ltd., 1955.

Hegelund, Hugo, "The Multiplier Theory," *Lund Social Science Studies*, 9, 1954.

Heilperin, Michael A., *The Trade of Nations*, New York: Alfred A. Knopf, 1947.

Henderson, Sir Hubert D., "The Function of Exchange Rates," *Oxford Economic Papers*, January, 1949.

Henry, James A., "South Africa and the Free Gold Market," *The Journal of the Institute of Bankers in South Africa*, March, 1949.

Hickman, Bert G., "Capacity, Capacity Utilization, and the Acceleration Principle," in *Problems of Capital Formation*, Studies in Income and Wealth, Vol. 19, Princeton: Princeton University Press, 1957.

Hicks, J. R., "Mr. Keynes and the 'Classics': A Suggested Interpretation," *Econometrica*, V, 1937.

Hicks, J. R., *Value and Capital*, Oxford: The Clarendon Press, 1939.

Hicks, J. R., "Recent Contributions to General Equilibrium Economics," *Economica, New Series*, November, 1945.

Hicks, J. R., "Devaluation and World Trade," *Three Banks Review*, London, December, 1949.

Hicks, J. R., *A Contribution to the Theory of the Trade Cycle*, Oxford: The Clarendon Press, 1950.

Hicks, J. R., "The Long-run Dollar Problem. An Inaugural Lecture," *Oxford Economic Papers*, June, 1953.

Hicks, J. R., "A Rehabilitation of 'Classical' Economics?" *Economic Journal*, June, 1957.

Hilgerdt, F., *Industrialization and Foreign Trade*, Geneva: League of Nations, 1945.

Hilgerdt, F., "International Trade and Structural Disequilibrium," *Quarterly Journal of Economics*, November, 1952.

Hinshaw, R., "American Prosperity and the British Balance-of-Payments Problem," *Review of Economics and Statistics*, February, 1945.

Hinshaw, Randall, "Effect of Income Changes on American Imports of Goods and Services," Division of Research and Statistics, Board of Governors of the Federal Reserve System, March, 1946, mimeographed.

Hinshaw, Randall, "On the Elasticity of Import Demand Schedules," Division of Research and Statistics, International Section, Board of Governors of the Federal Reserve System, August 26, 1946, mimeographed.

Hinshaw, Randall, "Export Prices and the Dollar-Sterling Rate," Federal Reserve mimeographed memo (confidential), August 2, 1949.

Hinshaw, Randall, "Currency Appreciation as an Anti-Inflationary Device," *Quarterly Journal of Economics*, November, 1951 and February, 1952.

Hirschman, A. O., *National Power and the Structure of Foreign Trade*, Berkeley: University of California Press, 1945.

Hirschman, A. O., "Disinflation, Discrimination and the Dollar Shortage," *American Economic Review*, December, 1948.

Hirschman, A. O., "Devaluation and the Trade Balance," *Review of Economics and Statistics*, February, 1949.

Hobhouse, L. T., *Liberalism*, New York: Henry Holt & Co., 1911.

Hobson, C. K., *The Export of Capital*, London: Constable and Co., Ltd., 1914.

Hoffman, M. L., *The Economics of Fluctuating Exchanges*, unpublished Ph.D. dissertation, Department of Economics, University of Chicago, 1942.

Hoffman, M. L., "Capital Movements and International Payments in Post-War Europe," *Review of Economics and Statistics*, November, 1949.

Hoffmann, Walther G., *Wachstum und Wachstumformen der Englischen Industriewirtschaft von 1700 bis zur Gegenwart*, Jena: Gustav Fisher, 1940.

Hoffmann, Walther G., "The Growth of Industrial Production in Great Britain: A Quantitative Study," *Economic History Review*, 2nd series, Vol. II, No. 2, 1949.

Hoffmann, Walther G., *British Industry, 1700-1950*, trans. by W. O. Henderson and W. H. Chaloner, Oxford: Blackwell, 1955.

Hollander, J. H., "International Trade under Depreciated Paper: A Criticism," *Quarterly Journal of Economics*, August, 1918.

Hoselitz, Bert F., "Entrepreneurship and Capital Formation in France and Britain since 1700," in *Capital Formation and Economic Growth*, National Bureau of Economic Research, Inc., Princeton: Princeton University Press, 1955.

Hoselitz, Bert F., ed., *The Progress of Underdeveloped Areas*, Chicago: University of Chicago Press, 1952.

Hume, David, *Essays and Treatises on Several Subjects*, new edition, 2 vols., London, printed for T. Cadell, 1772.

Hume, David, *History of England*, 2 vols., Philadelphia: McCarty and Davis, 1840.

Hume, David, *Essays Moral, Political and Literary* (1752), T. H. Green and T. H. Gross, eds., London: Longmans, Green and Co., Ltd., 1889.

Humphrey, Don D., *American Imports*, New York: The Twentieth Century Fund, 1955.

Huszar, George B., ed., *New Perspectives on Peace*, Chicago: University of Chicago Press, 1944.

Hutt, W. H., *Economists and the Public: A Study of Competition and Opinion*, London: Jonathan Cape, 1935.

Imlah, Albert H., "Real Values in British Foreign Trade," *Journal of Economic History*, November, 1948.

Imlah, Albert H., "The Terms of Trade of the United Kingdom, 1798-1913," *Journal of Economic History*, November, 1950.

Imlah, Albert H., "British Balance of Payments and Export of Capital, 1816-1913," *Economic History Review* 2nd series, Vol. V, No. 2, 1952.

Ingram, J. C., "Capital Imports and the Balance of Payments," *Southern Economic Journal*, April, 1956.

International Monetary Fund, *Annual Report on Exchange Restrictions*, Washington.

International Monetary Fund, *International Financial Statistics*, Washington, monthly.

Isard, Walter, "Location Theory and Trade Theory: Short-run Analysis," *Quarterly Journal of Economics*, May, 1954.

Isard, Walter, and Peck, Merton J., "Location Theory and International and Interregional Trade Theory," *Quarterly Journal of Economics*, February, 1954.

Iverson, Carl, *Aspects of the Theory of International Capital Movements*, Copenhagen: Levin & Drunksgaard, 1935.

Jefferys, James B., and Walters, Dorothy, "National Income and Expenditure of the United Kingdom, 1870-1952," in *Income and Wealth*, Series V, National Bureau of Economic Research, Inc., Princeton: Princeton University Press, 1956.

Jenks, Leland H., *Migration of British Capital to 1875*, New York: Alfred A. Knopf, 1927.

Jevons, W. Stanley, *The Theory of Political Economy*, London: Macmillan and Co., Ltd., 1924.

Johnson, D. Gale, "The Supply Function for Agricultural Products," *American Economic Review*, September, 1950.

Johnson, D. Gale, "Agricultural Price Policy and International Trade," *Essays in International Finance*, Princeton: Princeton University Press, 1954.

Johnson, D. Gale, "Stabilization of International Commodity Prices," in *Policies to Combat Depression*, National Bureau of Economic Research, Inc., Princeton: Princeton University Press, 1956.

Johnson, E. A. J., *Predecessors of Adam Smith*, New York: Prentice-Hall, Inc., 1937.

Johnson, H. G., "The Case for Increasing the Price of Gold in Terms of All Currencies: A Contrary View," *Canadian Journal of Economics and Political Science*, May, 1950.

Johnson, H. G., "Increasing Productivity, Income-Price Trends and the Trade Balance," *Economic Journal*, September, 1954.

Johnson, H. G., "The Transfer Problem: A Note on Criteria for Changes in the Terms of Trade," *Economica*, May, 1955.

Johnson, H. G., "The Transfer Problem and Exchange Stability," *Journal of Political Economy*, June, 1956.

Kahn, A. E., *Great Britain in the World Economy*, New York: Columbia University Press, 1946.

Kahn, R. F., "Tariffs and the Terms of Trade," *Review of Economic Studies*, No. 1, 1947-1948.

Kaldor, Nicholas, "A Note on Tariffs and the Terms of Trade, *Economica*, November, 1940.

Kaldor, Nicholas, "Employment Policies and the Problem of International Balance," *International Social Science Bulletin*, Spring, 1951.

Kaldor, Nicholas, "The Relation of Economic Growth and Cyclical Fluctuations," *Economic Journal*, March, 1954, pp. 53-71.

Katz, Samuel I., "Leads and Lags in Sterling Payments," *Review of Economic Statistics*, February, 1953.

Katz, Samuel I., "The Canadian Dollar: A Fluctuating Currency," *Review of Economic Statistics*, August, 1953.

Katz, Samuel I., "Exchange Flexibility and the Stability of Sterling," *American Economic Review*, March, 1954.

Katz, Samuel I., "Le dollar canadien et le cours de change fluctuant," *Bulletin d'information et de documentation*, Banque Nationale de Belgique, May, 1955.

Katz, Samuel I., "Two Approaches to the Exchange-Rate Problem: The United Kingdom and Canada," *Essays in International Finance*, Princeton University, August, 1956.

Keilhau, W., "Basic Remarks on the Relations Between Internal Policy, Inflation and External Balances," *International Social Science Bulletin*, Spring, 1951.

Kelsen, Hans, "The Natural-Law Doctrine before the Tribunal of Science," *Western Political Science Quarterly*, December, 1949. Republished in *What is Justice?* Berkeley: University of California Press, 1957.

Kemp, M., "Unilateral Transfers and the Terms of Trade," *American Economic Review*, March, 1956.

Kendrick, John W., "National Productivity and its Long-Term Projection," in *Long-Range Economic Projection*, Studies in Income and Wealth, Vol. 16, Princeton: Princeton University Press, 1954.

Kennedy, C., "Devaluation and the Terms of Trade," *Review of Economic Studies*, Vol. XVIII, No. 1, 1949-1950.

Keynes, John Maynard, "The German Transfer Problem," *Economic Journal*, March, 1929; reprinted in *Readings in the Theory of International Trade*, Philadelphia: American Economic Association, 1949.

Keynes, John Maynard, *A Treatise on Money*, Vol. II, New York: Harcourt, Brace & Co., 1930.

Keynes, John Maynard, *A Tract on Monetary Reform*, London: Macmillan and Co., Ltd., 1932.

Keynes, John Maynard, "National Self-Sufficiency," *Yale Review*, June, 1933.

Keynes, John Maynard, *The General Theory of Employment, Interest and Money*, New York: Harcourt, Brace & Co., 1936.

Keynes, John Maynard, "Alternative Theories of the Rate of Interest," *Economic Journal*, June, 1937.

Keynes, John Maynard, *How To Pay for the War*, New York: Harcourt, Brace & Co., 1940.

Keynes, John Maynard, "The International Clearing Union," speech before the House of Lords, May 18, 1943.

Keynes, John Maynard, "The Objective of International Price Stability," *Economic Journal*, June-September, 1943.

Keynes, John Maynard, Préface pour l'edition française, *Theorie générale de l'emploi, de l'intérêt et de la monnaie*, Paris: Payot, 1943. Translated from French by A. T. Peacock, *International Economic Papers*, No. 4, New York: The Macmillan Co., 1954.

Keynes, John Maynard, "The International Monetary Fund," speech before the House of Lords, May 23, 1944; reprinted in *The New Economics*, Seymour E. Harris, ed., New York: Alfred A. Knopf, 1947.

Keynes, John Maynard, "The Balance of Payments of the United States," *Economic Journal*, June, 1946.

Kindleberger, Charles P., *International Short-term Capital Movements*, New York: Columbia University Press, 1937.

Kindleberger, Charles P., *The Dollar Shortage*, New York: John Wiley & Sons, Inc., and Technology Press of M.I.T., 1950.

Kindleberger, Charles P., *International Economics*, Homewood (Ill.): R. D. Irwin, 1953.

Kindleberger, Charles P., "Industrial Europe's Terms of Trade on Current Account," *Economic Journal*, March, 1955.

Kindleberger, Charles P., *The Terms of Trade: A European Case Study*, New York: John Wiley & Sons, Inc., 1956.

Kindleberger, Charles P., "The Dollar Shortage Re-Revisited," *American Economic Review*, June, 1958.

Kindleberger, Charles P., *Economic Development*, New York: McGraw-Hill Book Co., 1958.

Klein, Lawrence R., *The Keynesian Revolution*, New York: The Macmillan Co., 1947.

Knapp, J., "The Theory of International Capital Movements and its Verification," *Review of Economic Studies*, No. 2, Summer, 1943.

Knorr, Klaus, "Strengthening the Free World Economy," Center of International Studies Conference, Memorandum No. 3, Princeton, December 16-17, 1952.

Kruse, Alfred, ed., "Die Mechanismen des Zahlungsbilanzausgleichs," in *Wirtschaftstheorie und Wirtschaftspolitik: Festgabe fur Adolf Weber*, Berlin, 1951.

Kubinski, Z., "The Elasticity of Substitution between Sources of British Imports, 1921-1938," *Yorkshire Bulletin of Economic and Social Research*, January, 1950.

Kung, Emil, *Die Selbstregulierung der Zahlungsbilanz: Eine Untersuchung uber die automatischen Methoden des Zahlungsbilanzausgleiches*, St. Gallen, 1948.

Kuznets, Simon, *National Income: A Summary and Findings*, New York: National Bureau of Economic Research, Inc., 1946.

Kuznets, Simon, *Economic Change*, New York: W. W. Norton & Co., Inc., 1953.

Kuznets, Simon, "Quantitative Aspects of the Economic Growth of Nations," *Economic Development and Cultural Change*, October, 1956 and July, 1957.

Kuznets, Simon, "International Differences in Capital Formation and Financing," *Capital Formation and Economic Growth*, Princeton: Princeton University Press, 1956.

Kuznets, Simon, *Toward a Theory of Economic Growth*, Baltimore: The Johns Hopkins University Press, 1956.

Kuznets, Simon, Moore, Wilbert E., and Spangler, Joseph J., eds., *Economic Growth: Brazil, India, Japan*, Durham: Duke University Press, 1955.

Lachmann, L. M., "A Note on the Elasticity of Expectations," *Economica, New Series*, November, 1945.

Landes, David S., "Entrepreneurship in Advanced Industrial Countries: The Anglo-German Rivalry," *Entrepreneurship and Economic Growth*, Cambridge: Harvard University Research Center in Entrepreneurial History, November, 1954.

Lange, Oscar, "The Rate of Interest and the Optimum Propensity to Consume," *Economica*, V, L.S., 1938.

Lange, Oscar, "Say's Law: A Restatement and Criticism," in *Studies in Mathematical Economics and Econometrics*, O. Lange, F. McIntyre, and T. O. Yntema, eds., Chicago: University of Chicago Press, 1942.

Lange, Oscar, "On the Theory of the Multiplier," *Econometrica*, July-October, 1943.

Lange, Oscar, "Economic Controls after the War," *Political Science Quarterly*, March, 1945.

Lange, Oscar, *Price Flexibility and Employment*, Bloomington: Principia Press, 1945.

Laursen, Svend, "Production Functions and the Theory of International Trade," *American Economic Review*, September, 1952.

Laursen, Svend, "Productivity, Wages, and the Balance of Payments," *Review of Economics and Statistics*, May, 1955.

Laursen, Svend, and Metzler, Lloyd A., "Flexible Exchange Rates and the Theory of Employment," *Review of Economics and Statistics*, November, 1950.

Laursen, Svend, and Metzler, Lloyd A., "Reply" to W. H. White's "The Employment-insulating Advantages of Flexible Exchanges: A Comment on Professors Laursen and Metzler," *Review of Economics and Statistics*, May, 1954.

League of Nations, *The Network of World Trade*, Geneva: League of Nations, 1942.

League of Nations, *Economic Stability in the Postwar World*, Geneva: League of Nations, 1945.

League of Nations, *Industrialization and Foreign Trade*, Geneva: League of Nations, 1945.

League of Nations, *Review of World Trade*, Geneva: League of Nations, (various issues).

League of Nations, *Statistical Yearbook*, Geneva: League of Nations, (various issues).

Lederer, Walther, "Major Developments Affecting the United States Balance of International Payments," *Review of Economics and Statistics*, May, 1956.

Lehfeldt, R. A., "Rate of Interest on British and Foreign Investments," *Journal of the Royal Statistical Society*, January, 1913.

Leibenstein, Harvey, *A Theory of Economic-Demographic Development*, Princeton: Princeton University Press, 1954.

Leibenstein, Harvey, *Economic Backwardness and Economic Growth*, New York: John Wiley & Sons, Inc., 1957.

Lekachman, Robert, ed., *National Policy for Economic Welfare at Home and Abroad*, New York: Doubleday & Co., 1955.

Leontief, Wassily, "The Use of Indifference Curves in the Analysis of Foreign Trade," *Quarterly Journal of Economics*, May, 1933; reprinted in *Readings in the Theory of International Trade*, Philadelphia: American Economic Association, 1949.

Leontief, Wassily, "Note on the Pure Theory of Capital Transfer," in *Explorations of Economics: Notes and Essays Contributed in Honor of F. W. Taussig*, New York: McGraw-Hill Book Co., 1936.

Leontief, Wassily, "Domestic Production and Foreign Trade: The American Capital Position Re-examined," *Proceedings of the American Philosophical Society*, September, 1953; reprinted in *Economia Internazionale*, February, 1954.

Lerner, Abba P., "Diagrammatical Representation of Cost Conditions in International Trade," *Economica*, August, 1932.

Lerner, Abba P., "Diagrammatical Representation of Demand Conditions in International Trade," *Economica*, August, 1934.

Lerner, Abba P., "The Symmetry Between Import and Export Taxes," *Economica*, August, 1936.

Lerner, Abba P., *The Economics of Control*, New York: The Macmillan Co., 1944.

Lerner, Abba P., "Factor Prices and International Trade," *Economica*, February, 1952. *Essays in Economic Analysis*, New York: St. Martins Press, Inc., 1953; contains the four essays mentioned above.

Letiche, J. M., *Reciprocal Trade Agreements in the World Economy*, New York: King's Crown Press, 1948.

Letiche, J. M., "Isaac Gervaise on the International Mechanism of Adjustment," *Journal of Political Economy*, February, 1952.

Letiche, J. M., "Reflections on the future of the Bretton Woods System," *American Economic Review, Papers and Proceedings*, May, 1953.

Letiche, J. M., "A Note on the Statistical Results of Studies on Demand Elasticities, Income Elasticities, and Foreign Trade Multipliers," *Nordisk Tidsskrift for Teknisk Okonomi*, Lobe No. 39, 1953.

Letiche, J. M., "Introduction to Gervaise, Isaac," *The System or Theory of the Trade of the World*, Baltimore: The Johns Hopkins Press, 1954.

Letiche, J. M., "Differential Rates of Productivity Growth and International Imbalance," *Quarterly Journal of Economics*, August, 1955.

Letiche, J. M., "Die sowjetische Aussenwirtschaftspolitik," *Handel und Hilfsprogramme*, September, 1957.

Letiche, J. M., "Balance of Payments," *Encyclopaedia Britannica*, 1954, 1958.

Lewis, W. A., "World Production Prices and Trade, 1870-1960," *Manchester School of Economic and Social Studies*, May, 1952.

Lewis, W. A., *The Theory of Economic Growth*, London: George Allen and Unwin, Ltd., 1955.

Lewis, W. A., "World Trade in Manufactures: Percentage Shares, 1883-1954," November, 1956, mimeographed.

Lewis, W. A., and O'Leary, P. J., "Secular Swings in Production and Trade, 1870-1913," *Manchester School of Economics and Social Studies*, May, 1955.

Lindahl, Erik, *Studies in the Theory of Money and Capital*, London: George Allen and Unwin, Ltd., 1950.

Lindahl, Erik, "On Keynes' Economic System," *Economic Record*, May and November, 1954.

Lindahl, Erik, "Full Employment Without Inflation," *Three Banks Review*, Edinburgh, March, 1957.

Lindahl, Erik, *Spelet om penningvärdet*, Stockholm: Kooperativa förbundets bokförlag, 1957.

Lindahl, Erik, ed., *Knut Wicksell: Selected Papers on Economic Theory*, London: George Allen and Unwin, Ltd., 1958.

25 Economic Essays in Honor of Erik Lindahl, Stockholm: Ekonomisk Tidskrift, 1956.

Lipson, E., *The Economic History of England*, London: Adam and Charles Black, 1943.

Longfield, Mountifort, *Lectures on Political Economy*, Dublin: R. Milliken and Son, 1834, Series of Reprints of Scarce Tracts in Economic and Political Science, No. 8, London: London School of Economics and Political Science, 1938.

Lovasy, Gertrud, "International Trade under Imperfect Competition," *Quarterly Journal of Economics*, August, 1941.

Lovasy, Gertrud, "Prices of Raw Materials in the 1953-54 U.S. Recession," *International Monetary Fund Staff Papers*, February, 1956.

Lubell, Samuel, *The Revolution in World Trade and American Economic Policy*, New York: Harper & Brothers, 1955.

Lundberg, Erik, *Studies in the Theory of Economic Expansion*, New York: Kelley and Millner, Inc., 1955.

Lundberg, Erik, and Hill, Malcolm, "Some Points of View on the Long-Term Balance of Payments Problems of Australia," *Economic Record*, January, 1956.

Lutz, F. A., and Ellis, Howard, S., *Building the World Economy*, New York: The Twentieth Century Fund, 1947.

Luxemburg, Rosa, *The Accumulation of Capital*, London: Routledge and Kegan Paul, Ltd., 1951.

Macaulay, Frederich R., *The Movements of Interest Rates, Bond Yields and Stock Prices in the United States Since 1856*, New York: National Bureau of Economic Research, Inc., 1938.

MacDougall, G. D. A., "Britain's Foreign Trade Problem," *Economic Journal*, 1947.

MacDougall, G. D. A., "British and American Exports: A Study Suggested by the Theory of Comparative Costs, Part I," *Economic Journal*, December, 1951.

MacDougall, G. D. A., "British and American Exports: A Study Suggested by the Theory of Comparative Costs, Part II," *Economic Journal*, September, 1952.

MacDougall, G. D. A., "Flexible Exchange Rates," *The Westminster Bank Review*, August, 1954.

MacDougall, G. D. A., "Does Productivity Rise Faster in the United States?" *Review of Economics and Statistics*, May, 1956.

MacDougall, G. D. A., *The World Dollar Problem*, London: Macmillan and Co., Ltd., 1957.

Machlup, Fritz, *International Trade and the National Income Multiplier*, Philadelphia: The Blakiston Company, 1943.

Machlup, Fritz, "The Theory of Foreign Exchanges," *Economica*, November, 1939, and February, 1940; reprinted in *Readings in the Theory of International Trade*, Philadelphia: American Economic Association, 1949.

Machlup, Fritz, "Elasticity Pessimism in International Trade," *Economia Internazionale*, February, 1950.

Machlup, Fritz, "Three Concepts of the Balance of Payments and the So-called Dollar Shortage," *Economic Journal*, March, 1950.

Machlup, Fritz, "Dollar Shortage and Disparities in the Growth of Industry," *The Scottish Journal of Political Economy*, October, 1954.

Machlup, Fritz, "Relative Prices and Aggregate Expenditure in the Analysis of Devaluation," *American Economic Review*, June, 1955.

Machlup, Fritz, "The Terms-of-trade Effects of Devaluation upon Real Income and the Balance of Trade," *Kyklos*, Fasc. 4, 1956.

McKenzie, Lionel W., "Specialisation and Efficiency in World Production," *Review of Economic Studies*, No. 3, 1953-1954.

Macrae, N., *The London Capital Market*, London: Staples Press, 1954.

Maizels, A., discussion of C. T. Saunders' paper, "Consumption of Raw Materials in the United Kingdom: 1851-1950," *Journal of the Royal Statistical Society*, Series A, general, Vol. CXV, Part III, 1952.

Malthus, Thomas R., *An Essay on the Principle of Population*, London: T. Bensley, 1803.

Malthus, Thomas R., *Principles of Political Economy*, Boston: Wells and Lilly, 1821.

Manoilesco, M., *Theory of Protection and International Trade*, London: P. S. King & Son, Ltd., 1931.

Marcus, E., "Countercyclical Weapons for the Open Economy," *Journal of Political Economy*, December, 1954.

Maroni, Yves R., *The Theory of International Trade under Monopolistic Competition*, unpublished Ph.D. dissertation, Harvard University, 1946.

Marsh, Donald Bailey, *World Trade and Investment: The Economics of Interdependence*, New York: Harcourt, Brace and Co., 1951.

Marshall, Alfred, *The Pure Theory of Domestic Values*, 1879; reprinted London: The London School of Economics and Political Science, 1930.

Marshall, Alfred, *The Pure Theory of Foreign Trade*, 1879; reprinted London: The London School of Economics and Political Science, 1930.

Marshall, Alfred, "Memorandum on the Fiscal Policy of International Trade," 1903, in *Official Papers of Alfred Marshall*, London: Macmillan and Co., Ltd., 1926.

Marshall, Alfred, *Industry and Trade*, London: Macmillan and Co., Ltd., 1921.

Marshall, Alfred, *Money, Credit and Commerce*, London: Macmillan and Co., Ltd., 1929.

Martin, K., "Capital Movements, the Terms of Trade, and the Balance of Payments," *Bulletin of the Oxford University Institute of Statistics*, November, 1949.

Martin, K., and Thackeray, F. G., "The Terms of Trade of Selected Countries, 1870-1938," *Bulletin of the Oxford University Institute of Statistics*, November, 1948.

Mason, E. S., "The Doctrine of Comparative Cost," *Quarterly Journal of Economics*, November, 1926.

Mason, E. S., "Raw Materials, Rearmament, and Economic Development, *Quarterly Journal of Economics*, August, 1952.

Matthews, R. C. O., "The Trade Cycle in Britain, 1790-1850," *Oxford Economic Papers*, February, 1954.

Matthews, R. C. O., *A Study in Trade-Cycle History: Economic Fluctua-*

tions in Great Britain, 1833-42, Cambridge: University Press, 1954.

Maynard, G. W., "The Principles of the Foreign Trade Multiplier," *Economica Internationale*, August, 1951.

Meade, J. E., "National Income, National Expenditure and the Balance of Payments," *Economic Journal*, December, 1948, and March, 1949.

Meade, J. E., *The Balance of Payments*, London: Oxford University Press, 1951.

Meade, J. E., *A Geometry of International Trade*, London: George Allen and Unwin, Ltd., 1952.

Meade, J. E., *Problems of Economic Union*, Chicago: University of Chicago Press, 1953.

Meade, J. E., "The Case for Variable Exchange Rates," *Three Banks Review*, September, 1955.

Meade, J. E., *Trade and Welfare*, London: Oxford University Press, 1955.

Meade, J. E., *Trade and Welfare, Mathematical Supplement*, London: Oxford University Press, 1955.

Meier, Gerald M., "The Poverty of Nations," *Weltwirtschaftliches Archiv*, Band 78, Heft 1, 1957.

Meier, Gerald M., and Baldwin, Robert E., *Economic Development: Theory, History, Policy*, New York: John Wiley & Sons, Inc., 1957.

Menderhausen, H., *The Trade Balance of the United States since 1914 and the International Order*, unpublished paper for the New York Federal Reserve Bank, April 22, 1949.

Menderhausen, H., "America's Trade Balance and the International Order," *World Politics*, October, 1949.

Metzler, Lloyd A., "Underemployment Equilibrium in International Trade," *Econometrica*, April, 1942.

Metzler, Lloyd A., "The Transfer Problem Reconsidered," *Journal of Political Economy*, June, 1942.

Metzler, Lloyd A., review of Machlup's *International Trade and the National Income Multiplier*, in *Review of Economics and Statistics*, February, 1945.

Metzler, Lloyd A., "The Theory of International Trade," in *A Survey of Contemporary Economics*, Howard S. Ellis, ed., Philadelphia: The Blakiston Co., 1948.

Metzler, Lloyd A., "Tariffs, the Terms of Trade, and the Distribution of National Income," *Journal of Political Economy*, February, 1949.

Metzler, Lloyd A., "Tariffs, International Demand and Domestic Prices," *Journal of Political Economy*, August, 1949.

Metzler, Lloyd A., "Graham's Theory of International Values," *American Economic Review*, June, 1950.

Metzler, Lloyd A., "A Multiple-Region Theory of Income and Trade," *Econometrica*, October, 1950.

Metzler, Lloyd A., "A Multiple-Country Theory of Income Transfers," *Journal of Political Economy*, February, 1951.

Metzler, Lloyd A., and Ellis, Howard S., *Readings in the Theory of International Trade*, Philadelphia: The Blakiston Co., 1948.

Metzler, Lloyd A., and Laursen, Svend, "Flexible Exchange Rates and the Theory of Employment," *Review of Economics and Statistics*, November, 1950.

Metzler, Lloyd A., and Laursen, Svend, "Reply" to W. H. White's "The Employment-insulating Advantages of Flexible Exchanges: A Comment on Professors Laursen and Metzler," *op. cit.*, May, 1954.

Meyer, F. V., *Britain's Colonies in World Trade*, London: Oxford University Press, 1948.

Mikesell, R. F., "Gold Sales as an Anti-Inflationary Device," *Review of Economics and Statistics*, May, 1948.

Mikesell, R. F., "International Disequilibrium and the Postwar World," *American Economic Review*, June, 1949.

Mikesell, R. F., *United States Economic Policy and International Relations*, New York: McGraw-Hill Book Co., 1952.

Mikesell, R. F., *Foreign Exchange in the Postwar World*, Baltimore: The Lord Baltimore Press, 1954.

Mildmay, William, *The Law and Policy of England, Relating to Trade*, London: 1765.

Mill, John Stuart, *Essays on Some Unsettled Questions of Political Economy*, 1844; reprinted London: The London School of Economics and Political Science, 1948.

Mill, John Stuart, *On Liberty*, New York: Henry Holt & Co., 1873.

Mill, John Stuart, *Letters*, Hugh Elliot, ed., London: Longmans, Green and Co., Ltd., 1910.

Mill, John Stuart, *A System of Logic*, 8th ed., London: Longmans, Green and Co., Ltd., 1919.

Mill, John Stuart, *Principles of Political Economy*, W. J. Ashley, ed., London: Longmans, Green and Co., Ltd., 1929.

Mints, Lloyd W., "A Symposium on Fiscal and Monetary Policy," *Review of Economic Statistics*, May, 1946.

Mints, Lloyd W., *A History of Banking Theory in Great Britain and the United States*, Chicago: University of Chicago Press, 1945.

Mints, Lloyd W., *Monetary Policy for a Competitive Society*, New York: McGraw-Hill Book Co., 1950.

Mishan, E. F., "The Long-run Dollar Problem: A Comment," *Oxford Economic Papers*, n.s., June, 1955.

Modigliani, Franco, "Liquidity Preference and the Theory of Interest and Money," *Econometrica*, January, 1944; reprinted in *Readings in Monetary Theory*, New York: The Blakiston Co., 1951.

Modigliani, Franco, "New Developments on the Oligopoly Front," *Journal of Political Economy*, June, 1958.

Morgan, E. V., "The Theory of Flexible Exchange Rates," *American Economic Review*, June, 1955.

Mosak, Jacob L., *General-Equilibrium Theory in International Trade*, Bloomington (Ind.): The Principia Press, Inc., 1944.

Mun, Thomas, *England's Treasure by Forraign Trade*, 1664, New York: The Macmillan Co., 1903.

Myrdal, Gunnar, *Monetary Equilibrium*, London: William Hodge & Co., Ltd., 1939.

Myrdal, Gunnar, *An International Economy: Problems and Prospects*, New York: Harper & Brothers, 1956.

Myrdal, Gunnar, *Economic Theory and Under-developed Regions*, London: General Duckworth and Co., Ltd., 1957.

Nash, E. F., "The Sources of Our Food Supplies," *Agriculture in the British Economy*, London: Imperial Chemical Industries, Ltd., 1957.

National Bureau of Economic Research, Inc., Studies in Income and Wealth, Vol. 15, New York: National Bureau of Economic Research, Inc., 1952.

National Bureau of Economic Research, Inc., *Long-Range Economic Projections*, Studies in Income and Wealth, Vol. 16, Princeton: Princeton University Press, 1954.

National Bureau of Economic Research, Inc., *Capital Formation and Economic Growth*, Princeton: Princeton University Press, 1955.

Nef, John U., *The Rise of the British Coal Industry*, London: George Routledge and Sons, 1932.

Nef, John U., *War and Human Progress*, Cambridge: University Press, 1952.

Neisser, H., "The Significance of Foreign Trade for Domestic Employment," *Social Research*, September, 1946.

Neisser, H., and Modigliani, Franco, *National Incomes and International Trade*, Urbana: University of Illinois Press, 1953.

New Zealand Census and Statistics Department, *The New Zealand Official Yearbook*.

Newton, Isaac, *Scholium*, Book I of the *Principia*, 1687, in *Sir Isaac Newton's Mathematical Principles*, translated by Andrew Motte, 1729, and revised by Florian Cajori, Berkeley: University of California Press, 1934.

North, Sir Dudley, *Discourses upon Trade*, 1691, Baltimore: The Johns Hopkins Press, 1907.

Nourse, Edwin G., *America's Capacity to Produce*, Washington: Brookings Institution, 1934.

Noyes, C. R., "Stable Prices versus Stable Exchanges," Econometrica, April, 1935.

Nurkse, Ragnar, International Currency Experience, Princeton: Princeton University Press, 1944.

Nurkse, Ragnar, "Conditions of International Monetary Equilibrium," Essays in International Finance, Spring, 1945.

Nurkse, Ragnar, "Domestic and International Equilibrium," in The New Economics: Keynes' Influence on Theory and Public Policy, Seymour E. Harris, ed., New York, 1948.

Nurkse, Ragnar, "Some International Aspects of the Problem of Economic Development," American Economic Review, Papers and Proceedings, May, 1952.

Nurkse, Ragnar, Problems of Capital Accumulation in Underdeveloped Countries, Oxford: Blackwell, 1953.

Nurkse, Ragnar, "A New Look at the Dollar Problem and the U.S. Balance of Payments," Economia Internazionale, February, 1954.

Nurkse, Ragnar, "International Investment Today in the Light of Nineteenth Century Experience," Economic Journal, December, 1954.

Nurkse Ragnar, "The Relation between Home Investment and External Balance in the Light of British Experience, 1945-1955," Review of Economics and Statistics, May, 1956.

Ohlin, Bertil, "The Reparation Problem: A Discussion," Economic Journal, June, 1929; reprinted in Readings in the Theory of International Trade, Philadelphia: American Economic Association, 1949.

Ohlin, Bertil, "The Inadequacy of Price Stabilization," Index, VII, No. 96, 1933.

Ohlin, Bertil, Interregional and International Trade, Cambridge: Harvard University Press, 1933.

Ohlin, Bertil, and Viner, Jacob, National Policy for Economic Welfare at Home and Abroad, Robert Lekachman, ed., New York: Doubleday & Co., 1955.

Ojala, E. M., Agriculture and Economic Progress, Oxford: Oxford University Press, 1952.

Oldmixon, John, The British Empire in America, Vol. I, London: J. Nicholson, B. Tooke, etc., 1708.

Orcutt, Guy H., "Measurement of Price Elasticities in International Trade," Review of Economics and Statistics, May, 1950.

Orcutt, Guy H., "Exchange Rate Adjustment and Relative Size of the Depreciating Bloc," Review of Economics and Statistics, February, 1955.

Organization for European Economic Cooperation, Prolongation of the European Payments Union to 30th June 1956 and Adoption of a European Monetary Agreement and of Amendments to the Code of Liberalisation, Paris: O.E.E.C., August, 1955.

Organization for European Economic Cooperation, *European Monetary Agreement*, Paris: O.E.E.C., August 5, 1955.

Organization for European Economic Cooperation *Agricultural Policies in Europe and North America*, Paris: O.E.E.C., 1956.

Organization for European Economic Cooperation, *Liberalisation of Europe's Dollar Trade*, Paris: O.E.E.C., 1956.

Paish, F. W., "Banking Policy and the Balance of International Payments," *Economica*, November, 1936; reprinted in *Readings in the Theory of International Trade*, Philadelphia: American Economic Association, 1949.

Paish, Sir George, "Great Britain's Capital Investments in Other Lands," *Journal of Royal Statistical Society*, September, 1909.

Patinkin, Don, "A Reconsideration of the General-Equilibrium Theory of Money," *Review of Economic Studies*, No. 45, 1949-1950.

Patinkin, Don, *Money, Interest, and Prices*, Evanston: Row, Peterson and Co., 1956.

Pearce, I. F., "A Note on Mr. Spraos' Paper," *Economica*, May, 1955.

Perroux, François, "The Quest for Stability: The Real Factors," International Economic Association First Congress, Rome, September 6-11, 1956, mimeographed.

Pesmazoglu, J. S., "Some International Aspects of British Cyclical Fluctuations," *Review of Economic Studies*, No. 3, 1947-1950.

Pigou, Arthur C., "The Foreign Exchanges," *Quarterly Journal of Economics*, November, 1922.

Pigou, Arthur C., ed., *Memorials of Alfred Marshall*, London: Macmillan and Co., Ltd., 1925.

Pigou, Arthur C., "Reparations and the Ratio of International Interchange," *Economic Journal*, December, 1932.

Pigou, Arthur C., *A Study in Public Finance*, London: Macmillan and Co., Ltd., 1947.

Pigou, Arthur C., "Unrequited Imports," *Economic Journal*, June, 1950.

Pigou, Arthur C., "Long-run Adjustments in the Balance of Trade," *Economica*, November, 1953.

Plumptre, A. F. W., "Variable or Fixed Exchange Rates?" in *Central Banking in the Dominions*, Toronto: University of Toronto Press, 1940.

Polak, J. J., "Balance of Payments Problems of Countries Reconstructing with the Help of Foreign Loans," *Quarterly Journal of Economics*, February, 1943.

Polak, J. J., "Exchange Depreciation and International Monetary Stability," *Review of Economics and Statistics*, August, 1947.

Polak, J. J., *An International Economic System*, Chicago: University of Chicago Press, 1953.

Polak, J. J., and Chang, T. C., "Effect of Exchange Depreciation on a

Country's Export Price Level," *International Monetary Fund Staff Papers*, February, 1950.

Polak, J. J., and Haberler, G., "The Foreign Trade Multiplier," *American Economic Review*, December, 1947.

Polak, J. J., and Liu, Ta-Chung, "Stability of the Exchange Rate Mechanism in a Multi-Country System," *Econometrica*, July, 1954.

Polak, J. J., and White, W. H., "The Effect of Income Expansion on the Quantity of Money," *International Monetary Fund Staff Papers*, August, 1955.

Predohl, Andreas, *Aussenwirtschaft: Weltwirtschaft, Handelspolitik und Wahrungspolitik*, Grundiss der Sozialwissenschaft, 17, Göttingen: Vandenhoeck & Ruprecht, 1949.

President's Materials Policy Commission, *Resources for Freedom*, Vols. I-IV, Washington: Government Printing Office, 1952.

Prest, A. R., "National Income of the United Kingdom, 1870-1946," *Economic Journal*, March, 1948.

Prest A. R., "Some Experiments in Demand Analysis," *Review of Economics and Statistics*, February, 1949.

Puckle, James, *A New Dialogue between a Burgermaster and an English Gentleman*, London: J. Southby, 1697.

Ramaswami, V. K., "Trade Imbalance, Gains from Trade and National Income Change," *Economic Journal*, September, 1955.

Rangnekar, S. B., *Imperfect Competition in International Trade*, Oxford: Oxford University Press, 1947.

Read, Conyers, ed., *The Constitution Reconsidered*, New York: Columbia University Press, 1938.

Reder, M. W., *Studies in the Theory of Welfare Economics*, New York: Columbia University Press, 1946.

Rees, G. L., "Price Effects and the Foreign Trade Multipliers," *Review of Economic Studies*, No. 3, 1952-1953.

Ricardo, David, *The High Price of Bullion, A Proof of the Depreciation of Bank Notes*, 1810; Piero Sraffa, ed., with the collaboration of M. H. Dobb, *The Works and Correspondence of David Ricardo*. Vol. III, Cambridge: Cambridge University Press, 1951.

Ricardo, David, *The Principles of Political Economy and Taxation*, 1st ed., 1817, London: J. M. Dent and Sons, Ltd., 1937.

Robbins, Lionel, "The International Economic Problem," *Lloyds Bank Review*, January, 1953.

Robbins, Lionel, *The Theory of Economic Policy*, London: Macmillan and Co., Ltd., 1953.

Robbins, Lionel, *The Economist in the Twentieth Century*, London: Macmillan and Co., Ltd., 1954.

Robbins, Lionel, *Robert Torrens and the Evolution of Classical Economics*, London: Macmillan and Co., Ltd., 1958.

Robertson, D. H., A *Study of Industrial Fluctuation*, 1915, reprinted London: London School of Economics and Political Science, 1948.

Robertson, D. H., *Banking Policy and the Price Level*, London: P. S. King and Son, Ltd., 1926.

Robertson, D. H., "The Transfer Problem (1929)," in Pigou, A. C., and Robertson, D. H., *Economic Essays and Addresses*, London: P. S. King and Son, Ltd., 1931.

Robertson, D. H., "The Future of International Trade," *Economic Journal*, March, 1938.

Robertson D. H., "Mr. Keynes and 'Finance,'" *Economic Journal*, March, 1938.

Robertson, D. H., "Mr. Keynes and the Rate of Interest," in *Essays in Monetary Theory*, London: Staples Press, Ltd., 1940.

Robertson, D. H., "The Revolutionists' Handbook," *Quarterly Journal of Economics*, February, 1950.

Robertson, D. H., "The Terms of Trade," *International Social Science Bulletin*, Spring, 1951.

Robertson, D. H., *Utility and All That*, London: George Allen and Unwin, Ltd., 1952.

Robertson, D. H., *Britain in the World Economy*, London: George Allen and Unwin, Ltd., 1954.

Robertson, D. H., "Stability and Progress: The Richer Countries' Problem," First Congress of the International Economic Association, September, 1956, mimeographed.

Robertson, D. H., *Economic Commentaries*, London: Staples Press, Ltd., 1956.

Robertson, D. H., "Wage Inflation," Address to School of Central Bank Officials, Bank of England, May 27, 1957.

Robinson, Austin, "The Future of British Imports," *Three Banks Review*, London, March, 1953.

Robinson, E. A. G., "John Maynard Keynes," *Economic Journal*, March, 1947.

Robinson, E. A. G., "The Changing Structure of the British Economy," *Economic Journal*, September, 1954.

Robinson, E. A. G., "Agriculture's Place in the National Economy," *Agriculture in the British Economy*, London: Imperial Chemical Industries, Ltd., 1957.

Robinson, Joan, *The Economics of Imperfect Competition*, London: Macmillan and Co., Ltd., 1945.

Robinson, Joan, "The Pure Theory of International Trade," *Review of Economic Studies*, No. 2, 1946-1947; reprinted in Joan Robinson, *Collected Economic Papers*, Oxford: Blackwell, 1951.

Robinson, Joan, *Essays in the Theory of Employment*, 2nd ed., London: Macmillan and Co., Ltd., 1947.

Robinson, Joan, "The Foreign Exchanges," *Essays in the Theory of Employment*, Oxford, 1947; reprinted in *Readings in the Theory of International Trade*, American Economic Association, Philadelphia: The Blakiston Co., 1949.

Robinson, Joan, *The Rate of Interest and Other Essays*, London: Macmillan and Co., Ltd., 1952.

Robinson, Joan, *The Accumulation of Capital*, Homewood (Ill.): Richard D. Irwin, Inc., 1956.

Robinson, Romney, "A Graphical Analysis of the Foreign Trade Multiplier," *Economic Journal*, September, 1952.

Rolph, Earl R., *The Theory of Fiscal Economics*, Berkeley: University of California Press, 1954.

Rosenson, A., "International Commodity Reserve Standard Reconsidered," *Review of Economics and Statistics*, May, 1948.

Rosenstein-Rodan, P. N., "Problems of Industrialization of Eastern and South-eastern Europe," *Economic Journal*, June–September, 1943.

Rosenstein-Rodan, P. N., "The International Development of Economically Backward Areas," *International Affairs*, April, 1944.

Rostas, L., *Comparative Productivity in British and American Industry*, Cambridge: Cambridge University Press, 1948.

Rostas, L., "Changes in the Productivity of British Industry, 1945-1950," *Economic Journal*, March, 1952.

Rostow, W. W., *British Economy of the Nineteenth Century*, Oxford: Oxford University Press, 1948.

Rostow, W. W., "The Historical Analysis of the Terms of Trade," *Economic History Review*, 2nd series, Vol. IV, No. 1, 1951.

Rostow, W. W., *The Process of Economic Growth*, New York: W. W. Norton & Co., Inc., 1952.

Rostow, W. W., "The Take-Off into Self-sustained Growth," *Economic Journal*, March, 1956.

Rothschild, K., "The Effects of Devaluation on the Terms of Trade," *International Economic Papers*, No. 5, 1955.

Royal Institute of International Affairs, *The Problem of Foreign Investment*, Oxford: Oxford University Press, 1937.

Salera, Virgil, and Enke, Stephen, *International Economics*, 2nd ed., New York: Prentice-Hall, Inc., 1951.

Salter, Sir Arthur, *Foreign Investment*, Essays in International Finance, Princeton University, February, 1951.

Sammons, Robert L., "International Transactions by Major Foreign Areas," *Survey of Current Business*, November, 1948.

Samuelson, Paul A., "Welfare Economics and International Trade," *American Economic Review*, June, 1938.

Samuelson, Paul A., "The Gains from International Trade," *Canadian Journal of Economics and Political Science*, May, 1939; reprinted in

Readings in the Theory of International Trade, Philadelphia: American Economic Association, 1949.

Samuelson, Paul A., *Foundations of Economic Analysis*, Cambridge: Harvard University Press, 1947.

Samuelson, Paul A., "International Trade and the Equilization of Factor Prices," *Economic Journal*, June, 1948.

Samuelson, Paul A., "Disparity in Postwar Exchange Rates," in *Foreign Economic Policy for the United States*, Seymour Harris, ed., Cambridge: Harvard University Press, 1948.

Samuelson, Paul A., "International Factor Price Equilization Once Again," *Economic Journal*, June, 1949.

Samuelson, Paul A., "The Transfer Problem and Transport Costs, the Terms of Trade when Impediments are Absent," *Economic Journal*, June, 1952.

Samuelson, Paul A., "The Transfer Problem and Transport Costs, II: Analysis of Effects of Trade Impediments," *Economic Journal*, June, 1954.

Saul, S. B., "Britain and World Trade, 1870-1914," *Economic History Review*, 2nd series, Vol. XII, No. 1, August, 1954.

Saunders, C. T., "Consumption of Raw Materials in the United Kingdom: 1851-1950," *Journal of the Royal Statistical Society*, series A, general, Vol. CXV, Part III, 1952.

Say, J. B., *Traité d'économie politique*, Paris: Chez Deterville, 1803.

Say, J. B., *A Treatise on Political Economy*, trans. by C. R. Prinsep, Boston: Wells and Lilly, 1824.

Sayers, R. S., "Review of A. E. Kahn's *Great Britain in the World Economy*," in *Economic History Review*, 2nd series, Vol. I, No. 1, 1948.

Sayers, R. S., "The New York Money Market Through London Eyes," *Three Banks Review*, December, 1955.

Schelling, Thomas C., *National Income Behavior*, New York: McGraw-Hill Book Co., 1951.

Schelling, Thomas C., "American Foreign Assistance," *World Politics*, July, 1955.

Schelling, Thomas C., "International Cost-Sharing Arrangements," *Essays in International Finance*, September, 1955.

Schelling, Thomas C., "An Essay on Bargaining," *American Economic Review*, June, 1956.

Schelling, Thomas C., "American Foreign Assistance and the Newly Independent Countries of Asia and Africa," November, 1956, mimeographed.

Schelling, Thomas C., *International Economics*, Boston: Allyn and Bacon, Inc., 1958.

Schiff, E., "Direct Investments, Terms of Trade, and Balance of Payments," *Quarterly Journal of Economics*, February, 1942.

Schlesinger, Eugene R., *Multiple Exchange Rates and Economic Development*, Princeton: Princeton University Press, 1952.

Schlesinger, Eugene R., *et al.*, *The Pattern of United States Import Trade Since 1923*, New York: Federal Reserve Bank of New York, 1952.

Schlote, Werner, *Entwicklung und Strukturwandlungen des englischen Aussenhandels von 1700 bis zur Gegenwart*, Jena: Gustav Fisher, 1938.

Schlote, Werner, *British Overseas Trade from 1700 to the 1930's*, trans. by W. O. Henderson and W. H. Chaloner, Oxford: Blackwell, 1953.

Schultz, Theodore W., *Agriculture in an Unstable Economy*, New York: McGraw-Hill Book Co., 1945.

Schultz, Theodore W., *Production and Welfare of Agriculture*, New York: The Macmillan Co., 1949.

Schultz, Theodore W., *The Economic Organization of Agriculture*, New York: McGraw-Hill Book Co., 1953.

Schultz, Theodore W., "Latin-American Economic Policy Lessons," *American Economic Review, Papers and Proceedings*, May, 1956.

Schultz, Theodore W., "Economic Prospects for Primary Products," International Economic Association, Rio de Janeiro, August, 1957.

Schumpeter, J. A., *Theory of Economic Development*, trans. by Redvers Opie, Cambridge: Harvard University Press, 1934.

Schumpeter, J. A., *Business Cycles*, New York: McGraw-Hill Book Co., 1939.

Schumpeter, J. A., "John Maynard Keynes, 1883-1946," *American Economic Review*, September, 1946.

Schumpeter, J. A., "Theoretical Problems of Economic Growth," The Tasks of Economic History, *Journal of Economic History*, Supplement VII, 1947.

Schumpeter, J. A., *History of Economic Analysis*, New York: Oxford University Press, 1952.

Scitovsky, Tibor, "Capital Accumulation, Employment and Price Rigidity," *Review of Economic Studies*, Vol. VIII, 1940-1941.

Scitovsky, Tibor, "A Reconsideration of the Theory of Tariffs," *Review of Economic Studies*, No. 2, Summer, 1942; reprinted in *Readings in the Theory of International Trade*, American Economic Association, Philadelphia: The Blakiston Co., 1949.

Scitovsky, Tibor, "Economies of Scale, Competition, and European Integration," *American Economic Review*, March, 1956.

Scitovsky, Tibor, "The Theory of the Balance of Payments and the Problem of a Common European Currency," *Kyklos*, Vol. X, Fasc. 1, 1957.

Scitovsky, Tibor, "The Doctrine of Comparative Advantage and the European Coal and Steel Community," *Economia Internazionale*, February, 1958. (The last three essays are reprinted in Tibor Scitovsky, *Economic Theory and Western European Integration*, Stanford: Stanford University Press, 1958.)

See, Henri E., *L'evolution commerciale et industrielle de la France sous l'ancien régime*, Paris: M. Girard, 1925.

Senior, Nassau, *Three Lectures on the Transmission of Precious Metals*, 1st ed., London: J. Murray, 1828; reprinted London: London School of Economics, 1931.

Senior, Nassau, *Four Introductory Lectures on Political Economy*, London: Browen, Green and Longmans, 1852.

Seton F., "Productivity, Trade Balance and International Structure," *Economic Journal*, December, 1956.

Sheffield, John, earl of, *Observations on the abuses and false interpretations of the Poor Laws*, London: J. Hatchard, 1818.

Shinohara, M., "The Multiplier and the Propensity to Import," *American Economic Review*, September, 1957.

Silberner, Edmund, *The Problem of War in Nineteenth Century Thought*, Princeton: Princeton University Press, 1946.

Singer, H. W., "The Distribution of Gains between Investing and Borrowing Countries," *American Economic Review, Papers and Proceedings*, May, 1950.

Singer, H. W., "Problems of Industrialization of Under-Developed Areas," Round Table on Economic Progress, International Economic Association, Santa Margherita Ligure, Italy, 1953, mimeographed.

Sismondi, M. de, *Political Economy and the Philosophy of Government*, London: John Chapman, 1847.

Smith, Adam, *Wealth of Nations*, Edwin Cannan, ed., New York: The Modern Library, 1937.

Smith, W. L., "Effects of Exchange Rate Adjustments on the Standard of Living," *American Economic Review*, December, 1954.

Smithies, Arthur, "Devaluation with Imperfect Markets and Economic Controls," *Review of Economics and Statistics*, February, 1950.

Smithies, Arthur, "Modern International Trade Theory and International Policy," *American Economic Review, Papers and Proceedings*, May, 1952.

Smithies, Arthur, "Economic Fluctuations and Growth," *Econometrica*, January, 1957.

Solow, Robert, "A Contribution to the Theory of Economic Growth," *Quarterly Journal of Economics*, February, 1956.

Spengler, Joseph J., "Theories of Socio-Economic Growth," *Problems in the Study of Economic Growth*, New York: National Bureau of Economic Research, Inc., 1947.

Spraos, J., "Consumers' Behaviour and the Conditions for Exchange Stability," *Economica*, May, 1955.

Staehle, Hans, "Some Notes on the Terms of Trade," *International Social Science Bulletin*, Spring, 1951.

Stafford, J., "The Future of the Rate of Interest," *The Manchester School of Economic and Social Studies*, No. 2, 1937.

Staley, Eugene, *The Future of Underdeveloped Countries*, New York: Harper & Brothers, 1954.

Statistisches Jahrbuch fur das Deutsche Reich, Internationalen Ubersuchten, Berlin, 1938.

Stephen, Leslie, *The English Utilitarians*, Vol. I, London: Duckworth & Co., 1900.

Stolper, Wolfgang F., "The Volume of Foreign Trade and the Level of Income," *Quarterly Journal of Economics*, February, 1947.

Stolper, Wolfgang F., "Notes on the Dollar Shortage," *American Economic Review*, June, 1950.

Stolper, Wolfgang F., and Samuelson, Paul A., "Protection and Real Wages," *Review of Economic Studies*, November, 1941; reprinted in *Readings in the Theory of International Trade*, Philadelphia: American Economic Association, 1949.

Stone, Lawrence, "Elizabethan Overseas Trade," *Economic History Review*, 2nd series, Vol. II, 1949.

Stuvel, Dr. G., *The Exchange Stability Program*, Leiden: H. E. Stenfert Kroese, 1950.

Svennilson, Ingvar, *Growth and Stagnation in the European Economy*, Geneva: United Nations Economic Commission for Europe, 1954.

Tarshis, Lorie, *Introduction to International Trade and Finance*, New York: John Wiley & Sons, Inc., 1955.

Taussig, F. W., "International Trade under Depreciated Paper: A Contribution to Theory," *Quarterly Journal of Economics*, May, 1917.

Taussig, F. W., "A Rejoinder," *Quarterly Journal of Economics*, August, 1918.

Taussig, F. W., *International Trade*, New York: The Macmillan Co., 1933.

Explorations in Economics: Notes and Essays Contributed in Honor of F. W. Taussig, New York: McGraw-Hill Book Co., 1936.

Terbogh, George, "Purchasing Power Parity Theory," *Journal of Political Economy*, April, 1926.

Thomas, Brinley, "Migration and the Rhythm of Economic Growth, 1830-1913," *The Manchester School of Economic and Social Studies*, September, 1951.

Thomas, Brinley, *Migration and Economic Growth: A Study of Great Britain and the Atlantic Economy*, Cambridge: University Press, 1954.

Thornton, Henry, *An Inquiry into the Nature and Effects of the Paper Credit of Great Britain*, F. A. V. Hayek, ed., New York: Farrar and Rinehart, Inc., 1939.

Thorp, Willard L., *Trade, Aid, or What*, Baltimore: The Johns Hopkins Press, 1954.

Timlin, Mabel F., *Keynesian Economics*, Toronto: Toronto University Press, 1942.

Tinbergen, Jan, *International Economic Cooperation*, Amsterdam: Elsevier, 1946.

Tinbergen, Jan, "The Equilization of Factor Prices between Free-trade Areas," *Metroeconomica*, April, 1949.

Tinbergen, Jan, "Anomalien im Zahlungsbilanzmechanismus," *Weltwirtschaftliches Archiv*, 63. 1949.

Tinbergen, Jan, "The Contribution of Econometrics to the Understanding of the Transfer Mechanism," trans. from *Revista Brasileira de Economica*, III, 1949, pp. 71 ff., mimeographed.

Tinbergen, Jan, "The Relation Between Internal Inflation and the Balance of Payments," Banca Nazionale del Lavoro, *Quarterly Review*, October-December, 1952.

Tinbergen, Jan, *On the Theory of Economic Policy*, Amsterdam: North-Holland Publishing Co., 1952.

Tinbergen, Jan, *International Economic Integration*, 2nd ed., Amsterdam: Elsevier, 1954.

Tinbergen, Jan, *Economic Policy: Principles and Design*, Amsterdam: North-Holland Publishing Co., 1956.

Tinbergen, Jan, *The Design of Development*, Baltimore: The Johns Hopkins Press, 1958.

Torrens, Robert, *An Essay on the External Corn Trade*, London: printed for J. Hatchard, 1815.

Torrens, Robert, *An Essay on the Production of Wealth*, London: Langman, Hurst, Rees, Orme, and Brown, 1821.

Towle, Lawrence W., *International Trade and Commercial Policy*, New York: Harper & Brothers, 1956.

Trevelyan, George Macauley, *British History in the Nineteenth Century*, 1782-1901, New York: Longmans, Green & Co., 1928.

Triantis, S. G., "Cyclical Changes in the Balance of Merchandise Trade of Countries Exporting Chiefly Primary Products," *American Economic Review*, March, 1952.

Triffin, Robert, *Monopolistic Competition and General Equilibrium Theory*, Cambridge: Harvard University Press, 1941.

Triffin, Robert, "National Central Banking and the International Economy," *Review of Economic Studies*, No. 36, 1946-1947.

Triffin, Robert, "International Monetary Policies," Board of Governors of the Federal Reserve System, Washington: Government Printing Office, 1947.

Triffin, Robert, *Europe and the Money Muddle*, New Haven: Yale University Press, 1957.

Turk, Sidney, "Foreign Exchange Market in Canada," *The Canadian Chartered Accountant,* August, 1953.

Tyszynski, H., "World Trade in Manufactured Commodities, 1889-1950," *The Manchester School of Economics and Social Studies,* September, 1951.

United Nations, Department of Economic Affairs, *International Capital Movements during the Inter-War Period,* Lake Success (N.Y.): United Nations Press, 1949.

United Nations, Department of Economic Affairs, *National and International Measures for Full Employment,* Lake Success (N.Y.): United Nations Press, 1949.

United Nations, Department of Economic Affairs, *Relative Prices of Exports and Imports of Under-developed Countries,* Lake Success (N.Y.): United Nations Press, 1949.

United Nations, Department of Economic Affairs, *Measures for the Economic Development of Under-developed Countries,* New York: United Nations Press, 1951.

United Nations, Department of Economic Affairs, *Instability in Export Markets of Under-developed Countries,* New York: United Nations Press, 1952.

United Nations, Department of Economic and Social Affairs, *Analyses and Projections of Economic Development, I. An Introduction to the Technique of Programming,* New York: United Nations Press, 1955.

United Nations, Department of Economic and Social Affairs, *Processes and Problems of Industrialization in Under-Developed Countries,* New York: United Nations Press, 1955.

United Nations, Department of Economic and Social Affairs, *World Economic Survey, 1956,* New York: United Nations Press, 1957.

United Nations, Department of Economic and Social Affairs, *World Economic Survey, 1957,* New York: United Nations Press, 1958.

United Nations, Economic Commission for Latin America, *The Economic Development of Latin America and its Principal Problems,* Lake Success (N.Y.): United Nations Press, 1950.

United Nations, Economic Commission for Latin America, *Economic Survey for Latin America, 1951-52,* New York: United Nations Press, 1953.

United Nations, Food and Agricultural Organization, *The State of Food and Agriculture, 1956,* Rome: F.A.O., 1956.

United Nations, Statistical Office, *National Income and its Distribution in Underdeveloped Countries,* New York: United Nations Press, 1951.

United Nations, Statistical Office, *Monthly Bulletin of Statistics,* New York: United Nations Press. (Various issues.)

United Nations, Statistical Office, *Yearbook of International Trade Statistics,* New York: United Nations Press. (Various issues.)

United States, Board of Governors of the Federal Reserve System, *Federal Reserve Bulletin*, Washington: Government Printing Office. (Various issues.)

United States, Bureau of Agricultural Economics, *Agricultural Outlook Charts*, Washington: Government Printing Office. (Various issues.)

United States, Bureau of Agricultural Economics, *Agricultural Prices*, Washington: Government Printing Office. (Various issues.)

United States, Bureau of Agricultural Economics, *Farm Income Situation*, Washington: Government Printing Office. (Various issues.)

United States, Bureau of Agricultural Economics. *Farm Labor*, Washington: Government Printing Office, February, 1950.

United States, Bureau of Agricultural Economics, *Farm Population Estimates, 1910-1942*, Washington: Government Printing Office, November, 1942.

United States, Bureau of Agricultural Economics, *Foreign Agricultural Trade of the United States*, November, 1955, and March, 1956.

United States, Bureau of Agricultural Economics, *United States Farm Products in Foreign Trade*, Statistical Bulletin No. 112.

United States, Bureau of Census, *Foreign Commerce and Navigation of the United States*, Washington: Government Printing Office. (Various issues.)

United States, Bureau of the Census, *Historical Statistics of the United States, 1789-1945*, Washington: Government Printing Office, 1949.

United States, Bureau of the Census, *Quarterly Summary of Foreign Commerce of the United States*, Washington: Government Printing Office. (Various issues.)

United States, Bureau of the Census, *Statistical Abstract of the United States*, Washington: Government Printing Office. (Various years.)

United States, Bureau of Foreign Commerce, *World Trade Information Service*, Washington: Government Printing Office. (Various issues.)

United States, Bureau of Foreign and Domestic Commerce, *Foreign Trade of the United States, 1936-1949*, Washington: Government Printing Office, 1951.

United States, Commission on Foreign Economic Policy, *Report*, Washington, 1954, mimeographed.

United States, Commission on Foreign Economic Policy, *Staff Papers*, Washington: Government Printing Office, 1954.

United States, Congress, Joint Committee on the Economic Report, *Foreign Economic Policy*, Hearings, 84th Cong., 1st Sess., Washington: Government Printing Office, 1955.

United States, Department of Commerce, "Balance of Payments of the United States, 1919-1953," in *Survey of Current Business*, Washington: Government Printing Office, July, 1954.

United States, Department of Commerce, *International Transactions of the United States During the War 1940-45,* prepared by Robert L. Sammons, Washington: Government Printing Office, 1950.

United States, Department of Commerce, *Survey of Current Business,* Washington: Government Printing Office. (Various issues.)

United States, Department of Commerce, *The United States in the World Economy,* prepared by Hal Lary and Associates, Washington: Government Printing Office, 1943.

United States, Department of Labor, *Handbook of Labor Statistics,* 1947 ed., Bulletin 916, Washington: Government Printing Office.

Unwin, George, *Industrial Organization in the Sixteenth and Seventeenth Centuries,* Oxford: The Clarendon Press, 1904.

Upgren, A. R., "Devaluation of the Dollar in Relation to Exports and Imports," *Journal of Political Economy,* February, 1936.

Valavanis-Vail, Stefan, "Leontief's Scarce Factor Paradox," *Journal of Political Economy,* December, 1954.

Valavanis-Vail, Stefan, "An Econometric Model of Growth—USA—1869-1953," *American Economic Review, Papers and Proceedings,* May, 1955.

Vernon, Raymond, "Trade Policy in Crisis," *Essays in International Finance,* March, 1958.

Viner, Jacob, *Canada's Balance of International Indebtedness, 1900-1913,* Cambridge: Harvard University Press, 1924.

Viner, Jacob, "Angell's Theory of International Prices," *Journal of Political Economy,* October, 1926.

Viner, Jacob, "Adam Smith and Laissez Faire," *Journal of Political Economy,* April, 1927.

Viner, Jacob, "International Trade Theory," in *Encyclopedia of the Social Sciences,* Vol. 8, New York, 1932.

Viner, Jacob, "Mr. Keynes and the Causes of Unemployment," *Quarterly Journal of Economics,* November, 1936.

Viner, Jacob, "Professor Taussig's Contribution to the Theory of International Trade," in *Explorations in Economics: Notes and Essays Contributed in Honor of F. W. Taussig,* New York: McGraw-Hill Book Co., 1936.

Viner, Jacob, *Studies in the Theory of International Trade,* New York: Harper & Brothers, 1937.

Viner, Jacob, "Clapham on the Bank of England," *Economica,* May, 1945.

Viner, Jacob, "International Finance in the Post-War World," *Lloyd's Bank Review,* October, 1946; reprinted in *Journal of Political Economy,* April, 1947.

Viner, Jacob, "America's Lending Policy," *Proceedings of the Academy of Political Science,* January, 1947.

Viner, Jacob, "Benthan and Mill: The Utilitarian Background," *American Economic Review*, March, 1949.

Viner, Jacob, "Full Employment at Whatever Cost," *Quarterly Journal of Economics*, August, 1950.

Viner, Jacob, *The Customs Union Issue*, New York: Carnegie Endowment for International Peace, 1950.

Viner, Jacob, *International Economics; Studies*, Glencoe (Ill.): Free Press, 1951.

Viner, Jacob, *Rearmament and International Commercial Policies*, Foreign Service Institute, U.S. Department of State, 1951.

Viner, Jacob, *International Trade and Economic Development*, Glencoe (Ill.): Free Press, 1952.

Viner, Jacob, "International Trade Theory and Its Present Day Relevance," *Economics and Public Policy*, Washington: The Brookings Institution, 1955.

Viner, Jacob, "Stability and Progress: The Case for the Poorer Countries," First Congress International Economic Association, September, 1956, mimeographed.

Viner, Jacob, "Some International Aspects of Economic Stabilization," in *The State of the Social Sciences*, Leonard D. White, ed., Chicago: University of Chicago Press, 1956.

Viner, Jacob, *The Long View and the Short*, Glencoe (Ill.): Free Press, 1958.

von Stackelberg, Heinrich, "Die Theorie der Wechselkurse bei vollstandiger Konkurrenz," *Jahrbuch fur Nationalokonomie und Statistik*, September, 1949. English translation in *International Economic Papers*, No. 1, New York: The Macmillan Co., 1951.

von Waltershausen, A. Sartorius, *Die Entstehung der Weltwirtschaft*, Jena: Gustav Fisher, 1931.

Waight, Leonard, *The History and Mechanism of the Exchange Equalisation Account*, Cambridge: University Press, 1939.

Wallich, H. C., "Underdeveloped Countries in the International Monetary Mechanism," in *Money, Trade, and Economic Growth*, New York: The Macmillan Co., 1951.

Wallich, H. C., and Adler, John H., *Public Financing in a Developing Country—El Salvador: A Case Study*, Cambridge: Harvard University Press, 1951.

Webb, Sidney and Beatrice, *English Local Government from the Revolution to the Municipal Corporations Act: The Parish and the County*, London: Longmans, Green and Co., Ltd., 1906.

Webb, Sidney and Beatrice, *English Poor Law History: Part II—The Last Hundred Years*, London: Longmans, Green and Co., Ltd., 1929.

Weber, B., and Handfield-Jones, S. J., "Variations in the Rate of Economic Growth in the U.S.A., 1869-1939," *Oxford Economic Papers,* June, 1954.

Whale, P. B., "International Short-term Capital Movements," *Economica,* February, 1939.

White, W. H., "The Employment-insulating Advantages of Flexible Exchanges: A Comment on Professors Laursen and Metzler," *Review of Economics and Statistics,* May, 1954.

Whitin, T. M., "Classical Theory, Graham's Theory and Linear Programming in International Trade," *Quarterly Journal of Economics,* November, 1953.

Whitworth, Sir Charles, *State of the Trade of Great Britain in its Imports and Exports, Progressively from the Year 1697,* London: G. Robinson, 1776.

Wicksell, Knut, "International Freights and Prices," *Quarterly Journal of Economics,* February, 1918.

Wicksell Knut, *Selected Papers on Economic Theory,* London: George Allen and Unwin, Ltd., 1958.

Wijnolds, H. W. J., "Some Observations on Foreign Exchange Rates in Theory and Practice," *South African Journal of Economics,* December, 1947.

Williams, J. B., *International Trade under Flexible Exchange Rates,* Amsterdam: North-Holland Publishing Co., 1954.

Williams, John H., *Argentine International Trade under Inconvertible Paper Money, 1880-1900,* Cambridge: Harvard University Press, 1920.

Williams, John H., "The Balance of International Payments of the United States for the year 1920, with a Statement of the Aggregate Balance July 1, 1914–December 31, 1920," *Review of Economic Statistics,* Supplement, Preliminary Vol. 3, June, 1921.

Williams, John H., "The Theory of International Trade Reconsidered," *Economic Journal,* June, 1929; reprinted in *Readings in the Theory of International Trade,* American Economic Association, Philadelphia: The Blakiston Co., 1949.

Williams, John H., "World's Monetary Dilemma, Internal Stability versus External Monetary Stability," *Proceedings of the Academy of Political Science,* 1934.

Williams, John H., "The Adequacy of Existing-Currency Mechanisms under Varying Circumstances," *American Economic Review,* Supplement, 1937.

Williams, John H., *Postwar Monetary Plans and Other Essays,* New York: Alfred A. Knopf, 1944.

Williams, John H., "An Appraisal of Keynesian Economics," *American Economic Review,* May, 1948; reprinted in *Economic Stability in a Changing World,* New York: Oxford University Press, 1953.

Williams, John H., "International Trade Theory and Policy—Some Current Issues," *American Economic Review, Papers and Proceedings,* May, 1951.

Williams, John H., *Money, Trade, and Economic Growth,* Essays in Honor of J. H. Williams, New York: The Macmillan Co., 1951.

Williams, John H., *Economic Stability in the Modern World,* London: Athlone Press, 1952.

Williamson, Harold F., and Buttrick, John A., eds., *Economic Development: Principles and Patterns,* New York: Prentice-Hall, Inc., 1954.

Wilson, Thomas, *Discourse Upon Usury,* R. H. Tawney, ed., New York: Harcourt, Brace and Co., 1925.

Wilson, Thomas R., "The British Imperial Preference System," *Foreign Commerce Weekly,* June 3, 1944.

Wilson, Roland, *Capital Imports and the Terms of Trade, Examined in the Light of Sixty Years of Australian Borrowings,* Melbourne: Melbourne University Press, 1931.

Woolley, Herbert B., "On the Elaboration of a System of International Transaction Accounts," *Problems in the International Comparison of Economic Accounts,* Studies in Income and Wealth, Vol. 20, Princeton: Princeton University Press, 1957.

Woytinsky, W. S. and E. S., *World Population and Production—Trends and Outlook,* New York: The Twentieth Century Fund, 1953.

Wu, Chi-Yuen, *An Outline of International Price Theories,* London: G. Routledge & Sons, Ltd., 1939.

Yntema, Theodore O., *A Mathematical Reformulation of the General Theory of International Trade,* Chicago: University of Chicago Press, 1932.

Youngson, A. J., "Investment Decisions, Trade Cycle, and Trade," *Oxford Economic Papers,* September, 1954.

Zassenhaus, H. K., "Direct Effects of a United States Recession on Imports: Expectations and Events," *Review of Economics and Statistics,* August, 1955.

Indexes

Index of Names[1]

Adler, J. H., 189 n., 311 n., 321, 362
Alai, H., 321
Alexander, S. S., 57 n., 321
Allely, J. S., 321
Allen, R. G. D., 143 n., 321
Allen, William R., 321
Angell, James W., 322
Appleton, Nathan, 14
Arndt, H. W., 322
Ashley, W. J., 21
Ashton, T. S., 9 n., 189 n., 220 n., 221 n., 222 n., 322
Atallah, M. K., 322
Attwood, Thomas, 81, 82, 322
Aubrey, Henry G., 177 n., 311 n., 322

Baghot, Walter, 322
Bain, Joe S., 285 n., 322
Baines, E., 322
Baldwin, Robert E., 322, 346
Balogh, T., 57 n., 179 n., 322-323
Bastable, Charles, 44, 94, 323
Bauer, P. T., 323
Baumol, W. J., 80 n., 323
Beach, Walter E., 323

Becker, G. S., 80 n., 323
Beckerman, W., 323
Bell, P. W., 323
Bendix, Reinhard, 221 n., 323
Benham, Frederic, 323
Bensusan-Butt, D. M., 324
Bentham, Jeremy, 16-18, 324
Bernstein, E. M., 179 n., 324
Beveridge, William H., 324
Bezanson, Anne, 324
Bickerdike, C. F., 324
Black, J. D., 156 n., 324, 331
Blank, John, 324
Bloch, E., 324
Bloomfield, Arthur I., 49 n., 118 n., 279 n.
Bourneuf, Alice, 324
Bowley, A. L., 77 n., 324
Bowley, Marian, 324
Brems, H., 325
Bresciani-Turroni, C., 325
Bridgman, P. W., 4, 325
Brisman, S., 325
Brofenbrenner, M., 325
Brown, A. J., 325
Brown, E. H. Phelps, 253 n., 257 n., 260 n., 262 n., 301 n., 325
Brown, George Hay, 172 n., 325

[1] Italicized numbers indicate bibliographical lists.

367

Waight, Leonard, 49 n., 362
Wallich, H. C., 321, 362
Walras, L., 78
Walters, Dorothy, 244 n., 262 n., 338
Webb, Sidney and Beatrice, 13 n., 14,
  222 n., 362
Weber, B., 253 n., 301 n., 325, 362-
  363
Westerborg, E. Van, 311 n.
Whale, P. B., 363
Wheatley, J., 94
White, W. H., 174 n., 363
Whitin, T. M., 363
Whitworth, Sir Charles, 363
Wicksell, Knut, 82, 94 n., 149 n.,
  363
Wijnolds, H. W. J., 363
Williams, J. B., 363

Williams, John H., 42 n., 84 n., 98 n.,
  179 n., 272 n., 275 n., 277 n., 326,
  363-364
Williamson, Harold F., 364
Wilson, Roland, 364
Wilson, Thomas, 364
Wilson, Thomas R., 364
Woolley, Herbert B., 268 n., 269 n.,
  364
Woytinsky, W. S. and E. S., 268 n.,
  364
Wright, J. F., 219 n.
Wu, Chi-Yuen, 364

Yntema, T. O., 80 n., 364
Youngson, A. J., 364

Zassenhaus, H. K., 364

Index of Subjects[1]